Architectures for the Intelligent AI-Ready Enterprise

Building real-world solutions
with MongoDB

Boris Bialek, Sebastian Rojas Arbulu, Taylor Hedgecock

‹packt›

Architectures for the Intelligent AI-Ready Enterprise

Portfolio Director: Sunith Shetty
Relationship Lead: Sathya Mohan
Project Managers: Aniket Shetty & Sathya Mohan
Content Engineers: Siddhant Jain, David Sugarman, & Divya Poliyath
Technical Editor: Aniket Shetty
Copy Editor: Safis Editing
Indexer: Pratik Shirodkar
Proofreader: Siddhant Jain
Production Designer: Deepak Chavan

First published: September 2025

Production reference: 1290825

Published by Packt Publishing Ltd.
Grosvenor House
11 St Paul's Square
Birmingham
B3 1RB, UK.

ISBN 978-1-80611-715-4
www.packtpub.com

Foreword

If you had told me a few years ago that I'd be writing the foreword to a book on AI, I might've raised an eyebrow. And yet, here we are, right in the middle of one of the fastest-moving technological shifts in modern history.

Unlike prior technological shifts, what is different this time is the pace. Change is not unfolding over years; it is happening in months, weeks, sometimes even days.

The question facing every organization is not whether AI will reshape their business; it is how fast they can adapt and whether they will lead or fall behind.

Throughout my career, I have seen what separates the companies that thrive during moments like these from those that fall behind. It is rarely just the technology. It is the mindset—the willingness to rethink how you operate, how you deliver value, and how you use data to drive better outcomes. AI, especially generative and agentic systems, demands exactly that kind of rethink.

At MongoDB, we have worked closely with thousands of organizations across various industries, including financial services, healthcare, insurance, retail, and manufacturing, as they navigate their AI journeys. And the pattern is clear: the companies that succeed do not start with algorithms or models. They start with the foundation. That foundation is the **data**.

Consider a major financial institution that transitioned from traditional batch-based fraud detection to real-time monitoring using MongoDB Atlas, reducing rollout times from weeks to minutes and saving millions annually. Or consider a global pharmaceutical company that used MongoDB and generative AI to cut clinical report generation from twelve weeks to just ten minutes. These AI-enabled systems were transformational for both businesses and were made possible by modern, flexible infrastructure built to support intelligent workloads at scale.

The lesson is clear: if you want to implement AI successfully, your data foundation has to come first.

That is why this book matters.

It doesn't just talk about what is possible with AI; it shows you **how to make it a reality**. You will find hard-earned lessons from those already deploying AI in production, plus architectural blueprints and implementation strategies that you can apply immediately across any industry.

You will also learn why document-based data models are quickly becoming central to AI applications, how vector search unlocks meaning from unstructured data, and why blending operational and analytical capabilities creates real architectural leverage.

Just as important, this book addresses the often-overlooked realities of trust, governance, security, and scale. Building powerful AI is one thing. Making it responsible, resilient, and production-ready is something else entirely.

Whether you are a technology leader, architect, engineer, data scientist, or anyone responsible for implementing AI in your organization, this book offers a clear, practical path forward.

I am excited to see what you will build next.

Jim Scharf

Chief Technology Officer,

MongoDB, Inc.

Note from the author

The advent of **large language models (LLMs)**, predicated on transformer-based architectures, began in 2018. At the same time, advancements in GPU technology facilitated greater parallel computational capabilities, culminating in the Nvidia V100 and catalyzing the **generative AI (GenAI)** domain. Natural language processing moved beyond reliance on rule-based systems and narrow subject area training, benefiting from comprehensive internet data and yielding significant advancements. The 2022 public beta release of ChatGPT, along with the introduction of competing LLMs, most notably Google Gemini and Anthropic Claude (utilized in AWS Bedrock), precipitated a shift in software development paradigms. Software design, coding, and business use cases expanded in unprecedented ways.

My preliminary investigations into vector utilization for semantic search and enhancements to MongoDB's existing text search functionality predated these developments. The domains of embeddings, models, and nearest neighbors converged with the emerging field of LLMs. This convergence enabled the rapid development of a preliminary **retrieval-augmented generation (RAG)** solution, which facilitated the interpretation of PDF documents and the generation of responses based on natural language queries and vectorized document data. The MongoDB Industry Solutions team recognized the innovative potential and expedited implementation through the MongoDB Atlas platform. The advantages of an integrated platform over multi-component systems were substantial. However, the proliferation of components and permutations created challenges, particularly the overreliance on singular, nascent components. Consequently, the focus shifted toward solution design with specific business outcomes, referred to as the *art of the possible*. Client requests increasingly emphasized implementation details (*how*) rather than conceptualization (*what*).

During 2023 and 2024, reference architectures and established designs were developed, warranting broader dissemination. Solutions originating in specific use cases demonstrated cross-industry applicability. The concept of the consolidated data store was refined and required further documentation.

In the summer of 2025, a directive was issued to the team to compile industry-specific solution designs, based on current agentic AI patterns and templates, into a comprehensive publication. Foundational chapters were subsequently incorporated to accommodate varied experience levels.

Collaboration with strategic business partners has provided diverse perspectives, enriching the content. The insights of the CXO Advisory team, focused on application modernization and the use of generative AI tools for legacy system enhancement, have also been incorporated.

It is anticipated that this publication will serve as a valuable resource for those interested in industry solutions leveraging GenAI.

Boris Bialek

Vice President and Field CTO,

MongoDB, Inc.

Acknowledgements

Every book has its origin story, and ours began with a simple yet overwhelming challenge. As MongoDB's Industry Solutions team, we specialize in presenting MongoDB as a solution for specific industries. We speak our customers' language and understand their industry needs, roadblocks, market trends, and competitors.

Over the years, we have spent countless hours documenting industry solutions across our blogs, the MongoDB solution library, and numerous articles and presentations that we have passionately created to help developers and organizations solve their most challenging data problems. But when clients asked us to help them navigate this wealth of knowledge, we faced an uncomfortable truth: having thousands of scattered links, no matter how valuable each one might be, had become overwhelming rather than helpful.

It was Raghu Viswanathan, our remarkable leader in education and documentation, who identified the opportunity we hadn't yet seen. In a conversation that began as a brainstorm about how to better serve our community, he suggested something that felt both obvious and audacious: *"Why not turn all these insights into a book?"* Without his clarity and persistent encouragement, this project would have remained nothing more than a collection of good intentions instead of becoming something real.

Writing a book in the technology space is never a solo endeavor. This is especially true when discussing real-world architectures and solutions. We are deeply grateful to the teams at Iguazio (acquired by QuantumBlack, AI by McKinsey), Fireworks AI, Dataworkz, Encore, Cognigy, and RegData, whose real-world implementations and feedback helped us understand what actually works in practice. Equally important are our technology partners such as Amazon Web Services, Microsoft Azure, Google Cloud, Confluent, Capgemini, and others. Their platforms and expertise make the solutions we discuss possible.

We would also like to thank our publishing partners at Packt, who proved that the best collaborations happen when expertise meets passion. Through countless revision cycles, they pushed us to think about our readers at every step. They asked the hard questions that helped transform our technical expertise into something both authoritative and accessible.

And to our colleagues across Industry Solutions, Product, and other internal teams, you know who you are. Your fingerprints are on every chapter.

This book is for every builder, architect, and strategist working to solve what comes next with AI. It is for you.

Contributors

About the authors

Boris Bialek has worked in the IT industry since the 1990s and was one of the initial drivers of Linux in Europe, delivering the first SAP port to Linux, conducting the first benchmarks, and securing the first clients. Since then, he has led product and development teams across IBM and FIS, driving innovation for both the end product and development productivity. Boris Bialek joined MongoDB in 2019, igniting a focus on industry solutions based on MongoDB's document model. Promoted to global field CTO and VP of industries, he drives technical design. He works directly with numerous clients, helping them gain the benefits of the MongoDB Atlas data platform. Boris holds a master's in computer science from the Karlsruhe Institute of Technology.

Sebastian Rojas Arbulu is an industry solutions specialist at MongoDB, where he collaborates with numerous stakeholders across diverse industries to help customers realize the transformative value of MongoDB through tailored, data-driven solutions, particularly for AI integration. Sebastian also leads his team's content strategy, including numerous additions such as blogs, white papers, magazines, and other thought leadership pieces. With a background in IT consulting, marketing, and digital transformation, among other areas, he has extensive experience in identifying customer needs and developing innovative solutions that prepare data for intelligent applications and unlock new possibilities. He holds a bachelor of business administration degree.

Taylor Hedgecock is a strategic program leader and transformation partner who turns vision into velocity. With a career spanning startups to multinationals, she brings a mix of operational rigor, narrative clarity, and cross-functional orchestration. At MongoDB, she has led high-impact programs across AI, partner ecosystems, and services modernization, often serving as the connective tissue between vision and execution. Her work has guided C-level priorities, enabled go-to-market readiness, and driven large-scale change, establishing her as a trusted leader in aligning stakeholders, translating strategy into story, and driving outcomes that last. Taylor currently serves as senior program manager on the industry solutions team, partnering with ISVs and AI innovators to bring next-generation solutions to market. Previously, she was chief of staff for professional services leadership, where she helped launch new offerings and guided modernization strategy, shaping MongoDB's vision for applying AI to its hardest problems.

Benjamin Lorenz has been a key contributor to MongoDB since 2016, driving growth across the Central European sales region. With deep expertise in strategic customer initiatives, he partners with decision-makers to align tailored solutions with business goals—leveraging the power of MongoDB's developer data platform. As industry solutions principal for telco & media, Benjamin guides global clients through digital transformation, helping them unlock innovative, data-driven revenue streams.

Francesc Mateu is a principal of industry solutions at MongoDB, with 20+ years in B2B SaaS and IT innovation, including 15 years in digital health. As a startup founder and product leader, he possesses an entrepreneurial mindset aimed at helping healthcare organizations modernize their data architectures. His work includes designing digital platforms that support patient-centered care and value-based models, including telemedicine solutions for capturing patient-reported outcomes. At MongoDB, he works globally with sales, partners, and product teams to help healthcare systems adopt AI-ready, standards-based architectures—leveraging technologies such as FHIR and openEHR—to create tailored solutions to meet each organization's unique needs.

Genevieve Broadhead is the global lead for retail solutions at MongoDB, based in Barcelona. She helps global retailers and retail software companies modernize data architectures for real-time personalization, omnichannel experiences, and AI-powered operations. With a computer engineering degree from Trinity College Dublin and a decade of experience in system design, Genevieve has extensive experience bridging business needs with cutting-edge technology. A recognized thought leader, she speaks regularly on cloud-native data pipelines, AI adoption, and composable commerce. She also serves on the MACH Alliance tech council, shaping standards for modern retail architectures.

Dr. Humza Akhtar is the smart manufacturing and automotive expert at MongoDB. Prior to joining MongoDB, he worked at Ernst & Young Canada in its digital operations consultancy practice. After completing his education in Singapore, he worked in the Singapore manufacturing industry for many years on Industry 4.0 research and implementation. He has spent his entire career enabling connected factories and connected cars for global manufacturing and automotive clients. He is a published author on Industry 4.0, and these days, his interest lies in enabling the use of generative AI within the automotive sector. Humza holds a master's degree in embedded systems and a doctorate in computer science from Nanyang Technological University, Singapore.

Jeff Needham is MongoDB's insurance industry expert, with nearly 30 years of experience in software delivery. As former senior director of architecture at Travelers, he led one of the industry's most successful MongoDB adoptions. His career spans leadership at major software companies and healthcare giants such as Aetna/CVS. Jeff's technical expertise and strategic insight drive exceptional outcomes for MongoDB's complex enterprise engagements, helping organizations navigate digital transformation. He holds a master's in political strategy from George Washington University.

Ken Wiebke has been working in the software development industry for over 30 years, with a career spanning development, architecture, and leadership. Throughout his career, Ken has driven change in organizations ranging from small to Fortune 500, including the shift from waterfall to agile. Serving in leadership roles for over 15 years, Ken's focus has been on driving efficiencies and building high-performance teams that consistently deliver on time and within budget. Ken joined MongoDB in December 2024 as a CxO advisor to help organizations leverage the power of MongoDB and transform their legacy software to modern tech stacks.

Luis Pazmino Diaz holds over two decades of experience in the technology sector, particularly within banking and finance. Previously, he served as global strategy architect for Backbase, director of innovation at Temenos, and solutions advisor at major enterprise software firms such as SAP and Oracle. As MongoDB's industry principal for financial services, he delivers strategic guidance to clients and solution partners across Europe, the Middle East, and Latin America. Based in Madrid, Spain, Luis has been widely recognized as a financial innovation expert.

Peyman Parsi began his career in financial services software engineering at SS&C, focusing on building wealth management software for the banking industry. In 2001, he joined the Toronto Stock Exchange (TSX), leading the development of capital markets solutions. Over 18 years at TSX, Peyman delivered several large-scale transformations and held the position of chief technology delivery officer. In 2020, he embarked on a new journey in FinTech, serving as CTO at Blanc Labs, with a primary focus on banking and digital lending solutions. Peyman is a member of the advisory board of the CIO Association of Canada and joined MongoDB in 2024 as senior principal of financial services industry solutions for the Americas.

Prashant Juttokonda is an expert in enterprise data architecture and modernization at MongoDB. Previously, he held leadership roles at EPAM, TCS, and IBM, advising global clients on cloud adoption, data transformation, and AI-ready architectures. With over 30 years of experience across banking, retail, and energy sectors, he has led large-scale modernization programs and driven the adoption of frameworks such as Data Mesh and Data Fabric. He is a frequent speaker and published thought leader in data strategy. His focus is on enabling generative AI and resilient data platforms. He holds a B.Sc. in mathematics and numerous certifications in cybersecurity and cloud technologies.

Raphael Schor is a mechanical engineer with 20+ years of experience in mechanical development, plant engineering, and industrial maintenance. He has served as CTO in the automotive and packaging industries, leading R&D and digital transformation. Since 2023, Raphael has served as principal for manufacturing and motion at MongoDB. In this role, he bridges the gap between industrial engineering challenges and modern data architecture. His focus includes digital twins, smart factories, and generative AI. Raphael holds a bachelor's in mechanical engineering and a Master of Advanced Studies in Management, Technology, and Economics from ETH Zurich.

Rodrigo Leal, with over 20 years in the technology industry, is the principal retail industry solutions for Latin America at MongoDB. Prior to MongoDB, Rodrigo served as a senior principal solution specialist at Qualtrics, enhancing employee, customer, brand, and product experiences. Earlier, he was part of NCR's Walmart Global Team, playing a role in launching self-checkout technology in Mexico and Central America, and was recognized with two NCR President's Club awards. He previously worked with Oracle and MicroStrategy as an account manager and sales engineer. Known for strengths in consultative multi-product selling, he is dedicated to uncovering customer needs and crafting solutions that often reveal previously unseen opportunities.

Thorsten Walther boasts over 25 years in tech leadership, blending enterprise expertise, entrepreneurial drive, and deep technical acumen to drive digital transformation. He founded and led INSPIFY, an AI-powered SaaS platform for luxury retail. His career spans leadership roles at Credit Suisse and SOFGEN Services, as well as extensive advisory work in finance, retail, pharmacy, and enterprise software. Currently, as managing director, CXO advisory for Asia at MongoDB, he guides senior executives on digital transformation. Uniquely, Thorsten was a professional footballer in Germany's Bundesliga and France's Ligue 1 and 2. He holds an MBA from the University of Liverpool.

Wei You Pan is the global director of financial services industry solutions at MongoDB. With over 25 years spanning fintech, data architecture, and financial services, he empowers institutions to overcome complex data challenges and drive innovation. His expertise includes trading, loan origination, risk management, and sustainability, supported by credentials in enterprise architecture (SCEA), financial risk management (FRM), and climate risk (SCR). His cross-disciplinary background enables him to uniquely bridge technology and business, helping organizations realize the full value of their data.

About the reviewers

Coral Parmar serves as lead product manager on MongoDB's search portfolio, bringing more than 20 years of technology and systems experience to help developers navigate modern data challenges across diverse verticals. His career spans leadership roles in MongoDB technical services, AdTech companies, and data development at UPS, providing deep expertise in scaling customer solutions for complex data systems across supply chain, logistics, and advertising technologies. Throughout his career, he has maintained a passion for solving complex problems and empowering teams to build effective, scalable solutions in rapidly evolving technical landscapes. He holds a master's in information systems from New Jersey Institute of Technology.

James Osgood is a staff solutions architect at MongoDB with over 30 years of experience spanning software development and financial services. He began his career in the audio and video industry before moving into financial services, where he specialized in low-latency trading and market surveillance systems. Since joining MongoDB in 2017, James has partnered with major customers across London and Europe. Today, his focus is on helping global enterprises transform mission-critical financial systems and modernize broader application estates with purpose-built AI-driven modernization solutions.

Jim Blackhurst is a distinguished solutions architect at MongoDB, with more than 20 years of experience designing and delivering distributed data systems. He currently works with MongoDB's application modernization team, helping some of the world's largest organizations modernize their estates through purpose-built AI modernization tools, liberating them from the grip of legacy technologies. Before joining MongoDB, Jim spent his career in the video game industry, architecting and operating backend systems for some of the most iconic global gaming brands, working with data at scale before "scale" became a thing. Based in London, Jim continues to focus on pushing the boundaries of distributed systems design and helping enterprises unlock new possibilities with data.

Julia Pak is a product manager at MongoDB on the enterprise initiatives and tools team. She currently focuses on developing internal products that enhance organizational productivity through data centralization and AI-powered features. Prior to joining MongoDB, Julia worked in the insurance and advertising technology industries, building external products from the ground up. She earned her bachelor of arts degree in history from Princeton University.

Shash Thakor is a senior product manager at MongoDB, primarily responsible for Atlas networking. He has 15+ years of product and engineering leadership experience in developing highly distributed, scalable, and secure software systems. Before moving into product management, he was a software developer with Cisco Systems and Juniper Networks, responsible for developing switching and routing software systems deployed in many data centers across the world and used by hyperscalers, big enterprises, and small businesses. He has multiple patents in distributed systems, security, and zero-touch provisioning. He holds a master's in computer science from the University of Maryland, College Park (UMCP).

Table of Contents

Chapter 2: What Sets GenAI, RAG, and Agentic AI Apart   15

Chapter 3: The System of Action 45

Chapter 9: Cognigy's Voice and Chatbots in the Time of Agentic AI　　209

Chapter 10: Harnessing AI to Transform the Retail Industry   223

Part 3: The Future of Intelligent Enterprise   405

Chapter 17: Enterprise Document Management with MongoDB and AI   407

Chapter 18: Democratizing Agentic AI for Enterprise with Dataworkz and MongoDB   417

Chapter 19: Outlook: Beyond Today's AI   431

Afterword   **445**

Index   **449**

Other Books You May Enjoy   **463**

Preface

This book is about how organizations can move beyond surface-level AI adoption and implement AI as a true driver of business transformation. It explains the strategic importance of distinguishing between modernization and innovation, and how both are essential for successful AI deployment. Through real-world implementations, success stories, and practical frameworks, it provides a roadmap for navigating the AI inflection point, aligning data infrastructure with AI goals, and building trustworthy, scalable, and context-aware AI systems.

The book is organized into three parts. The first part lays the foundation, covering core AI concepts, system architectures, governance, and modernization approaches that prepare organizations for large-scale adoption. The second part explores industry applications, showing how agentic and **generative AI (GenAI)** can reshape sectors such as manufacturing, media, retail, financial services, insurance, and healthcare. The final part looks ahead, presenting advanced implementation patterns, governance models, and emerging technologies such as **Model Context Protocol (MCP)** and causal AI, equipping readers with strategies to sustain innovation and adapt to the next wave of intelligent systems.

How this book will help you

Inside, you will learn the core patterns for building intelligent architectures, with a focus on GenAI, **retrieval-augmented generation (RAG)**, and agentic systems powered by AI agents. You will see how these capabilities are applied across industries, supported by mapped reference architectures and detailed implementation guidance. The book also explores emerging directions such as causal intelligence, MCP, and advanced multi-agent design patterns. Whether you are modernizing legacy infrastructure or creating new platforms, it equips you with the vocabulary, frameworks, and practical context to move faster, reduce guesswork, and build reliable, scalable, and context-aware AI systems.

Who this book is for

This book is for:

- **IT decision-makers** exploring where to place strategic AI bets
- **Enterprise and solution architects** rethinking their data and application stack
- **Technical ears and curious builders** who want to understand how intelligent systems are structured and deployed
- **Business strategists and domain owners** seeking to translate AI hype into domain-specific outcomes

You don't need deep AI experience to get value from this book, but you should feel comfortable thinking in terms of data systems, application layers, and business architecture. If you're already experienced with AI concepts covered here, feel free to skip the early chapters and jump into the real-world case studies and future-focused content.

What this book covers

Chapter 1, AI Modernization to Innovation, outlines the difference between modernization and true innovation and how to structure teams, data, and processes to turn AI experiments into business outcomes.

Chapter 2, What Sets GenAI, RAG, and Agentic AI Apart, defines GenAI, RAG, and agentic systems, and explains when to use each approach.

Chapter 3, The System of Action, describes the document-oriented system of action and why unified, low-latency access to multimodal data and embeddings is critical for AI workloads.

Chapter 4, Trustworthy AI, Compliance, and Data Governance, summarizes governance, privacy, explainability, and risk management practices required for production AI.

Chapter 5, Modernization Using AI, gives practical patterns for using AI to accelerate legacy modernization while preserving correctness and governance.

Chapter 6, Practical Applications of Agentic and GenAI in Manufacturing – Part 1, focuses on supply-chain and inventory use cases, including embedding-driven classification and autonomous procurement helpers.

Chapter 7, Practical Applications of Agentic and GenAI in Manufacturing – Part II, focuses on factory-floor operations, including predictive maintenance, quality inspection, and multi-agent production orchestration.

Chapter 8, AI-Driven Strategies for Media and Telecommunication Industries, covers personalization, search experiences, AI operations, and fraud detection tailored to media and telecom sectors.

Chapter 9, Cognigy's Voice and Chatbots in the Time of Agentic AI, examines voice and chat systems for high-throughput, goal-oriented customer interactions.

Chapter 10, Harnessing AI to Transform the Retail Industry, explains personalization, demand forecasting, inventory optimization, and real-time decision-making in retail.

Chapter 11, Financial Services and the Next Wave of AI, outlines the sector's next AI transformation, from customer insight and compliance automation to AI-enhanced risk management and service models.

Chapter 12, RegData, MongoDB, and Voyage AI: Semantic Data Protection in FSI, describes semantic protection and audit approaches that enable compliant use of **large language models (LLMs)** in finance.

Chapter 13, Driving Client Success in Banking with GenAI Copilots, shows how banking copilots can automate advisor tasks, surface research, and support compliant client communications.

Chapter 14, Delivering Business Value with AI in Insurance, outlines converged datastores and AI patterns to improve underwriting, claims, and customer outcomes.

Chapter 15, Automating Insurance Underwriting with Fireworks AI and MongoDB, details an end-to-end underwriting pipeline using retrieval-grounded AI for faster, more accurate policy intake and quoting.

Chapter 16, AI-Powered Transformation of Healthcare and Life Sciences, addresses clinician overload with FHIR facade patterns, clinical RAG, and multi-agent care coordination to achieve better patient outcomes.

Chapter 17, Enterprise Document Management with Encore and MongoDB, demonstrates how to turn unstructured enterprise *dark* data into enriched, searchable knowledge for operational and AI use.

Chapter 18, Democratizing Agentic AI for Enterprise with Dataworkz and MongoDB, provides architectural guidance, governance practices, and real-world cases for deploying safe, observable, and effective agentic AI.

Chapter 19, Outlook: Beyond Today's AI, looks ahead to MCP, memory-driven agents, and causal AI as drivers of the next wave of intelligent systems.

To get the most out of this book

No specific tooling expertise is required, though a working understanding of enterprise systems and data architecture will help you engage more deeply with the material. Readers interested in implementation details, can explore:

- MongoDB Solutions Library: `https://www.mongodb.com/docs/atlas/architecture/current/solutions-library/`
- MongoDB for Artificial Intelligence: `https://www.mongodb.com/solutions/use-cases/artificial-intelligence`

Download the color images

We also provide a PDF file that has color images of the screenshots/diagrams used in this book. You can download it here: `https://packt.link/gbp/9781806117154`.

Conventions used

There are a number of text conventions used throughout this book.

`CodeInText`: Indicates code words in text, database table names, folder names, filenames, file extensions, pathnames, dummy URLs, user input or prompts, and Twitter handles. For example: "In the relational model, fields use names such as `FIRST_NAME`."

A block of code is set as follows:

```
{
  "_id": "67c20cf886f35bcb8c71e53c",
  "agent_id": "default_agent",
  "profile": "Default Agent Profile",
  "instructions": "Follow diagnostic procedures meticulously.",
  "rules": "Ensure safety; validate sensor data; document all steps.",
  "goals": "Provide accurate diagnostics and actionable recommendations."
}
```

Bold: Indicates a new term, an important word, or words that you see on the screen. For example: "The terms **prompting** and **prompt engineering** are frequently used in the same breath as LLMs and GenAI."

Warnings or important notes appear like this.

Tips and tricks appear like this.

Customer stories and other real-world examples appear like this.

Get in touch

Feedback from our readers is always welcome.

General feedback: If you have questions about any aspect of this book or have any general feedback, please email us at customercare@packt.com and mention the book's title in the subject of your message.

Errata: Although we have taken every care to ensure the accuracy of our content, mistakes do happen. If you have found a mistake in this book, we would be grateful if you reported this to us. Please visit http://www.packt.com/submit-errata, click **Submit Errata**, and fill in the form.

Piracy: If you come across any illegal copies of our works in any form on the internet, we would be grateful if you would provide us with the location address or website name. Please contact us at copyright@packt.com with a link to the material.

If you are interested in becoming an author: If there is a topic that you have expertise in and you are interested in either writing or contributing to a book, please visit http://authors.packt.com/.

Share your thoughts

Once you've read *Architectures for the Intelligent AI-Ready Enterprise*, we'd love to hear your thoughts! Scan the QR code below to go straight to the Amazon review page for this book and share your feedback.

https://packt.link/r/1806117150

Your review is important to us and the tech community and will help us make sure we're delivering excellent quality content.

Download a free PDF copy of this book

Thanks for purchasing this book!

Do you like to read on the go but are unable to carry your print books everywhere?

Is your eBook purchase not compatible with the device of your choice?

Don't worry, now with every Packt book you get a DRM-free PDF version of that book at no cost.

Read anywhere, any place, on any device. Search, copy, and paste code from your favorite technical books directly into your application.

The perks don't stop there, you can get exclusive access to discounts, newsletters, and great free content in your inbox daily.

Follow these simple steps to get the benefits:

1. Scan the QR code or visit the link below:

https://packt.link/free-ebook/9781806117154

2. Submit your proof of purchase.
3. That's it! We'll send your free PDF and other benefits to your email directly.

Part 1:
AI and Key Concepts

The following set of chapters lays the conceptual and architectural foundation for building intelligent systems with generative and agentic AI. It introduces the shift from modernization to innovation. It also explains the importance of real-time, document-based data models, and it describes the new architectural thinking required to implement AI at scale in a secure and responsible way.

This part of the book includes the following chapters:

- *Chapter 1, AI Modernization to Innovation*
- *Chapter 2, What Sets GenAI, RAG, and Agentic AI Apart*
- *Chapter 3, The System of Action*
- *Chapter 4, Trustworthy AI, Compliance, and Data Governance*
- *Chapter 5, Modernization Using AI*

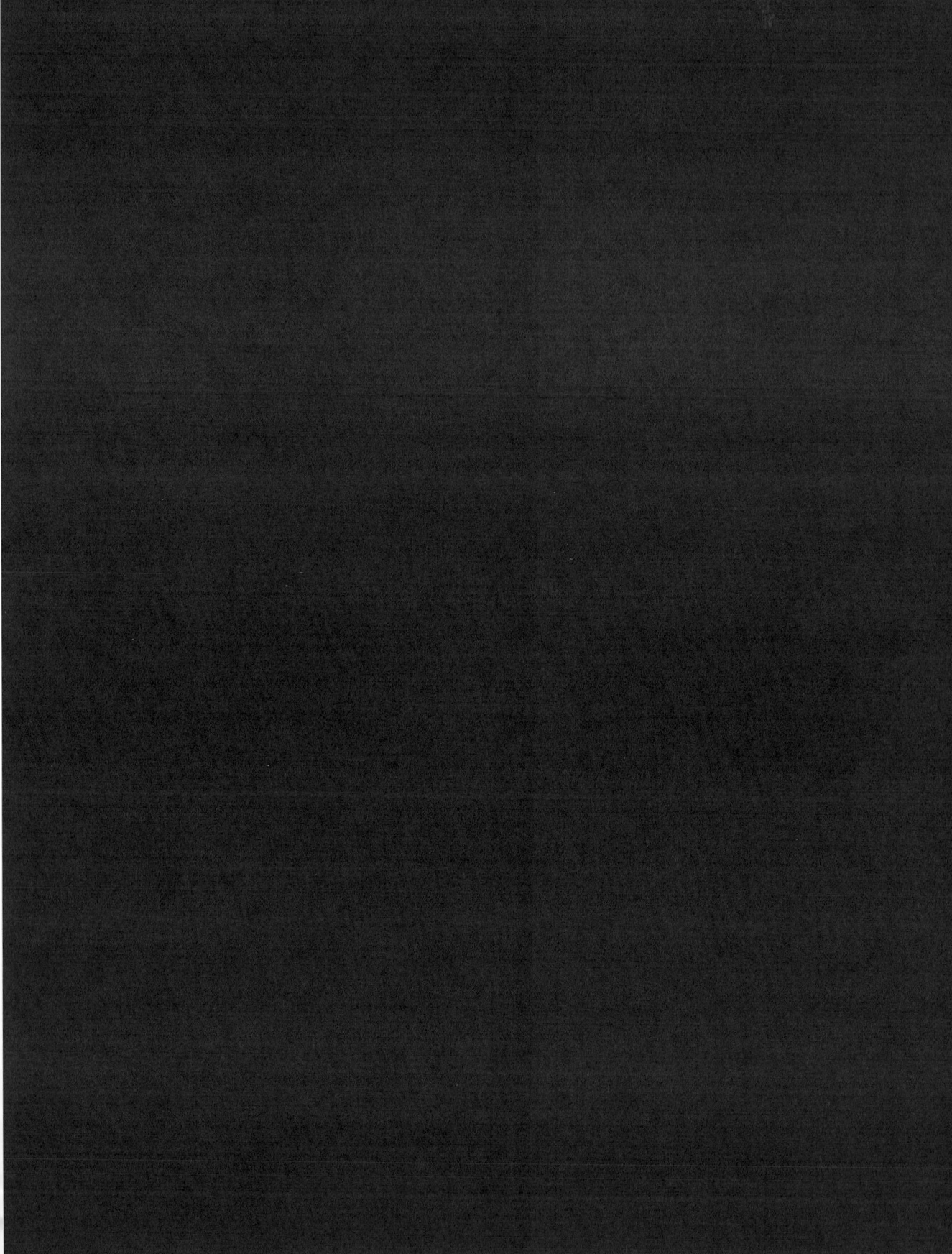

1

AI Modernization to Innovation

Many readers are at different stages of their AI journey, from initial exploration to active implementation planning. Some are leading teams tasked with *doing something with AI*. Others are watching competitors announce AI initiatives while wondering what their next move should be. Still others have tried AI pilots that showed promise in demos but somehow never made it to production. If any of this sounds familiar, you've found the right resource.

While countless publications theorize about AI's promise, this book takes a different approach: it's a field guide built *by* practitioners *for* practitioners, designed to help you navigate past the endless testing phase and move toward real-world AI implementation at scale.

Across industries, we've gathered hard-won lessons from teams that have actually done the work. These aren't abstract frameworks or vendor pitches; they're playbooks forged in the fire of enterprise constraints, integration realities, and performance expectations. We also look beyond the buzzwords. Though we cover **generative AI (GenAI)** and AI agents, we also discuss the data architectures, governance models, and design patterns that make this technology actually work. Because in the end, AI transformation isn't just about adopting new tools; it's about rethinking how your systems, teams, and business strategy fit together.

This practical focus matters now more than ever. While the AI revolution promises unprecedented productivity growth potential, the reality is that most organizations remain trapped in a cycle of modernization without innovation. Nearly all companies are investing in AI technologies, but few have integrated them deeply enough to deliver game-changing results. The difference lies in their approach [1].

How do you close this gap? It starts with distinguishing between two concepts that often get conflated: **modernization** and **innovation**. In this chapter, we'll untangle those definitions and show why understanding the difference is strategic. You'll learn how modernization sets the stage for AI success, how innovation extends its reach, and how both become essential when navigating a moment of rapid disruption.

At the end of this chapter, you will walk away with a sharper grasp of the core dynamics shaping successful AI adoption, including:

- The fundamental differences between innovation and modernization, and why both matter in AI deployments
- How Andy Grove's theory of strategic inflection points applies to today's AI revolution
- Why modernizing legacy systems and data infrastructure is essential for successful AI implementation
- How to avoid common pitfalls organizations face when pursuing AI initiatives without proper foundations
- How to implement practical approaches to balancing innovation and modernization in your AI strategy

Understanding innovation: Creating new value

Before you can effectively harness AI to modernize or innovate, you need a practical understanding of what these terms actually mean and how they differ in both execution and impact.

Innovation, at its core, *is the process of creating and implementing new ideas, methods, products, or services that add value or improve upon existing ones.* It involves turning creative concepts into practical solutions that meet real-world needs or solve problems more effectively.

Innovation can take many forms, including the following:

- **Product innovation**: Developing new or significantly improved goods or services. Think of the move from paper maps to GPS apps.
- **Process innovation**: Introducing new ways of producing or delivering products. **Robotic process automation (RPA)** has revolutionized standardized processes and decision-making, leading to innovations such as autonomous underwriting or real-time claims management for insurance companies.
- **Business model innovation**: Redefining how a company creates and captures value. Probably the most famous of all innovations was Netflix's multi-level innovation, first shipping DVDs to people's homes, rather than *picking them up at Blockbuster*, and then delivering content via streaming to make it even easier than mail.

- **Social innovation**: Using new technologies to address environmental and societal needs. AI is accelerating **environmental, social, and governance (ESG)** progress. This includes everything from smart energy systems to automated carbon tracking. In places such as Brazil, platforms such as PicPay are expanding access to financial tools and social programs for underserved communities.

Each of these examples started with an idea, but became an innovation only once it was applied to solve a problem at scale. In this sense, innovation requires more than invention. It requires execution.

Strategic inflection points: Andy Grove's theory applied to AI

Few frameworks better explain what's at stake in today's AI race than Andy Grove's theory of strategic inflection points, introduced in his book *Only the Paranoid Survive*. Grove describes these moments as times when the fundamentals of a business (or an entire industry) undergo dramatic, irreversible change. These shifts can be triggered by new technology, regulatory upheaval, competitive pressure, or all three at once.

Grove's central insight? *You don't see an inflection point clearly until you're in it.* And by then, it's often too late to catch up. Companies that adapt early can leap ahead. Those that hesitate, resist, or cling to old models often don't survive.

Strategic inflection points require leadership to do more than just optimize; they demand reinvention. Grove famously said: *"Only the paranoid survive."* In his view, success requires constant vigilance, relentless questioning of assumptions, and the courage to bet on transformation before the path is proven.

The best-known example? Intel.

In the 1980s, Intel dominated the memory chip business. But competitors from Japan began producing faster, cheaper, and higher-quality alternatives. Grove and then-CEO Gordon Moore made a bold call: they abandoned their legacy business and pivoted entirely to microprocessors. At the time, this market was small and uncertain. But the gamble paid off. Intel's chips became the backbone of the personal computing revolution, transforming the company into one of the most important tech players of the modern era.

Today, AI presents a similar inflection point. The introduction of **large language models (LLMs)**, **retrieval-augmented generation (RAG)**, and agentic systems may prove to be as foundational to the AI era as the first microprocessors were to the PC era. These technologies are not just new features; they're new substrates for how business is done.

Unlike the microprocessor revolution, which unfolded over decades, AI is evolving at unprecedented speed. Expectations are rising faster than infrastructure can keep up. And many organizations haven't even started modernizing their foundations.

If you're feeling the urgency, you should be. This is what an inflection point feels like.

Navigating the AI inflection point

Organizations that recognize this moment as a true inflection point can prepare their infrastructure and capabilities for the AI-driven future. Beyond new tools, success demands a fundamental rethink of how data, technology, and business processes work together.

At the core of this transformation are five critical capabilities:

- **Flexible, future-ready data infrastructure**: Legacy systems face significant challenges with AI requirements. Rigid database schemas and monolithic architectures often cannot support dynamic AI applications. Organizations need infrastructure that can adapt to rapidly evolving AI capabilities without requiring complete system overhauls. This means adopting platforms that support schema flexibility, can handle diverse data types from structured databases to unstructured documents and multimedia content, and can scale both vertically and horizontally as AI workloads grow. The infrastructure must also support real-time data processing and streaming, as many AI applications require immediate access to the most current information.

- **Fluency in vector embeddings and semantic search technologies**: These technologies form the backbone of many modern AI applications. Vector embeddings allow AI systems to understand and process human language, images, and other complex data types by converting them into mathematical representations that machines can work with. While many AI implementations can succeed without deep technical knowledge of embeddings, organizations pursuing more sophisticated or differentiated AI solutions will benefit from teams that understand how to generate, store, and query these embeddings effectively. This includes knowledge of different embedding models, understanding when to use pre-trained versus custom embeddings, and expertise in vector databases and similarity search algorithms. This expertise becomes particularly valuable when building AI applications that can truly understand and reason about complex, domain-specific data.

- **Architectures that bridge AI and operations**: Too often, AI initiatives are built separately from the data sources and business systems they're meant to enhance. That leads to data silos, synchronization problems, and AI applications that work with stale or incomplete information. Successful organizations design architectures where AI capabilities are deeply integrated with operational systems, allowing for real-time insights and automated decision-making based on current business data. This integration requires careful consideration of data flow, API design, and event-driven architectures that can propagate changes across both traditional and AI systems.

- **Strategies for maintaining data consistency between systems**: This becomes critical when AI applications need to work alongside legacy systems during transition periods, though this remains one of the most challenging aspects of AI implementation. Organizations cannot typically replace all their systems overnight, so they need approaches for managing data synchronization across multiple platforms, even when perfect consistency may not be achievable. This includes implementing change data capture mechanisms, designing data validation processes, and establishing clear data governance policies. The strategy must also account for the fact that AI systems may process and transform data differently than traditional applications, requiring new approaches to data lineage and quality management. Organizations should expect this to be an ongoing challenge rather than a problem with straightforward solutions.

- **Guardrails for responsible AI**: As pressure builds to move fast, the temptation to cut corners grows. But without robust governance frameworks, organizations risk deploying systems that are biased, brittle, or out of compliance. Practical AI governance means codifying policies for data privacy and security, algorithmic bias and fairness, model explainability and transparency, and regulatory compliance across different jurisdictions. The governance framework must be enforceable, providing clear guidelines for AI development teams while not slowing down innovation unnecessarily. Done well, governance becomes a catalyst, not a constraint.

These approaches address a critical challenge at the AI inflection point: the need to bridge operational data and AI capabilities without creating new data silos or overly complex architectures. Organizations that successfully navigate this inflection point will find themselves with significant competitive advantages, while those that fail to adapt risk being left behind as AI transforms their industries. The key is to start building these capabilities now, before the competitive pressure becomes overwhelming.

Understanding modernization: The often-overlooked prerequisite

In addition to the high impact potential of innovation, there's another critical lever in the transformation toolkit: modernization. While modernization itself is a broader term often used to describe physical infrastructure, **technical modernization** refers to the *upgrading or replacement of outdated technologies, systems, or processes with newer, more efficient, and more advanced ones to improve performance, productivity, and competitiveness*. Key elements of technical modernization include the following:

- **Digitalization** using technologies such as automation, AI, cloud computing, or **Internet of Things (IoT)**
- **Digitization** of analog processes, for instance, replacing paper records with digital systems
- **System upgrades**, such as modernizing legacy IT infrastructure or software (commonly referred to as refactoring)
- **Integration** of modern tools into existing workflows to increase efficiency and reduce costs
- **Cybersecurity improvements** that address evolving threats and meet industry standards

The goal of modernization is to **enhance capabilities, reduce operational risks,** and **remain competitive** in a fast-changing technological landscape.

In the context of this book, modernization comes in two distinct forms. The first form involves modernization through the adoption of advanced technologies to address what is arguably the most significant challenge facing many enterprises today: **legacy systems**. Here, the term *legacy system* is used in a broad sense. While these systems often undergo physical upgrades every three to five years (a cycle deeply familiar in the mainframe world and certainly impacting IBM results), the software running on these systems often remains outdated. This leads to situations where companies are running decades-old business logic and software, despite having upgraded to newer hardware. The underlying code and business processes can be as old as half a century, creating significant challenges for modernization efforts.

The second approach, which is often the best way to go in scenarios such as this, is a complete system replacement built from scratch. But, as is often the case in business, the direct approach may not be available as the reasons for not touching a system as such are plenty: implicit business know-how, regulatory compliance, connectivity to existing machines, and more.

Common modernization strategies

Modernizing legacy applications isn't one size fits all. According to industry research and best practices [2], there are several common modernization strategies that organizations can employ:

- **Refactoring**: When a company refactors, developers update the code base, improving the code structure, performance, and maintainability. This can involve enhancing existing code without changing functionality, or migrating from older languages and frameworks to more modern alternatives. For example, an application built in Ruby might be refactored into Rust, or a system using an old version of Java with Spring might be refactored to modern Java with Quarkus. This action allows for independent scaling, easier maintenance, and access to current development tools and practices.

- **Replatforming**: This involves updating parts of an application's platform, such as the underlying database, and typically necessitates some code base modifications as well.

- **Rehosting or redeploying**: Sometimes called *lift and shift*, this method involves moving applications to a public cloud, private cloud, hybrid cloud, or multi-cloud environment. It's a straightforward way to gain some of the cloud's benefits without extensive rework, but it does not attempt to address any problems with the application as is.

- **Rearchitecting**: This may involve updating the code base to leverage modern architectures, such as containers or microservices.

- **Rebuilding**: Starting from scratch, while preserving the application's scope and specifications, is also an option and is useful when the existing application is too outdated or inefficient for modernization.

- **Replacing**: This involves starting over with a completely new code base, beginning from basic requirements upward. Rather than replicating the legacy application, this approach goes back to the business to collect current, modern requirements and build from there. Many applications aren't worth modernizing because business processes have evolved significantly since they were originally built, making replacement often the most sensible path forward. This allows organizations to eliminate outdated features while incorporating new capabilities that align with current business needs.

The choice between these strategies depends on several factors, including the current state of the application, business requirements, available resources, and timeline constraints. Organizations often find that a hybrid approach works best, combining multiple strategies across different components of their systems. For instance, they might refactor critical applications while rehosting less critical ones, or rebuild core systems while replacing outdated peripheral applications.

Each strategy involves trade-offs between cost, risk, and potential benefits. Refactoring and replatforming offer lower risk but more limited improvements, while rebuilding and replacing provide greater transformation potential but require more significant investment and carry higher implementation risks. The key is aligning the modernization approach with business objectives and technical constraints.

While these strategies outline how modernization can be approached at the application level, executing them effectively often depends on the foundation provided by modern data platforms.

Where innovation meets modernization: The AI intersection

This is where AI-driven innovation and infrastructure modernization converge. Over the last 20 years, many companies have offered elaborate *modernization approaches* or full-scale practices, often involving reviews of existing software and processes to ultimately do a de facto rewrite from scratch, essentially rebuilding entire systems from the ground up while calling it *modernization*.

However, as we will discuss further in *Chapter 5, Modernization Using AI*, these complete rewrites have significant pitfalls. They lack the repeatability and transparency required to drive true modernization of existing systems, often becoming resource-intensive, one-off projects that risk losing embedded business logic and institutional knowledge.

AI shifts the equation. Instead of defaulting to wholesale replacement, it enables smarter, more sustainable modernization, preserving what works while evolving what doesn't. AI can analyze legacy code, convert it to more digestible, modern formats (such as different programming languages or paradigms), and facilitate comprehensive architecture changes from monolithic systems to modern distributed, n-tier architectures, including microservices-based designs. It accelerates test generation, improves maintainability, and bridges the gap between brittle systems and modern workflows. These strategies, explored further in *Chapter 5, Modernization Using AI*, equip organizations to evolve systems iteratively without starting over.

The AI implementation pitfall: When innovation lacks foundation

The second part, where modernization and AI innovation align, is more subtle. The strong push through the business for AI solutions and utilizing AI to improve business functionality may lead to quick solutions that are neither sustainable nor fit the definition of production readiness.

When AI projects don't make it to production

Consider this real-world scenario. A large multinational company with an elaborate innovation process received a mandate from business leadership to deliver AI across the organization. Excited by the possibilities, the company initiated a broader evaluation that ultimately spawned 500 independent projects, all focused on implementing some form of AI capability. The organization invested significant resources, assembled teams across multiple business units, and generated considerable enthusiasm for the AI transformation. Twelve months later, when these projects underwent formal evaluation for production deployment, none made the cut to move forward. Not a single project among the 500 initiatives demonstrated sufficient business value, technical reliability, or operational readiness to justify continued investment.

Analysis showed that there was a disconnect between resolving actual business problems and implementing solutions that, while appealing from an IT perspective, had no measurable impact. Second, each project was driven by independent research conducted by individuals or smaller teams, which ignored fundamental discussions about production deployment or continuous integration into workflows. Lastly, data integration was overlooked, as people worked with sample data that did not reflect the requirements of real-time use cases. Any changes or updates to these datasets could have led to unexpected results on the LLM side beyond simple hallucinations. For example, changing datasets with different calibrations (such as a software upgrade in a manufacturing line), could've resulted in, at best, unsellable products and, at worst, dangerous goods.

In other words, modernizing underlying data infrastructure is a prerequisite for such use cases to move beyond experimentation and begin actual implementation. AI applications require a substantially different approach to data infrastructure compared to legacy applications that utilize the same schema for decades; they must handle diverse data types, support real-time processing, and accommodate rapidly evolving business requirements and integration needs.

In this context, modernization is not an optional, nice-to-have side effect but a hard prerequisite for the production implementation of AI functionality. As a side effect, the modernization of data landscapes will simplify the discussion with the business about the actual value of AI.

So, what does a solid foundation look like in practice? It starts with modern data platforms designed to balance both the agility of innovation with the rigor of modernization.

Modern data platforms: The backbone of AI-ready transformation

Modern data platforms are not just an infrastructure upgrade; they are foundational to enabling AI-driven transformation, supporting both innovation and modernization simultaneously. In an era defined by rapid change, traditional systems are too rigid to meet the evolving needs of businesses pursuing AI. A modern platform bridges this gap by offering the flexibility, speed, and scalability that both innovation and modernization demand.

Why modern data platforms are necessary

At the heart of modernization and AI readiness is the ability to manage and operate on diverse, rapidly changing data. Many enterprises rely on relational databases with fixed schemas and monolithic architectures that require significant modification to support dynamic AI applications. Modern data platforms, especially those built around document-based or non-relational architectures, offer enhanced capabilities for contemporary workloads, including schema flexibility, real-time processing, and horizontal scaling, which AI applications typically require.

This flexibility is a strategic necessity. Modern business requirements often include real-time decisions, multi-format data, and agile development, none of which are feasible with legacy data systems. As organizations pursue AI transformation, their ability to innovate, modernize, and scale depends directly on the underlying data infrastructure.

Enabling innovation through agility and speed

Traditional databases force developers to spend weeks defining exact data structures before writing any code. If you want to add a new field or change how data connects, you need database administrators to manually update schemas, often taking days or weeks. Modern platforms let developers start coding immediately with whatever data structure makes sense. Need to add customer preferences to your insurance app? Just start storing that data. Want to test a new claims workflow? Build it without waiting for schema changes.

This means a team can go from idea to working prototype in days instead of months. Teams can build, test, and iterate on new solutions, such as autonomous underwriting or real-time claims processing, without relying on manual changes to rigid database structures.

Additionally, platforms such as MongoDB accommodate natural data formats such as images, documents, and time-series data, enabling a wider range of use cases. For example, by removing the need for complex data transformations, organizations can bring together previously siloed data sources to develop new applications faster, increasing time to value.

This flexibility and speed are essential because innovation is a continuous process that requires ongoing development and iteration. As ideas mature, modern data architectures evolve with them, supporting product growth, feature expansion, and user-driven feedback loops without requiring disruptive migrations.

Simplifying modernization without starting over

Modernization efforts are notoriously difficult, especially when legacy systems contain decades of embedded business logic and regulatory dependencies. Modern data platforms reduce the risk and cost of modernization by supporting incremental migration paths.

Instead of forcing big-bang rewrites, these platforms enable hybrid deployments where legacy and modern systems coexist. Seamless integration tools analyze existing schemas, map legacy structures into modern formats, and maintain data integrity during transitions. These platforms keep old and new systems synchronized automatically; when a customer updates their address in your legacy system, that change instantly appears in your new system too. This means you can migrate customers and functions gradually instead of risking a complete system shutdown. Furthermore, cloud-native deployment capabilities offer the flexibility to scale infrastructure on demand, reducing upfront costs and allowing experimentation with new architectures in sandbox environments. This makes it possible to modernize without losing institutional knowledge or disrupting core operations.

Powering AI at scale

AI applications depend on more than just models; they require infrastructure capable of storing, retrieving, and reasoning over complex data. Modern databases meet this need by supporting advanced AI workflows, including vector embeddings and semantic search.

By storing vector representations of data such as those generated by LLMs alongside operational records, organizations can implement capabilities such as similarity search, context-aware recommendations, and intelligent automation. Integrated support for vector search eliminates the need for disjointed pipelines and enables tighter coupling between operational data and AI decision-making.

Additionally, real-time data processing capabilities ensure that AI systems work with current information rather than static snapshots. As AI systems evolve rapidly with new models and architectures emerging every few months, modern platforms offer the agility needed to adapt without reengineering foundational systems.

Summary

This chapter explored the critical distinction between innovation and modernization in the context of AI transformation. It examined Andy Grove's strategic inflection points theory and demonstrated how today's AI revolution represents a comparable inflection point to the computing revolution of the 1980s.

The discussion illustrated why modernizing legacy systems and data infrastructure is essential for successful AI implementation through both cautionary tales and success stories. The chapter established that AI innovation requires a solid foundation. Modernization addresses the burden of legacy infrastructure, particularly in data systems.

By understanding the relationship between innovation and modernization, and leveraging modern data platforms that support both, organizations can successfully navigate the AI inflection point and create a sustainable competitive advantage.

The next chapter demystifies the AI landscape. You'll understand how the core technologies, that is, semantic search, LLMs, RAG, and agentic AI, fit together to create business value.

References

1. *Superagency in the workplace: Empowering people to unlock AI's full potential*: https://www.mckinsey.com/capabilities/mckinsey-digital/our-insights/superagency-in-the-workplace-empowering-people-to-unlock-ais-full-potential-at-work

2. *Why Application Modernization is Vital for Business Growth*: https://www.mongodb.com/resources/solutions/use-cases/application-modernization#common-modernization-strategies

2
What Sets GenAI, RAG, and Agentic AI Apart

Organizations today face a critical challenge: separating real AI capabilities from marketing hype, while aligning future strategies in a rapidly changing environment. With newly minted AI terms flooding every proposal, pitch, and product demo, even experienced technologists find themselves navigating conversations where the fundamental differences between technologies remain unclear. At best, these differences are unclear; more often, they are incomprehensible. Whether you're evaluating solutions, architecting systems, or advising on strategic investments, this isn't just about understanding buzzwords; it's about making informed decisions that define your organization's competitive advantage.

Three concepts have emerged as the cornerstone technologies defining modern AI applications: **generative AI (GenAI)**, which enables systems to create new content from learned patterns; **retrieval-augmented generation (RAG)**, which connects AI models to external knowledge sources for improved accuracy; and agentic AI, which powers autonomous systems that can plan, reason, and execute complex workflows with minimal human intervention. Understanding how these technologies interconnect and build upon one another is essential for making strategic decisions about AI implementation. Even these widely accepted terms have a myriad of interpretations, and while we do not claim to present the single truth, we aim to provide you with a solid fundamental baseline.

This chapter serves as your entry point into the world of GenAI. If you already possess extensive experience with AI architectures and clearly understand the distinction among these technologies, you may choose to advance to subsequent chapters. But for those seeking to build solid foundational knowledge, this chapter will provide the essential groundwork for everything that follows.

By the end of this chapter, you will have a clear understanding of the following:

- An exploration of the historical evolution of AI and how GenAI emerged from earlier approaches
- The fundamental role of **large language models (LLMs)** and how they process and generate information
- How embedding models transform data into vectors, the foundation for AI reasoning
- The critical role of vector databases in storing, managing, and enabling efficient similarity searches
- The distinction between semantic search, RAG, and hybrid search approaches
- What makes agentic AI different from previous AI systems, and how it enables autonomous decision making
- The core components of AI agents, including memory, orchestration, tools, models, and data services
- How these components work together in practical applications to solve real business problems

How AI evolved: From theory to ChatGPT

To understand today's AI landscape, we need to trace the technological journey that brought us here. This evolution spans decades of research breakthroughs, from symbolic logic and expert systems to the transformer architectures powering today's LLMs. By examining this progression, we can better appreciate how current capabilities emerged and why architectural decisions continue to shape today's systems.

When we talk about *models* in GenAI, we are referring to a mathematical system trained to recognize and replicate patterns found in data. We use the word *model* because, like a model of a building or a climate system, it's a simplified, structured version of something complex; in this case, language, images, or behavior. A GenAI model is trained on large datasets to learn how elements (such as words or pixels) typically relate to each other. Once trained, it can generate new, realistic-like content based on that learned structure. It doesn't store exact answers; it models how things work, then uses that understanding to create new outputs.

We'll trace that evolution across three major inflection points: the early foundations of AI, the breakthrough emergence of LLMs, and how these developments culminated in the GenAI systems we know today.

A small walk into history

AI has arguably become the most talked-about technology in the IT community since the advent of the mouse through Xerox PARC. It's fascinating how widespread the belief is that *AI was magically invented overnight, emerging fully formed when OpenAI released ChatGPT to the public.* But today's capabilities did not appear overnight. To understand them, we need to trace the evolution of today's *GenAI* in the context of time.

The term **artificial intelligence** was coined in 1955 by John McCarthy and colleagues, and first used at the Dartmouth Workshop in 1956, a pioneering event that brought together leading scientists to define and advance the field[1]. According to the Oxford dictionary, AI is:

> *The theory and development of computer systems able to perform tasks normally requiring human intelligence, such as visual perception, speech recognition, decision making, and translation between languages [2].*

From that starting point, several different approaches emerged, each shaped by the computing capabilities and research priorities of their time. Among them: symbolic logic systems, fuzzy logic (1980s), early neural networks (1990s), and eventually machine learning, which became increasingly practical and widespread in the early 2000s.

As experimentation accelerated, two key technological advances converged to enable large-scale AI development. First, parallel compute power was established through early support of graphics cards (GPUs) via software interfaces such as **CUDA** (released in 2007), which allowed programmers to harness the massive parallel processing power of graphics cards for general computing tasks. Second, frameworks such as **Apache Spark** (open-sourced in 2010) helped overcome a core limitation of earlier distributed computing platforms such as **Hadoop MapReduce**.

Hadoop MapReduce was an early system for splitting large computing jobs across multiple computers, but it was slow for machine learning because it had to repeatedly read and write data to disk. Spark revolutionized this by keeping data in computer memory between processing steps, making iterative algorithms essential for machine learning run orders of magnitude faster. Together, these advances meant researchers could finally process and analyze massive datasets efficiently, a breakthrough that became crucial for training the large-scale AI models we see today.

AlphaGo and the turning point in AI

In March 2016, another milestone unfolded. On a Go board in Seoul, South Korea, **AlphaGo**, an AI system developed by DeepMind, faced off against Lee Sedol, one of the most accomplished Go players in history. What followed was a stunning 4–1 victory for the machine, and a turning point in the story of modern AI.

Why was this such a big deal? Go, unlike chess, had long resisted computer mastery. Its search space is vast, with more possible board states than atoms in the universe. It demands intuition, pattern recognition, and strategic depth. For decades, AI researchers believed Go was beyond the reach of brute-force computation, requiring a form of reasoning once thought uniquely human.

AlphaGo shattered that belief. Combining deep neural networks with **reinforcement learning** and Monte Carlo tree search, it marked a radical shift in approach. Rather than relying solely on predefined rules or exhaustive search, AlphaGo learned. First, from human expert games, and then by playing millions of games against itself. It was one of the first public demonstrations of deep reinforcement learning at scale, showing the power of systems that could improve through experience rather than being programmed line by line.

The emergence of LLMs

If AlphaGo marked a turning point in decision-making AI, **transformers** redefined how machines understand language.

Starting from a 2006 proposal, IBM developed *Watson*, a deep question-answering system that won *Jeopardy!* in 2011, a significant breakthrough for **natural language processing (NLP)** on unstructured data[3]. Watson combined knowledge bases, ML, and sophisticated question-answering systems, marking an important milestone in AI's ability to understand and process human language.

But today's LLMs followed a different evolutionary path. In 2017, Google researchers published *Attention Is All You Need*, introducing the **transformer** architecture, critical for building modern language models[4]. The key innovation of transformers was the self-attention mechanism, allowing models to process entire sequences simultaneously and capture long-range dependencies in text more effectively than previous sequential approaches.

Transformers became the foundation for modern LLMs, which truly entered the mainstream with models such as GPT-3 in 2020 and ChatGPT in 2022, ushering in the **GenAI era**.

The turning point

While Watson showcased engineered systems and curated knowledge bases to win, transformer-based LLMs took a radically different route. Instead of being programmed with what to say, they learned to *predict* it, spotting patterns across massive datasets and generating fluent, often human-like responses. Between those milestones, AlphaGo's victory revealed something new: that AI could not only answer but adapt, learn, and surprise. That shift helped pave the way for today's generative and agentic systems.

This recent history underscores that today's GenAI systems aren't the product of a single breakthrough, but the result of decades of incremental innovation, infrastructure evolution, and compounding research progress. While the broader history of AI includes both progress and periods of reduced funding known as *AI winters*, the trajectory leading directly to GenAI has accelerated sharply in recent years. Modern data platforms have been crucial in this recent evolution, providing the infrastructure needed to store, process, and analyze the massive datasets required to train today's most powerful models.

The development of LLMs continues to evolve rapidly. While early leaders such as OpenAI (ChatGPT) and Anthropic dominate the market in 2025, new approaches are emerging. Companies such as DeepSeek are exploring divide-and-conquer methodologies to reduce LLM complexity and costs, while others such as Zhipu are developing router-based architectures with specialized *experts*. Despite these varied approaches, the core concept of LLMs serving as knowledge bases and reasoning engines will likely remain central to AI systems in the foreseeable future.

GenAI: Creating new content from patterns

LLMs form the foundation of any GenAI solution. While often perceived as the sole requirement for implementing GenAI capabilities, today's LLMs, despite achieving substantial reasoning abilities, still depend critically on an external resource to provide useful context: **data**.

The terms **prompting** and **prompt engineering** are frequently used in the same breath as LLMs and GenAI. Prompting refers to crafting queries for an LLM, while prompt engineering involves systematically optimizing these queries for better results. Early LLM interactions heavily emphasized standalone prompt engineering and led to the overnight phenomenon of millions of prompt engineers on LinkedIn.

However, the emergence of advanced architectural patterns such as RAG, which combines LLMs with external knowledge retrieval systems, has shifted the focus toward more comprehensive solutions that embed LLMs within broader systems rather than treating them as isolated tools. (We'll explore RAG in detail later in this chapter.) Effective prompting now involves crafting queries that optimally leverage rich contextual data provided by these patterns, making the quality of context as crucial as the prompt itself.

More advanced prompting techniques, such as **Chain-of-Thought (CoT)** prompting, give us a way to help AI think step by step, similar to showing your work in math class, which further improves the quality of the responses. By asking it to `"think step by step"`, you make it more likely to reason correctly, especially for harder problems in math, logic, or multi-part tasks. This approach is particularly effective when dealing with complex scenarios that benefit from systematic breakdown; for instance, when processing large documents such as insurance claims, you might prompt the LLM first to identify key components, then analyze each section methodically, and finally synthesize the findings.

As with any data system, the old phrase *garbage in, garbage out* applies. In the case of LLMs, poor input quality can result in **hallucinations**, responses that often generate incorrect answers that initially appear to be reasonable output but, upon inspection, turn out to be complete fabrications by the LLM. Approaches to mitigate these issues have evolved beyond simple prompt tuning to include better context framing, improved data validation, and sophisticated filtering mechanisms to prevent information drift and ensure output reliability.

How GenAI works

GenAI refers to AI systems that can create new content, such as text, images, code, or other media, based on patterns learned from existing data. Unlike traditional AI systems that follow explicit rules, GenAI learns patterns and relationships from vast datasets and then uses this understanding to generate new, original content that resembles the training data. Understanding the foundational nature of LLMs can help organizations assess their resource implications and effectively leverage these technologies.

However, the reality is that LLMs are black boxes and non-deterministic, meaning that the same input doesn't always produce the same output. There is some truth in the idea that we still don't fully understand the internal workings of LLMs. While a lot of research is being done on this, a clear and accurate understanding of what actually happens inside an LLM is tantalisingly out of reach. Anthropic, one of the leaders in the field of AI safety, wrote a paper on this, concluding that:

Understanding the representations the model uses doesn't tell us how it uses them; even though we have the features, we still need to find the circuits they are involved in. And we need to show that the safety-relevant features we have begun to find can actually be used to improve safety. There's much more to be done.

Recognizing both the capabilities and limitations of LLMs, such as their limited context windows and potential for hallucinations, becomes crucial for setting realistic expectations and planning for necessary safeguards and augmentation strategies. Furthermore, decisions around using pre-trained models versus fine-tuning or building custom models directly impact budget, timelines, and infrastructure choices, knowledge that proves invaluable for vendor negotiations and platform selection.

The GenAI process follows key sequential steps, as illustrated in *Figure 2.1*.

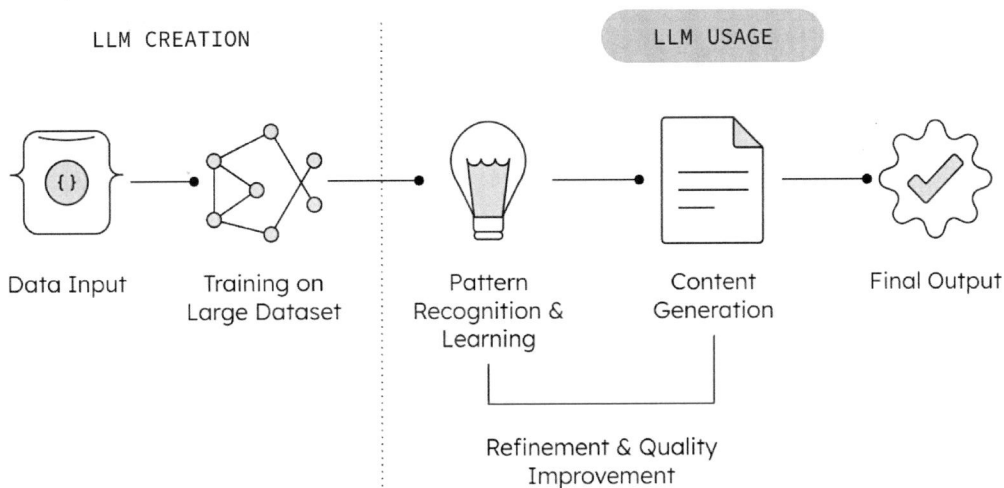

LLM CREATION   LLM USAGE

Data Input   Training on   Pattern   Content   Final Output
                  Large Dataset   Recognition &   Generation
                                     Learning

                                     Refinement & Quality
                                     Improvement

Figure 2.1: GenAI process flow

The diagram depicts a process flow that involves five key stages. Firstly, a giant training dataset is assembled, typically many petabytes in size. This is then used to train the LLM. During training, and with subsequent use, the model begins to recognize patterns and build connections between disparate pieces of data. The model is then prompted by an end user, and output is generated. Often, these prompts and outputs will be monitored internally and fed back into the model for constant refinement and quality improvement.

This sequential process demonstrates a fundamental principle: GenAI's ability to create novel content stems directly from its comprehensive understanding of existing patterns. The more diverse and high-quality the training data, the more sophisticated and accurate the generated outputs become. This understanding is crucial for organizations planning GenAI implementations, as it highlights the critical importance of data quality and the iterative nature of achieving optimal results.

Limitations and challenges of GenAI

While GenAI has made remarkable progress, it faces several significant limitations that organizations must consider:

- **Training data limitations**: LLMs are fundamentally constrained by their training data. If the data is outdated, biased, or lacks diversity, the model's outputs will reflect these flaws, potentially generating irrelevant information or perpetuating harmful stereotypes.

- **Hallucinations and factual inaccuracy**: Models can confidently generate plausible-sounding but factually incorrect or nonsensical information, a phenomenon known as *hallucination*. This makes them unreliable for applications requiring high levels of factual accuracy without proper safeguards such as RAG.

- **Lack of explainability**: The complex, *black-box* nature of many LLMs makes it difficult to understand their internal reasoning. This lack of transparency, often called the challenge of explainability or interpretability, can be a significant barrier in regulated industries or critical applications where understanding the *why* behind a decision is essential.

- **Context and reasoning limitations**: Models can struggle with nuanced understanding, commonsense reasoning, and maintaining context over long interactions. They may misinterpret ambiguous queries or fail to grasp complex, multi-step instructions.

- **Ethical and societal risks**: The widespread use of GenAI introduces significant ethical challenges, including the potential for generating misinformation and deepfakes, perpetuating biases, infringing copyright, and creating new avenues for malicious use.

Modern data platforms help address some of these challenges by providing flexible, scalable infrastructure for storing and processing the diverse data types needed for AI training and operation. Document-based data models are particularly well-suited for AI applications, as they can adapt to changing requirements and store heterogeneous data types in their natural form, a foundational step in building more reliable and grounded AI systems. Furthermore, accessing a broad range of data sources, rather than being limited to legacy siloed systems, often requires concepts such as dynamic systems of action, which we'll discuss in the next chapter.

From data to vectors

Building on the introduced flexible data storage capabilities, the next step in enabling AI reasoning requires transforming data into a format that computers can process and manipulate mathematically. This is where the concept of vectors comes in; they serve as the universal language that enables GenAI to work with any type of structured or unstructured data. Think of vectors as coordinates on a map, but instead of just showing location with latitude and longitude, they can represent the *meaning* of any piece of data in hundreds or thousands of dimensions. A vector might capture what makes a product description appealing, why certain customer reviews are similar, or how different documents relate to each other. While the representation of text in three dimensions is still easy to grasp, the representation of movie segments in hundreds of dimensions defies any visualization, and we leave the concept as a mental exercise. A use case for movie segments could be digital rights management and identification of identical versus derived movies, so this is not something unusual.

Here's the key insight: similar things end up close together in vector space.

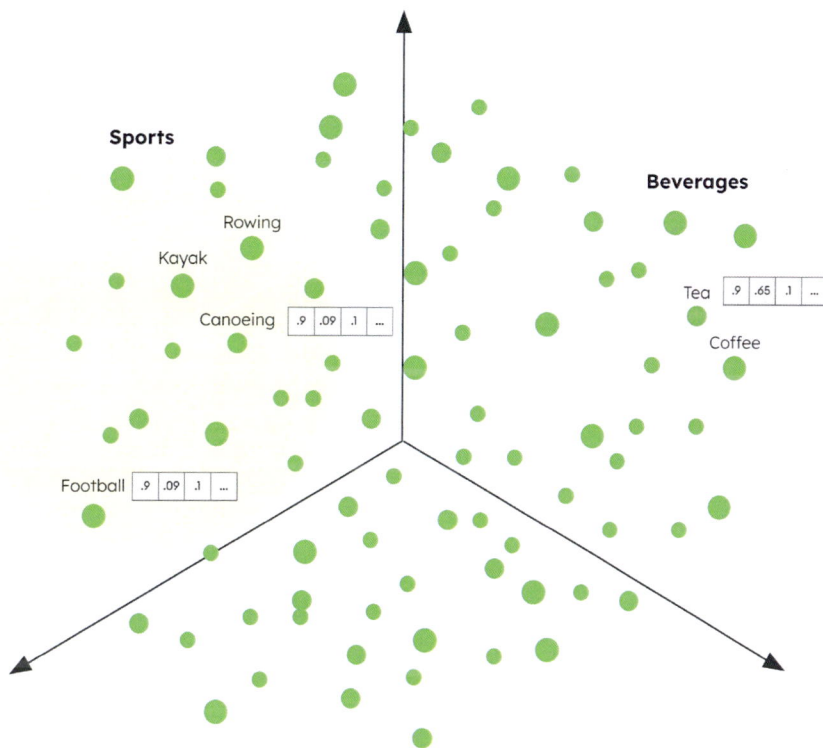

Figure 2.2: Vector space visualization – similar concepts cluster together

Figure 2.2 illustrates this concept in action. Each colored dot represents a different piece of data that has been converted into vector form. Notice how related concepts naturally group together, sports-related terms cluster in one area, beverages form their own region, and specific activities such as basketball and football sit close to their broader sports category. This isn't a coincidence; it's the mathematical representation of meaning that makes AI systems so powerful.

But what does this look like in action in business applications? When a customer asks about `payment issues`, the AI system can instantly locate not just documents containing those exact words, but also related content about `billing problems`, `account charges`, and `subscription fees`, because they all exist in the same neighborhood of vector space.

The embedding models and "embedders"

But now you might ask, "*How do I transform my data into vectors?*" Data gets represented as vectors through specialized algorithms called embedding models. These models, often incorporating machine learning or mathematical functions, can transform a wide variety of data types into numerical representations in the form of vectors that enable AI systems to understand relationships and find similarities across multiple dimensions. Text, pictures, video, and voice are the most common applications, but embedding models can represent virtually any data type and even complex combinations of data that capture specific states or contexts.

The tools that perform this data transformation, commonly called *embedders*, are where the real mathematics happens. Not every dataset is identical, and clearly, a video has different embedding requirements than simple text. The embedder is the engine for vector generation and often becomes the most sought-after piece of the overall system design. It is not unheard of that clients do A/B testing (comparing two different approaches to see which performs better) of different embedders to identify the one that fits best for their specific needs (every embedder has its own mathematical undercarriage, and something that works well for German insurance documents may not be great for healthcare documents in Malaysia).

Depending on whether teams come from the application development side or the data science side, embedders are viewed quite differently. Application developers often see them as basic tools to serialize data into a usable format, while data scientists and AI specialists recognize them as critical components that can determine the success or failure of an entire AI solution. The choice of embedding model can dramatically impact search relevance, semantic understanding, and overall system performance.

A good example of high-performance embedding models is Voyage AI's suite of embedding models, which are specifically optimized for retrieval tasks and offer state-of-the-art performance across different domains and data types. These models demonstrate how specialized embedders can significantly improve the quality of vector representations and, consequently, the effectiveness of AI applications.

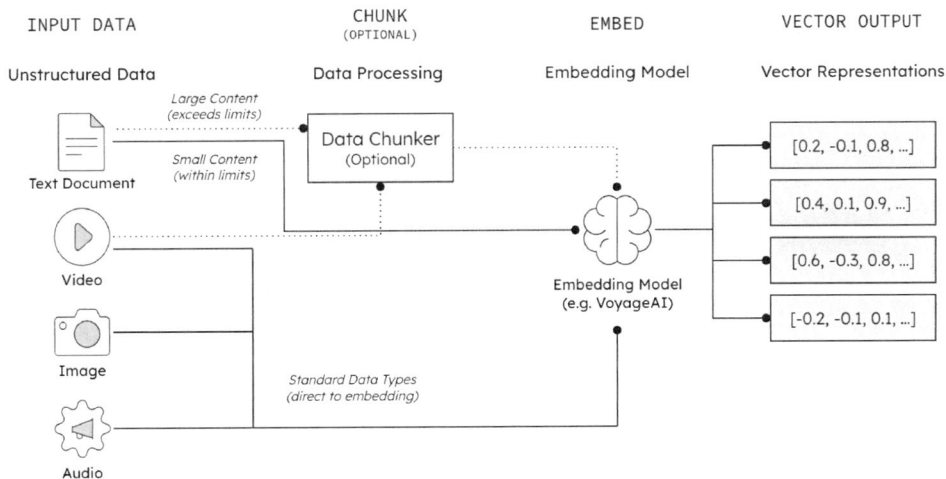

Figure 2.3: How embedding models convert diverse unstructured data types into vector representations

Figure 2.3 demonstrates how embedding models, such as Voyage AI, convert unstructured data into vector representations for AI processing. The visualization shows the transformation process through several key stages:

1. **Input data**: Various unstructured data types (text documents, images, audio, and video) serve as the starting point for the embedding process.

2. **Optional data processing**: Depending on the size and complexity of the input data, some content may require preprocessing to ensure it fits within the embedding model's capacity limits. This optional step, called **chunking**, is most commonly needed for large text documents that exceed model limitations, though it can apply to other data types as well. We'll explore chunking strategies and best practices in detail later in this chapter.

3. **Embedding transformation**: The embedding model (such as Voyage AI) converts all data, whether processed or direct, into numerical vector representations that capture the semantic meaning and relationships within the original content.

4. **Vector output**: The result is a collection of numerical vectors that enable AI systems to mathematically understand and compare the meaning of different pieces of content.

The diagram illustrates that while some data follows a direct path to the embedding model, other content may require intermediate processing based on size or complexity constraints. All paths ultimately lead to the same outcome: vector representations that enable efficient search, retrieval, and AI reasoning across diverse data types.

Learn more about Voyage AI's embedding models here: https://www.voyageai.com

Vector databases and their importance

Once embedding models have transformed your data into vectors, you need a system to store, manage, and efficiently search through these vector representations, either through dedicated vector databases or databases with built-in vector search functionality. The built-in approach offers the advantage of keeping your original data and its vector representations in a single place, eliminating the need for complex joins across multiple databases.

The storage of vectors themselves can be achieved in a simple JSON format, aligned with the actual source dataset. This approach has significant advantages: multiple vectors can be stored alongside the data, and datasets can have different vectors attached for various purposes, such as customer sentiment, purchase behavior, or next-best-offer recommendations, covering a range of typical retail use cases.

The second part of the work involves fast search capabilities. Once you have millions of vectors stored, you need a way to quickly find the most similar ones when you run a query. This search functionality is really the core of what *vector databases* provide. Here's where it gets interesting: traditional databases store and retrieve exact data (such as customer names or order amounts). But vector databases are primarily about similarity search, finding vectors that are *close* to your query vector (as shown previously). In that sense, they're more like sophisticated search engines than traditional databases. Naturally, the vendors of *pure vector databases* may violently disagree with this position, so we keep the term vector database in this context as an industry standard term.

Vector databases store organizational information, which AI systems can query and use as additional context. The more data you can store and the more precisely you can represent it, the broader your information space becomes for addressing specific business problems. It's important to recognize that both models and vectors may need frequent updates based on new research, evolving requirements, or simply discovering that the chosen embedding model isn't optimal for the task.

These specialized systems are critical components in modern AI applications for several key reasons:

- **Efficient similarity search:** At their core, vector databases excel at performing rapid similarity searches, often using **Approximate Nearest Neighbor (ANN)** algorithms, sometimes enhanced with techniques such as K-means clustering, to find the most similar vectors from billions of entries. This capability is fundamental for applications such as semantic search, recommendation engines, and anomaly detection.

- **Scalability:** They are built to handle the massive datasets required by today's AI, providing the infrastructure to manage and query billions of vectors without compromising performance.

- **Multimodal support:** These databases can store vector representations of various data types, including text, images, audio, and time series data in a unified system.

- **Integration capabilities:** Vector databases are designed to connect seamlessly with various AI frameworks and tools, facilitating their integration into broader AI and MLOps workflows.

To achieve these capabilities, vector databases employ several advanced technologies. A key innovation is the use of advanced indexing algorithms to accelerate similarity searches. One of the most prominent and widely adopted implementations is the **Hierarchical Navigable Small World (HNSW)** algorithm[5]. HNSW constructs a hierarchical graph structure that allows for efficient traversal and searching, significantly speeding up query times compared to brute-force methods. This algorithm is not only highly performant but also adaptable, making it a popular choice for databases such as MongoDB and Pinecone.

Another relatively new capability in leading vector databases is vector quantization. Quantization is the process of shrinking full-fidelity vectors into fewer bits. It reduces the amount of main memory required to store each vector in a vector search index by indexing the reduced representation vectors instead. This allows for the storage of more vectors or vectors with higher dimensions. Therefore, quantization reduces resource consumption and improves speed.

For enterprise deployments, additional considerations become critical. In regulated industries, both embedding models and their generated vectors may need to be preserved for significant periods. Organizations often require multiple vector embeddings for the same document to represent different aspects or modalities. For instance, a wildlife database might store both `description_embedding` (vector representation of the textual description) and an `image_embedding` (vector representation of the animal's photograph), or use different embedding models optimized for various search tasks. Additionally, implementing **time-to-live** (**TTL**) index technology that acts as an expiry timer and archives historical data becomes critical for maintaining compliance while managing storage costs. TTL functionality allows organizations to retain vector embeddings and associated documents for required regulatory periods (such as 7 years for financial records) while automatically purging outdated data to prevent storage costs from growing indefinitely.

Document-based databases such as MongoDB with integrated vector search capabilities offer additional advantages. By storing the original data alongside its vector representation within a single document, they can often entirely eliminate the need for complex joins between different databases (e.g., a relational database for metadata and a dedicated vector store). This unified approach simplifies the overall architecture, reduces data duplication, and can lead to significant performance improvements for AI applications.

These technical capabilities combine to make vector databases essential infrastructure for modern AI applications. However, before we can effectively leverage these systems, we need to understand how to optimally prepare our data through strategic chunking approaches.

Chunking strategies for AI applications

Earlier, we introduced chunking as an optional preprocessing step for data that exceeds embedding model capacity limits. Now that you understand how vectors work and where they're stored, let's explore how to implement chunking strategically to maximize the effectiveness of your AI applications.

Chunking is more than just splitting large documents into smaller pieces; it's about finding the optimal balance between preserving context and staying within technical constraints. Poor chunking can break logical connections, leading to irrelevant search results and degraded AI performance. Effective chunking, however, ensures that each piece contains meaningful, self-contained information that AI systems can reason about accurately.

Every chunking strategy involves three key decisions:

- **Splitting technique**: Where to place chunk boundaries based on paragraph breaks, sentence boundaries, semantic content, or programming language-specific separators
- **Chunk size**: The maximum number of characters or tokens allowed per chunk, typically constrained by your embedding model's limits
- **Chunk overlap**: Overlapping content between adjacent chunks to preserve context across boundaries, usually specified as a percentage of chunk size

Let's explore how to use chunking strategically to enhance your AI applications:

- **Fixed-size chunking** splits documents into chunks with a predetermined number of tokens. While simple to implement, this approach can break sentences or concepts midway, potentially losing important context.

- **Fixed-size with overlap** adds overlapping content between chunks to preserve contextual continuity. For example, with 20% overlap, each chunk shares some content with its neighbors, helping maintain narrative flow and reducing information loss at boundaries.

- **Recursive chunking** attempts to split text at natural boundaries such as paragraphs, then sentences, then words, keeping related content together as much as possible while respecting size limits.

- **Semantic chunking** groups content based on meaning rather than size, using embedding similarity to identify where topics change and creating chunks around these semantic boundaries.

The optimal chunking strategy depends on your content type and use case and may evolve throughout the implementation process. Technical documentation with a clear hierarchical structure benefits from recursive chunking that respects headings and sections. Conversational content or narratives often work better with semantic chunking that preserves conceptual flow. As with choosing embedding models, we recommend testing different chunking strategies on a representative sample of your data and evaluating their impact on retrieval quality.

When designing your chunking approach, keep in mind key practical factors that impact performance, cost, and accuracy. Start with your embedding model's token limits as a hard constraint, typically around 8,000 tokens for most models. Tokens are the basic units that AI models use to process text; think of them as individual words or parts of words that the model reads and understands. Since AI services typically charge based on token usage, tokens essentially become the currency of AI operations, comparable to coins in many online games, where you pay for each action or feature you want to use. Consider your typical query patterns: if users ask broad conceptual questions, larger chunks with more context may perform better. For specific factual queries, smaller, focused chunks often provide more precise results.

Remember that chunking decisions compound through your entire AI pipeline. Well-chunked data improves semantic search accuracy, enhances RAG response quality, and enables more effective agent reasoning, all of which we'll explore in the following sections.

Modern document databases such as MongoDB make experimenting with different chunking strategies straightforward, allowing you to test multiple approaches and optimize for your specific use case without complex infrastructure changes.

Learn more about chunking at `https://www.mongodb.com/resources/basics/chunking-explained`.

Semantic search: Putting vectors to work

Having established how to chunk data effectively for maximum AI performance, we're ready to put these optimized vectors to work through semantic search capabilities. To utilize these vectors effectively, we implement vector search indexes that enable semantic alignment between queries and stored information. This process of matching a query vector with the nearest neighbors in our vector space is called **semantic search**.

When you perform a vector search, the system returns multiple results automatically ranked by similarity scores. These scores indicate how close each result is to your original query in the multi-dimensional vector space, with the most similar results (highest scores) appearing first based on mathematical distance calculations between vectors. These initial similarity rankings can be further refined through reranking techniques, which we'll explore later, to improve the relevance and quality of retrieved results.

To illustrate this concept, `Lemon` and `Banana` would be positioned close together in vector space as they share attributes such as being yellow and fruit, but would be quite distant from `Cat` and `Dog`, which cluster together due to shared mammalian and pet characteristics. `Monkey` might fall somewhere between these groups, sharing mammalian traits while also having associations with fruit consumption.

Semantic search represents a fundamental shift from traditional information retrieval methods and opens up powerful new possibilities for AI applications. Let's explore how this technology works in practice and examine its expanding capabilities across different types of data.

Beyond keyword matching

Semantic search alone is already a powerful tool and allows the use of vectorized data and embedding models without the need to reach out to an LLM. Unlike traditional keyword-based search that matches exact terms, semantic search understands the meaning and context of a query, returning results based on relevance rather than exact matches.

This works because (as with the preceding mammal and fruit example) embedding models position semantically related concepts close together in multi-dimensional vector space. Concepts such as `wind turbines`, `solar panels`, and `hydroelectric power` are all clustered near `renewable energy` because they share conceptual relationships and similar semantic meaning.

A semantic search for renewable energy solutions might return results about solar panels, wind turbines, and hydroelectric power, even if those exact terms weren't used in the query. This capability is particularly valuable for applications where understanding intent and context is crucial.

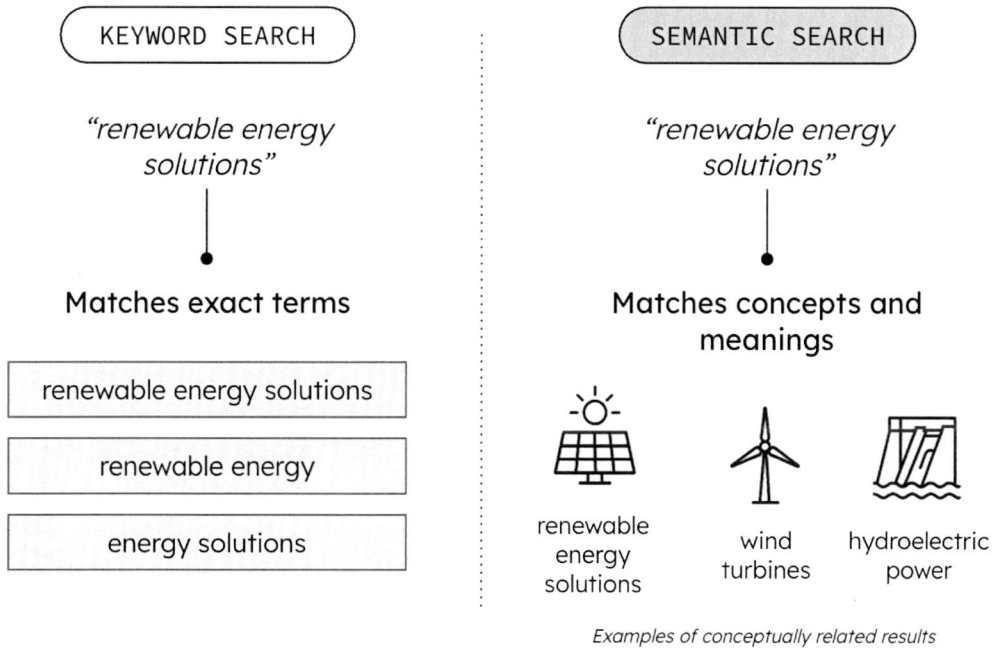

Figure 2.4: Keyword search versus semantic search comparison

Figure 2.4 illustrates the fundamental difference between traditional keyword search and semantic search approaches. On the left, a keyword search for `renewal energy solutions` performs exact term matching, returning content that includes all or part of the search phrase, such as `renewable energy solutions`, `renewable energy`, and `energy solutions`. On the right, a semantic search understands the underlying meaning and context of the query, retrieving **conceptually related results**, including `renewable energy solutions`, `wind turbines`, and `hydroelectric power`, even if those exact terms do not appear in the text.

Learn more about Atlas Vector Search here: `https://www.mongodb.com/products/platform/atlas-vector-search`

Multimodal applications of semantic search

Semantic search can be applied across various data types, not just text. For instance, it can be used to search for similar images, audio patterns, or video content. A powerful example of multimodal semantic search would be a system of action that can find relevant content across different media types based on a single query.

Consider a retail application where a customer uploads an image of a product they like. The system uses an LLM to determine what the product in the photo is, and then performs a semantic search to find similar products across the catalog, matching visual features, style, and characteristics, regardless of whether the product descriptions use similar terminology. This capability enables more intuitive and user-friendly search experiences that mirror how humans naturally think about similarity.

Modern data platforms with vector search capabilities built in make implementing these advanced search features straightforward. By storing vector embeddings alongside the original data, they enable efficient semantic search across large datasets without increasing tech sprawl or requiring specialized knowledge.

Understanding semantic search is fundamental to realizing the potential of modern AI applications. By transforming data into vectors and enabling similarity-based retrieval, semantic search bridges the gap between human language and machine understanding. This capability forms the foundation of more sophisticated AI patterns such as RAG, where the quality of semantic search directly impacts the accuracy and relevance of AI-generated responses. As we'll see in the next section, combining semantic search with LLMs unlocks even greater potential for creating intelligent, context-aware applications.

RAG: Enhancing LLMs with contextual data

While semantic search provides powerful retrieval capabilities, combining it with LLMs unlocks even greater potential. RAG represents the synthesis, a pattern where vector search results enhance user queries to LLMs, providing specific context that produces more accurate, grounded responses with fewer or no hallucinations.

RAG architectures enable organizations to build applications that securely ground AI in trusted company data, thereby reducing risks associated with hallucinations, ensuring factual accuracy, and enabling domain-specific solutions. To be effective with RAG, organizations must prioritize data strategies that allow proprietary, up-to-date information to be accessible for retrieval. Architecturally, planning for RAG implementations influences decisions on how LLMs integrate with existing data stores and the necessity of robust vector database capabilities.

RAG uses the company's proprietary corporate, domain-specific data to add context to a prompt, such as providing a customer history record or a product description, which narrows down the *ask* to the LLM and delivers more precise, less hallucinatory answers. The ability to provide hyper-personalization through RAG implementations represents a significant competitive differentiator that can really add value to customer interactions and lift mundane online chores into pleasant, collaborative experiences.

While this concept sounds complex, its implementation is actually quite simple, as can be seen in the following figure.

How RAG works

Figure 2.5 illustrates a comprehensive RAG implementation that demonstrates how organizations can leverage their proprietary data to enhance LLM responses.

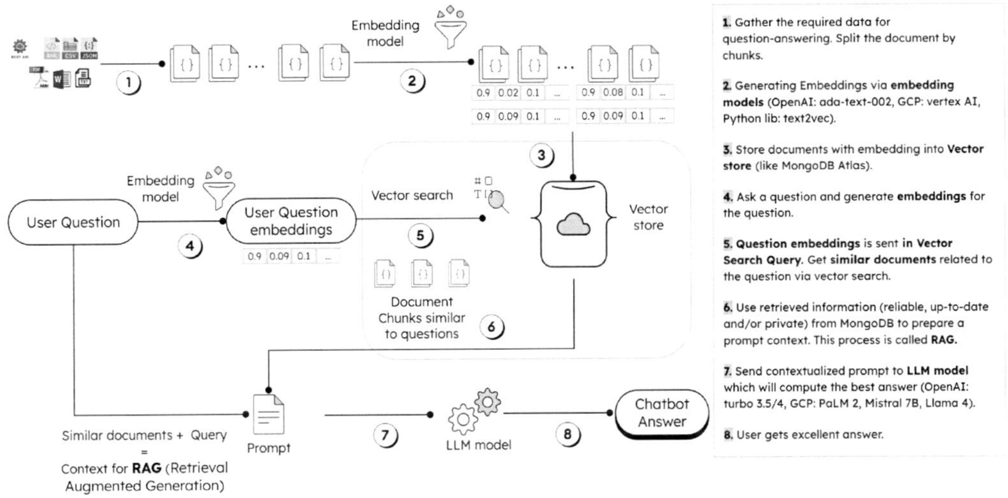

Figure 2.5: Basic RAG process flow

While RAG architectures can vary in complexity, from basic three-step workflows (retrieval, augmentation, generation) to more sophisticated multi-step implementations, this diagram shows a detailed eight-step process that provides complete visibility into the RAG workflow:

1. **Document preparation**: The system gathers required data for question-answering and splits large documents into manageable chunks to ensure they fit within embedding model constraints.

2. **Vector generation**: Embedding models such as Voyage AI convert each document chunk into numerical vector representations that capture semantic meaning.

3. **Vector storage:** These document embeddings, the vectors, are stored in databases such as MongoDB, and then the vector database search index is created on top. It creates a searchable knowledge base of organizational information.

4. **Query processing:** When a user or application asks a question, the system generates embeddings for that query using the same embedding model to ensure compatibility.

5. **Vector search:** The question embeddings are used in a vector search query to find document chunks with similar semantic meaning, retrieving the most relevant information from the knowledge base.

6. **Context augmentation:** The retrieved information, whether reliable, up-to-date, or private organizational data, is used to prepare an enhanced prompt context. This contextual enhancement is the core of RAG.

7. **Enhanced generation:** The contextualized prompt is sent to an LLM (such as OpenAI's GPT-4, GCP's PaLM 2, Mistral 7B, or Llama 4), which generates responses based on both its pre-trained knowledge and the retrieved context.

8. **Optimized output:** Users receive accurate, contextually relevant answers that are grounded in the organization's specific data and knowledge.

This approach addresses several limitations of standalone LLMs:

- **Reduces hallucinations:** By grounding responses in retrieved facts
- **Provides up-to-date information:** By retrieving current data not available during model training
- **Enables domain specialization:** By incorporating domain-specific knowledge
- **Improves transparency:** By citing sources for information

A typical use case is a chatbot that augments information about the case being discussed with additional information, such as airline tickets, actual location, and flight status, so the answer from the LLM is context-relevant for the individual and puts the actual need in the center.

Organizations across industries are implementing RAG to enhance their AI applications:

- **Customer support:** Augmenting responses with product documentation and support history.
- **Healthcare:** Providing medical professionals with relevant research and patient history.
- **Financial services:** Incorporating regulatory information and market data into advisory services.

- **Manufacturing:** Integrating equipment manuals and maintenance records into operational guidance. Product and engineering documents can be made accessible.
- **Insurance:** Evaluating insurance claim documents.
- **Public sector:** Providing information about public works projects.

Modern document databases excel at supporting RAG implementations because they can store both the original data and its vector representations in a unified model. This approach simplifies the architecture and improves performance by eliminating the need to join data across multiple systems.

Beyond RAG: Hybrid search approaches

RAG can be further enhanced by utilizing regular text search as a verbatim recall of information alongside vector search. The combination of text and vector search is called **hybrid search** and is still just a flavor of RAG. Nonetheless, it is powerful and allows the extension of refining the LLM input with additional data points.

Traditional text search and vector search have complementary strengths:

- **Text search:** Excels at finding exact matches and specific keywords
- **Vector search:** Better at understanding meaning and finding semantically similar content

Hybrid search combines these approaches to deliver comprehensive and relevant results. For example, a hybrid search system might use vector search to understand the semantic intent of a query while using text search to ensure specific terms are present in the results.

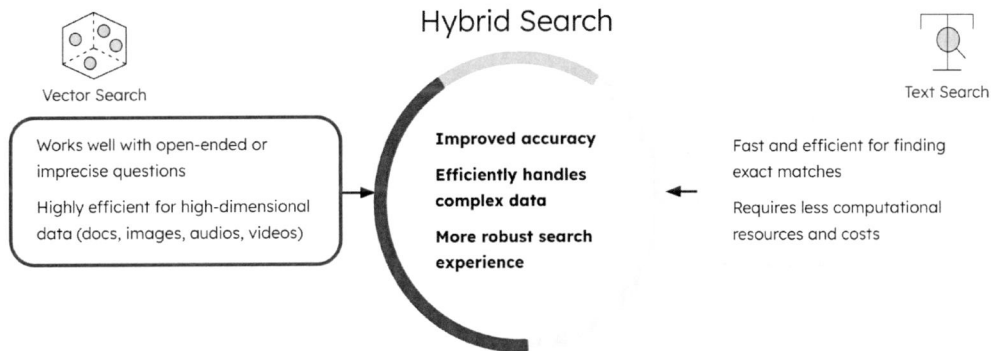

Figure 2.6: Hybrid search architecture combining text and vector search

Figure 2.6 demonstrates how hybrid search enhances RAG by combining both text search and vector search capabilities. The system processes queries through two parallel paths: vector search (left) handles semantic understanding and finds conceptually similar content, while text search (right) performs exact keyword matching and precise term identification. The results from both approaches are merged through a fusion algorithm that delivers improved accuracy by leveraging the complementary strengths of semantic understanding and specific term matching before augmenting the LLM prompt.

Reranking: Refining search results

The final enhancement in the retrieval pipeline is reranking, a process that improves the retrieved context before serving it to the LLM. As the name suggests, reranking reorders search results based on a deeper understanding of their relevance to the original query. This typically involves four steps:

1. **Initial retrieval**: Gathering a larger set of potentially relevant documents
2. **Contextual evaluation**: Assessing each document's relevance to the specific query in context
3. **Prioritization**: Reordering results based on this deeper evaluation
4. **Selection**: Choosing the most relevant documents to include in the LLM prompt

This process significantly improves the quality of information provided to the LLM, resulting in more accurate and helpful responses. Modern data platforms with integrated search capabilities make implementing these sophisticated retrieval patterns straightforward, allowing developers to focus on application logic rather than infrastructure.

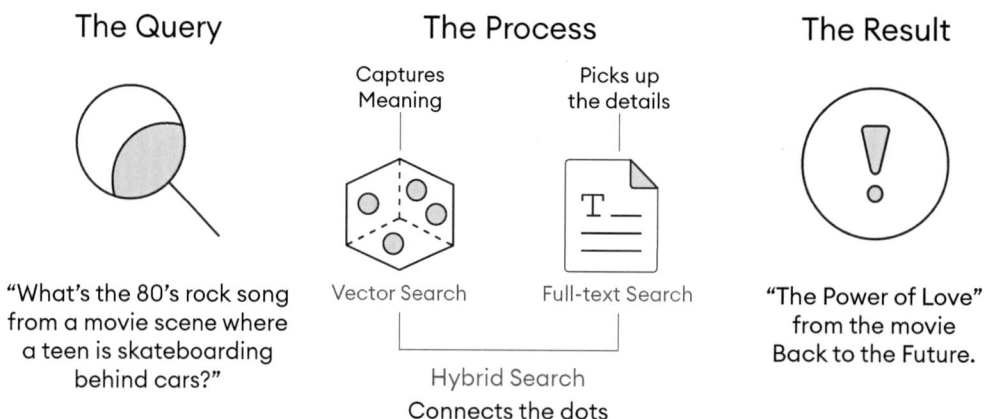

Figure 2.7: Hybrid search process

Figure 2.7 illustrates a practical example of hybrid search in action, showing how the system processes a complex natural language query: `"What's the 80s rock song from a movie scene where a teen is skateboarding behind cars?"` The process demonstrates vector search capturing the semantic meaning of the query, while full-text search identifies specific keywords such as `movie`, `skateboarding`, and `cars`. The hybrid approach connects these complementary search methods to successfully identify `"The Power of Love"` from the movie `Back to the Future`, showcasing how combining semantic understanding with precise keyword matching delivers accurate results that neither approach could achieve independently.

As illustrated in the figure, hybrid search excels at handling complex, natural language queries that traditional search methods would struggle with. The following steps occur in this example:

1. Vector search captures the semantic meaning of the query about an 80s rock song in a skateboarding scene.
2. Full-text search identifies specific keywords such as `movie`, `skateboarding`, and `cars`.
3. Hybrid search combines these approaches to connect the conceptual dots.
4. The system successfully identifies `"The Power of Love"` from the movie `Back to the Future` as the answer.

This example demonstrates how hybrid search can understand both the context (a memorable movie scene) and specific details (skateboarding behind cars) to deliver precise results that neither approach could achieve alone.

Agentic AI: Automating decision-making and reasoning

While RAG and hybrid search enhance LLMs with external knowledge, they still require human initiation and oversight. The next evolutionary step removes this limitation, creating systems that can autonomously pursue goals and make decisions within their designated domain. This is the realm of agentic AI.

This transition from human-guided to autonomous AI systems represents more than just a technological advancement; it's a fundamental shift in how we conceptualize AI's role in business operations. Where RAG systems excel at providing enhanced responses to specific queries, agentic AI systems can independently identify problems, formulate strategies, and execute solutions across extended workflows. Collaborating agentic AI instances build out a broader functional scope that represents the concept of a digital expert, functioning like a subject matter expert within an organization.

Agentic AI foundation

Agentic AI incorporates an orchestrator layer that manages task execution in workflows. AI agents can operate in either a fully autonomous or semi-autonomous way, with a **human-in-the-loop (HITL)**. AI agents are equipped with advanced tools, models, memory, and data storage. Memory leverages both long- and short-term contextual data for informed decision-making and continuity of the interactions. Tools and models enable the AI agents to decompose tasks into steps and execute them cohesively. The data storage and retrieval are pivotal to AI agent effectiveness and can be advanced by embedding and vector search capabilities.

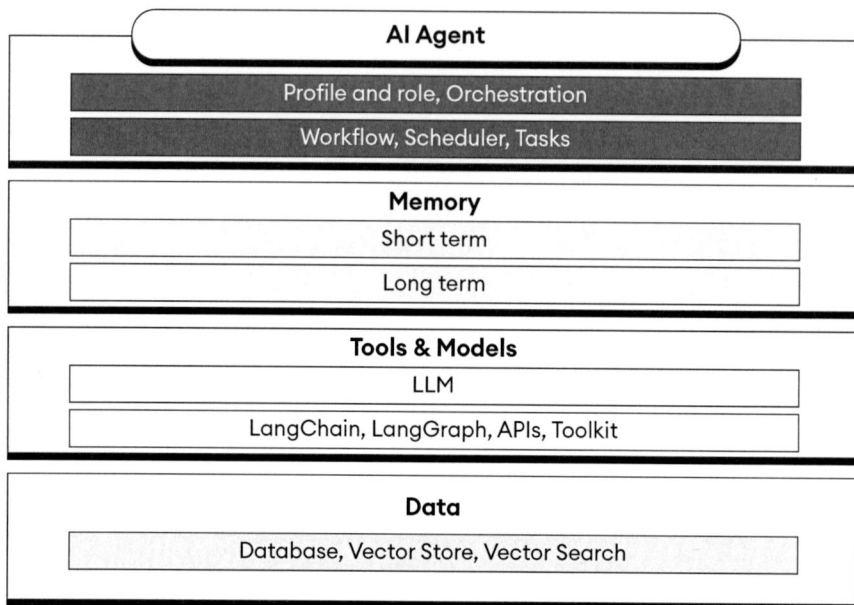

Figure 2.8: Agentic AI foundation

Figure 2.8 illustrates the foundational layers of agentic AI systems, showing how the orchestrator manages task execution workflows. The visualization depicts the relationship between AI agents, their tools, models, and memory systems that enables autonomous or semi-autonomous operation with HITL capabilities.

Here are some key characteristics of an AI agent:

- **Autonomy:** The ability to make decisions based on the situation dynamically and to execute tasks with minimal human intervention
- **Chain of thought:** The ability to perform step-by-step reasoning and break complex problems into logical, smaller steps for better judgment and decision-making

- **Context-aware**: AI agents continuously adapt their actions based on the environment, changing conditions
- **Learning**: AI agents improve their performance over time by adapting and enhancing

Agentic AI represents a significant leap towards automating complex workflows and decision-making, marking the next evolutionary step in our AI journey. Organizations may begin strategic planning for how these autonomous systems will integrate into enterprise architecture, considering data access, security protocols, and governance frameworks. The development and deployment of AI agents and digital experts will require new skill sets and potentially new roles within IT and business operations, making it essential for forward-looking leaders to start assessing these needs now.

Building upon these retrieval and generation capabilities is the automation of processes and reasoning in a contained environment, leading to the concept of agentic AI. While decision-making agents based on rule engines have existed for a long time, the concept of agentic AI is much more refined. These sophisticated systems rely heavily on robust, accessible, and well-structured data, as well as advanced orchestration capabilities. This reinforces the critical importance of a modern, flexible data platform that can serve as the 'memory' and 'tool-access layer' for these agents.

What is an agent?

An AI agent is an autonomous system that can perceive its environment, make decisions, and take actions to achieve specific goals. Unlike simpler AI systems that perform specific tasks in isolation, agents operate with a degree of autonomy and can adapt their behavior based on feedback and changing conditions.

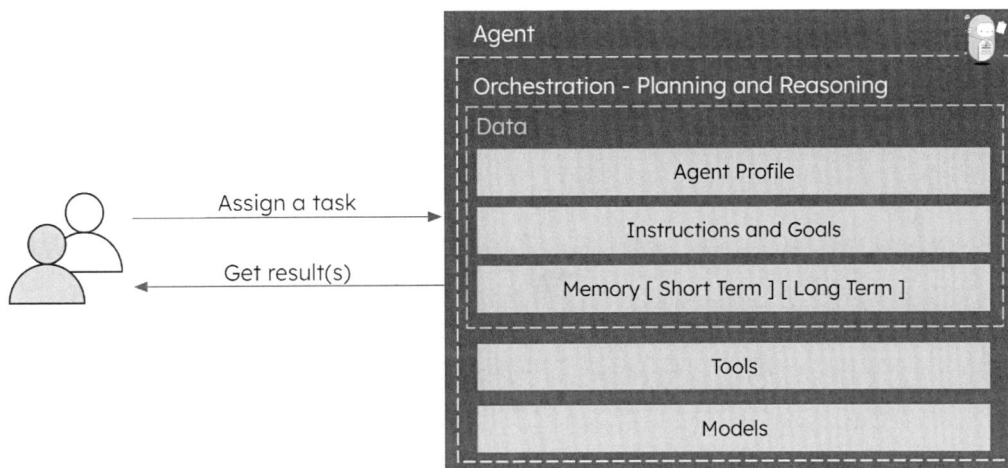

Figure 2.9: AI agent architecture and core components

Figure 2.9 illustrates the fundamental structure of an AI agent system, showing how users assign tasks and receive results through the agent's core components. The architecture demonstrates how these components work together to enable autonomous decision making and task execution, with the agent able to perceive its environment, process information, and take actions to achieve specific objectives while adapting based on feedback and changing conditions.

The core components of an AI agent include the following:

- **Instructions and goals**: The agent's purpose and objectives that guide all decision-making processes
- **Memory**: Both short-term (for current task context) and long-term (for persistent knowledge), which enables continuity across interactions
- **Orchestration**: Planning and reasoning capabilities that determine actions and coordinate between different components
- **Tools**: Specific capabilities the agent can use to interact with its environment and execute tasks
- **Models**: The underlying AI models that power the agent's capabilities, from language understanding to decision-making
- **Data**: The information the agent can access and use, stored in various formats and updated dynamically

Agentic AI is being applied across various domains to automate complex decision-making processes: financial services deploy portfolio management agents that analyze market trends, assess risk, and recommend investment strategies. Healthcare organizations use diagnostic agents that review patient history, symptoms, and medical literature to suggest potential diagnoses and treatments. Manufacturing and logistics companies implement agents that optimize routing, inventory, and scheduling based on real-time conditions. Modern data platforms with document models and vector search capabilities are ideal for supporting these applications. They provide the flexible, scalable infrastructure needed for both agent memory (short-term and long-term) and diverse data storage, while enabling the fast, context-aware retrieval essential for effective decision-making.

Digital experts or multi-agent systems: Collaborative problem-solving

Multi-agent systems represent the next level of sophistication, where multiple AI agents collaborate to solve complex tasks. Each agent specializes in specific capabilities, enabling more sophisticated problem-solving through collaboration.

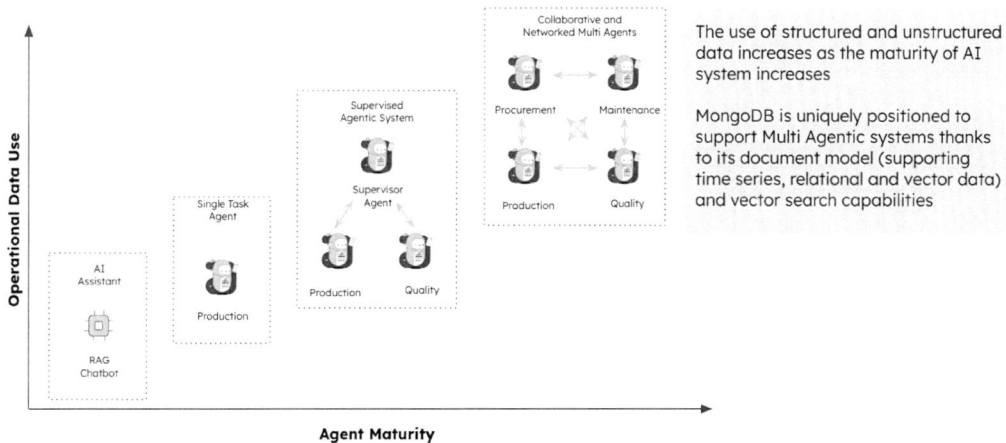

Figure 2.10: Evolution from RAG to multi-agent systems

Figure 2.10 illustrates the evolution from simple RAG chatbots to sophisticated multi-agent systems. As agent maturity increases (*x* axis), so does organizational complexity (*y* axis), progressing from single AI assistants to specialized collaborative agents working across different domains such as production and quality management.

In a multi-agent system, different agents can do the following:

1. **Specialize in different domains**: Some might excel at data analysis, others at natural language understanding, and others at planning
2. **Collaborate on complex tasks**: Breaking down problems into manageable components
3. **Communicate and share information**: Passing relevant data and insights between agents
4. **Provide checks and balances**: Verifying each other's work and catching errors

As AI systems mature, their use of structured and unstructured data increases exponentially. Systems supporting flexible data models (accommodating time series, relational, and vector data) with integrated vector search capabilities become essential for effective multi-agent deployments.

How agentic AI works

From a technical perspective, user interaction with agentic systems follows familiar API patterns but with sophisticated processing underneath. The agent engages in multi-stage planning to accurately interpret user intent and contextualize queries.

This approach fundamentally differs from deterministic software, which follows a prescribed path. Agents dynamically determine their approach based on context and goals, marking where the true value of the GenAI approach emerges.

The agent leverages various tools, including vector search, text search, and data augmentation, to create a comprehensive context. This can incorporate long-term information such as historical trends, transaction data, and statistical analyses. By synthesizing this broad information spectrum and accessing its own data stores and vectorizations, the agent can provide rich context to the LLM for reasoning and retrieval. After reranking responses, it structures formal answers for the requesting client.

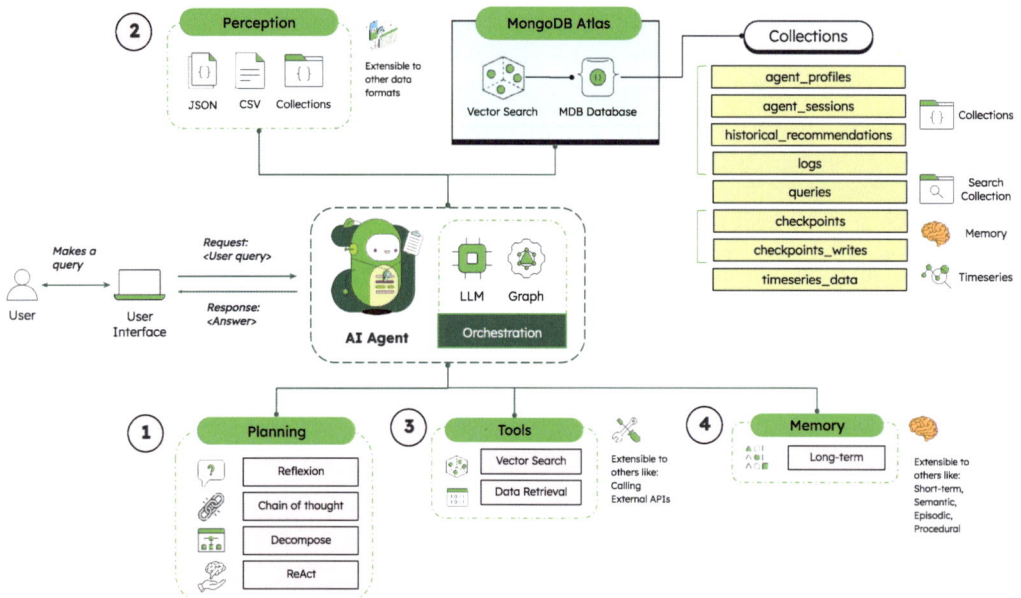

Figure 2.11: Agentic AI system workflow and architecture

Figure 2.11 illustrates the complete workflow of an agentic AI system, showing how user queries are processed through four main stages: **Planning**, **Perception**, **Tools**, and **Memory**.

The system processes each user query by moving through these four interconnected stages to deliver intelligent, contextual responses:

1. **Planning**, where the agent uses reflection to analyze what the user is asking, employs a chain of thought to break down reasoning into logical steps, uses decomposition to split complex tasks into smaller parts, and applies ReAct to plan reasoning and action steps iteratively while determining the overall strategy for responding to the query.

2. **Perception**, which involves data collection from various sources, including JSON, CSV, and collections, while database systems such as MongoDB Atlas serve as the central data hub. For unstructured data, this stage will utilize vector search to process data for semantic understanding, gather information from multiple databases and formats, and contextualize data relevant to the user's specific query.

3. **Tools**, where vector search tools find semantically similar information, data retrieval tools access specific information from databases, specialized processing tools manipulate and analyze gathered data, external integrations provide additional capabilities as needed, and the system executes specific functions required to answer the query.

4. **Memory**, which maintains long-term memory to store persistent knowledge and past experiences, short-term memory to maintain current conversation context, learning integration to update the agent's knowledge base, context preservation for handling follow-up questions, and historical data storage in database collections for future reference.

Throughout this process, the central AI agent coordinates all four stages to provide contextualized, intelligent responses, and the system dynamically adapts its approach based on context and goals rather than following predetermined paths.

This proposed framework represents the practical realization of the AI evolution we've traced from basic RAG systems to autonomous agents. By building on your existing data infrastructure and search capabilities, organizations can rapidly deploy agents that provide immediate business value while establishing the foundation for more advanced multi-agent systems.

The key insight is that successful agent deployment isn't about replacing existing systems; it's about intelligently orchestrating them to create autonomous, goal-oriented capabilities that scale with your organization's needs.

Summary

This chapter traced the evolution of AI from its origins in the 1950s to today's sophisticated GenAI systems. We explored the fundamental components powering modern AI applications, including LLMs, embedding models that transform data into vectors, and the semantic search capabilities that enable AI reasoning.

We clarified the distinctions between semantic search (understanding meaning in queries), RAG (enhancing LLMs with external context), hybrid search approaches (combining semantic and keyword matching), and agentic AI systems (autonomous decision-making). More importantly, we examined how these components build upon each other to create increasingly sophisticated capabilities.

Throughout these advancements, modern data platforms have played a crucial role in enabling AI innovation. Choosing the right data platform, one that is flexible, scalable, and natively supports these diverse AI workloads, from vector search to complex data models for agentic memory, becomes a critical enabler for innovation and competitive advantage in the era of GenAI. By understanding these concepts and their relationships, organizations can make more informed decisions about how to leverage AI to drive business value.

The next chapter will examine why data is the key differentiator for companies investing in innovation. It will discuss why consolidating operational data into a single layer is critical for moving forward with AI initiatives, covering real-time data requirements, the importance of well-structured data, data flow, and integration approaches.

References

1. A Very Short History Of Artificial Intelligence (AI): https://www.forbes.com/sites/gilpress/2016/12/30/a-very-short-history-of-artificial-intelligence-ai/

2. Oxford Reference: https://www.oxfordreference.com/display/10.1093/acref/9780198609810.001.0001/acref-9780198609810-e-423

3. What Ever Happened to IBM's Watson?: https://www.nytimes.com/2021/07/16/technology/what-happened-ibm-watson.html

4. Attention Is All You Need: https://arxiv.org/abs/1706.03762

5. What is a Hierarchical Navigable Small World?: https://www.mongodb.com/resources/basics/hierarchical-navigable-small-world

3

The System of Action

Data is the foundation for turning GenAI into measurable business outcomes. AI-enabled capabilities such as vector-encoding of unstructured data, real-time synthesis across silos, and agents-in-the-loop are changing *how* we transact business. Enterprises that master these capabilities can move from reactive, siloed decisions to proactive, intelligence-driven operations, responding to market changes in real time, lowering operational expenses, and driving stronger customer outcomes.

Augmenting and automating business workflows with agents-in-the-loop places increased demands on the underlying data layer. Agents may access and analyze a myriad of siloed sources, build rich context, and inform business decisions. But where does that context persist? How can business users view, interact with, or even edit that information?

To support this evolution, enterprises must move beyond static *systems of record*, which passively store and serve data, toward dynamic *systems of action*: systems designed for real-time decisions, automation, and collaboration between humans, AI-assisted users, and fully autonomous agents to *act* on data. While traditional systems of record excel at maintaining data integrity and compliance, systems of action can autonomously trigger decisions, execute workflows, and learn from outcomes. For example, in retail, an AI agent could reorder inventory in real time as customer demand shifts.

This chapter explores how systems of action transform data into decisions: a shift that is becoming unavoidable. They must handle data in many forms (from original sources and text search indices to vector embeddings) and even LLM inputs requiring context-sensitive reranking, a process for prioritizing the most relevant results. Meeting those demands requires a unified, contextualized view of enterprise data that exceeds what their system of record and *system of insight* predecessors can provide. This shift also introduces new challenges in scalability, performance, security, and governance.

By the end of this chapter, you'll understand how:

- System of action databases support real-time AI and RAG applications by breaking traditional data modeling constraints and enabling signal processing with responsive, document-based data layers
- Unified data access enables GenAI to process diverse formats such as source data, embeddings, and real-time signals within a coherent framework
- Data quality and consistency reduce hallucinations and improve reliability through full lineage tracking and provenance awareness
- AI-ready data architectures break from traditional warehouses and systems of insight, supporting dynamic, multimodel workloads
- Governance and security strategies align with AI-specific needs such as privacy, access controls, and encryption
- Model training and fine-tuning pipelines prepare and optimize data for GenAI applications
- Implementation patterns follow the flow from signal ingestion through enrichment to intelligent response, providing deployment blueprints

Building an AI-ready data foundation

Delivering on the promise of systems of action requires a new kind of data foundation—one built for speed, context, and adaptability.

Agentic AI systems fundamentally differ from traditional systems of record in their operational demands. Where legacy systems focus on capturing and storing historical transactions, systems of action powered by agentic AI require real-time decision-making, dynamic data synthesis, and immediate response capabilities. This shift demands that our data architecture choices move beyond the rigid, siloed structures of traditional enterprise systems.

A unified view of core enterprise is essential. It must bring together the diverse data types that autonomous agents rely on (real-time operational signals, contextual documents, vector embeddings) into a single, coherent platform. That platform must be built on flexible data structures that can adapt as agent behaviors evolve.

The transition from supporting passive systems of record to enabling active systems of action introduces six critical architectural requirements that distinguish agentic AI infrastructure from legacy approaches:

- **Unified data access** to eliminate the complexity of managing multiple disparate datastores
- **Data quality and consistency** mechanisms that reduce hallucinations and errors from systems out of sync
- **Real-time context** capabilities that enable immediate signal processing for RAG applications
- **Scalability and performance** characteristics that support operational AI rather than only backward-looking analytics
- **Governance and security** frameworks that protect sensitive information while enabling innovation
- **Efficient model training workflows** that optimize data preparation for GenAI applications

Together, these elements form the data foundation for autonomous, intelligent systems. As we examine each in the sections ahead, we'll see how a system of action database departs from traditional data management and enables more intelligent, responsive, and scalable AI applications.

What is a system of action?

Systems of action are a new class of enterprise application, designed to execute decisions and drive workflows in real time. They enable collaboration between people, AI-assisted users, and AI agents, supporting everything from assisted decision-making to fully autonomous execution.

Unlike systems of record, which passively store historical transactions, or systems of insight, which analyze data retrospectively, systems of action operate in the moment. They process dynamic context, trigger decisions, and execute tasks through AI agents. For instance, they might reroute a delayed flight in real time or automatically adjust hospital staffing during a sudden surge.

Building systems of action requires more than analytical capabilities. They must ingest streaming signals, reason across unstructured and structured sources, and respond in real time. They require specialized database architectures capable of managing high-velocity, multimodal data streams and supporting complex state transitions over time. Most legacy systems, designed for static, batch-oriented workflows, simply cannot support this kind of continuous intelligence.

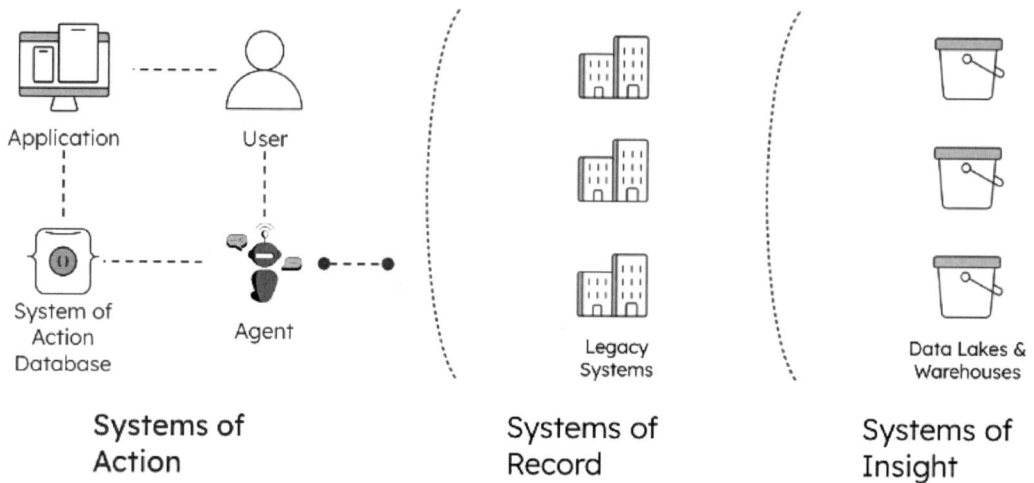

Figure 3.1: Enterprise system landscape: from system of record to system of action

Figure 3.1 illustrates this evolution across the enterprise landscape. Unlike traditional systems that passively store or retrospectively analyze data, systems of action enable real-time interaction between users, applications, and agents; all powered by a live, adaptable data layer.

Unified data access architecture

The foundation of any GenAI system begins with access to diverse, multimodal data, at speed, in formats AI can reason with. Unfortunately, this is also where most enterprises struggle. Traditional enterprise data architectures are fragmented across dozens of incompatible systems, each optimized for narrow use cases. The result is integration pain, access friction, and massive overhead.

Modern AI applications demand a fundamental departure: unified access must be treated not as a convenience but as a prerequisite.

Today's models must navigate a wide variety of inputs: text documents, application logs, product catalogs, support transcripts, and streaming sensor data. Relational and legacy systems often store semi-structured data (like JSON or XML) as **binary large objects (BLOBs)** or **character large objects (CLOBs)**, limiting their usability for AI systems. In these cases, the actual data is hidden inside a single entry and must be extracted and interpreted before it can be reasoned over or acted upon. This was tolerable when the goal was to store and retrieve files. But for GenAI systems, where models need immediate access to both structured and semi-structured data, often in the same query, this format becomes a bottleneck. Even a video can have its own addressable metadata structure, rather than existing solely as an opaque BLOB, illustrates the shift needed to support AI-native reasoning.

Beyond the format problem lies a more urgent challenge: **fragmentation**.

An AI application might need to stitch together context from a CRM (customer profiles and account hierarchies), a product catalog (SKU-level details, pricing, availability), a data warehouse (historical transactions), a streaming platform (real-time behavioral signals), and a document store (contracts, support transcripts, policy documents). Each source has its own schema, access pattern, and often its own API. This complexity creates two persistent challenges:

- **Developer integration friction**: Each layer introduces its own headaches, from authentication and authorization to schema mismatches, brittle connectors, and inconsistent formats
- **System fragility/maintenance drag**: Over time, these integrations accumulate, introducing silent failures, versioning issues, and downstream reliability risks that make innovation slower and more expensive

MongoDB's document model takes a fundamentally different approach. Instead of forcing diverse data into rigid schemas or hiding it in unreadable blobs, it enables rich, hierarchical data structures that mirror how businesses actually operate [1]. Developers can model a full customer, order, or event in a single document, including nested context, version history, and behavioral attributes. This eliminates the need for complex joins while preserving the relationships critical for effective agentic reasoning.

Even more critically, *flexible schema design*, meaning the ability to store and query data without locking into a rigid blueprint, allows fields and document shapes to adapt as requirements change. This lets data evolve—new attributes can be added without downtime, and new types of signals can be integrated without costly migrations. For AI systems (especially those that learn, adapt, and extend themselves), this agility is essential.

This architectural convergence enables structured transactions, real-time signals, and unstructured content together in a single query or operation. Model updates, enrichment jobs, or downstream agent actions can all be triggered directly from the same data platform [2]. That unified model lays the groundwork for sophisticated, AI-native workflows.

Perhaps more importantly, unified data access transforms developer productivity. Instead of spending cycles reconciling formats or debugging brittle connectors, teams can focus on building intelligent systems. And, as we'll see in the sections ahead, everything from data quality and governance to real-time orchestration builds on this foundation.

Ensuring data quality and consistency

Data quality and consistency are non-negotiable for GenAI solutions. Unlike traditional analytics, where data quality issues might simply yield incorrect reports or delayed insights, poor data quality in AI systems can cause hallucinations, introduce biased outputs, and fundamentally unreliable behavior that undermines user trust and business value.

Legacy quality approaches tried to solve this through normalization, deduplication, and validation against external sources. Consider a familiar failure mode: a system validates `Joe Miller, 12 High Street`, through postal APIs and credit checks, yet fails to distinguish between three different Joe Millers (grandfather, father, and son) at the same address. For entity analytics, where precise relationship mapping matters, this is a critical flaw.

In this scenario, an online store might unknowingly treat all three individuals as the same customer, losing the ability to tailor interactions or offers. Relational star schemas exacerbate this problem by fragmenting contextual information across multiple tables. When customer data is split between fact tables, dimension tables, and lookup tables, the rich context that enables accurate entity resolution becomes scattered and difficult to reconstruct.

In our Joe Miller example, a document-based approach would maintain separate documents for each individual, complete with detailed demographic information, purchase history, behavioral patterns, and relationship data that enables clear differentiation.

Within a document, you can store original values alongside enrichments and enhancements within the same dataset. This approach improves output reliability and reduces hallucinations or contradictory results. When an AI system generates an output, the complete chain of data sources, transformations, and reasoning steps can be traced back through the document structure, enabling both debugging and compliance reporting.

This lineage capability proves essential for improving output reliability and reducing hallucinations or contradictory results. When AI models can access not just the current state of data but also its provenance and transformation history, they can make more informed decisions about data reliability and confidence levels. For example, customer service AI might weigh recent direct customer interactions more heavily than older inferred preferences, or flag potential inconsistencies when multiple data sources provide conflicting information.

For organizations implementing document-based data quality strategies, MongoDB offers comprehensive best practices, as well as compatibility with industry-leading tooling for data modeling and cataloging that make advanced quality management achievable at scale [3]. When high-quality, lineage-aware data becomes the default, AI systems can deliver results that are accurate, explainable, and trustworthy.

Real-time context and RAG

The definition of *real-time* varies significantly by use case and industry, but the real-time requirements of data in use with GenAI cannot be overstated. Hedge fund trading systems, for example, require millisecond responses, while life insurance underwriting processes measure time in days. While application response times continue to decrease, many architectures use caching layers that create an illusion of real-time performance at the expense of freshness of data.

A typical real-time environment follows a simple pattern where an interaction generates a signal that enables immediate interpretation. These signals may originate from diverse sources, such as a retail website recording shopping cart additions, a smart meter transmitting electricity usage, or a pathology lab completing cancer analysis data. All signals, when combined with existing datasets, enable text search, vector search, and LLM processing for reasoning and causal analysis. This applies equally to interactive systems, such as retail shopping carts, and autonomous agentic systems, such as automated insurance claim processing.

Real-time integration of signals with metadata, reference data, and historical information generates new knowledge instantaneously. Consider how this has evolved. Traditional rule-based systems might suggest "You ordered a burger, would you like fries?" In contrast, an AI-powered system recognizes patterns such as "You order cat food bi-weekly, always the same brand", and reasons contextually with suggestions such as "Based on your purchase history, you might be interested in our new, healthier formula. Would you like us to send you a free sample?" The system identifies repeat customers and enhances their experience through reasoning that connects purchase patterns with product recommendations, requiring deeper knowledge about customer preferences and pet characteristics.

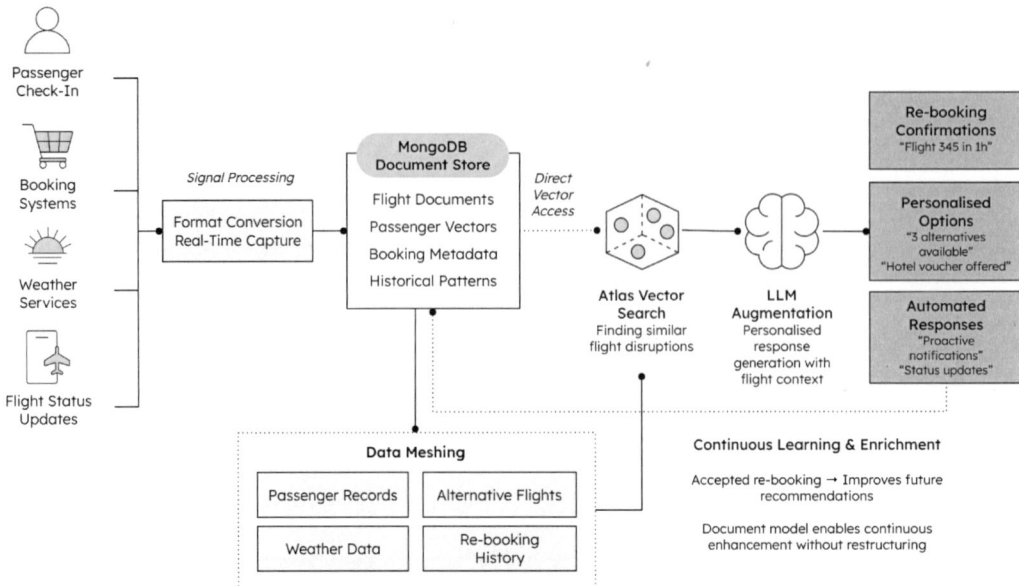

Figure 3.2: Real-time AI data flow

The architectural flow in *Figure 3.2* demonstrates how modern AI applications process real-time signals through a system of action database using an airline passenger assistance scenario. The flow begins with diverse signal sources on the left: **Passenger Check-In**, **Booking Systems**, **Weather Services**, and **Flight Status Updates**, which feed into **Signal Processing** and **Format Conversion/Real-Time Capture** components. These signals are then ingested into the central **MongoDB Document Store**, which contains **Flight Documents**, **Passenger Vectors**, **Booking Metadata**, and **Historical Patterns** with **Direct Vector Access** capabilities.

The system processes this data through **Atlas Vector Search** (finding similar flight disruptions) and **LLM Augmentation** (generating personalized responses with flight context) to produce three types of intelligent outputs: **Re-Booking Confirmations**, **Personalized Options**, and **Automated Responses**. At the foundation sits the **Operational Data Layer (ODL)**, an architectural pattern that centrally integrates and organizes siloed enterprise data, serving as an intermediary between existing data sources and consuming applications. In this case, the ODL enriches signals with contextual information from passenger records, alternative flights, weather data, and rebooking history.

A continuous learning and enrichment feedback loop ensures that every interaction outcome, whether accepted re-bookings or user preferences, flows back to improve future recommendations. The document model enables continuous enhancement without requiring system restructuring, creating a system that grows smarter with each passenger interaction while delivering real-time, context-aware responses vital for modern AI applications.

Critically, the feedback loop ensures continuous improvement, ensuring every interaction outcome enriches the system of action database, making future responses more accurate and contextual. This circular flow embodies the key advantage of document-based architectures: *the ability to evolve and improve without the schema rigidity that constrains traditional relational systems*. The result is a system that grows smarter with each interaction, delivering real-time, context-aware responses that modern AI applications require.

Scalability, availability, and performance

Historically, enterprise data warehouses represented the largest database implementations, with denormalized, column-oriented star schemas designed for analytical queries. These systems perform well with queries such as "`Display yogurt sales by region`", where large datasets are filtered by specific criteria (region, store, price) to generate insights. The integration of multiple sources led to the development of **extract**, **transform**, **load** (**ETL**) processes and master data management systems. While these platforms have added machine learning features and now claim to support GenAI capabilities, they remain primarily designed for backward-looking analytical tools, unsuited to real-time, agentic, and causal AI applications.

Consider the contrast. A chatbot assisting an airline passenger who missed a connection requires fundamentally different capabilities than answering "`How many passengers experienced day-long delays in Frankfurt last year?`" The chatbot and its underlying agentic system must address immediate needs, finding available seats, offering mitigation services, and responding empathetically to frustrated passengers. The required data is real-time, context-sensitive, and simply not available from a historic warehouse.

To be successful in the request for the passenger, the system needs both real-time seat information access (easy to achieve with an API to the usual booking systems), as well as more important detailed context and information about the passenger and their situation. Is it a family stranded, or a single adult? What other ticket dependencies exist? Can the passenger be rerouted via a different track, or is the best option to stay overnight?

This scenario demands that all passenger data reside in an up-to-date system of action database, as real-time interactions fail without current information. As these systems achieve global coverage, non-functional requirements mandate not only 24/7/365 availability but also the ability to handle transaction volume fluctuations from quiet periods to peak travel seasons such as Thanksgiving. Even minimal outages become unacceptable, and caching solutions that simply solve a data availability challenge compromise on data *accuracy* by introducing data staleness issues.

Document-based architectures, such as those provided by MongoDB, offer advantages in specific scenarios for this type of data availability and scalability. Rather than requiring complex joins across multiple tables to reconstruct user context, document models can store complete contextual information in a single, efficiently retrievable record. This approach reduces the computational overhead of context reconstruction while enabling more sophisticated caching and optimization strategies.

The performance characteristics of AI workloads also differ significantly from traditional analytical patterns. While analytical queries typically process large volumes of data to generate aggregate results, AI applications often require rapid access to specific, contextually relevant information. This pattern favors architectures optimized for high-concurrency, low-latency access to individual records, rather than bulk processing of large datasets.

Governance, security, and compliance

Governance and compliance requirements stem from a fundamental need to protect individuals from flawed decision-making in systems that lack adequate self-regulation. These safeguards exist to prevent real harms, from biased loan approvals to unsafe product recommendations.

GenAI faces intense scrutiny regarding accuracy, with media coverage of hallucinations bringing this concern to the forefront. Therefore, transparency in data lineage, reasoning processes, and result interpretation becomes critical for any GenAI solution. The document model in a system of action database enables tracking of all changes, transformations, and actions related to specific datasets. Unlike legacy relational databases, documents offer the flexibility for enhancement and enrichment throughout the process without requiring upfront planning.

From a governance perspective, this enables precise and comprehensive tracking of communication and decision-making processes. It facilitates decision auditing and corrective actions when compliance challenges arise, often due to gradual shifts in decision criteria requiring adjustment.

Security represents an additional critical dimension. MongoDB's Queryable Encryption keeps data absolutely protected from unauthorized access. While passenger data may have moderate sensitivity, healthcare provider consultations about potential illnesses require the highest security levels. The system of action database enables transparent security implementation, significantly more challenging when coordinating multiple data sources with potentially incompatible security and policy systems [4].

Model training and fine-tuning

Training or fine-tuning models requires large volumes of clean, labeled, and diverse data. The system of action database ensures efficient data curation, sampling, and preprocessing for training pipelines. Data enrichment becomes key, as features such as MongoDB's aggregation pipeline enable data annotation and continuous analysis of criteria such as minimum or maximum values and moving averages to validate reasoning processes.

The subject of data preparation for GenAI is often misunderstood, stemming from the evolution of early AI solutions supporting ML systems (systems that were derived from **business intelligence (BI)** architectures). This sometimes leads to the mistaken assumption that all data for AI usage and interaction must first be prepared, or readied, in lakes, warehouses, or marts, requiring extensive transformation and data pipeline processing. The resulting data objects are often stored as star schemas with fact tables, each containing hundreds of columns and accompanying dimension tables. Star schemas, a data modeling format originally designed to solve the problem of performant analytics queries executed against relational database objects, introduce the need for complex queries and join operations to extract insight, an architecture still employed by platforms such as Snowflake.

Apache Spark object-storage implementations, such as Databricks, offer more complex query capabilities through distributed computing frameworks and in-memory processing, representing a significant advancement over traditional batch processing systems. Both approaches, star schemas and Spark-manipulated object storage files, share a foundation in backward-looking data warehousing, regardless of contemporary terminology such as *data lake* or *lakehouse*.

These systems are optimized for processing large volumes of homogeneous data aligned along dimensional axes. Real-time access to individual datasets for operational processing falls outside their design parameters. Historically, this was the realm of **online transaction processing (OLTP)** systems. While transactional logging isn't central to GenAI data structures, the access patterns remain similar.

Often, the example of building models for embeddings is referenced as justification for why the data warehouse must be the source of data for GenAI, but this is misleading. Firstly, many business solutions successfully deploy standard embedding models for PDFs, images, and audio, without the need for custom development. Secondly, and more importantly, the comparison doesn't hold, as warehouses analyzing quarterly sales have no relevance to point-of-sale operations and transaction booking.

Practical considerations for AI data design

While the theoretical foundations of system of action databases provide the conceptual framework for AI-ready system of action architectures, successful implementation requires attention to practical design principles and operational realities. This section examines three critical aspects that determine the success of real-world GenAI implementations: the fundamental importance of well-structured and organized data, patterns of data movement through AI systems, and the operational considerations necessary for deploying and maintaining these architectures at scale.

A good data structure is critical

Well-organized data, such as documents, indexes, and embeddings, enable fast and relevant information access, essential for RAG.

In contrast, traditional relational database storage patterns create fundamental impedance mismatches with GenAI applications, which require unified, contextually rich data objects that preserve semantic relationships and business meaning. When business entities span reference data, metadata, and operational information across multiple normalized tables, extensive join operations and additional application-layer code are often required to reconstruct fragmented data into coherent business objects, ready for AI processing. This relational fragmentation not only degrades query performance and increases system complexity but also obscures the natural data relationships essential for effective AI consumption, creating artificial boundaries that require ongoing maintenance of interdependent schema relationships. Consequently, GenAI applications demand data architectures that can natively represent complex, hierarchical business entities without extensive reconstruction logic, favoring document-based architectures that align more naturally with how AI models consume data and that is, rich, contextual objects, rather than decomposed, normalized fragments.

A well-designed system of action database based on the document model is a solution that addresses all the above challenges while also delivering a wealth of non-tangible benefits, including reducing developer cognitive load and infrastructure tech sprawl.

The combination of various sources enhances metadata understanding and improves the accuracy and relevance of the models. From a developer perspective, document structures enable superior prompt construction, as denormalized documents are much easier for both developers and LLMs to work with, thereby improving the quality of the prompts. Additionally, the simpler structure with reduced normalization reduces the number of data objects required to generate appropriate context. The fewer the number of data objects, the easier it is to ensure data quality for the purposes of reducing hallucinations and improving factuality.

In the previous airline example, multiple models might contribute different reasoning aspects: a general LLM to handle chatbot communication, and a domain-specific fine-tuned model for determining routing options. Secondary LLMs might specialize in summarization versus data validation, demonstrating why relying on a single LLM likely may not achieve reasonable quality in agentic systems.

The document model enhances output quality through iterative enrichment, evolving with use cases rather than requiring re-architecting or refactoring to accommodate new or changed requirements (an unavoidable pain point in relational systems). Ultimately, enriched documents improve the fluency, coherence, and creativity of reasoning-based agentic systems.

Poor data retrieval design, stemming from loosely organized sources, results in slow performance, irrelevant results, or inaccurate information. Conversely, well-aligned architectures ensure fast, contextually relevant retrieval that supports meaningful model output.

In short, when data structure and model design are thoughtfully aligned, the result is a more accurate, responsive, and scalable GenAI solution.

Data flow

GenAI solution data flow typically begins with transactional data captured during machine, process, or human interactions. It may then be enriched with related unstructured artifact vector-encoding, or even existing reference data, so that it can be made actionable within agentic system workflows. This real-time business object enrichment in MongoDB results in a single document consisting of all relevant information enriched to the maximum extent. In a legacy architecture design, by contrast, the data would be referenced only from its sources, requiring, at best, calls to APIs, and at worst, possible direct access to databases.

Data flow with a document-based approach allows the passing of all contextual information in one object and format, facilitating collaborative work between multiple agentic systems for a single process or workflow. In our example, the flight interruption is compiled into a single document, managing all different aspects of the case, including passenger interactions, flight information, contractual data, and even situation factors such as weather conditions.

This enables multiple agentic systems to collaborate on different aspects of the same business object or transactional interaction. For example, while a chatbot communicates with the passenger and provides real-time status updates, another system component proactively works on the underlying issue, having been triggered by the transactional system detecting a flight delay and calculating the probability that the passenger will miss their connecting flight. This means the *case* begins processing before the passenger even initiates contact.

During this case creation process, the system generates multiple vectors through specific embeddings and performs semantic searches against similar historical cases. This allows the LLM to prepare natural language responses, such as `"We identified multiple flight options…"`, at the earliest possible moment. In an optimal scenario, the agentic system can proactively generate multiple solutions and communicate them to the passenger with a message such as `"We are sorry you missed your flight. We have three available options to continue your journey…"`.

Once the case is successfully resolved, the document is enriched with comprehensive outcome data, such as `"Passenger accepted rebooking on Flight 345 departing in one hour, expressed satisfaction with proactive communication, and declined meal voucher offer"`. The interactions with the passenger can then be interpreted, and the overall outcome classified. This allows critical quality assurance, helps identify emerging trends, and validates and tests newer models and their suggested outcomes.

Operationalizing a system of action database

Moving from architectural principles to production deployment requires addressing the operational complexities that distinguish AI data systems from traditional databases. The unique characteristics of GenAI workloads, including real-time vector search, continuous model evolution, and dynamic schema requirements, demand specialized approaches to deployment, monitoring, and maintenance that extend far beyond conventional database administration practices.

Deployment patterns

Implementing a system of action database requires careful planning around deployment architecture. Organizations typically follow one of three primary patterns: greenfield implementations for new AI initiatives, gradual migration strategies that slowly transition away from legacy systems, or hybrid approaches that maintain existing systems while building new AI capabilities alongside them.

Cloud-native deployments offer the greatest flexibility and scalability, with managed services such as MongoDB Atlas, providing automatic scaling, backup, and security features. On-premises deployments may be necessary for organizations with strict data sovereignty requirements, while hybrid cloud approaches can balance security needs with operational efficiency.

Performance monitoring and optimization

Real-time AI applications demand continuous performance monitoring across multiple dimensions. Query performance metrics must track not just response times but also relevance scores for vector searches and accuracy metrics for AI-generated outputs. Document-based systems require monitoring of collection sizes, index effectiveness, and aggregation pipeline performance.

Key performance indicators should include throughput metrics for data ingestion, latency measurements for retrieval operations, and resource utilization patterns during peak AI processing loads. Automated alerting systems should trigger when performance degrades below acceptable thresholds, particularly for real-time applications where delays directly impact user experience.

Cost management and resource allocation

The economics of AI data infrastructure differ significantly from traditional database systems. Vector storage and similarity searches consume different resource patterns than relational queries, requiring new approaches to capacity planning and cost optimization.

Storage costs scale with both document size and embedding dimensions, while compute costs vary based on model complexity and query frequency. Organizations should implement tiered storage strategies, moving older or less frequently accessed data to less frequently accessed, lower-cost storage tiers while maintaining frequently accessed, or hot data in high-performance systems for real-time access.

Maintenance workflows and data lifecycle management

Document-based AI systems require specialized maintenance procedures that account for schema evolution, embedding model updates, and data quality drift over time. Unlike traditional databases, where schema changes require careful migration planning, document stores allow for more flexible evolution, but this flexibility doesn't negate the need for governance frameworks that ensure data consistency.

Regular re-processing of embeddings becomes desirable as newer, more effective models become available. Automated pipelines should be utilized to manage embedding updates while maintaining high system availability, potentially utilizing blue-green deployment strategies to minimize system disruptions during major model transitions.

Migration strategies from legacy systems

Organizations rarely start with a clean slate when implementing systems of action data stores. The necessary migration of data from existing relational systems, data warehouses, and disparate operational systems requires phased approaches that minimize business disruption while maximizing the benefits of unified data access.

Experience from a wide range of customers across many industries has shown that the most successful migrations begin with pilot projects that demonstrate value quickly, then expand scope incrementally. Data synchronization strategies should maintain business data parity between old and new systems during transition periods, with automated validation ensuring data integrity throughout the migration process.

Team training and adoption considerations

Successfully operationalizing a system of action databases requires investment in team capabilities. Traditional database administrators may need training in document modeling principles, while application developers may need to learn new query patterns and optimization techniques specific to AI workloads.

Data scientists and ML engineers require an understanding of how document structures impact model training and inference performance, while DevOps teams need familiarity with AI-specific monitoring and scaling requirements. Cross-functional collaboration becomes essential as the boundaries between data engineering, AI development, and operations blur in system of action architectures.

Summary

This chapter explored the crucial role of system of action databases in order to build effective GenAI solutions. We examined the limitations of traditional data management approaches and presented an alternative paradigm centered on the document model. Key aspects discussed include unified access to diverse data sources, improved data quality and consistency, real-time context for RAG, scalability, security and governance, and the importance of aligning data structures with model design for optimal performance and accuracy.

The primary benefit of a well-designed system of action database, based on the document model, is its ability to provide real-time, context-sensitive, and holistic access to diverse data, essential for reasoning, causal analysis, and generating accurate, relevant outputs. This approach differs from traditional data warehousing by providing a unified view of enriched data optimized for RAG, model training, and fine-tuning. This results in GenAI solutions that are safer, more accurate, responsive, scalable, and secure.

In the next chapter, we will explore the critical foundations of trustworthy AI, examining how organizations can navigate the complex landscape of ethical frameworks, regulatory compliance, and data governance requirements. As AI systems become increasingly embedded in critical decision-making processes, ensuring they operate within the boundaries of ethics, law, and society becomes paramount. We will discuss how proper data governance, the foundation we've established with system of action databases, enables organizations to build AI systems that are transparent, fair, accountable, and compliant with evolving regulations across different industries and jurisdictions.

References

1. *MongoDB's document model approach*: https://www.mongodb.com/docs/manual/data-modeling/

2. *A comprehensive guide to data modeling*: https://www.mongodb.com/resources/basics/databases/data-modeling

3. *Implementing effective data quality patterns*: https://www.mongodb.com/developer/products/mongodb/modernizing-rdbms-schemas-mongodb-document/

4. *MongoDB's advanced security features*: https://www.mongodb.com/docs/manual/core/queryable-encryption/

4

Trustworthy AI, Compliance, and Data Governance

As AI transforms industries, organizations must balance its power with ethical, legal, and societal responsibilities.

This chapter explores how trustworthy AI, compliance frameworks, and data governance work together as the foundation of responsible AI. You will learn how to navigate regulatory complexity while building systems that earn (and maintain) trust through transparency, fairness, and accountability.

By the end of this chapter, you will understand the following:

- Core principles of trustworthy AI and why they matter
- How ethical frameworks translate into practical implementation strategies
- Key regulatory shifts across industries and regions
- Essential data protection and privacy requirements for AI systems
- Practical approaches for risk assessment and management
- Techniques for achieving AI transparency and explainability
- Strategies for operationalizing trustworthy AI in your organization

Why ethical AI matters

To meet the growing challenges of AI adoption and build systems that can withstand scrutiny while delivering value, organizations need a clear understanding of what trustworthy AI entails in practice. Good intentions are not enough. Building trustworthy AI requires clear principles, deliberate execution, and structured governance frameworks.

The rising stakes of AI implementation

As AI becomes increasingly embedded in critical systems, such as healthcare diagnostics, financial decision-making, and autonomous transportation, the consequences of failures grow more severe. Trust isn't just a philosophical concern. It's a strategic imperative. When AI systems shape people's lives and rights, they must operate ethically.

The expanding threat landscape presents significant challenges. On average, it takes nearly 200 days to identify a breach, and the full lifecycle can stretch to 300 days, leaving organizations exposed far longer than they may realize [1]. At the same time, regulations are tightening. Laws such as the **Health Insurance Portability and Accountability Act (HIPAA)** and cybersecurity regulations introduced by the United States **Securities and Exchange Commission (SEC)** now enforce stricter security requirements for safeguarding sensitive data. It's essential to ensure AI systems are built and managed with these risks in mind.

Defining the core concepts

To lay a strong foundation for understanding trustworthy AI, let's clarify three interconnected concepts:

- **Trustworthy AI** refers to systems designed and operated to be explainable, fair, safe, and secure. It represents a framework for reducing the diverse risks associated with AI deployment, aiming to build confidence and operate within ethical boundaries. As organizations increasingly rely on AI for high-stakes decision-making, trustworthy AI ensures alignment with human values and societal expectations. This alignment is critical for both ethical reasons and long-term business sustainability, since untrustworthy systems often face rejection by users, regulatory scrutiny, and legal exposure.

- **AI compliance** encompasses the decisions, practices, processes, standards, and frameworks that ensure AI systems operate in accordance with applicable laws, regulations, ethical guidelines, data privacy requirements, security protocols, fairness principles, and accountability mechanisms. Organizations must also stay current with evolving regulations and continuously adapt their AI systems to remain both compliant and responsible.

- **AI data governance** is the structured oversight of how data is collected, managed, and used in AI systems. It ensures that data is accurate, secure, and ethically applied while addressing challenges such as algorithmic transparency, traceability, and bias amplification. Strong governance lays the groundwork for AI compliance and trustworthiness. Without it, organizations risk undermining the integrity and accountability of their AI systems.

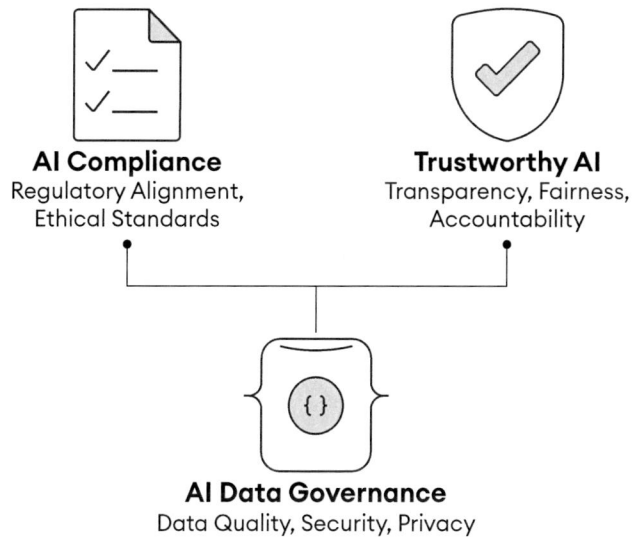

AI Compliance
Regulatory Alignment,
Ethical Standards

Trustworthy AI
Transparency, Fairness,
Accountability

AI Data Governance
Data Quality, Security, Privacy

Figure 4.1: AI data governance as the foundation for compliance and trustworthy AI

Figure 4.1 shows how these three concepts form an interconnected framework for responsible AI implementation. Robust AI data governance serves as the essential foundation for both trustworthy AI and AI compliance, ensuring the quality, integrity, security, and ethical handling of the data that fuels AI systems. Understanding these core concepts provides the groundwork for applying ethical frameworks, which translate principles into actionable guidelines for implementing AI.

Ethical frameworks: From principles to practice

Ethical frameworks offer guiding principles to help organizations develop and deploy AI systems responsibly. One of the most widely cited is the **European Union (EU)**'s *Ethics Guidelines for Trustworthy AI*, which outlines seven key requirements that have become a global benchmark:

- **Human agency and oversight**: AI systems should support human decision-making and remain subject to oversight. In practice, this means establishing *human-in-the-loop* processes for critical decisions, such as loan approvals or medical diagnoses, where humans can review and intervene as needed.

- **Technical robustness and safety**: AI must be secure, resilient, and safe, with fallback mechanisms to mitigate vulnerabilities or adversarial attacks. This includes rigorous testing protocols, secure architecture, and continuous monitoring to prevent misuse.

- **Privacy and data governance**: AI systems must respect individual privacy and maintain data quality, integrity, and security throughout the lifecycle. Techniques include data minimization, anonymization, and secure handling from collection to deletion.

- **Transparency**: AI capabilities, limitations, and decision-making processes should be understandable and traceable. Documentation should explain how AI affects outcomes and provide accessible explanations of decisions.

- **Diversity, non-discrimination, and fairness**: AI must be designed and tested to prevent unfair bias and promote equitable treatment across demographic groups. This includes using diverse training data and conducting audits to detect and address discriminatory patterns in outcomes such as hiring, lending, or healthcare.

- **Societal and environmental well-being**: AI should support societal progress and reduce negative environmental impacts. This includes evaluating job displacement risks, tracking environmental costs, and aligning systems with broader sustainability goals.

- **Accountability**: Clear ownership should be established for AI decisions and outcomes. Organizations need audit mechanisms, mitigation protocols, and ways to respond when harm occurs.

Learn more about these guidelines here: `https://digital-strategy.ec.europa.eu/en/library/ethics-guidelines-trustworthy-ai`

Ethical gaps create real operational and reputational risk. Regulatory penalties are increasing, and once trust is broken, it can be difficult to restore. Several major tech companies have already retired AI products due to bias or oversight failures. In a competitive environment where accountability matters, organizations that neglect responsible AI practices risk falling behind.

IntellectAI's Purple Fabric and trustworthy AI in finance

A strong example of trustworthy AI in a high-stakes environment comes from IntellectAI, a pioneer in AI solutions for the **banking, financial services, and insurance (BFSI)** sector. The company created **Purple Fabric**, an *Open Business Impact AI* platform designed to help enterprises meet complex regulatory and compliance demands.

One of its most notable users is a sovereign wealth fund with over $1 trillion in assets under management. The fund relies on Purple Fabric's orchestration of AI agents, powered by advanced RAG techniques and MongoDB Atlas Vector Search, to extract critical intelligence from millions of unstructured documents across its 9,000 portfolio companies. This enables differentiated portfolio management and supports a custom sustainability matrix that extends beyond standard frameworks, strengthening internal reporting and strategic initiatives.

Purple Fabric processes unstructured enterprise data through its **Enterprise Knowledge Garden (EKG)**, powered by MongoDB Atlas Vector Search, and activates that intelligence using **Enterprise Digital Experts (EDE)**, a multi-agent system that orchestrates AI across enterprise workflows.

Purple Fabric illustrates the principles of trustworthy AI in action:

- **Privacy and data governance**: Built on MongoDB Atlas, the platform securely manages unstructured data at scale, particularly from the retrieval use case just described. Fine-grained access controls limit data and AI agent exposure to only authorized users. The platform's EKG processes diverse content while preserving enterprise-grade governance over sensitive information.

- **Technical robustness and safety**: Purple Fabric meets industry compliance requirements, including SOC 2, ISO 27001, ISO 27017, ISO 27018, and AWS architecture reviews. Its infrastructure continuously monitors agent behavior and data pipelines to support reliable, safe deployment of AI at scale.

- **Transparency and accountability**: Purple Fabric's governance suite provides full data source lineage and traceability of AI outputs, ensuring AI agents are grounded in trusted source data. TRACES ensures explainability across multi-agent operations with a clear audit trail. The *Model Optimization Hub* allows teams to benchmark LLMs across speed, cost, and accuracy, and supports model selection from multiple providers or onboarding custom models. This gives users clear visibility and control over AI decisions at scale.

By combining a secure data foundation with robust monitoring, explainability, and user controls, IntellectAI has built a powerful AI platform in Purple Fabric that helps enterprises adopt AI responsibly while delivering real business impact [2].

Bridging principles and implementation

Organizations worldwide are developing practical ways to bring ethical AI to life. IBM, for example, emphasizes empathy and stakeholder engagement in its AI governance practices, ensuring alignment with broader societal values [3].

In practice, organizations are operationalizing ethics through efforts such as:

- **Bias audits**: Regularly testing AI systems for unfair bias across different demographic groups
- **Ethical review boards**: Creating diverse committees to evaluate AI applications against ethical standards
- **Transparent documentation**: Maintaining clear records of development decisions, data sources, and model limitations
- **Stakeholder engagement**: Involving affected communities in AI design, deployment, and governance decisions

Each of these practices helps translate high-level ethical principles into repeatable actions that foster trust, reduce risk, and support long-term AI sustainability.

Bias audits

Bias audits systematically evaluate AI systems, particularly LLMs, to identify and mitigate prejudicial behavior. These evaluations often test how models perform across varying demographic attributes or sensitive contexts.

A Stanford-led study applied this approach to LLMs used in hiring. Researchers collected 801 real job applications for K-12 teaching positions, then generated synthetic versions that differed only by race and gender-associated cues (such as names and pronouns) [4]. When submitted to eight independent models, the results revealed consistent disparities in scoring: female applicants were rated moderately higher than male applicants, and Black, Hispanic, and Asian applicants were generally rated moderately higher than their White counterparts. These gaps persisted even when resumes were redacted, prompts reworded, or geographic context changed.

This experiment highlights a critical challenge: even well-aligned models can exhibit demographic preferences that affect real-world decisions. Bias audits like these are therefore essential in high-stakes domains, such as hiring, where fairness, transparency, and accountability must be actively verified rather than assumed.

Ethical review boards

Ethical review boards play a vital role in the responsible development of AI. They provide structured oversight, surface risks such as bias or privacy concerns, and ensure that systems align with organizational values and societal expectations. When integrated effectively, these boards help teams make better decisions earlier, increase transparency, and earn the trust of users and stakeholders.

IBM offers a leading example. Its internal AI Ethics Board includes diverse leaders from across the company and has formal authority to oversee AI development. The board reviews use cases, shapes policy, and holds product teams accountable through a repeatable governance process.

IBM's approach operates across four key areas:

- **Principles-driven**: The board translates IBM's AI principles into specific requirements and checkpoints. For example, the principle "*AI augments human intelligence*" led to a mandate for meaningful human oversight in all systems, especially those with real-world consequences. "*Data belongs to its creator*" was reflected through strict governance protocols that protect client data and enforce consent. Transparency was addressed by requiring explainability standards and documentation throughout the development lifecycle.

- **Use case assessment**: The board reviews AI projects with heightened ethical considerations. Each project moves through a structured evaluation process that includes risk assessment, stakeholder impact analysis, and compliance checks. Depending on findings, teams may receive approval, be required to make changes, or, in some cases, be asked to stop work altogether. For instance, AI applications that affect hiring decisions underwent enhanced bias testing, while healthcare projects required additional privacy safeguards, including domain validation.

- **Workstreams and education**: The board supports company-wide education on AI ethics, including training programs and policy guidance. These efforts help embed responsible design practices into engineering and product development teams.

- **Accountability**: The board helps uphold IBM's public commitments to ethical AI by ensuring that ethics reviews are taken seriously and integrated into decision-making. It serves as a governance function while also shaping the company's culture over time [5].

To be effective, ethical review boards need more than good intentions. They require diverse representation, defined processes, and the ability to influence both product development and company norms. Without this foundation, even strong ethical principles risk being overlooked during implementation.

Transparent documentation

Transparent documentation gives stakeholders a clear window into how AI systems are designed, trained, and governed. This visibility fosters trust by demystifying complex AI models and enabling accountability for their decisions and outcomes. By carefully recording data sources, model architectures, evaluation methodologies, and potential biases, organizations can identify and mitigate risks, support regulatory compliance, and ensure responsible AI deployment.

Despite its importance, transparent documentation is often undervalued. Technical teams may deprioritize it in favor of speed, creating gaps in critical information when systems move to production. Inconsistent standards across departments make it difficult to compile coherent records for governance. The rapid pace of AI development can outstrip documentation updates, and concerns about intellectual property sometimes limit what gets recorded.

Successful organizations take a different approach. Documentation is built into development workflows from the start. Automated tools capture model metadata, training data, and performance metrics as development unfolds. Templates ensure consistency, version control keeps records current, and routine reviews flag missing or outdated information. Cross-team audits close the loop before compliance risks emerge.

Strong documentation connects teams. Legal can assess risk when data sources and model behavior are clearly logged. Business leaders can make informed decisions when system limitations are documented. Risk managers can act quickly when they have insight into training data, evaluation procedures, and known biases.

With a shared view across stakeholders, collaboration improves, and AI systems are more likely to meet technical, legal, and ethical expectations. The result is not just better compliance, but more reliable and sustainable AI systems.

Stakeholder engagement

Engaging stakeholders in AI governance ensures that systems align with the needs, values, and expectations of the people they affect. This includes users, communities, experts, and regulators who help surface risks, provide feedback, and build trust before deployment. Done well, this collaborative approach leads to stronger and more broadly supported AI solutions [6].

Many organizations struggle to do this effectively. Identifying the right stakeholders isn't always straightforward, especially when AI systems have far-reaching impacts. Competing interests require time, facilitation, and tradeoff decisions. Development timelines and resource constraints can limit how much engagement actually happens. Even when feedback is collected, teams may lack the structures to turn it into actionable changes.

The consequences of insufficient stakeholder engagement are increasingly visible. Microsoft's Copilot tool, for example, faced criticism when early versions surfaced biased or insecure code suggestions. Experts later linked the issue to gaps in engagement with the developer communities most affected. Google's Gemini image-generation tool was paused after producing offensive and historically inaccurate imagery, revealing a lack of input from diverse perspectives, especially during training and evaluation.

These cases demonstrate the risk of sidelining stakeholder voices. Reputational damage, product suspensions, and regulatory scrutiny can follow, but more importantly, so can systems that fail to serve the very people they were built for.

Successful organizations embed engagement throughout the AI lifecycle. Advisory groups bring together **users**, **domain experts**, **advocacy organizations**, and **impacted communities**. Feedback loops begin early and continue through deployment. Pilot programs and public consultations surface concerns before they become crises. Clear, ongoing communication builds trust and ensures that conversations go deeper than marketing claims.

Crucially, stakeholder input must influence how systems are built, not just how they are presented. When organizations integrate this input into design and development, AI systems become more capable of meeting real-world needs. They earn trust quicker, perform more effectively, and are better equipped to navigate regulatory and social scrutiny over time.

Navigating the regulatory landscape

AI regulations vary by industry and jurisdiction due to differing risks, maturity levels, and end-user impacts. Yet common themes are emerging across regions. EY identifies six global trends that shape the evolving landscape of AI governance [7]:

- **Core principles**: Frameworks often begin with universal commitments such as respect for human rights, sustainability, transparency, and robust risk management. These principles are reflected in guidelines from the **Organization for Economic Co-operation and Development (OECD)** and the G20.
- **Risk-based approach**: Regulations increasingly focus on the severity of potential harm. Stricter requirements apply to high-risk use cases that could affect public safety, civil rights, or health outcomes.
- **Sector-agnostic and sector-specific rules**: Some standards apply across industries, while others are tailored to sectors such as healthcare and finance.

- **Policy alignment:** AI regulations are being woven into broader digital policy domains, including cybersecurity, data privacy, and digital rights.
- **Private-sector collaboration:** Regulatory sandboxes, innovation hubs, and public-private partnerships enable safe experimentation with defined oversight.
- **International collaboration:** As AI systems cross borders, regulators are coordinating on shared standards and enforcement, especially with frontier models that present unknown risks.

While these trends offer directional clarity, they do not replace the need for local compliance and regulations. Each jurisdiction imposes its own requirements, timelines, and enforcement mechanisms.

To remain agile, organizations should adopt compliance strategies that combine long-range regulatory awareness with adaptive architecture. Flexible governance capabilities allow systems to meet evolving requirements without disrupting operations.

In the sections that follow, we'll look at two heavily regulated industries: healthcare and financial services. We'll examine how these global trends manifest in concrete compliance challenges.

Healthcare

Healthcare AI is subject to heightened regulatory scrutiny due to its direct impact on patient safety and privacy. As of this writing, the global regulatory landscape is evolving rapidly, but several key themes have emerged that help frame compliance strategies.

The **World Health Organization (WHO)** outlines four foundational considerations for AI regulation in healthcare:

- **Transparency and documentation:** Maintaining clear records of AI development and lifecycle management to establish trust and enable regulatory assessment. This includes tracing the development process and guarding against biases and data manipulation. Healthcare providers must be able to demonstrate how AI systems were developed, validated, and deployed to ensure safety and compliance.
- **Risk management:** Addressing intended use, continuous learning capabilities, and cybersecurity risks across the product lifecycle. *Intended use* refers to pre-specifying and documenting the exact medical purposes and clinical contexts for which the AI system is designed, ensuring it's not misused outside its validated scope. *Continuous learning*

addresses the unique challenge of AI systems that can update their algorithms based on new data, requiring ongoing monitoring to ensure they don't drift from their original safety and efficacy standards. These factors, combined with cybersecurity threats, must be managed throughout the entire product lifecycle.

- **Data quality**: Conducting rigorous pre-release evaluations to prevent bias amplification and ensure population representativeness. Inadequate training data, which can result in systemic errors, particularly for underrepresented groups, should be mitigated through more comprehensive training.

- **Collaboration**: Engaging patients, healthcare professionals, regulators, and industry stakeholders to improve the safety and quality of AI technologies. Multilateral coordination strengthens oversight, accelerates innovation, and supports regulatory alignment throughout the product lifecycle.

In the US, HIPAA governs the protection of patient data, while new legislative proposals target specific use cases, such as the use of AI in utilization management decisions [8]. In the EU, the AI Act classifies most healthcare AI applications as high-risk, triggering stricter compliance obligations, including conformity assessments, data governance audits, and post-market monitoring [9].

To meet these demands, healthcare organizations are adopting technologies that support both security and adaptability. Document-oriented databases with field-level encryption and granular access controls can enforce patient privacy without limiting AI innovation. For example, MongoDB enables sensitive health data to be encrypted at rest and in use, ensuring only authorized users can access designated attributes. Combined with role-based access and comprehensive auditing, this architecture helps satisfy HIPAA and other regulatory requirements [10].

As healthcare AI continues to expand, these regulatory guardrails will become increasingly essential. They support not just compliance, but also public confidence and clinical effectiveness. Organizations that align technical practices with emerging oversight standards will be better positioned to scale safely and sustainably.

Financial services

Financial institutions face a fragmented and fast-moving AI regulatory landscape. While no global standard has been established, governments and supervisory bodies are actively shaping policies that strike a balance between innovation and risk management. This section captures key developments as of the time of writing and outlines themes likely to shape future oversight.

Emerging themes in regulatory discussions include consumer protection, fairness, explainability, accountability, and cybersecurity. Key developments include:

- **US executive order on AI**: Executive orders promote innovation while managing risks. They direct federal agencies to assess AI's impact across sectors, including financial services, and develop best practices for safe, secure, and trustworthy AI. These orders also emphasize the need for systems capable of managing diverse data sources for comprehensive model training and validation while addressing cybersecurity and potential systemic financial instability [11].

- **EU AI Act**: This landmark regulation applies a risk-based framework. Financial AI systems, such as credit scoring and payment and settlement systems deemed high-risk, face strict requirements including conformity assessments, robust data and metadata governance, transparency, and human oversight mandates [9].

- **UK approach**: The **United Kingdom (UK)** has adopted a more sector-specific strategy. Regulators, such as the **Financial Conduct Authority (FCA)** and the **Prudential Regulation Authority (PRA)**, are integrating AI considerations into their existing supervisory approaches. These emphasize the need for firms to maintain strong controls over AI systems and apply fairness, transparency, and accountability principles to financial services specifically [12].

- **AI regulation in APAC**: The Asia-Pacific region follows varied, often sector-specific approaches. Singapore's **Monetary Authority of Singapore (MAS)** has led with its **fairness, ethics, accountability, and transparency (FEAT)** principles. Though non-binding, they offer clear guidance to financial institutions. China has adopted more prescriptive rules in areas such as algorithmic recommendations and deepfakes. India is shaping its regulatory framework with an emphasis on data privacy and ethical use. Japan and South Korea are advancing industry-led guidelines that prioritize ethical development.. This fragmented landscape across the APAC region reflects differing AI adoption rates and regulatory priorities, requiring businesses to strengthen internal governance and maintain region-specific compliance strategies [13].

To navigate this evolving landscape and turn compliance into a competitive advantage, financial institutions can build upon a modern data foundation designed for agility and scale. These platforms allow the seamless integration of complex and evolving data structures. They support the rapid development and iteration of AI models and can efficiently scale to handle the vast data volumes and processing demands of AI. This comprehensive approach is crucial for meeting compliance requirements while enabling responsible AI innovation.

Building trustworthy and responsible AI

Having established ethical principles and regulatory frameworks, the next step is to put them into practice. This requires a comprehensive approach across four interconnected areas: safeguarding data, managing risk, ensuring transparency, and embedding governance. Together, these elements form the foundation for responsible AI implementation that maintains stakeholder trust while delivering business value.

Safeguarding data

Data protection is the foundation of trustworthy AI. It encompasses both regulatory compliance and operational discipline. As AI systems process sensitive personal information at increasing scale, organizations must navigate privacy requirements while building governance structures that preserve data quality, integrity, and ethical use.

This section examines how organizations can meet modern privacy expectations and establish governance frameworks that support innovation without sacrificing oversight.

Protection and privacy requirements

AI systems often process vast amounts of personal data, making data protection an essential pillar of trustworthy AI. The stakes are high: while AI's effectiveness depends on broad access to data, this same appetite introduces serious privacy risks. Unlike traditional software, which may rely on limited datasets, AI systems continuously ingest, analyze, and learn from personal information, creating complex challenges around consent, data minimization, and user rights. The opaque nature of many AI models further complicates matters, especially when organizations must explain how personal data influences outcomes to meet modern transparency requirements.

To reconcile these tensions, organizations must implement technical and organizational safeguards that protect individual rights while enabling innovation. Techniques such as differential privacy and causal modeling (discussed later in this book) can help bridge that gap.

Key regulations include:

- **General Data Protection Regulation (GDPR)**: Requires transparency, data minimization, and the right to explanation for AI systems processing the data of EU residents [14]. This is especially relevant to machine learning models, which are often referred to as black boxes. Organizations must explain how automated decisions are made and ensure users understand their rights.

- **California Consumer Privacy Act (CCPA)**: Grants consumers the right to access, delete, and opt out of data collection [15]. AI systems that rely on continuous data collection for training and personalization must now provide mechanisms to remove user data, which may require model retraining or adjustments.

- **HIPAA**: Protects patient health information in U.S. healthcare AI applications [16]. AI systems that analyze medical records, diagnostic images, or patient data must use encryption and strict access controls. Breaches can result in significant penalties and erode patient trust.

- **China's Personal Information Protection Law (PIPL)**: Imposes stringent rules on data handling and cross-border transfers [17]. Global AI providers must navigate PIPL's localization mandates and obtain explicit consent before using Chinese user data, which can affect how AI models are trained and deployed internationally.

To comply, organizations adopt privacy-by-design principles, apply anonymization and differential privacy techniques, and implement strong encryption and access controls. For example, an AI model used for disease diagnosis must encrypt patient data to meet HIPAA standards and ensure that only authorized users can access sensitive attributes.

Building robust AI data governance

AI data governance provides the infrastructure for trustworthy and compliant AI by ensuring the quality, integrity, security, and ethical handling of the data that drives AI systems. Key practices include:

- **Data quality management**: Ensuring data is accurate, complete, and representative of the population it serves

- **Data security**: Applying queryable field-level encryption at rest, strong encryption in flight, and full auditing of data access to protect sensitive information

- **Data privacy**: Using anonymization (removing identifiers), pseudonymization (replacing identifiers with pseudonyms), differential privacy (adding statistical noise), and data minimization (limiting collection to only necessary information)

- **Data lineage tracking**: Maintaining clear records of data sources, transformations, and downstream usage

- **Access control**: Enforcing role-based permissions and authentication mechanisms

- **Data retention and deletion**: Defining policies for how long data is stored and when it should be deleted

These practices function as a system. A weakness in even one area can compromise the entire governance framework and undermine the trustworthiness of AI systems.

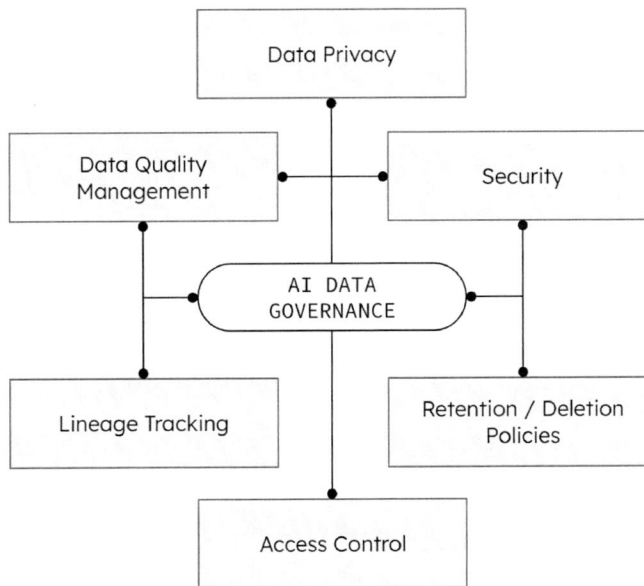

Figure 4.2: Key components of the AI data governance framework

Figure 4.2 shows how effective governance requires a holistic approach. Data quality depends on reliable lineage tracking. Privacy is strengthened by resilient security controls. Access policies allow retention protocols to function as intended. Together, these components create a foundation that supports ethical outcomes and regulatory compliance throughout the AI lifecycle, from data ingestion to model deployment.

Governance becomes more difficult when the AI stack is fragmented. Each component enforces its own security model, which can lead to inconsistencies. This challenge underscores the value of a unified data platform, such as MongoDB Atlas, which simplifies security and access controls across the entire stack.

Success depends on treating governance as an integrated framework rather than a disconnected set of tasks. Organizations that embrace this mindset reduce compliance risk, improve data quality, and strengthen stakeholder trust. As AI systems scale and regulations evolve, governance becomes a strategic enabler for innovation. It supports all other dimensions of responsible AI, including risk management, transparency, and accountability.

Managing risk: assessment and mitigation strategies

While strong data governance lays the groundwork for trustworthy AI, organizations must also address the unique risks that AI systems introduce. Unlike traditional software, AI can amplify bias, create new privacy threats, and generate unpredictable outcomes that affect critical business and societal decisions.

Proactive risk management involves two complementary efforts: assessing risks early and implementing strategies to mitigate them. Together, these steps help organizations anticipate challenges *before* they escalate into failures.

Risk assessment

Risk assessment systematically identifies and evaluates AI-specific threats, such as bias, security vulnerabilities, or ethical lapses. A structured process typically includes:

- **Risk identification**: Cataloging risks across technical, ethical, legal, and business domains
- **Risk evaluation**: Estimating the likelihood and impact of each risk
- **Risk prioritization**: Focusing resources on the most critical issues
- **Control implementation**: Developing safeguards to prevent or reduce risks
- **Monitoring and review**: Continuously evaluating controls for effectiveness

For example, a healthcare AI might undergo demographic audits to ensure diagnostic equity. A financial model could be tested for robustness against adversarial attacks.

Practical risk management approaches

To mitigate risks in practice, organizations can adopt a combination of technical, procedural, and cultural strategies:

- **Continuous monitoring**: Regular performance and compliance testing with automated alerts to detect drift or degradation
- **Incident response plans**: Predefined protocols for AI failures or breaches that reduce downtime and recovery. Having predefined response procedures minimizes harm
- **Stakeholder engagement**: Involving diverse communities in AI design and testing to uncover risks that technical teams might miss
- **Adversarial testing**: Deliberate attempts to manipulate AI systems to expose vulnerabilities before bad actors do
- **Redundancy and failsafe**: Backup systems and human oversight for continuity of operations when AI systems fail unexpectedly

EY recommends coupling regulatory literacy with strong governance and active regulator engagement [18]. IBM has found that 80% of business leaders view explainability and ethics as barriers to AI adoption (*a reminder that strong risk management isn't just about compliance concerns but also a strategic differentiator*) [19].

Modern data platforms support these strategies through features such as audit logging (which tracks all data interactions) and resource policies (which automate access controls and enforce compliance rules).

Learn more here: `https://www.mongodb.com/blog/post/simplify-security-at-scale-resource-policies-mongodb-atlas`

With a strong foundation in ethical principles and regulatory compliance, the next crucial aspect is ensuring the transparency and explainability of AI systems.

Transparency in action: Explainability mechanisms

Explainability and transparency build trust by making AI decisions understandable and system operations clear. While **transparency** provides high-level insight into how an AI system works overall, **explainability** dives into the specifics of why it made a particular choice in a specific situation. Both are important for building responsible and trustworthy AI systems.

AI transparency

Transparency in AI refers to the ability to provide meaningful insight into how a system was designed, what data it uses, and how it functions at a system level (as opposed to explainability, which focuses on individual outputs). It includes disclosing the types of data used, the model's structure, and the decision-making approaches it employs.

Organizations ranked **data privacy and security** as the top priorities for AI implementation, followed by performance and scalability [20]. From the perspective of a compliance officer or auditor, transparency is essential to demonstrate control over risk.

Organizations need transparency to align AI initiatives with business objectives and ensure systems operate as intended:

- **Data usage:** Clear documentation of data sources, formats, and processing methods enables risk assessment, auditability, and compliance.

- **General patterns:** Transparency into how AI models make decisions (especially in high-risk use cases) allows organizations to ensure systems follow defined business rules, fairness thresholds, and regulatory obligations.

- **Model structure**: Knowing whether a system uses rule-based logic, traditional machine learning, or deep neural networks informs expectations around maintainability, oversight, and failure risks.

Transparency also strengthens stakeholder communication. Business leaders need clarity when AI systems drive customer decisions. Legal and risk teams need documented evidence to respond to inquiries or defend outcomes. Internal developers need a shared understanding of how models were created and where their limits lie.

When implemented consistently, transparency reduces institutional blind spots and supports responsible scaling of AI systems. It becomes a structural input (not a last-mile output), for governance, compliance, and innovation.

AI explainability

Explainability focuses on answering *why* an AI system made a specific decision. While methods for achieving explainability are advancing, many remain technically challenging due to the inherent complexity of modern AI models. The trade-offs between model accuracy and interpretability, along with the need to make outputs understandable to humans, have led to several approaches now widely used across industries:

- **Local Interpretable Model-agnostic Explanations (LIME)**: Builds simpler, interpretable surrogate models that show how changes to input features influence outputs. LIME might be used to explain why a specific customer was denied a loan by isolating which input values most affected the decision.

- **SHapley Additive exPlanations (SHAP)**: Uses cooperative game theory to assign each input feature a *Shapley* value representing its contribution to a specific prediction. In a loan model predicting a 70% approval chance, SHAP might show that a high credit score adds +20%, stable income adds +15%, late payments subtract -5%, and high debt-to-income ratio subtracts -10%, clarifying how the model arrived at the final prediction.

- **Attention mechanisms**: Typically used in natural language processing and computer vision, attention mechanisms highlight which parts of the input the model focused on. In medical imaging, attention layers can show which regions of an X-ray influenced a diagnosis, allowing clinicians to validate AI decisions more easily.

- **Intrinsically interpretable models**: Simpler models such as decision trees or rule-based systems offer full transparency (although likely less accurate than complex neural networks and LLMs). A decision tree, for instance, might read: *"If credit score > 700 AND income > $50,000 AND debt-to-income < 30%, then approve loan."*

Explainability serves multiple business-critical functions. It enables model debugging and improvement by revealing when AI systems make decisions for the wrong reasons, builds stakeholder confidence through transparent decision-making, and supports regulatory audits by providing clear documentation of AI reasoning. Organizations implementing explainable AI often discover that the insights gained from understanding model behavior lead to improved model performance, better data quality, and enhanced trust from both internal teams and stakeholders. This combination of technical and business benefits makes explainability a strategic capability rather than simply a compliance requirement.

The business case for explainable AI

Explainability and transparency go beyond technical accuracy. They shape how organizations manage risk, earn trust, and meet accountability standards.

- **Building trust**: Users are more likely to trust AI systems when they understand how and why decisions are made
- **Accountability**: Explainability clarifies responsibility when issues arise
- **Fairness assessment**: Transparent systems make it easier to detect and address bias or discrimination
- **Regulatory compliance**: Many industries require explainable AI, especially for high-stakes or consumer-facing use cases
- **Continuous improvement**: Understanding model behavior helps teams identify failure points, refine logic, and improve performance over time

Explainability should be prioritized from the design phase. Teams can select appropriate techniques based on the system's intended use, risk level, and applicable regulations.

Technique	Strengths	Weaknesses	Typical Use Cases
LIME (Local Interpretable Model-agnostic Explanations)	Model-agnostic; fast local explanations; highlights key features per prediction	Valid only locally; unstable for complex models; approximate, not exact	Quick checks, debugging individual predictions, fast instance-level insights
SHAP (Shapley Additive exPlanations)	Grounded in game theory; consistent feature attribution; supports local and global explanations	Computationally intensive; slow on large datasets or complex models	Regulatory reporting, fairness audits, high-stakes decisions needing detailed explanations
Attention Mechanisms	Visualizes model focus; naturally integrated in deep learning models (NLP and vision); intuitive for sequence data	Not a guaranteed explanation (shows focus, not causality); limited scope beyond attention layers	NLP (translation, summarization), vision tasks, any case where knowing model focus aids understanding
Intrinsically Interpretable Models	Transparent by design; decision logic traceable; fast and lightweight	Limited accuracy; misses complex patterns; weak on unstructured data	Finance, healthcare, or domains needing critical interpretability with simple models (e.g., decision trees, linear regression)

Table 4.1: Comparison of AI explainability techniques: strengths, weaknesses, and use cases

Table 4.1 summarizes four common explainability techniques and compares them across strengths, limitations, and typical use cases. These side-by-side insights help teams choose the right method based on regulatory requirements, model complexity, and operational needs.

Operationalizing trustworthy AI through governance

Turning principles into practice requires effective governance structures that ensure AI systems are developed, deployed, and monitored responsibly. Organizations can choose from several models based on their scale, structure, and regulatory environment:

- **Centralized governance**: A single team or department oversees all AI initiatives. This ensures consistent standards and accountability across the organization but may introduce bottlenecks or slow decision-making.

- **Decentralized governance**: Individual business units manage their own AI governance. This offers flexibility and speed but increases the risk of inconsistency and misalignment with company-wide standards.

- **Hybrid governance**: Combines centralized standards with decentralized implementation. This approach balances consistency with agility and is well-suited to large or global organizations with diverse use cases.

Regardless of the model, AI governance should align with the organization's broader corporate governance structures. This includes integrating legal, technical, operational, and ethical responsibilities into a coordinated system that supports both compliance and innovation.

The road ahead: Emerging trends and future directions

As organizations implement the trustworthy AI frameworks outlined in this chapter, it is equally important to remain aware of where the field is heading. AI governance is undergoing rapid transformation, driven by new technologies, shifting regulations, and growing pressure from customers, employees, and the public to ensure the development of ethical and responsible systems.

This forward-looking section explores two dimensions: the trends that will shape AI governance in the coming years and the persistent challenges organizations must navigate to sustain trust and compliance at scale.

Evolution of AI governance

Several key trends are redefining how organizations approach AI governance:

- **AI auditing**: Independent third-party assessments of AI systems to verify compliance with ethical and regulatory standards
- **Global regulatory harmonization**: International efforts to align AI-related laws and standards across jurisdictions
- **Automated compliance tools**: AI-based solutions for tracking, monitoring, and documenting compliance in real time
- **Standardized documentation**: Tools such as Model Cards and Datasheets that provide consistent, transparent reporting on AI models
- **Collaborative governance**: Involvement of industry, regulators, academia, and civil society in shaping governance frameworks

Together, these trends promise to make AI systems more trustworthy, transparent, and easier to audit. They also reduce compliance burdens through standardization and automation.

Persistent challenges and opportunities

Despite progress, several challenges remain:

- **Scaling ethical practices**: Applying responsible AI principles consistently across large, distributed organizations
- **Balancing innovation and regulation**: Ensuring compliance while preserving flexibility and creativity

- **Technical complexity**: Making advanced systems transparent, explainable, and auditable
- Evolving threats: Addressing new security and privacy risks introduced by emerging AI capabilities
- **Keeping pace with AI advancement**: Adapting governance frameworks to technologies such as GenAI, which evolve faster than regulations

These challenges also present an opportunity for organizations that lead in trustworthy AI, allowing them to turn governance into a differentiator.

Modern data platforms with flexible governance capabilities help lay the foundation for AI that merits trust at scale.

Learn more here: `https://www.mongodb.com/resources/basics/data-management-strategy`

Summary

Trustworthy AI cannot be achieved solely through intention. This chapter examined how ethical frameworks, regulatory shifts, and data governance practices must be actively implemented to ensure transparency, fairness, and accountability in AI systems.

We explored practical concepts of trustworthy AI, including bias audits, explainability techniques, ethical review boards, stakeholder engagement, and transparent documentation. These methods help organizations operationalize trust while navigating legal and societal expectations. Case studies from healthcare, finance, and industry pioneers like IntellectAI showed what success looks like when strong governance supports real-world impact.

With these foundations in place, the next chapter turns toward execution. We explore how AI can drive large-scale modernization across complex systems, from transforming legacy applications to designing next-generation platforms.

References

1. *IBM Cost of a Data Breach Report*: `https://www.ibm.com/reports/data-breach`
2. *IntellectAI Unleashes AI at Scale With MongoDB*: `https://www.mongodb.com/company/blog/innovation/intellect-ai-unleashes-ai-at-scale-with-mongodb`
3. *What is AI Governance?* `https://www.ibm.com/topics/ai-governance`
4. *Bias Audits for LLMs in Hiring Processes*: `https://arxiv.org/html/2404.03086v1`
5. *AI Ethics*: `https://www.ibm.com/artificial-intelligence/ai-ethics`

6. *Data Management Strategy*: https://www.mongodb.com/resources/basics/data-management-strategy

7. *How to Navigate Global Trends in Artificial Intelligence Regulation*: https://www.ey.com/en_gl/insights/ai/how-to-navigate-global-trends-in-artificial-intelligence-regulation

8. *Regulation of AI in Healthcare Utilization Management*: https://www.hklaw.com/en/insights/publications/2024/10/regulation-of-ai-in-healthcare-utilization-management

9. *EU AI Act: First Regulation on Artificial Intelligence*: https://www.europarl.europa.eu/topics/en/article/20230601STO93804/eu-ai-act-first-regulation-on-artificial-intelligence

10. *WHO Considerations for AI Health Regulation*: https://pmc.ncbi.nlm.nih.gov/articles/PMC12076083/

11. *Removing Barriers to American Leadership in Artificial Intelligence*: https://www.whitehouse.gov/presidential-actions/2025/01/removing-barriers-to-american-leadership-in-artificial-intelligence/

12. *AI Regulation: A Pro-Innovation Approach*: https://www.gov.uk/government/publications/ai-regulation-a-pro-innovation-approach

13. *The Landscape of AI Regulation in the Asia-Pacific*: https://lawtech.asia/the-landscape-of-ai-regulation-in-the-asia-pacific/

14. Data Protection: https://commission.europa.eu/law/law-topic/data-protection_en

15. *California Consumer Privacy Act (CCPA)*: https://oag.ca.gov/privacy/ccpa

16. *HIPAA Compliance*: MongoDB Atlas: https://www.mongodb.com/products/platform/trust/hipaa

17. *Navigating AI in Regulated Industries: A Guide to Regulatory Considerations*: https://www.sodalessolutions.com/navigating-ai-in-regulated-industries-a-guide-to-regulatory-considerations/

18. *How to Navigate Global Trends in Artificial Intelligence Regulation*: https://www.ey.com/en_pk/insights/ai/how-to-navigate-global-trends-in-artificial-intelligence-regulation

19. AI Governance: https://www.ibm.com/think/topics/ai-governance

20. *Embracing AI in Internal Audit*: https://www.bakertilly.com/insights/embracing-ai-in-internal-audit

5

Modernization Using AI

In today's rapidly evolving digital landscape, businesses face a critical inflection point, a moment when they can either maintain the status quo or redefine what's possible. For organizations worldwide, this inflection point centers on the modernization of legacy systems that have become both essential to operations and increasingly difficult to maintain. According to recent studies, 80–90% of application modernization projects fail, highlighting the enormous challenges organizations face when attempting to update their critical systems [1,2].

This chapter explores how AI is transforming the modernization landscape, offering new approaches to overcome traditional barriers and accelerate the journey to modern, flexible, and scalable systems.

By the end of this chapter, you will understand the following:

- The fundamental challenges that cause most modernization projects to fail
- Why traditional approaches to modernization are increasingly unsustainable
- How AI can accelerate specific aspects of the modernization process
- The limitations of AI and where human expertise remains essential
- The role of modern data platforms, such as MongoDB, in successful modernization
- Practical approaches to implementing a repeatable modernization approach with AI
- How testing strategies can be enhanced with AI to reduce modernization risk
- Real-world results from a leading private bank's successful transformation

The modernization challenge

Businesses worldwide are struggling to modernize their outdated software. They face pressure to cut operational expenses, accelerate the delivery of new features, integrate AI, and meet security and compliance standards. The emergence of AI, particularly GenAI, has created renewed enthusiasm for tackling these modernization challenges.

However, getting there isn't easy. Some of the key obstacles to application modernization include the following:

- **Extended timelines and cost overruns**: Large-scale application rewrites are notoriously difficult to estimate accurately. They often stretch project timelines and budgets to unsustainable levels, creating financial strain and eroding organizational support. What begins as an 18-month project frequently extends to three years or more, with costs far exceeding initial expectations.

- **Leadership turnover and loss of momentum**: The prolonged nature of modernization projects can be subject to leadership changes, with initial champions of the rewrite moving on. This leaves new management to inherit an expensive, ongoing, and often poorly understood endeavor, which can erode confidence and lead to project abandonment.

- **The moving target phenomenon**: While the new system is being built, the legacy system continues to evolve. New features are added and bugs are fixed in the old code. The rewrite team must constantly play catch-up, trying to achieve feature parity with a moving target. This parallel development effectively doubles their workload, making it nearly impossible for the new system ever truly to replace the old one.

- **Undocumented complexities and the second-system effect**: Legacy systems often contain years of accumulated business logic, undocumented edge cases, and *features* that were originally bugs. A complete rewrite risks losing this critical institutional knowledge. Furthermore, developers may fall prey to the *second-system effect*, overdesigning the new system with excessive features and an overly generalized architecture, adding unnecessary complexity and delaying completion. As one study on mainframe application rewrites found, "*9 in 10 rewrite projects don't succeed on their initial attempt*," with reasons including complex integration and inadequate tools [3].

Figure 5.1 illustrates the vicious cycle many organizations face when attempting to modernize legacy systems. It shows how extended timelines lead to leadership changes, which cause shifting requirements and scope creep, ultimately resulting in project delays or failure. The cycle highlights why traditional approaches to modernization often fall short and why new AI-assisted methodologies are needed to break this pattern. Ultimately, these combined factors create a high probability of failure for large-scale rewrites, leading to significant financial losses and a reluctance within organizations to undertake similar modernization efforts in the future.

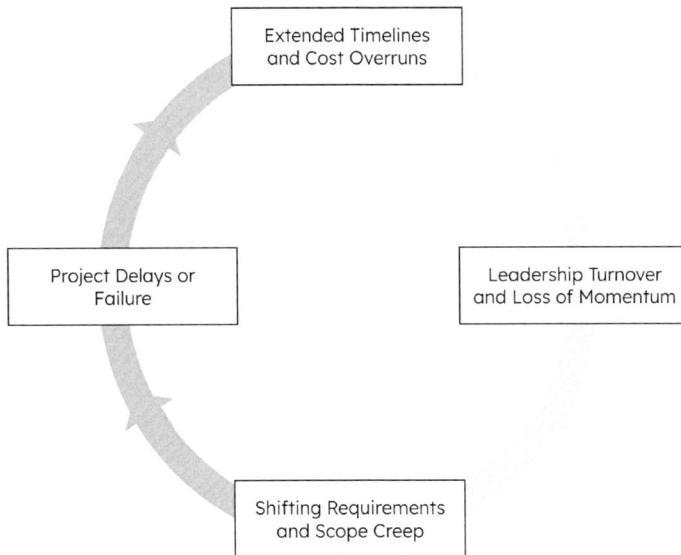

Figure 5.1: Vicious cycle when attempting legacy system modernization

MongoDB has developed a comprehensive approach to *modernization* that encompasses skilled engineers, comprehensive AI-powered tooling, and processes forged from the experience of working with many customers worldwide. Many of these customers talk about an ideal scenario that would involve an AI system autonomously managing the entire modernization lifecycle, from environment creation and code refactoring to testing and production migration. However, this level of automation remains a distant aspiration.

Motivations for modernization

Despite the challenges, organizations continue to pursue modernization initiatives because the cost of inaction outweighs the risk of change. Understanding these motivations provides important context for how AI can help address the underlying needs. There are two primary motivations behind modernization for most organizations: the fear of falling behind the competition due to a lack of agility caused by brittle, inflexible legacy systems, and the growing pressure and investment to just keep the lights on with old business-critical systems.

Business imperatives: Competitive pressure and innovation

Organizations don't modernize their technology stack simply because it's aging; they do so because legacy systems increasingly constrain business objectives. Modern digital infrastructure enables companies to pivot quickly as markets shift and customer expectations evolve. When competitors can launch new features in days rather than months, modernization becomes a strategic imperative, not a technical preference.

Against a backdrop of aggressive competition, legacy applications are an existential threat to most organizations, often creating invisible barriers to innovation. Development teams spend the majority of their time maintaining these brittle systems rather than investing in the new capabilities they need to compete effectively. By addressing these constraints, modernization frees both human and computational resources to focus on innovation and competitive differentiation, including the integration of AI, real-time services, and advanced analytics.

Technical limitations: The growing burden of legacy architecture

Behind most modernization initiatives lie several common technical challenges that eventually become impossible to ignore:

- **Architectural inflexibility**: Monolithic legacy applications resist change by their very nature. What might be a simple feature addition in a modern, modular system often requires cascading modifications across tightly coupled components in older architectures. This inflexibility dramatically increases the cost and risk of even minor changes, creating a growing backlog of needed improvements that get delayed time and again, because of the fear of disruption of service through unavoidable downtime.

- **Performance constraints**: Legacy systems typically weren't designed for cloud deployment or to handle today's transaction volumes and data growth. As demands increase, these systems hit performance ceilings that can't be overcome without fundamental redesign. These limitations become particularly acute when organizations attempt to implement AI capabilities that require real-time data processing and analysis.

- **Security exposure**: Outdated frameworks and unpatched components create growing security vulnerabilities. While many vendors happily provide extended support for these legacy systems, the cost of this is often breathtaking and far exceeds that of even the most complex modernization programs. This inability to update increases compliance risk, particularly as regulations such as GDPR, HIPAA, and PCI-DSS continue to evolve with more stringent requirements,. as discussed in greater detail in *Chapter 4, Trustworthy AI, Compliance, and Data Governance.*

The motivations for modernization are clear; there is no company of any significant size operating today that does not already have some kind of modernization program in place, operating with varying degrees of success. In fact, many companies have already begun to wonder whether this new world of GenAI, which promises so much, could be just the ticket they need to freedom from legacy chains.

Why AI alone isn't the answer

While AI tools offer impressive capabilities, any developer with even the briefest experience using them will quickly realize that they fall short as complete modernization solutions for several reasons:

- **Reliability concerns**: GenAI models produce non-deterministic output, meaning you cannot be guaranteed to get the same outcome with the same inputs. This unpredictability creates significant risk because AI-generated code may contain subtle logic errors, security vulnerabilities, or compliance issues that only surface in production environments.

- **Context limitations**: LLMs struggle with the scope and complexity of enterprise applications. Most modernization efforts involve interconnected systems with dozens or hundreds of components. LLMs lack the ability to maintain context across this breadth of code, making them prone to introducing errors at system boundaries where dependencies are most critical.

- **Engineering judgment**: AI systems cannot replicate the accumulated wisdom and nuanced decision-making that experienced architects and engineers bring to modernization projects. When evaluating legacy code, senior engineers make critical judgment calls about which components to refactor, replace, or retain based on business impact, risk assessment, and future scalability needs. While AI can analyze code, it cannot effectively balance immediate migration needs against long-term strategic goals or prioritize modernization efforts based on business value versus technical effort.

Coding assistants mark a transformative period for developer productivity by automating routine assignments. However, these assistants face inherent limitations mirroring those of GenAI, given their foundational reliance on such technologies. That hasn't stopped many developers, charged with modernizing applications, from picking up these coding tools and wondering how far they can push them towards their modernization goals. It quickly becomes obvious that the greater the complexity of work you give the coding assistants, the more time you spend hunting for and fixing bugs that the LLM has introduced. There is an obvious law of diminishing returns at play, to the point at which, without experience, processes, and tooling as support, it's easier and safer to just modernize by using traditional software development practices.

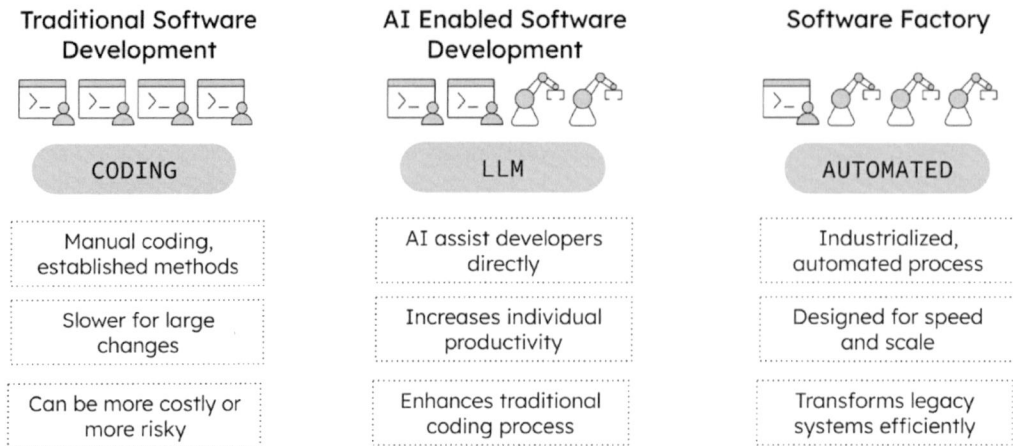

Traditional Software Development	AI Enabled Software Development	Software Factory
CODING	LLM	AUTOMATED
Manual coding, established methods	AI assist developers directly	Industrialized, automated process
Slower for large changes	Increases individual productivity	Designed for speed and scale
Can be more costly or more risky	Enhances traditional coding process	Transforms legacy systems efficiently

Figure 5.2: Evolution from traditional software development to software factory

Figure 5.2 illustrates three stages of software development evolution: traditional software development (manual coding with established methods, slower for large changes, more costly and risky), AI-enabled software development (LLM-assisted development that increases individual productivity and enhances traditional coding processes but struggles with complexity), and software factory (industrialized, automated processes designed for speed and scale that transform legacy systems efficiently). Each stage shows increasing levels of automation and capability, demonstrating how AI integration progresses from individual assistance to comprehensive automated development factories.

Unlocking innovation with AI-powered modernization

MongoDB's structured, proven approach to modernization helps organizations leverage AI to transform legacy applications into modern, scalable, and performant solutions. Developed in response to the fact that nearly 80% of enterprise applications still run on outdated technology, the approach combines AI-powered tools, specialized automation, and human software development expertise to reduce modernization risk and accelerate results [2].

At its core, MongoDB's modernization approach is a software-powered process that accelerates the individual steps of a modernization journey. It begins with application discovery, where AI tools analyze existing code bases and database structures, map system interdependencies, and generate early documentation. In close partnership with customers, the MongoDB team then generates test cases, particularly valuable for applications lacking formal testing frameworks, and iteratively converts legacy code into modern code, refining it based on test results until the system passes all quality checks. While not yet a fully automated *assembly line* process, the approach is evolving toward greater efficiency and automation with each iteration.

Achieving modernization at an enterprise scale and complexity necessitates a robust toolkit **leveraging AI**, **automation**, and a **modern data platform.** No single tool currently provides a complete end-to-end solution for complex code refactoring, dependency analysis, SQL conversion, and large-scale data migration. This is why MongoDB leverages a toolchain approach in its modernization efforts, integrating over 25 (and growing) specialized tools for distinct tasks.

The rest of this section will break down the essential components of that factory approach, from its data foundations and orchestration patterns to its GenAI-accelerated steps, testing principles, and real-world performance benchmarks.

Start with the right data foundation

Relational databases have served as enterprise workhorses for more than 40 years, but their design imposes fundamental constraints on modern application development. Developers must fragment data across multiple tables, implement complex joins, and maintain rigid schemas that resist change. As application needs evolve, this architectural mismatch slows velocity, increases cognitive load, and taxes innovation.

Today's workloads, including real-time analytics and AI-powered features, demand a data platform that can handle diverse data types, scale horizontally, and adapt quickly to changing requirements. Advanced document database platforms such as MongoDB provide that foundation. By aligning data storage with the way developers already structure information in their applications, document models remove the impedance mismatch that slows delivery and complicates system design.

MongoDB offers a unified data platform that natively supports a wide range of use cases: operational transactions, time series data, text and vector search, IoT telemetry, and more, all through a single document model and query interface. This eliminates the need for workload-specific databases, reducing the complexity, security risk, and operational cost, while accelerating innovation.

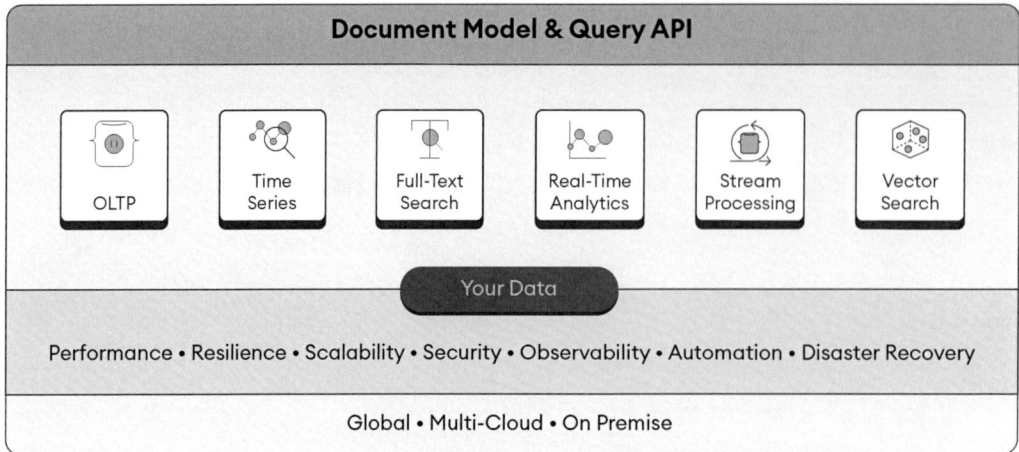

Figure 5.3: MongoDB's unified data platform architecture

Figure 5.3 illustrates how MongoDB enables diverse workloads through a single core dataset. All workloads operate on the same underlying architecture, optimized for performance, scalability, resilience, and security across global, multi-cloud, and on-premises environments.

Beyond operational efficiency, MongoDB's document model empowers developers to build modern AI-powered applications at a pace that legacy relational systems simply can't match. Because most modern applications already use JSON-formatted data for internal objects, APIs, events, and integrations, storing that data in the same shape unlocks meaningful benefits:

- **Natural data mapping**: Documents map directly to objects in languages such as Java, reducing boilerplate code and simplifying the use of modern frameworks and development libraries
- **Agility and developer productivity**: Flexible schemas align with agile development practices and rapid iteration common with modern languages, without the friction of complex SQL schema migrations
- **Readability and reduced cognitive load**: Developers can interact with full, self-contained objects (such as a user profile or product SKU) without having to stitch data together across multiple tables
- **Performance and infrastructure efficiency**: Denormalized JSON (BSON) documents reduce query complexity, speed up results, and improve infrastructure efficiency at scale

This contrast becomes especially clear when relational and document-based models are viewed side by side.

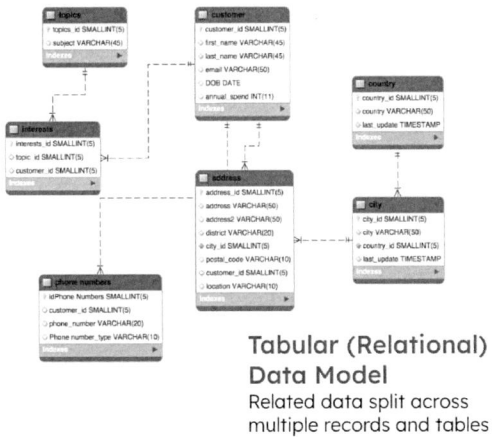

Figure 5.4: Contrasting relational and document data models

Figure 5.4 compares a normalized relational schema with a document-based model. On the left, related data is split across multiple tables, requiring joins to reassemble a complete record. On the right, MongoDB stores the full object in a single JSON document, mirroring how it's used in the application.

Together, the document model and unified data platform form a powerful foundation for software development. Already proven for modern applications, MongoDB is being embraced as the ideal solution for AI-powered applications too. Increasingly, organizations across all industry verticals are discovering that these same attributes are essential for scalable modernization. When combined with experienced engineering teams and a repeatable framework, this approach opens the door to large-scale application transformation at a pace the industry has not seen before.

Automating the modernization factory process

Any traditional factory relies on repeatable processes to deliver consistent and reliable outcomes. MongoDB's approach to modernization for enterprise applications follows the same principle: using automation to scale the transformation of legacy systems in a controlled and efficient way. Regardless of tooling, the modernization approach follows a common pattern. Within that pattern, each project has its own nuances, requiring humans to adapt tools and processes to the customer's unique environment, architecture, and priorities.

Each iteration of the factory includes the following:

1. **Analyze:** Understand the legacy system's structure, dependencies, and business logic.
2. **Test generation:** Build comprehensive tests to validate system behavior.
3. **Code transform and test:** Convert legacy code and data to modern formats while preserving functional equivalence.
4. **Deploy and migrate:** Move the transformed application to the new platform with minimal disruption.
5. **Repeat:** Apply these steps iteratively for each modernization phase.

The size and scope of each iteration depends on factors such as the customer's deployment strategy and tooling. In general, smaller and more frequent iterations reduce risk and provide earlier feedback.

This section explores how AI enhances and accelerates these processes while maintaining the necessary human oversight. First, we will examine how the factory itself is orchestrated and how AI optimizes the modernization process.

Orchestration: how the factory is automated

AI-focused workflows are ushering in a new era for orchestration tooling. MongoDB uses LangFlow as the foundation for automation within its modernization factories due to its tight integration with LLMs and speed to create and update agentic flows. One of the key capabilities enabled by this orchestration layer is the ability for LLMs not only to generate code or scripts, but also to diagnose and fix the errors they produce. These self-correcting workflows are designed using

LangFlow's visual interface, as shown in *Figure 5.5*.

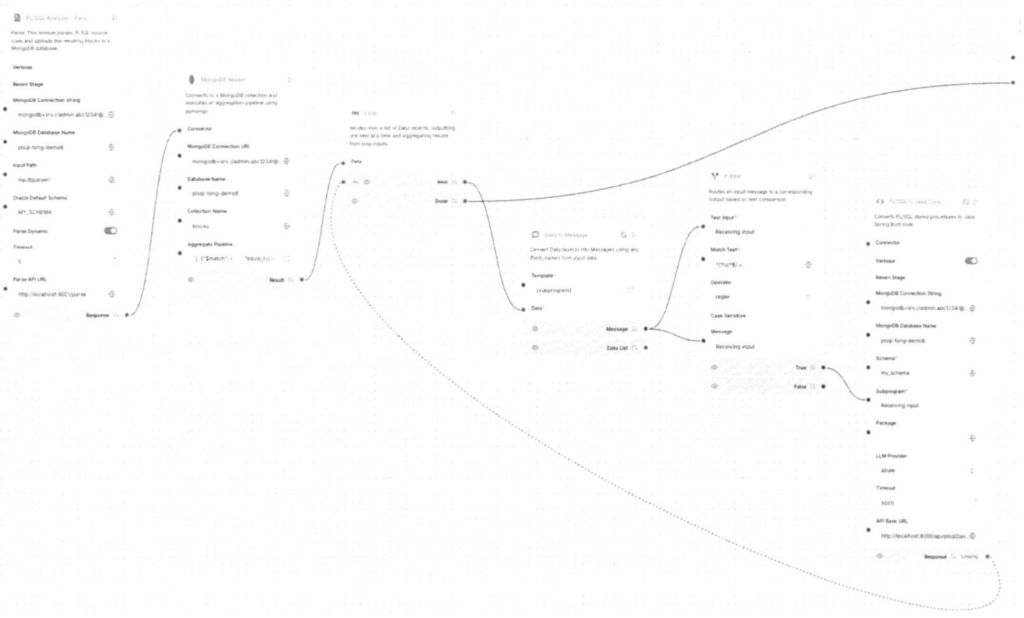

Figure 5.5: LangFlow orchestration workflow for AI agent development

Figure 5.5 shows the LangFlow visual workflow interface used in MongoDB's approach to modernization for creating and managing AI orchestration workflows. The interface displays a capability-based workflow design with various connected components, demonstrating how LangFlow enables tight integration with LLMs and provides a visual approach to creating and updating agentic workflows, simplifying the development of AI-powered automation processes through its drag-and-drop workflow builder.

Of course, orchestration only delivers value when paired with tools to automate. In the next section, we won't focus on specific tools, but on the strategic areas where AI is making the biggest impact across the modernization lifecycle. Given how quickly the tooling landscape evolves, focusing on *where* and *how* AI is used will offer more enduring value than analyzing individual tools.

Where AI accelerates the process

As discussed earlier, MongoDB's modernization approach does not treat GenAI as a magic wand. Anyone who's tried to fully automate modernization using LLMs knows the pitfalls: brittle output, hidden errors, and time-consuming rework that defeats the purpose. Instead, MongoDB engineers use AI as part of a carefully assembled toolkit to accelerate key tasks while maintaining control, precision, and accountability.

This section explores where AI is delivering the biggest performance and productivity gains, starting with analysis.

Analysis

The first step in any modernization effort is gaining a clear understanding of the legacy system, how it's constructed, what it does, and how complex it truly is. In one case, MongoDB's analysis revealed that a code base was nearly four times larger than the customer initially believed. This early insight helped right-size the project scope and avoid costly surprises later.

Here's how AI helps accelerate and enhance the analysis process:

- **System analysis and documentation**: Many large systems lack up-to-date documentation. LLMs help fill this gap by analyzing code to generate summaries of the application functionality and core capabilities. They can effectively provide an overview of an application and identify core domains, programming languages, frameworks, and business processes. Combined with static code parsers and database-specific tools, they can also extend their reach into stored procedures, triggers, and database schemas. However, one gap that often results from the system analysis is the downstream implications. While LLMs can help document direct integrations, they often lack the context of the entire ecosystem. This is where an organization's repository of architecture or integration models becomes valuable, as LLMs can use them to highlight key areas of focus for integrations.

- **Dependency mapping**: A crucial outcome of the AI-assisted dependency graphs helps teams visualize deep interdependencies across the code base. Starting with *leaf nodes*, components with few or no dependencies, enables faster, lower-risk progress. This targeted approach helps avoid the inefficiency of attempting to resolve a large, interconnected code base in its entirety. Modernization efforts often involve the migration to a microservices architecture. Dependency graphs provide valuable insights into helping identify potential bounded contexts and service interdependencies. While LLMs provide reasonable recommendations, subject matter experts are still required to ensure that the services are appropriate.

- **Schema transformation**: One major area of analysis involves understanding the database schema and determining the appropriate document collections and structures. First, MongoDB's **Relational Migrator** (**RM**) tool leverages AI behind the scenes to do just this. Besides providing a recommendation, RM allows the user to tweak the document structures. Secondly, leveraging LLMs to evaluate the application entities, such as **Plain Old Java Objects** (**POJOs**) or **Enterprise JavaBeans** (**EJBs**), provides additional insight into the structure of the application. Often, there are nuances or contextual considerations that LLMs cannot account for, and a human in the loop is necessary. One critical point to remember is that MongoDB's flexibility means it is very easy to change document structures as you progress. Not spending endless hours debating every detail of the document allows teams to start converting code, saving valuable time and money. When the team uncovers something that needs to change in the document, the cost of change is very low.

- **Knowledge augmentation**: Using MongoDB Atlas Vector Search, teams can create RAG systems to store and semantically search project documentation, code, and best practices. Leveraging RAG is useful for creating internal chatbots or search tools that enable developers to query vast amounts of project documentation, code, analysis reports, and modernization best practices. Having an easily accessible, current knowledge base is another time-saver made possible by AI.

For leaders, all of this contributes to greater confidence. Modernization can be done safely, at scale, and without disrupting core operations. As we'll see in the next section, this analysis foundation is what makes a test-first strategy not only possible, but essential.

Test generation

Focusing on testing in the early stages of modernization is critical for ensuring business functions remain intact. Many efforts stall, fail, or never begin due to the fear of breaking a solution that has worked for years. Proactively addressing this risk is essential for minimizing issues and fostering confidence throughout the modernization process.

End-to-end testing

Many large-scale applications lack adequate end-to-end tests, forcing subject matter experts to verify every change manually. While unit testing is essential (and covered in the next section), early modernization work benefits most from end-to-end behavioral testing, particularly when generated using real application activity rather than code prompts alone.

Figure 5.6 visualizes a more reliable strategy: capturing inputs, outputs, and database state changes during runtime to reflect real-world business workflows accurately. With this context in hand, including API traffic (HTTP, JSON, HTML), database state changes, and the underlying schema, LLMs can generate accurate, meaningful test cases.

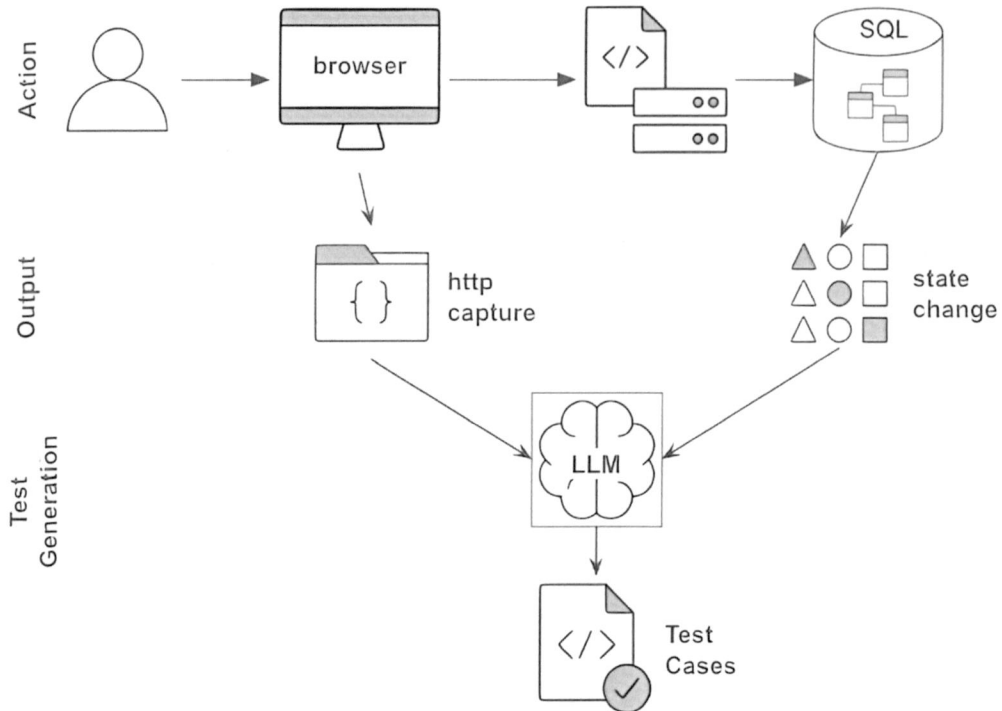

Figure 5.6: End-to-end test generation using application behavior capture

This method outperforms code-only prompting, which often fails due to missing business logic and application state. Once the behavioral context is captured, LLMs can generate tests in frameworks such as Cucumber, Karate, or others, thereby accelerating coverage in a format that integrates with existing QA pipelines. Additionally, vectorizing these generated tests and storing them in a knowledge base adds long-term value: developers can query the system's business logic semantically and reuse key patterns across domains.

Paper-based testing

Old applications often rely on static, human-readable test plans, stored as documents but never executed automatically. LLMs offer a quick path to automation here. Given access to digital test documents, they can parse and transform them into executable scenarios. If the documents are too long or inconsistently structured, teams can either split them manually or vectorize them to support semantic search and test generation through RAG.

It is a simple matter for an LLM to parse the document and generate a test scenario. However, the context limitations of LLMs can be problematic. There are several approaches to addressing this challenge. One is to manually break apart the tests, and another is to vectorize the documents. Vectorizing the documents enables someone to ask test-specific questions of the data and to generate tests.

Besides a lack of automated testing, many applications lack test data or test environments. It is beyond the scope of this book to address building test environments or defining your test data management strategy, as these items are unique to each organization and its testing maturity. After closing the most critical testing gaps, the next step is to start the actual code transformation.

Code transformation and testing

Modernizing applications comes in many different shapes and sizes. Modernization efforts may encompass one or more of the following areas: migrating logic out of stored procedures and migrating to MongoDB, replacing application servers/runtimes (such as JBoss and WebLogic), modernizing older frameworks (including Oracle Forms and WCF), and migrating to different languages (like Kotlin, Scala, etc.).

The general approach for modernization isn't unique and follows a common pattern:

- Test generation
- Code transformation and testing
- Comparative testing
- Code cleanup and optimization

Once all issues are resolved and the code is functionally equivalent, the effort to optimize becomes greatly reduced. Some teams may choose to optimize during the transformation phase, but that introduces more complexity and can make debugging more difficult. This chapter focuses on the core transformation process and doesn't delve into the post-transformation optimization process, as these situations are very unique to each modernization effort. Let's dive into the overall process.

By taking a test-driven approach, MongoDB's modernization strategy aims to deliver complex modernizations safely. Therefore, the first step is to close any lower-level testing gaps. Regardless of the testing technologies used, LLMs can dramatically reduce the time required to generate or improve tests.

- **Unit testing**: There are numerous preexisting solutions for generating unit tests, so this chapter doesn't go into depth on the topic. Newer, agentic tools are appearing on the market, such as Qodo Cover [5], that aim to identify and close unit testing gaps leveraging LLMs. One of the clever approaches in MongoDB's modernization solution leverages dependency reports to ensure that unit tests are generated for all dependent classes. This approach enables an iterative delivery approach while ensuring all dependent classes are testable. By automating test generation and leveraging dependency graphs, organizations can achieve a consistent and safe migration strategy.

- **Integration testing**: First, let's align on the term *integration testing*, which, for the context of this book, is testing code and other infrastructure components, such as databases. A different approach is needed for integration testing due to the increased complexity of testing a broader spectrum of an application. One effective strategy is to follow a similar pattern to end-to-end testing. Execute the code block (Java, stored proc, etc.) and capture the inputs, outputs, and state changes. Then feed this information, relevant source code, and the testing strategy (boundary tests, Fuzz, Monkey, etc.) to the LLM to generate the automated tests. To reduce the amount of labor involved to verify that the generated results are valid, utilize an LLM to score the output tests. This is done by feeding the original prompt, inputs, and generated test cases into the LLM and prompting it to score the tests. Humans can then inspect the test cases with lower scores to validate their effectiveness. Integration testing must address both the current solution and the new solution. At each step in the modernization process, equivalent tests should be run against the current and the new solution to ensure equivalence. This will be discussed in more detail in the *Comparative Testing* section.

- **End-to-end testing**: As additional test scenarios are identified, they will follow the preceding approach. It isn't uncommon for edge cases to be identified once teams focus on transformation-specific business capabilities.

AI-powered code transformation

Code modernization complexity varies greatly, but the following approach has proven successful regardless of complexity in accelerating delivery:

- **Recommend**: LLMs have dramatically improved in their ability to recommend an approach for transforming code. Prompt the LLM with the dependency reports and migration goals, such as converting Java to Kotlin, to provide a strategy for approaching the code transformation. You must include in the prompt basic details about how you want to approach the transformation, such as starting with capabilities without any dependencies or focusing on one business capability, such as adding a new customer. For the best results, review the LLM's response, identify any gaps or concerns, and ask it to improve the prompt with these details. After a few iterations, you will have a tailored prompt, specific to your modernization goals, that yields a well-planned approach for the modernization. This cannot replace subject matter experts who have context well beyond what the LLM can process, but it provides a solid foundation to begin.

- **Convert/compile/repair/test**: MongoDB's factory-based approach uses an agentic, closed-loop strategy to automate the conversion and eliminate a significant volume of mundane work. Humans are in the loop to direct the overall process and determine which aspects of the application to migrate. They are also in the loop to step in when the automated transform, build, test, and repair loop becomes stuck and the LLMs cannot correctly resolve the problems. *Figure 5.7* illustrates the automated, closed-loop, code transformation workflow. When tests pass, the process completes successfully. When tests fail, the system automatically loops back to an LLM repair phase that analyzes the failures and attempts to fix issues before re-entering the transformation cycle, creating a self-correcting automated modernization pipeline with human oversight only when the automated loop cannot resolve problems.

  Besides addressing issues in the process, humans are needed to review code and refine the code conversion prompts. Early in the process, you need to experiment with various prompts to determine what yields the best results. LLMs are becoming very skilled at generating and improving prompts. Provide the LLM with the original prompt and the improvements desired. Repeat this process for each unique aspect of the application. For example, prompts to convert EJBs to POJOs and repositories targeting databases will need to be altered for asynchronous communications.

Closed Loop Build Process

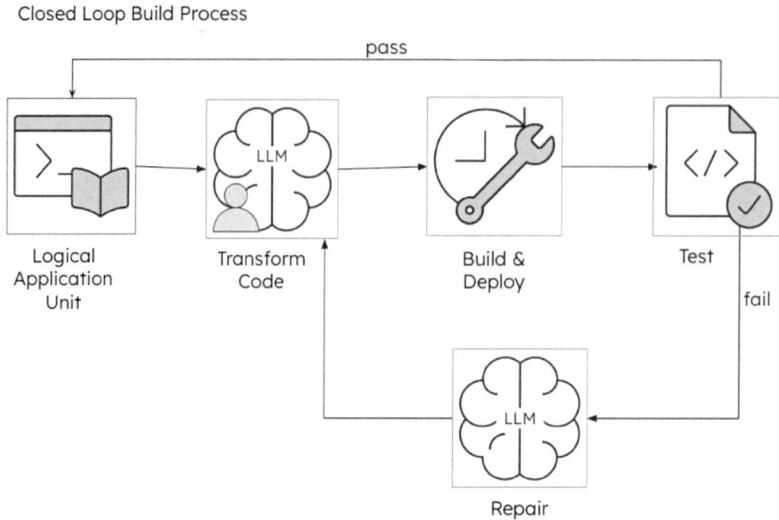

Figure 5.7: Closed-loop build process

Translation challenges

MongoDB's approach to modernization employs AI-powered tools and workflows tailored for specific code transformations, including SQL to Java, Java to Kotlin, SQL to **MongoDB Query Language (MQL)**, and more. Large language models require specific context to perform these translations effectively. For instance, converting PL/SQL to Java necessitates both the relevant database schema and the PL/SQL code.

To overcome challenges with large or complex code translations by LLMs, several strategies are employed and tailored to the situation. In many instances, the code is first broken down into logical units or code blocks. Then, the LLM transforms each code block and uses the previously converted code as input to the prompt. So, the transformed code is iteratively built one layer at a time.

However, in extreme cases, this iterative, compounding approach doesn't work due to the size of the code. To overcome these situations, we've developed a patent-pending technique that takes a different approach. This alternative approach avoids the compounding code challenges by building and testing in very small increments. Each increment is translated into the destination language and then tested. While the increments do build upon each other, each translation is independent, ensuring that the LLM isn't presented with too large a code file. By testing one increment at a time, any bugs are quickly identified.

As each logical unit is modernized, it is imperative to test that the old and new solutions produce the same results. The next section discusses where AI has proven incredible levels of acceleration at comparative testing.

Comparative testing

One of the most critical steps in modernization is comparing the legacy system and the new one to ensure the business logic remains intact, processes behave as expected, and data is preserved. MongoDB's modernization approach uses a like-for-like conversion strategy early in the process to minimize the challenges in comparing the results. At this stage, the performance and scale of the new system are suboptimal, but acceptable because the initial goal is modernization without breaking the business logic. Once the new code is confirmed to be correct, optimization for non-functional requirements begins, unlocking the true agility and performance of the modernized system.

While LLMs have not proven effective at directly comparing large or complex data results, they excel at generating the utilities and test scripts needed to validate data equivalence.

Figure 5.8 illustrates a simplified relational schema (left) alongside a modern document structure (right). In the relational model, fields use names such as FIRST_NAME, while the document model uses firstName and embeds related data such as job and department details. LLMs can identify these structural patterns and generate the code required to perform the side-by-side comparisons.

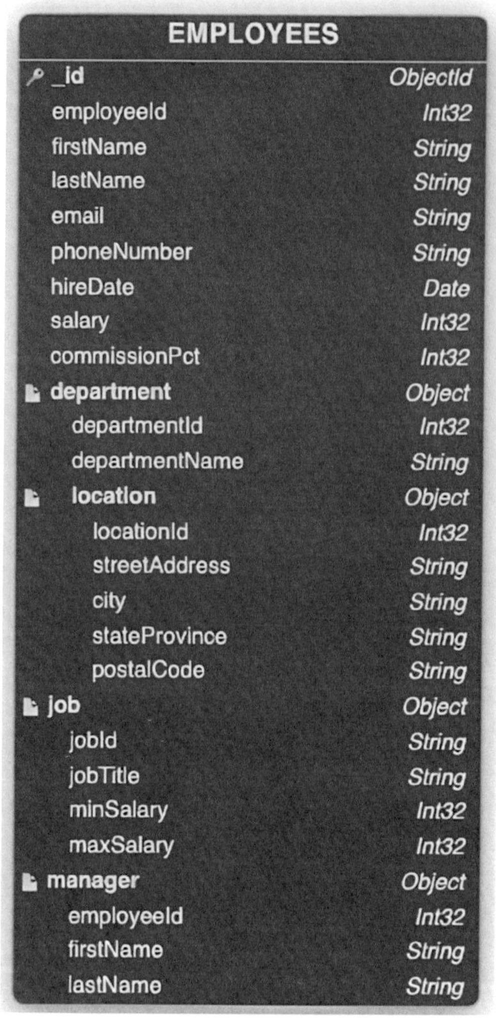

Figure 5.8: Database structures

With this iterative and test-driven approach, integration errors are typically easy to catch, especially when the data is isolated. More interesting challenges arise when downstream systems begin interacting with the data after it is written.

Once the code is validated and proven to be accurate, we can then start optimizing it.

Code cleanup and optimization

Once the transformed code has passed initial testing, there's a valuable opportunity to leverage LLMs for code improvements and system optimizations. Because adequate tests have been built throughout the process, these changes can be done iteratively, quickly, and safely:

- **Code comments**: LLMs have proven very effective at commenting code, even inferring the meaning of obscure variable names or acronyms. These comments can also serve as source material for other artifacts, such as Swagger API documentation or onboarding guides.

- **Code readability**: Another common practice is for LLMs to improve the readability of code. Common use cases include the following:

  - Improving variable and function names to make them more readable
  - Refactoring large methods into smaller, testable units
  - Rewriting complex conditional logic for maintainability
  - Enforcing code formatting to adhere to an organization's coding standards
  - Removing duplicate or unreachable code

- **Code optimization**: LLMs can help identify bottlenecks, but this process can be tricky and may yield some unexpected results. Always establish a clear performance baseline before embarking on code optimization. When used responsibly, LLMs can help to do the following:

  - Reduce memory usage
  - Improve execution speed
  - Optimize thread or concurrency handling

Deploying and migrating

Organizations have unique approaches for deploying code, including environment propagation, gated checks, use of feature toggles, CI/CD pipeline tooling, and more. AI can assist in these areas, but acceleration gains are often minimal due to the custom nature of each pipeline. However, most mature organizations have already automated these workflows, making them well-suited to a factory-type model.

With the additional tests generated throughout the process, there's an opportunity to further optimize pipelines for efficiency and automation. AI can recommend ongoing changes to improve deployment speed, reduce manual intervention, and increase reliability.

Each application modernization effort will have its own unique requirements for migrating to the new solution. Some teams may choose to run legacy and modern systems side by side and slowly migrate, while others may opt to carve out individual capabilities and migrate one piece at a time.

For a deeper exploration of migration strategies, we recommend Martin Fowler's *Patterns for Legacy Displacement* [4].

Establishing a repeatable modernization process

A key outcome of adopting a software factory approach to modernization, especially one enhanced by AI, is the ability to establish a repeatable process. Once successful patterns for test generation, code transformation, deployment, and migration are identified and refined for a specific type of legacy system or application component, these patterns can be repeated for similar modernization efforts. This repeatability is not about simply doing the same thing over and over, but about creating a well-defined, efficient, and continuously improving workflow.

The continuous improvement cycle is fueled by feedback from each modernization iteration. As teams complete transformations and deployments, they gather insights into the effectiveness of the AI tools, the accuracy of generated tests, the efficiency of the transformation workflows, and the challenges encountered during migration. This feedback is used to:

- Refine AI prompts and models: Improve the instructions given to LLMs for tasks like code recommendation, transformation, and test generation to yield better results in future iterations.
- Optimize workflows: Streamline the automated conversion, build, test, and repair loops to reduce manual intervention and accelerate the process.
- Enhance testing strategies: Adapt and improve testing methodologies based on the types of issues discovered in previous modernization efforts.
- Update documentation and best practices: Capture the lessons learned and successful techniques in documentation that can be used to guide subsequent modernization projects.

By actively incorporating these improvements, the repeatable modernization process becomes more efficient and effective over time. This allows organizations to tackle a larger volume of legacy modernization with increased speed and reduced risk, moving closer to a fully modernized digital landscape. The goal is to create a self-sustaining cycle where each completed modernization project contributes to making the next one smoother and more successful.

To illustrate these principles and their real-world impact, consider the following case study.

AI-powered modernization transforms core banking systems

A longstanding private bank faced the challenge of modernizing hundreds of legacy applications that had become a barrier to innovation. As part of a multi-year transformation initiative, the bank partnered with MongoDB to accelerate its modernization using GenAI-powered tooling and methodologies.

The effort began with two of the bank's most critical systems: its portfolio management platform and its online banking interface. MongoDB developed tailored AI tooling for the bank's architecture, combining scripts, prompts, and migration logic adapted to its technology stack. GenAI was applied across multiple modernization tasks, including:

- Legacy code analysis and translation
- Schema migration from relational models to MongoDB
- Data movement and transformation
- Middleware migration (from Java stacks to cloud-native runtimes)
- Functional test generation and automation

Working in tandem with MongoDB's experts, the bank adopted a test-first, iterative approach. This preserved business logic, reduced risk, and allowed value to be delivered continuously throughout the project.

The results were substantial:

- Code migration was up to 60 times faster than previous manual efforts
- Application migration accelerated by a factor of 20
- Regression testing dropped from days to hours
- Repetitive tasks were automated, freeing expert capacity and compressing timelines

Several core principles contributed to the bank's success:

- A document-based data model aligned naturally with application design
- Automated test scaffolding preserved business logic and reduced human error
- Human-AI collaboration enabled faster delivery without sacrificing control
- Incremental delivery supported early wins and broader adoption

This case underscores the transformative potential of GenAI when paired with the right data platform, technical expertise, and delivery approach. What was once considered too risky or complex is now achievable at enterprise scale.

This success story shows that when AI is paired with the right data model, expert oversight, and an iterative approach, modernization can be achieved at scale. While legacy transformation projects have historically failed at rates as high as 80–90%, these results demonstrate that this trend can be reversed through a combination of AI capabilities, proven methodologies, strong data foundations, and expert guidance This example has been anonymized for editorial clarity. To learn more, see: `https://mdb.link/private-bank-modernizes-legacy-banking-technology`.

Summary

Modernizing legacy systems represents one of the most challenging yet potentially rewarding initiatives an organization can undertake. While the risks are significant, with 80–90% of modernization projects failing due to extended timelines, leadership turnover, moving targets, and undocumented complexities, the cost of inaction continues to grow as legacy systems constrain business agility and innovation.

AI offers powerful new capabilities to accelerate and de-risk the modernization journey, but it's not a silver bullet. The non-deterministic nature of AI, its context limitations, and the continued need for human engineering judgment mean that AI works best as part of a comprehensive modernization approach that combines automated tools with human expertise.

MongoDB's approach to modernization embodies this hybrid strategy, leveraging AI for system analysis, test generation, and code transformation while maintaining human oversight for architectural decisions and business logic validation. The methodology emphasizes an iterative, testing-first approach that reduces risk through small increments and continuous validation. By generating comprehensive tests before transformation and using closed-loop automation for build-test-repair cycles, organizations can modernize with greater confidence and speed.

Starting with the right data foundation and moving beyond the limitations of relational databases to the flexibility and power of the document model, organizations can not only modernize their legacy systems but also position themselves for future innovation and growth. The document model's natural alignment with modern application development patterns eliminates impedance mismatches and enables the diverse workloads that AI-powered applications demand.

Throughout *Part 1, AI and Key Concepts*, we've explored the fundamental concepts, technologies, and approaches that enable AI-powered modernization. In *Part 2, Real-world case studies and implementations*, we'll examine how AI is being applied across various industry verticals, beginning with a focus on manufacturing and motion in the next chapter. These case studies will demonstrate how the principles and methodologies discussed so far translate into tangible business outcomes and competitive advantages.

References

1. *Why Technology Modernization Projects/Programs Fail!*: https://www.linkedin.com/pulse/why-technology-modernization-projectsprograms-fail-root-phil-harman/

2. *Why 84% Of Companies Fail At Digital Transformation*: https://www.forbes.com/sites/brucerogers/2016/01/07/why-84-of-companies-fail-at-digital-transformation/

3. *Most mainframe application rewrites fail the first time*: https://www.ciodive.com/news/mainframe-application-modernization-hybrid-cloud/727958/

4. *Patterns of Legacy Displacement*: https://martinfowler.com/articles/patterns-legacy-displacement/

5. *Qodo Cover*: https://github.com/qodo-ai/qodo-cover

Part 2:
Real-World Case Studies and Implementations

This set of chapters demonstrates how organizations across industries are putting generative and agentic AI into practice, turning strategy into architecture and architecture into outcomes. Each case study explores how domain-specific business challenges are solved through the use of real data models, scalable infrastructure, and intelligent orchestration.

This part of the book includes the following chapters:

- *Chapter 6, Practical Applications of Agentic and GenAI in Manufacturing – Part 1*
- *Chapter 7, Practical Applications of Agentic and GenAI in Manufacturing – Part 2*
- *Chapter 8, AI-Driven Strategies for Media and Telecommunication Industries*
- *Chapter 9, Cognigy's Voice and Chatbots in the Time of Agentic AI*
- *Chapter 10, Harnessing AI to Transform the Retail Industry*
- *Chapter 11, Financial Services and the Next Wave of AI*
- *Chapter 12, RegData, MongoDB, and Voyage AI: Semantic Data Protection in FSI*
- *Chapter 13, Driving Client Success in Banking with GenAI Copilots*
- *Chapter 14, Delivering Business Value with AI in Insurance*
- *Chapter 15, Automating Insurance Underwriting with Fireworks AI and MongoDB*
- *Chapter 16, AI-Powered Transformation of Healthcare and Life Sciences*

6

Practical Applications of Agentic and GenAI in Manufacturing – Part 1

As we transition from foundational concepts to real-world implementations in the second part of the book, we begin our industry-by-industry exploration of how organizations are putting AI into practice. Each industry presents unique challenges, data environments, and success metrics, from healthcare's patient privacy requirements and life-critical decisions to financial services' regulatory compliance and real-time fraud detection to retail's seasonal demand patterns and customer experience optimization. These distinct characteristics shape how AI implementations unfold, what success looks like, and which technologies prove most effective.

Let's start with manufacturing, because it offers an ideal proving ground: rich operational data flows from sensors and systems, complex multi-variable optimization problems, and measurable cost savings and efficiency gains. Given the breadth of AI applications in this sector, we'll explore manufacturing across two chapters. In this chapter, we will focus on where AI has become the cornerstone of modern manufacturing transformation, that is, supply chain optimization and inventory management, critical battlegrounds where intelligent systems deliver the most tangible results. We'll explore how **generative AI (GenAI)** and agentic systems are revolutionizing these operations, transforming traditional inventory management from reactive, rule-based approaches into intelligent, predictive systems that leverage both structured data and previously untapped unstructured information sources.

By the end of this chapter, you will understand the following:

- How AI is driving the next wave of supply chain transformation in manufacturing
- The evolution from traditional ABC analysis to AI-enhanced multi-criteria inventory classification
- The four-step methodology for implementing GenAI-powered inventory classification that incorporates unstructured data
- How to transform qualitative business insights into quantifiable inventory metrics using **natural language processing (NLP)**
- The practical implementation of agentic AI for autonomous raw material management and procurement optimization
- How MongoDB Atlas enables seamless integration of structured and unstructured data for intelligent inventory decisions
- Real-world examples and interactive demonstrations of AI-powered inventory optimization delivering measurable business outcomes
- Advanced demand forecasting techniques that leverage AI to predict requirements for both existing and new products

The path to success in manufacturing AI

While AI's transformative potential in manufacturing is widely recognized, the reality is that many organizations struggle to move beyond pilot projects to production-scale implementation. Research shows that the majority of companies remain in the early stages of AI adoption, with most manufacturers still relying on traditional methods and outdated equipment. The gap between successful proofs of concepts and real-world deployment represents one of the industry's most significant challenges, with many promising AI initiatives failing to achieve repetitive use and integration into operational business.

The difference between organizations that successfully deploy AI at scale and those that struggle to lies not in access to technology but in how well they orchestrate the complex interplay of technological infrastructure, organizational readiness, and human factors. Notably, research reveals that company size, technology intensity, and supply chain role don't significantly predict AI adoption success. Rather, it's the organization's digital readiness and foundational capabilities that matter most.

Understanding these patterns, successful organizations that have moved beyond pilots to full-scale AI deployment exhibit common traits across five key areas:

- **Identifying high-impact value drivers and AI use cases:** Efforts should be concentrated on domains where AI yields maximal utility, rather than employing it arbitrarily. According to a study by Capgemini, three use cases stand out for kickstarting a manufacturer's AI journey: demand planning, intelligent maintenance, and product quality control [1]. These use cases offer an optimal combination of clear business value, relative ease of implementation, and data availability.

- **Aligning AI strategy with data strategy:** Organizations must establish a strong data foundation with a data strategy that directly supports their AI goals. This alignment ensures that the right data is collected, processed, and made available to power AI applications effectively.

- **Continuous data enrichment and accessibility:** High-quality data, readily available and usable across the organization, is essential for the success of AI initiatives. Manufacturing environments generate vast amounts of data from sensors, equipment, and processes that must be properly captured and structured.

- **Empowering talent and fostering development:** By equipping their workforce with training and resources, organizations can empower them to leverage AI effectively. This human-centered approach ensures that AI augments human capabilities rather than replacing them.

- **Enabling scalable AI adoption:** Building a strong and scalable infrastructure is key to unlocking the full potential of AI by enabling its smooth and ongoing integration across the organization. This infrastructure must support the deployment of increasingly sophisticated AI agents and multi-agent systems.

These foundational principles become particularly evident when applied to one of manufacturing's most data-rich and optimization-intensive domains: supply chain management. Here, the convergence of vast operational datasets, clear ROI metrics, and immediate business impact creates an ideal environment for demonstrating AI's practical value.

GenAI-powered supply chain optimization

Modern manufacturing supply chains represent some of the most complex systems in business today, with interconnected networks spanning the globe. At the heart of these intricate operations lies a fundamental challenge: inventory optimization and management. Every organization faces the same critical trade-off: maintaining higher inventory levels provides a buffer against unexpected demand fluctuations, but comes with increased holding costs that ultimately impact profitability and competitive positioning.

This balancing act becomes even more challenging when considering the **bullwhip effect**, where sudden changes in demand can cascade through the supply chain, disrupting costs and performance across procurement and sourcing, manufacturing and production, distribution, logistics, and retail operations. Each player in the chain must navigate these complexities while striving to control operational costs and ensure on-time delivery to customers.

Enter the transformative potential of technological advancement. IoT and AI, particularly GenAI, are revolutionizing how organizations approach supply chain management. These technologies enable unprecedented transparency, efficiency, and adaptability through real-time monitoring, predictive analytics, and enhanced decision-making capabilities, turning what was once a reactive balancing act into a proactive, intelligent optimization system.

The automotive industry exemplifies this complexity, with its multi-tiered supplier networks, just-in-time requirements, and global interdependencies that make it an ideal case study for understanding modern supply chain challenges.

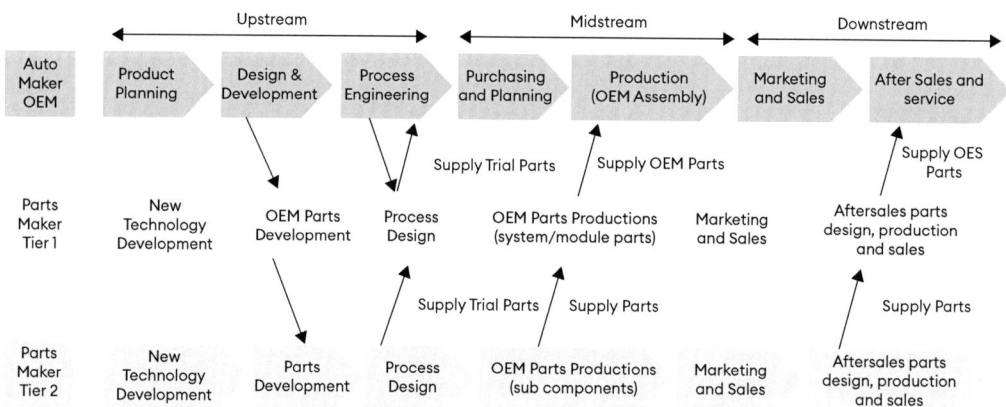

Figure 6.1: Supply chain management components and data flow

Figure 6.1 highlights the tightly interlinked nature of the automotive supply chain. It emphasizes how coordinated decision-making across upstream, midstream, and downstream functions, such as design, manufacturing, and sales, is essential to the efficient flow of information and parts. The complexity of these interactions shows the need for intelligent, flexible, and resilient supply chain management solutions for the automotive sector.

This automotive example illustrates a broader challenge facing all manufacturing sectors: traditional, manual approaches to supply chain management are no longer sufficient for managing such intricate networks. Each connection point represents potential bottlenecks, risks, and optimization opportunities that require real-time visibility and intelligent decision-making capabilities.

Inventory management emerges as essential for achieving the goals of efficient supply chains, controlling costs, and delivering to customers with minimal delays. It encompasses critical business processes, such as estimating material requirements at various points in the supply chain and determining necessary material amounts, ordering frequency, and safety stock levels. From demand forecasting and lead-time optimization to maintaining real-time inventory visibility across complex networks, these interconnected challenges require sophisticated coordination to ensure the right inventory is in the right place at the right time while minimizing system costs and meeting customer needs.

Multi-level planning approaches

The complexity illustrated in modern supply chains demands equally sophisticated planning approaches that can address different time horizons and organizational scopes simultaneously. Strategic and tactical planning are crucial to successful supply chain management, with the Pareto principle suggesting that 20% of efforts in strategic and tactical planning can deliver 80% of the total effect [2]. However, these processes face significant challenges, particularly in predicting long-term demand, market trends, and economic conditions due to extended time horizons that increase uncertainty as market conditions, consumer preferences, and technological advancements evolve. To address these challenges systematically, organizations must structure their planning processes across multiple levels of decision-making.

Companies typically conduct supply chain planning at three distinct levels:

1. **Strategic level**: High-level decisions affecting the entire organization, including scenario planning that examines internal and external data, such as global news, political developments, and scientific literature, to identify strategic concerns and trends that inform future scenarios.

2. **Tactical level**: Medium-term planning that focuses on resource allocation and the implementation of strategic decisions within defined timeframes and operational constraints.

3. **Operational level**: Short-term planning that addresses day-to-day operations, immediate needs, and real-time adjustments to maintain smooth supply chain flow.

This multi-layered approach provides the foundation for more sophisticated inventory management strategies, where each level of planning contributes essential inputs to the optimization process that will be enhanced through AI-powered classification and analysis techniques.

Inventory classification and optimization approaches

Effective inventory management begins with the proper classification of inventory items to determine appropriate control policies. Traditional approaches have progressed from classical ABC analysis, which categorizes items solely by dollar value, to **multi-criteria inventory classification** (**MCIC**), which incorporates multiple quantitative and qualitative factors for more precise categorizations. More recently, GenAI has unlocked the potential to transform unstructured data sources such as customer reviews and supplier communications into actionable inventory insights, creating entirely new possibilities for intelligent classification that go far beyond traditional methods.

ABC analysis and its limitations

ABC analysis is a widely used method to classify inventory items into categories based on their relative importance.

Optimize inventory by

- Prioritizing high-value items (A)
- Minimizing costs for low-value items (C)
- Balancing availability and cost for mid-value items (B)

Category A	Category B	Category C
20% of total inventory	30% of total inventory	50% of total inventory
80% of total sales	15% of total sales	5% of total sales

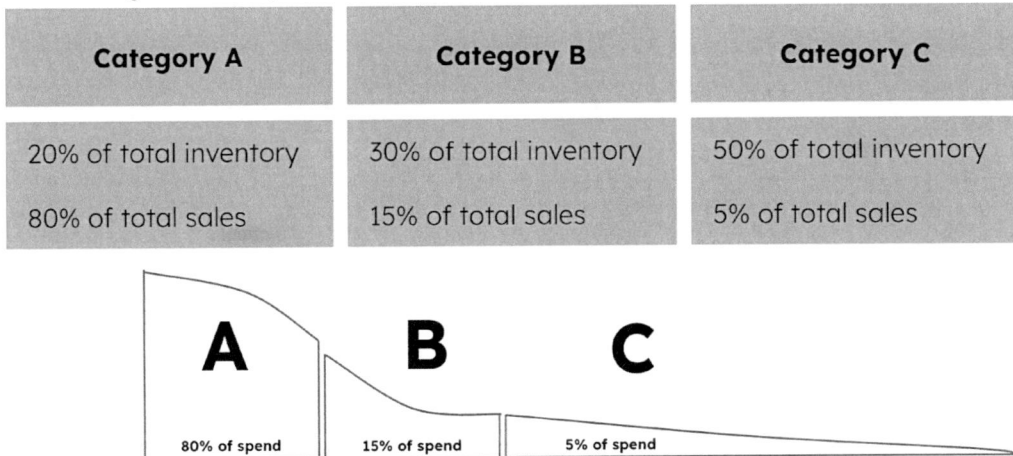

Figure 6.2: ABC analysis framework for inventory classification

Figure 6.2 illustrates the ABC analysis method, which categorizes inventory into three groups based on sales value: **Category A** includes 20% of items that generate 80% of total sales, **Category B** covers 30% of items contributing to 15% of sales, and **Category C** consists of 50% of items accounting for just 5% of sales. This classification helps optimize inventory by prioritizing high-value items (**A**), balancing availability and cost for mid-value items (**B**), and minimizing costs for low-value items (**C**). While ABC analysis is valued for its simplicity, it has been criticized for its exclusive focus on dollar usage. This has led to the development of more sophisticated approaches.

MCIC and the need for GenAI

MCIC expands beyond the dollar value to incorporate additional criteria that influence inventory decisions. These criteria include both quantitative features (measurable numerical data) and qualitative information (descriptive, subjective assessments). Some examples of criteria used for MCIC are both quantitative and qualitative factors.

Quantitative features that are typically considered are driven by the critical objective of achieving just-in-time inventory deliveries, which demands precise measurement and optimization of factors such as the following:

- Lead time (days)
- Inventory holding costs (percentage of item value)
- Order size requirements (units)
- Historical stockout frequency (occurrences per year)

Qualitative factors that may influence classification decisions represent lessons learned through decades of supply chain evolution. Auto parts suppliers and car manufacturers encountered these issues in the early days of globalizing supply chains and painfully factored these concerns into their order and inventory management systems through extensive trial and error:

- Commonality (how widely an item is used across products)
- Obsolescence risk (likelihood of becoming outdated)
- Durability (expected lifespan and reliability)
- Supplier reliability (consistency in delivery and quality)
- Strategic importance (alignment with business priorities)

The fundamental challenge in inventory classification lies in effectively combining these diverse types of information. While quantitative features can be directly incorporated into classification models, qualitative information must first be transformed into measurable values to be useful for systematic inventory categorization.

Traditionally, this transformation process faced several critical limitations:

- **Manual assessment burden:** Converting qualitative information into quantitative features typically required domain experts to manually rate each inventory item against each criterion, an extremely tedious process for large inventories
- **Consistency issues:** Human assessments of qualitative factors inevitably introduce subjectivity and inconsistency across different evaluators
- **Untapped data sources:** Valuable qualitative information often exists within unstructured data sources (customer reviews, maintenance records, and supplier communications) that remain inaccessible to traditional classification methods
- **Scalability constraints:** As inventory catalogs grow, the manual transformation of qualitative information becomes increasingly unsustainable

Advanced implementations of this approach can be applied through statistical clustering and other unsupervised machine learning techniques, creating a more nuanced understanding of inventory importance and appropriate management strategies, especially when both quantitative features and transformed qualitative information are available for analysis.

AI and MongoDB for inventory optimization

The convergence of AI and modern database technologies has created unprecedented opportunities to address these traditional limitations in inventory classification. AI-driven approaches can now automatically process vast amounts of both structured and unstructured data, transforming qualitative insights into quantitative features while maintaining the scalability and consistency that manual processes could never achieve. Modern platforms such as MongoDB Atlas provide the unified data foundation necessary for these advanced AI applications, enabling organizations to store, process, and analyze diverse data types from traditional inventory metrics to customer reviews and supplier communications within a single, flexible architecture. This technological foundation enables sophisticated inventory optimization approaches that were previously impossible to implement at scale.

GenAI-powered inventory classification

GenAI significantly enhances traditional MCIC by incorporating unstructured data that holds valuable information about demand and inventory consumption patterns. Unstructured data can be transformed into structured data for feature input into inventory classification models. The addition of unstructured data as features can improve classification results.

Product reviews can be used to extract qualitative metrics, such as probability of recommending the product, probability of buying it again, and expectation versus reality. Apart from rating scores, by analyzing the text and attached images, we can extract detailed information about the subjective perspective of our customers on a particular product, and that can potentially impact future demand.

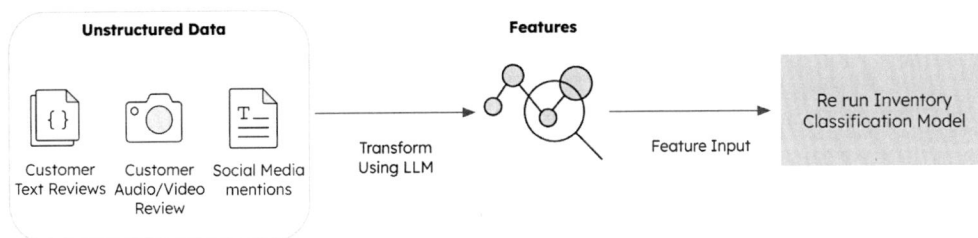

Figure 6.3: GenAI transformation of unstructured data for inventory classification

Figure 6.3 illustrates the core process through which GenAI transforms unstructured data into valuable features for inventory classification. On the left, we see diverse sources of unstructured data (customer text reviews, audio/video reviews, and social media mentions) that previously remained untapped in traditional inventory classification systems. The **large language model (LLM)** in the center acts as a powerful transformation engine, processing these diverse inputs and extracting meaningful patterns, sentiments, and insights. These are then structured as quantitative features that can be directly fed into inventory classification models alongside traditional metrics.

Methodology for implementing GenAI-powered inventory classification

While the conceptual transformation shown in *Figure 6.3* demonstrates the potential of GenAI for inventory classification, translating this vision into practice requires a systematic approach. Organizations need a clear roadmap that addresses the technical complexities of working with diverse data types, the challenge of creating meaningful evaluation criteria, and the integration requirements for existing inventory systems.

The methodology for implementing GenAI-powered inventory classification follows a four-step process:

1. Create and store vector embeddings from unstructured data.
2. Design and store evaluation criteria.
3. Create an agentic application to perform a transformation based on criteria.
4. Rerun the inventory classification model with enhanced features.

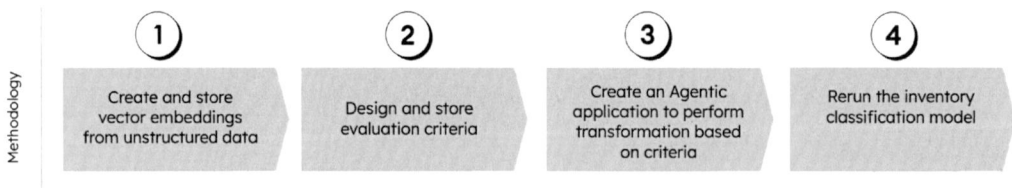

Figure 6.4: Four-step methodology for GenAI-powered inventory classification

This flowchart illustrates a sequential four-step process for implementing AI-enhanced inventory classification.

This integration of unstructured data represents a significant advancement over traditional inventory classification approaches, enabling organizations to factor in the voice of the customer, market sentiment, and other qualitative signals that often contain early indicators of changing demand patterns or product performance issues.

Each step in this methodology builds upon the previous one, creating a comprehensive framework that transforms how organizations approach inventory classification. Let's examine each step in detail to understand how this transformation unfolds in practice.

Step 1: Creating and storing vector embeddings from unstructured data

In this initial step, unstructured data sources such as customer reviews, social media mentions, and audio/video feedback are processed through embedding models to create vector representations. These vector embeddings capture the semantic meaning and nuanced information in the unstructured content.

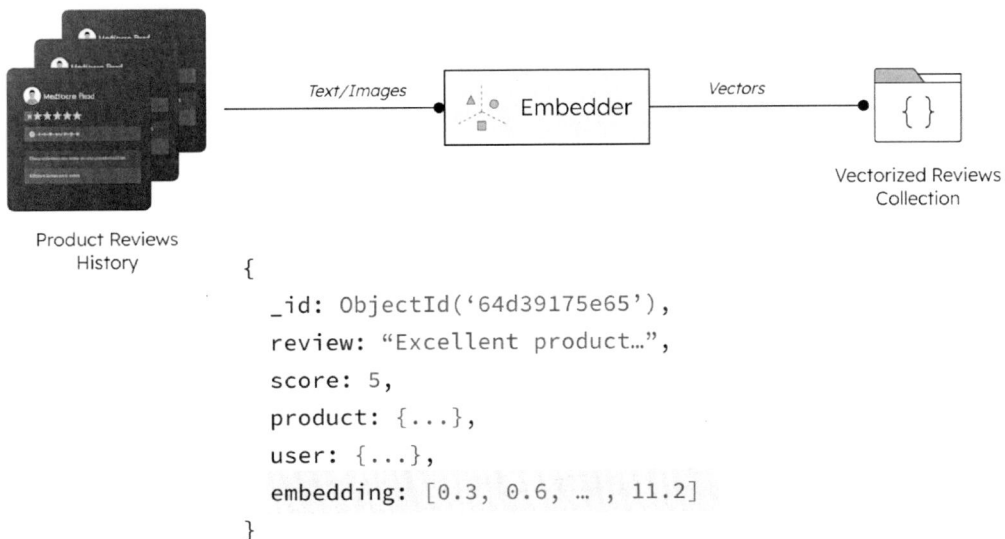

```
{
    _id: ObjectId('64d39175e65'),
    review: "Excellent product…",
    score: 5,
    product: {...},
    user: {...},
    embedding: [0.3, 0.6, … , 11.2]
}
```

Figure 6.5: Vector embedding process for unstructured data

This diagram shows how product reviews and images are processed through an embedder to create vector representations stored in a vectorized reviews collection. The embedding process transforms text, images, or other unstructured data into numerical vector arrays that can be efficiently stored and queried. For example, a product review such as "Excellent product..." is converted into a multi-dimensional vector (e.g., [0.3, 0.6, ..., 11.2]) that preserves its semantic meaning.

These embeddings are stored in MongoDB using a structure similar to the following:

```
{
    "_id": ObjectId('64d39175e65'),
    "review": "Excellent product...",
    "score": 5,
    "product": {...},
    "user": {...},
    "embedding": [0.3, 0.6, ..., 11.2]
}
```

The vectorization process makes previously unquantifiable information machine-readable and analyzable, creating a foundation for more sophisticated inventory classification that considers customer sentiment and feedback.

Step 2: Designing and storing evaluation criteria

A critical step in the implementation of GenAI for inventory classification is the development of evaluation criteria. Evaluation criteria are the explicit rules and guidelines that define how qualitative information is transformed into quantitative scores. These criteria serve as the **translation layer** between unstructured data and the numerical features required for inventory classification models.

This process involves multiple inputs and stakeholders to ensure that the AI system evaluates inventory items against relevant business objectives.

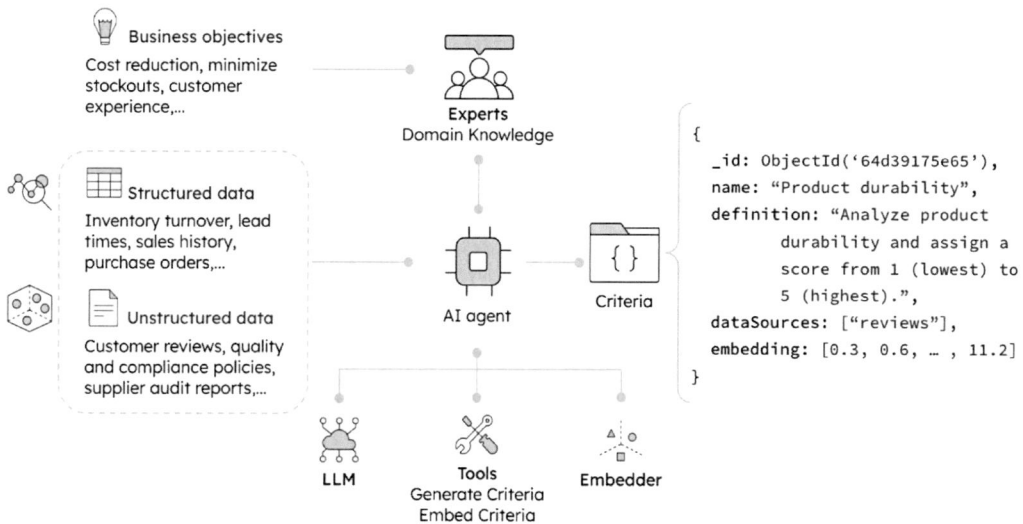

Figure 6.6: AI system generating business evaluation criteria

This diagram illustrates how an AI agent synthesizes multiple inputs, such as business objectives, expert domain knowledge, structured data (inventory turnover and sales history), and unstructured data (customer reviews and compliance policies), using LLMs, tools, and embedders to automatically generate evaluation criteria.

These evaluation criteria are designed to reflect both the organization's strategic priorities and its domain-specific expertise. The inputs can be broadly categorized as follows:

- **Business objectives**: These include cost reduction targets, stockout minimization goals, and customer experience requirements. Business leaders define these objectives based on corporate strategy and market demands.

- **Expert domain knowledge**: Subject matter experts provide insights on industry-specific factors that influence inventory decisions, ensuring that the classification system accounts for sector-specific considerations.

- **Structured data**: This is quantitative information such as inventory turnover rates, lead times, sales history, and purchase order patterns.

- **Unstructured data**: This is qualitative information from customer reviews, quality and compliance policies, and supplier audit reports.

The AI agent combines these inputs to generate evaluation criteria, which are then stored in a structured format. While the following example is simplified for illustration purposes, in practice, these criteria would be significantly more complex, often including multiple conditional evaluations, weighting schemes, and confidence thresholds:

```
{
    _id: ObjectId('64d39175e65'),
    name: "Product durability",
    definition: "Analyze product durability and assign a score from 1
(lowest) to 5 (highest).",
    dataSources: ["reviews"],
    embedding: [0.3, 0.6, … , 11.2]
}
```

The AI agent proactively suggests relevant data sources (in this case, "reviews") that contain information pertinent to the specific criterion being evaluated. By identifying which collections or data repositories contain valuable signals about each criterion, the AI system creates an intelligent bridge between disparate information sources and actionable inventory insights.

These criteria are subsequently vectorized to enable semantic matching with product information and reviews. This enables the AI to assess inventory items not just on traditional metrics but also on qualitative factors that might affect future demand or strategic importance.

MongoDB's document model and vector search capabilities provide an end-to-end solution for this approach, allowing organizations to store both structured inventory data and vector embeddings of unstructured information within the same database. This unified architecture eliminates data silos and provides a comprehensive view of inventory-related factors.

Step 3: Creating an agentic application to perform a transformation based on criteria

In this step, an AI agent is developed to systematically process each product in the inventory against the evaluation criteria established in *Step 2*. This agent serves as the operational engine that transforms qualitative data into quantifiable metrics.

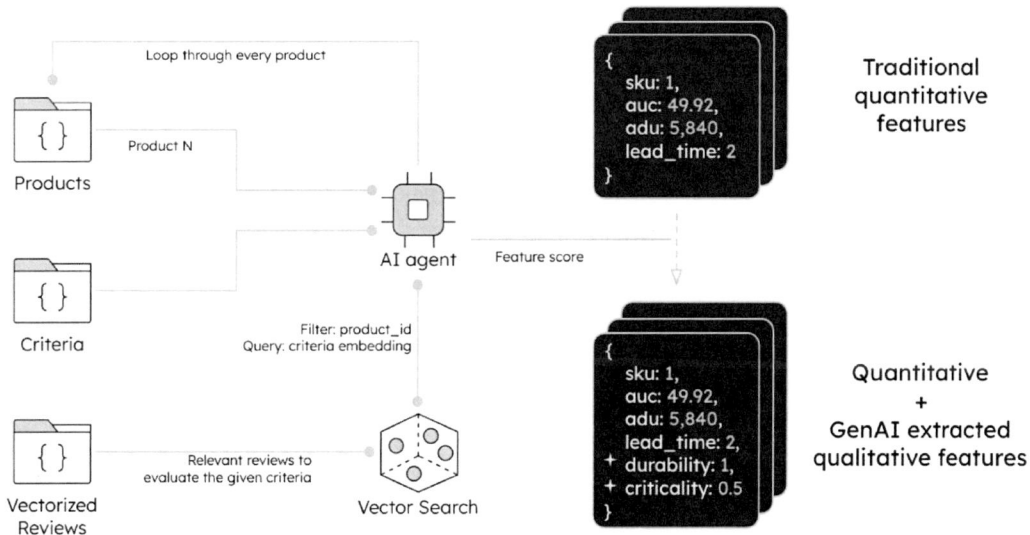

Figure 6.7: AI agent workflow for criteria-based transformation

This diagram shows how an AI agent systematically processes inventory products by combining traditional quantitative features with AI-extracted qualitative insights. The agent loops through each product, applies evaluation criteria, performs vector search on customer reviews, and outputs enhanced product data that includes both standard metrics (SKU, price, and lead time) and new AI-derived features (durability scores and criticality ratings) for improved inventory classification.

The agentic application follows a well-defined workflow:

1. **Product processing loop**: The system iterates through each product in the inventory catalog.

2. **Criteria matching**: For each product, the agent identifies relevant evaluation criteria.

3. **Vector search integration**: The agent uses vector search capabilities to find the most relevant customer reviews and other unstructured data pertaining to each product based on the criteria embeddings.

4. **Semantic analysis:** Using filters such as `product_ID` and semantic search queries, the agent locates and analyzes relevant reviews that contain information about the specific criteria being evaluated (such as durability, reliability, or user satisfaction).

5. **Feature extraction:** The agent processes this unstructured data to extract quantifiable scores for each criterion, transforming qualitative assessments into numerical values.

The output of this process is an enhanced product data structure that combines traditional quantitative metrics with new AI-extracted qualitative features.

For example, a product represented only with quantitative data might look like this:

```
{
  "sku": 1,
  "average_unit_cost": 49.92,
  "annual_dollar_usage": 5,840,
  "lead_time": 2
}
```

When enhanced with GenAI-extracted qualitative features, the same product data structure expands to include attributes such as durability and criticality:

```
{
  "sku": 1,
  "average_unit_cost": 49.92,
  "annual_dollar_usage": 5,840,
  "lead_time": 2,
  "durability": 1,
  "criticality": 0.5
}
```

This transformation process builds a comprehensive profile for each inventory item that captures both explicit quantitative attributes and implicit qualitative characteristics derived from customer feedback and other unstructured sources.

Step 4: Rerunning the inventory classification model with enhanced features

The final step involves utilizing the enhanced feature set to reclassify inventory items with greater accuracy and business relevance. This process incorporates both the traditional quantitative metrics and the newly generated qualitative features derived from unstructured data.

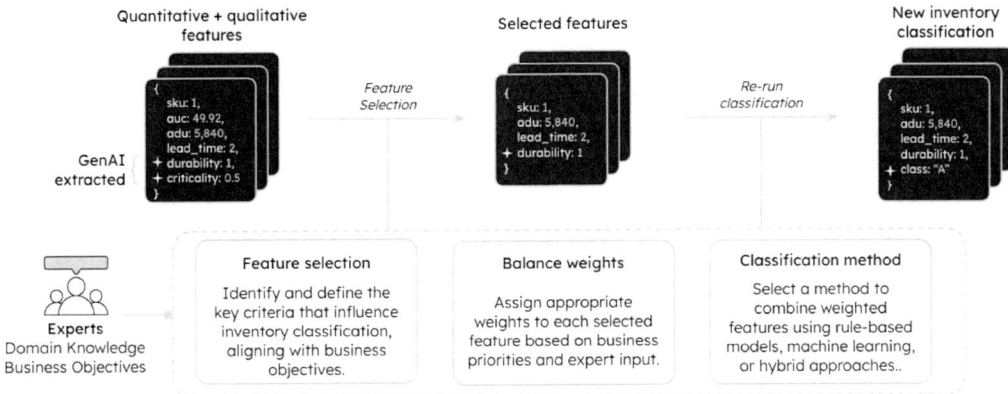

Figure 6.8: Inventory reclassification process with enhanced features

This diagram shows the final step where AI-extracted qualitative features are combined with traditional quantitative data through feature selection, weight balancing, and classification methods. The reclassification process includes several key components:

1. **Feature selection**: With guidance from domain experts and business objectives, the most relevant features for classification are identified. This might include traditional metrics such as **annual dollar usage (adu)** and lead time, along with new GenAI-derived features such as durability or customer satisfaction.

2. **Weight balancing**: Appropriate weights are assigned to each selected feature based on business priorities and expert input, ensuring that the classification reflects the organization's strategic goals.

3. **Classification method implementation**: A method is selected to combine these weighted features, which could involve rule-based models, machine learning algorithms, or hybrid approaches, depending on the complexity of the inventory and business requirements.

4. **Model execution**: The classification model is executed with the enhanced feature set, generating updated inventory classifications that reflect a more nuanced understanding of each item's importance.

The output of this process is a newly classified inventory with categorizations (e.g., A, B, C) that account for both traditional financial metrics and deeper qualitative aspects:

```
{
  "sku": 1,
  "annual_dollar_usage": 5,840,
  "lead_time": 2,
  "durability": 1,
  "class": "A"
}
```

This reclassification provides a more accurate and holistic view of inventory importance, enabling better-informed decisions about stock levels, ordering frequencies, and supplier management strategies.

Atlas: Unified AI infrastructure

MongoDB Atlas serves as the comprehensive foundation for modern inventory solutions, helping businesses enhance service quality and workforce efficiency and optimize stock management by enabling a single view of inventory, event-driven architectures, and real-time analytics. This solution lays the groundwork for advanced scenarios such as integrating IoT and RFID tags, delving into AI/ML forecasting for precise demand prediction and distributed logistics. The platform's flexibility allows its application not only from warehouse to point of sale but also across the entire supply chain, including manufacturing, transportation, retail, and reverse logistics, making it a valuable asset for diverse business domains. MongoDB's integrated suite of products supports each step of the AI-powered inventory classification process:

1. **Vector embeddings**: MongoDB Atlas Vector Search stores and indexes embeddings generated from unstructured data (customer reviews, social media, etc.), enabling efficient semantic searches.

2. **Evaluation criteria**: MongoDB's flexible document model stores complex evaluation criteria as JSON documents, including definitions, data source mappings, and vector representations for semantic matching.

3. **Agentic application**: MongoDB's query capabilities, combined with Atlas Vector Search, allow the AI agent to efficiently filter inventory items and find semantically similar reviews or documentation to evaluate qualitative criteria.

4. **Classification model**: For simpler classification methods, MongoDB's aggregation framework can be used to process the enhanced feature set to recalculate inventory classifications and store results in a format that integrates seamlessly with existing inventory systems. For more advanced methods, MongoDB integrates seamlessly with industry-leading AI frameworks and platforms to run the classification model.

The following figure provides a high-level overview of how MongoDB Atlas supports each stage of the AI-driven inventory classification workflow, integrating AI capabilities with data infrastructure requirements.

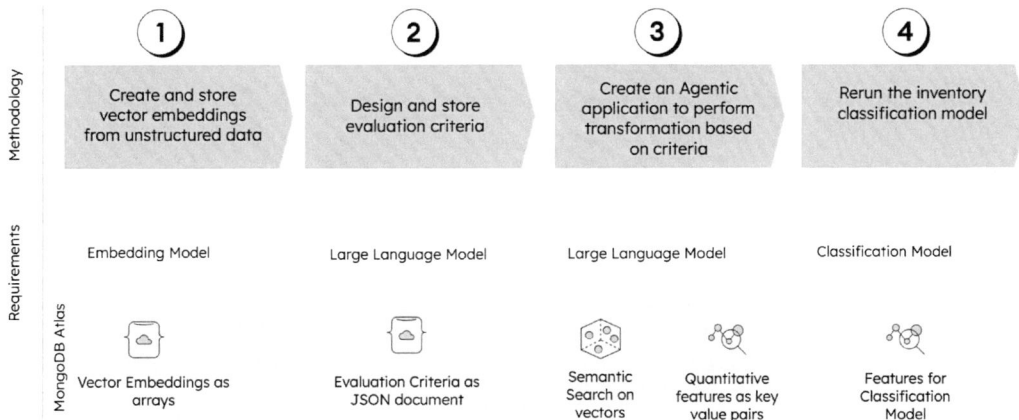

Figure 6.9: MongoDB Atlas AI-powered inventory classification pipeline

This diagram illustrates the seamless integration between AI capabilities and data infrastructure that makes sophisticated inventory classification possible at scale. The pipeline demonstrates how MongoDB Atlas serves as the unifying foundation that bridges the gap between raw data sources and actionable inventory insights. By supporting vector embeddings, flexible document storage, and native AI integration within a single platform, Atlas eliminates the complexity and technical debt typically associated with multi-system architectures, enabling organizations to focus on optimizing their inventory strategies rather than managing disparate technologies.

GenAI inventory classification demo: A visual walkthrough

Let's explore a real-world demonstration of how GenAI transforms inventory classification in action. This walkthrough shows how MongoDB Atlas moves beyond traditional metrics to create a truly intelligent inventory management system that captures both quantitative and qualitative factors.

Step 1: Starting with basic classification

The MongoDB **Inventory Optimization** interface initially presents a straightforward view of inventory items. This first screen displays products with conventional attributes such as **Product Code** and **annualDollarUsage**, along with a preliminary **Weighted Score** and **Class** assignment.

At this stage, classification is limited to basic quantitative metrics. As shown in the interface, only **annualDollarUsage** is actively considered with a default weight, resulting in a somewhat one-dimensional classification system. Notice how the products are sorted into classes (**A**, **B**, and **C**) based primarily on dollar value, missing many nuanced factors that could affect inventory decisions.

This starting point represents traditional inventory classification: functional but lacking the depth needed for truly optimized inventory management in complex supply chains. The weighted scores visible on this screen serve as our baseline for comparing the improvements made possible through GenAI.

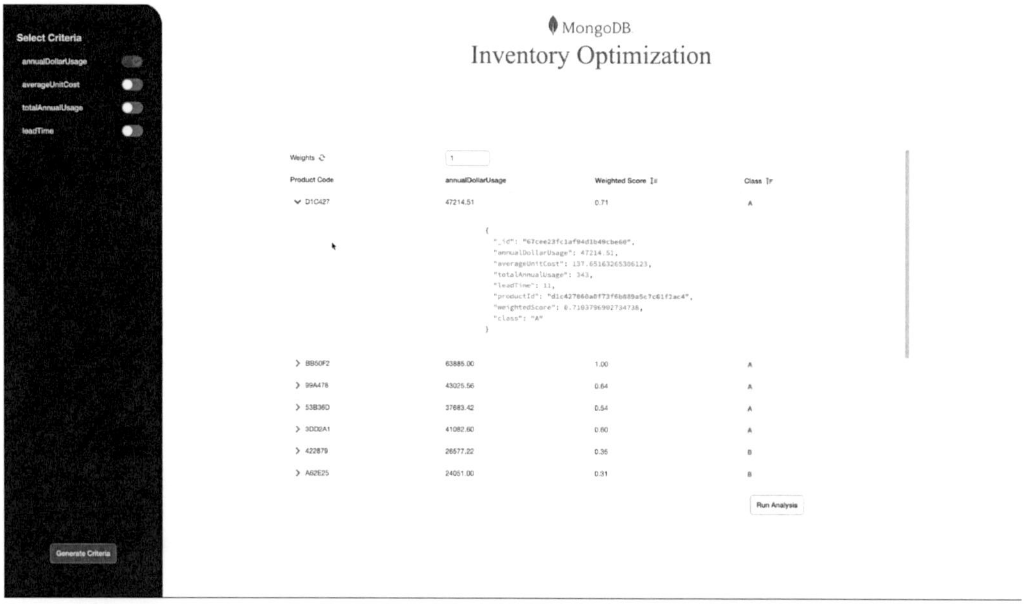

Figure 6.10: Initial MongoDB Inventory Optimization demo interface with basic classification

With this foundation established, we can now demonstrate how AI transforms this basic approach into something far more sophisticated and business-relevant.

Step 2: Generating new AI-powered criteria

The transformation begins when users click the **Generate Criteria** button, opening the intuitive **GenAI-Powered Criteria Generator** dialog shown in *Figure 6.11*. This interface bridges the gap between human expertise and AI capabilities by allowing business users to describe important factors in natural language.

In this example, a user has input: "Consider the customer level of satisfaction with a product to take into account the potential future value". The system processes this natural language description and automatically populates the following:

- **Criteria Name: Customer Satisfaction**
- **Criteria Definition:** A comprehensive definition explaining how customer satisfaction will be measured, including analysis of reviews for repeat purchase probability, sentiment extracted from star ratings, and overall perception of value relative to expectations
- **Data Sources:** The interface allows selection of relevant data repositories such as **REVIEWS** and **PRODUCTS**, which the AI will analyze to quantify this previously subjective criterion

This step represents a key innovation, translating qualitative business knowledge into quantifiable metrics using NLP. The system doesn't require technical expertise from the user; it translates business intent into technical implementation.

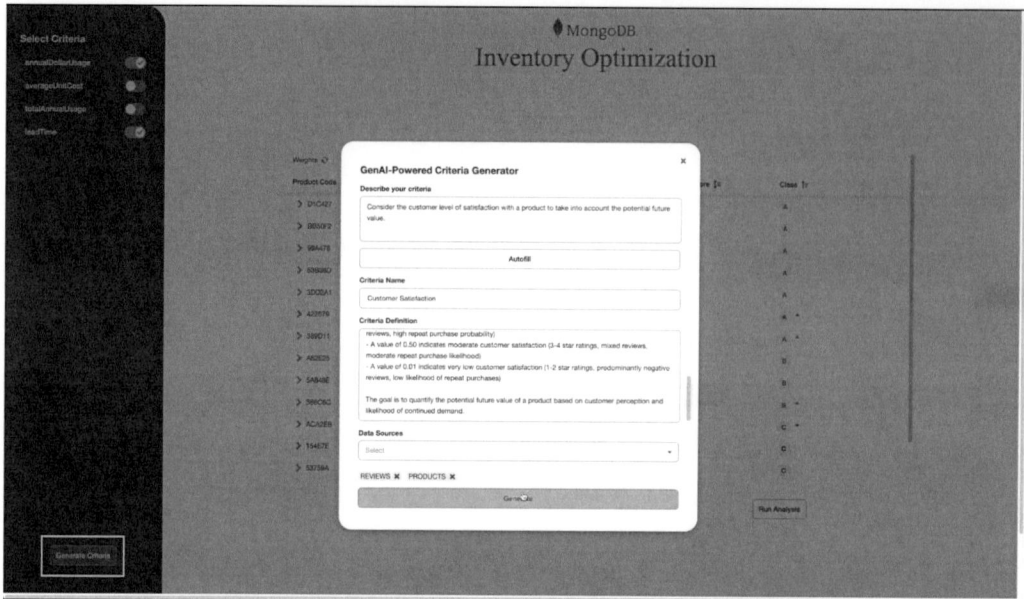

Figure 6.11: GenAI-Powered Criteria Generator demo dialog

The ease of this transformation demonstrates how AI democratizes advanced analytics, making sophisticated classification accessible to domain experts regardless of their technical background.

Step 3: Integrating new criteria into classification

After generation, the new AI-created **customerSatisfaction** criterion appears in the **Select Criteria** panel on the left side of the interface, now available alongside traditional metrics. When activated (as shown by the toggle switch), the system seamlessly integrates this new dimension into the inventory optimization model.

Notice how the interface updates to display this new metric as an additional column in the product listing. Each product now shows a numerical score for **customerSatisfaction**, effectively transforming what was previously an unmeasured qualitative factor into a quantitative value that can influence inventory decisions.

What's particularly valuable is how the system maintains a consistent framework; the new AI-generated criterion becomes a full-fledged component of the classification system, given equal consideration with traditional metrics. Products that might have seemed identical under conventional analysis now reveal important differences when customer satisfaction is considered.

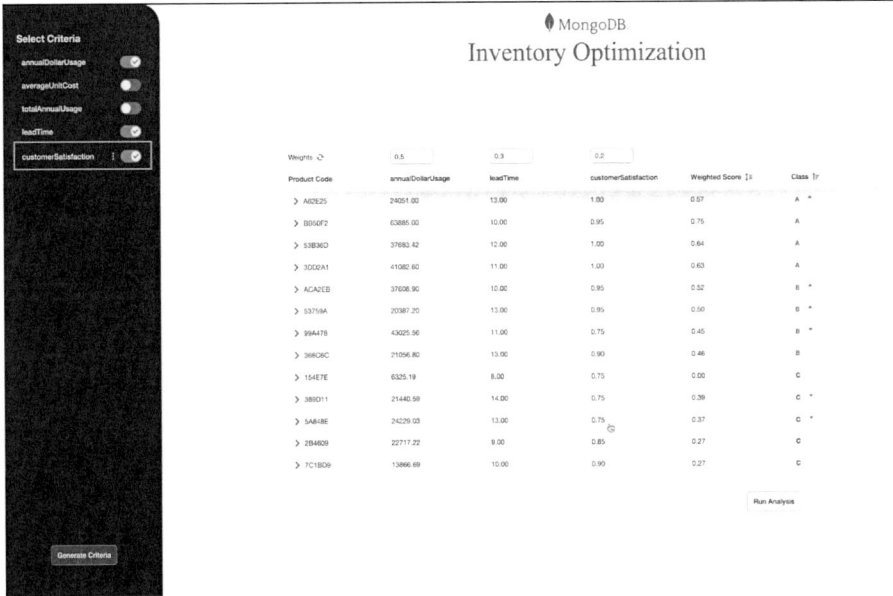

Figure 6.12: Inventory management demo interface after AI-created customer satisfaction integration

This integration showcases the true power of AI-enhanced classification: the ability to incorporate previously unmeasurable business factors into systematic decision-making processes.

Step 4: Weighting and running analysis

The final step demonstrates the flexibility and power of this enhanced classification system. As shown in *Figure 6.13*, users can assign relative importance to each criterion through intuitive weighting controls:

- 0.5 for **annualDollarUsage** (maintaining the importance of financial metrics)
- 0.3 for **leadTime** (acknowledging supply chain realities)
- 0.2 for **customerSatisfaction** (incorporating the newly quantified customer perspective)

After clicking the **Run Analysis** button, the system recalculates the weighted score for all inventory items based on this comprehensive set of criteria. The resulting **Class** assignments (**A**, **B**, and **C**) now reflect a more sophisticated analysis that balances multiple business priorities.

The real business impact becomes evident when comparing the before and after classifications. Products that previously received a lower classification based solely on dollar value might now be recognized as strategically important due to high customer satisfaction scores, which indicate potential for future growth. Conversely, high-value items with poor customer satisfaction might be flagged for closer evaluation.

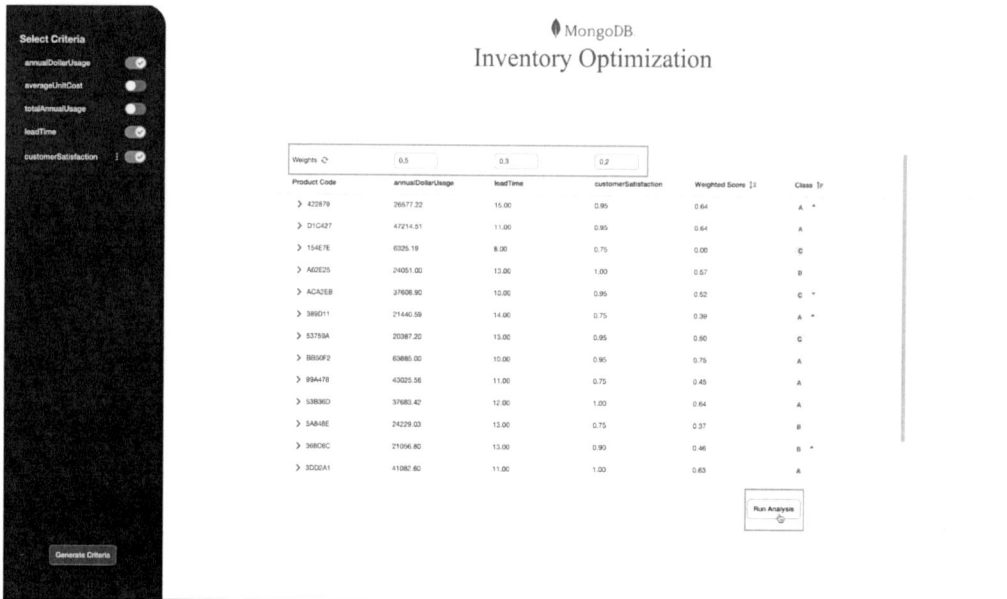

Figure 6.13: Weighting controls and analysis results

The iterative process shown in this demonstration enables continuous refinement of inventory management strategies. With an approach like this, customer subject matter experts are free to focus on strategy and business impact while the system handles the technical overhead. Organizations can progressively enhance their classification system by generating additional criteria for factors such as sustainability compliance, supply chain risk, or market trend alignment, all in one place. This approach transforms inventory classification from a static, retrospective analysis into a dynamic, forward-looking system that leverages the full potential of both structured and unstructured data through GenAI, allowing teams to spend more time on the customer-specific activities that drive positive business value and outcomes.

While GenAI-powered classification enhances how we categorize and understand inventory, the next frontier lies in automating the actions that result from these insights. Moving beyond decision support to autonomous decision-making, agentic AI systems can independently manage procurement processes, supplier relationships, and inventory replenishment based on the intelligent classifications we have established.

Raw material management via agentic AI

Let's now examine another cutting-edge application of AI in supply chain management: agentic AI for raw material management. While the previous section demonstrated how GenAI can enhance decision-making through improved classification, this approach takes automation a step further by deploying autonomous AI agents that can actively monitor, analyze, and take actions to optimize raw material inventory. This represents the evolution from AI-assisted decision-making to fully autonomous supply chain operations.

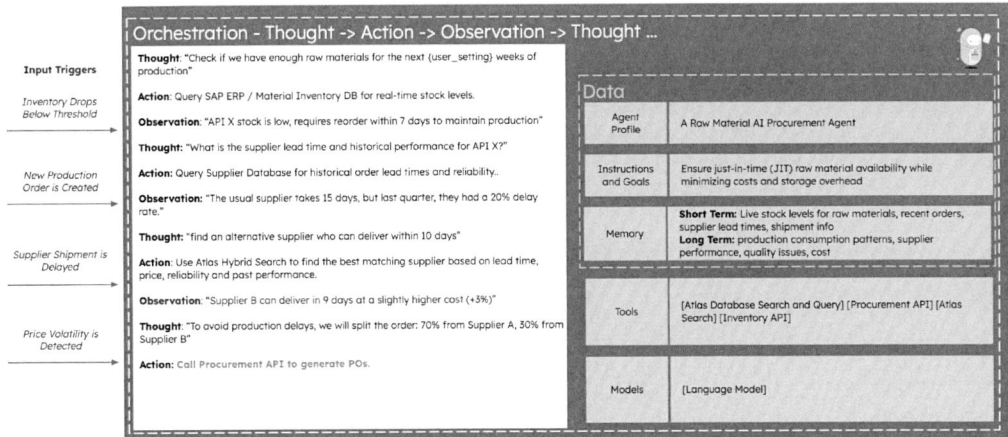

Orchestration - Thought -> Action -> Observation -> Thought ...

Input Triggers

- Inventory Drops Below Threshold
- New Production Order is Created
- Supplier Shipment is Delayed
- Price Volatility is Detected

Thought: "Check if we have enough raw materials for the next (user_setting) weeks of production"

Action: Query SAP ERP / Material Inventory DB for real-time stock levels.

Observation: "API X stock is low, requires reorder within 7 days to maintain production"

Thought: "What is the supplier lead time and historical performance for API X?"

Action: Query Supplier Database for historical order lead times and reliability..

Observation: "The usual supplier takes 15 days, but last quarter, they had a 20% delay rate."

Thought: "find an alternative supplier who can deliver within 10 days"

Action: Use Atlas Hybrid Search to find the best matching supplier based on lead time, price, reliability and past performance.

Observation: "Supplier B can deliver in 9 days at a slightly higher cost (+3%)"

Thought: "To avoid production delays, we will split the order: 70% from Supplier A, 30% from Supplier B"

Action: Call Procurement API to generate POs.

Data

Agent Profile	A Raw Material AI Procurement Agent
Instructions and Goals	Ensure just-in-time (JIT) raw material availability while minimizing costs and storage overhead
Memory	**Short Term:** Live stock levels for raw materials, recent orders, supplier lead times, shipment info **Long Term:** production consumption patterns, supplier performance, quality issues, cost
Tools	[Atlas Database Search and Query] [Procurement API] [Atlas Search] [Inventory API]
Models	[Language Model]

Figure 6.14: Orchestration and decision-making process of the raw material AI procurement agent

This diagram reveals the sophisticated reasoning capabilities that enable autonomous supply chain management. Unlike traditional rule-based systems that follow predetermined logic paths, this AI agent demonstrates dynamic problem-solving through its cyclical thought process. The agent's ability to evaluate multiple suppliers simultaneously; weigh competing factors, such as cost versus reliability; and make nuanced decisions, such as splitting orders, represents a fundamental shift from reactive to proactive supply chain management. This cognitive approach allows the system to handle complex scenarios that would typically require human judgment, such as balancing immediate cost savings against long-term supplier relationship risks.

The raw material management agent continuously monitors key event triggers and acts proactively to optimize inventory levels, procurement, supplier selection, and logistics. It ensures just-in-time material availability while minimizing costs and storage overhead. What makes this approach particularly powerful is the agent's ability to learn from each decision cycle, improving its reasoning over time and adapting to changing supply chain conditions without human intervention.

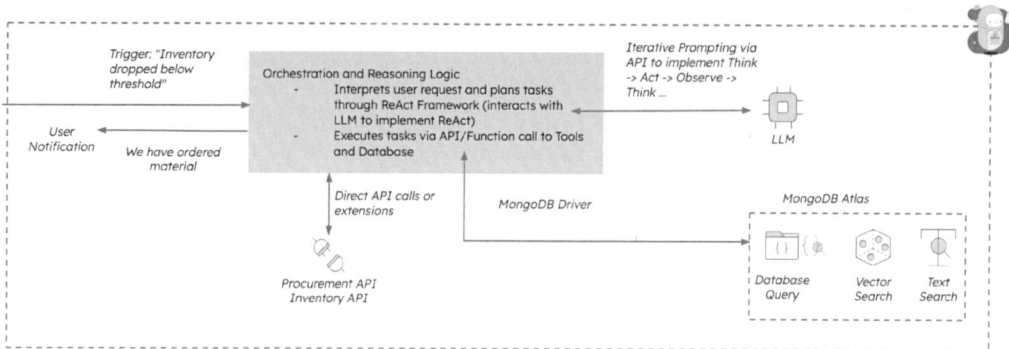

Figure 6.15: AI agent orchestration architecture for raw material management

This architecture demonstrates how event-driven design enables truly responsive supply chain automation. The central orchestration service acts as the intelligent coordinator, processing diverse triggers from inventory systems, production schedules, and market conditions, then determining the optimal sequence of actions. The integration with MongoDB Atlas as the central data platform ensures that all components, from inventory databases to supplier performance metrics, maintain data consistency while enabling real-time decision-making. This unified approach eliminates the data silos that traditionally plague supply chain systems, where inventory, procurement, and supplier information exist in separate systems. The architecture's modular design allows individual components to be updated or replaced without disrupting the entire system, providing the flexibility needed to adapt to evolving business requirements and new AI capabilities.

Demand forecasting and inventory optimization

Having established how AI enhances inventory classification and enables autonomous material management, we now turn to examine demand forecasting in greater detail. This capability has appeared throughout our discussion as a foundational element of intelligent supply chain operations.

AI-powered demand forecasting represents the predictive engine that drives both classification decisions and autonomous procurement actions. AI algorithms analyze complex datasets to predict future product and part requirements. Improvements in forecasting accuracy directly translate to more optimal inventory levels. Once demand is projected, AI systems can determine the most efficient stock levels by analyzing historical sales data, market trends, seasonal patterns, supply chain disruptions, and production schedules.

AI systems can also automate ordering based on predicted demand and targeted stock levels, reducing human error and administrative overhead. Additionally, AI can assist in supplier selection and relationship management by analyzing performance data to identify partners who best meet quality, delivery, and cost requirements.

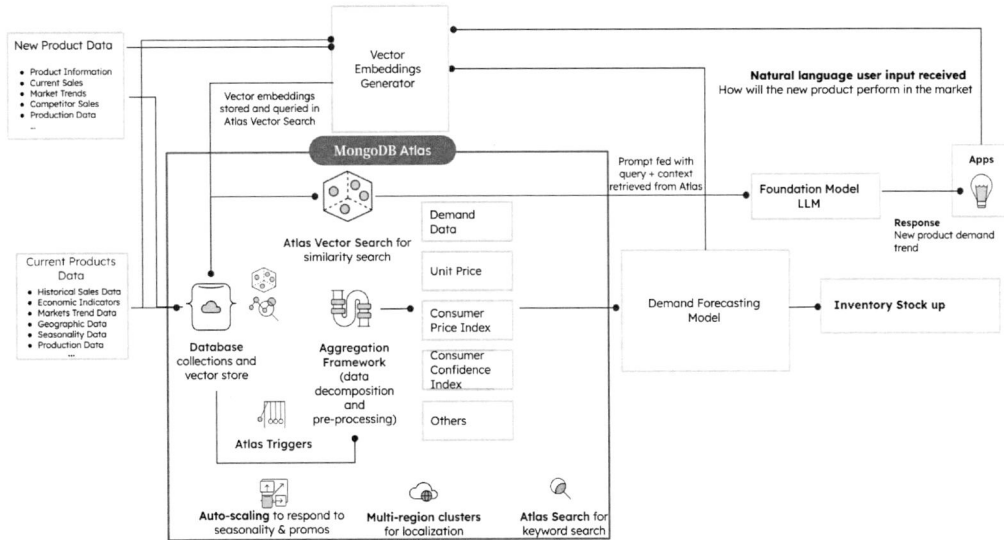

Figure 6.16: AI-powered demand forecasting and inventory optimization architecture

This diagram shows how MongoDB Atlas enables comprehensive demand forecasting by integrating new product data and current product data through vector embeddings and similarity search. The system processes natural language user input, utilizes foundation LLMs for context analysis, combines multiple data sources (demand data, unit price, and consumer indices) through an aggregation framework, and feeds into demand forecasting models that drive inventory stock optimization decisions, with Atlas triggers enabling auto-scaling and multi-region capabilities.

For new products without historical sales data, GenAI models can create synthetic data by learning patterns from similar existing products. MongoDB Atlas Vector Search enhances this capability by finding products with similar attributes and feeding that context into GenAI models, ensuring the synthetic data reflects realistic market conditions and customer behaviors.

Benefits of MongoDB for inventory management

The sophisticated AI applications we've explored, from GenAI-powered classification to autonomous agentic systems, all depend on a robust, flexible data foundation that can handle the complexity and scale of modern manufacturing supply chains. MongoDB Atlas provides this foundation through several key capabilities that directly enable the advanced inventory management approaches discussed throughout this chapter.

MongoDB Atlas provides significant advantages for AI-powered inventory management systems:

- **Document data model**: Handles complex inventory structures and hierarchies across multiple plants and suppliers
- **Vector search**: Enables semantic search capabilities for finding similar products or suppliers based on multiple criteria
- **Fine-grained security and access controls**: Ensures appropriate data access for different stakeholders in the supply chain
- **Time-series collections**: Efficiently stores and analyzes temporal data for trend detection and forecasting

These capabilities work together to create a unified platform that supports everything from basic inventory tracking to sophisticated AI-driven optimization. By eliminating the need for complex integrations between separate systems for structured data, vector embeddings, and real-time analytics, MongoDB Atlas enables organizations to focus on developing intelligent inventory strategies rather than managing technical infrastructure. This integrated approach accelerates the implementation of AI-powered solutions while providing the scalability and reliability needed for mission-critical supply chain operations.

Reimagining inventory management for Industry 5.0

Inventory management and optimization represent crucial components of efficient manufacturing operations. By leveraging advanced AI capabilities, particularly GenAI for unstructured data analysis and agentic AI for autonomous decision-making, organizations can achieve new levels of efficiency while balancing costs, availability, and responsiveness.

The integration of these technologies with flexible, scalable data platforms such as MongoDB Atlas enables manufacturers to do the following:

- Improve forecasting accuracy
- Optimize inventory levels

- Enhance supplier selection and management
- Respond proactively to supply chain disruptions
- Reduce carrying costs without sacrificing service levels

As manufacturing continues to evolve toward Industry 5.0, these AI-powered inventory optimization approaches will become increasingly essential for maintaining a competitive advantage in global markets. The transformation from reactive inventory management to predictive, intelligent systems represents just the beginning of AI's impact on manufacturing operations.

Summary

This chapter has explored how AI is revolutionizing supply chain and inventory management in manufacturing operations. We've examined the evolution from traditional inventory classification approaches such as ABC analysis to sophisticated MCIC enhanced by GenAI, which can now incorporate unstructured data from customer reviews, supplier communications, and market signals to create more nuanced and effective inventory categorization.

The four-step methodology for implementing GenAI-powered inventory classification, that is, creating vector embeddings, designing evaluation criteria, developing agentic applications, and enhancing classification models, demonstrates how modern data platforms can bridge the gap between qualitative business insights and quantitative decision-making. We've seen practical applications ranging from AI-powered classification systems that transform customer feedback into inventory insights to autonomous agentic systems that can independently manage raw material procurement and optimize supply chain decisions in real time.

Through detailed demonstrations and real-world examples, we've shown how MongoDB Atlas serves as the unified foundation that enables these sophisticated AI applications, providing the flexibility to handle both structured inventory data and unstructured market intelligence within a single platform. This integrated approach allows organizations to move from static, retrospective inventory analysis to dynamic, forward-looking optimization systems that adapt continuously to changing market conditions.

The next chapter continues our exploration of manufacturing AI by examining how these same principles extend beyond inventory management to transform broader manufacturing operations, including predictive maintenance, quality assurance, and production optimization across the entire manufacturing value chain.

References

1. *Europe is leading AI in manufacturing operations adoption*: https://www.capgemini.com/us-en/news/europe-is-leading-ai-in-manufacturing-operations-adoption/

2. *Supply chain planning & modeling for smart decisions*: https://www.anylogistix.com/resources/blog/supply-chain-strategic-planning-and-modeling-for-decision-support/

7

Practical Applications of Agentic and GenAI in Manufacturing – Part 2

Building on the supply chain foundations established in the previous chapter, we'll now venture into the next frontier of manufacturing AI: intelligent operational systems that don't just automate tasks, but collaborate, learn, and adapt in real time. While supply chain optimization demonstrates AI's power to transform reactive processes into predictive ones, the applications we'll explore in this chapter represent a fundamental shift toward truly autonomous manufacturing ecosystems where multiple AI agents work together to optimize complex, interconnected operations.

This chapter explores four critical domains where collaborative AI is redefining manufacturing excellence. We begin with predictive maintenance, where multi-agent systems coordinate across machine prioritization, failure prediction, repair planning, and maintenance guidance, transforming equipment management from scheduled downtime into intelligent, just-in-time interventions. We then examine how AI preserves and operationalizes decades of institutional knowledge, ensuring that retiring experts' insights remain accessible through semantic search and intelligent knowledge management systems. Moving beyond the factory floor, we investigate how GenAI is revolutionizing in-vehicle experiences through sophisticated voice assistants that understand context, access technical documentation, and provide personalized guidance. Finally, we explore fleet management optimization, where agentic AI systems autonomously coordinate complex logistics decisions, balancing routes, schedules, maintenance, and resource allocation in real time.

Each application demonstrates how modern data platforms enable these intelligent systems to seamlessly integrate structured operational data with unstructured knowledge sources, creating the comprehensive context these AI agents need to make sophisticated decisions autonomously.

By the end of this chapter, you will understand the following:

- How to implement a four-stage predictive maintenance strategy using multi-agent collaboration and RAG architectures
- The critical role of institutional knowledge preservation and how AI transforms tribal knowledge into searchable, actionable insights
- How GenAI powers next-generation automotive voice assistants through hybrid cloud-edge architectures
- Advanced chunking strategies for vehicle manuals and technical documentation that preserve critical context and relationships
- The implementation of agentic AI for autonomous fleet scheduling and optimization using the ReaAct framework
- How flexible document models, vector search, and time-series capabilities enable sophisticated multi-agent systems
- Real-world architectures and data models for connected fleet incident management and diagnostic systems
- The strategic advantages of AI-integrated manufacturing systems for operational excellence and competitive differentiation

Predictive maintenance and multi-agent collaboration

Having established how AI transforms supply chain decision-making through intelligent data integration, we'll now turn to another critical area where collaborative AI systems are revolutionizing manufacturing: predictive maintenance. While supply chain optimization focuses on materials flow and inventory management, predictive maintenance addresses the operational backbone of manufacturing: keeping production equipment running at peak performance through intelligent, proactive intervention.

A well-defined maintenance strategy can be a game-changer for any organization, driving significant revenue and cost savings. Here's how it works:

- First, identify the equipment that is most crucial for your operations. Downtime for this equipment can lead to bottlenecks, halting production.

- Second, equip these critical assets with sensors to enable condition monitoring. This allows you to monitor the health of the equipment in real time, identifying potential issues before they escalate into catastrophic failures.

- Third, based on the prediction, the system can generate work orders, schedule maintenance activities, and even provide guidance to maintenance personnel. This ensures that maintenance is performed only when necessary, optimizing resource allocation.

This series of activities delivers tangible benefits. Costs are reduced through saved labor hours and extended machine lifespan. Additionally, revenue increases as your machines operate at optimal performance levels.

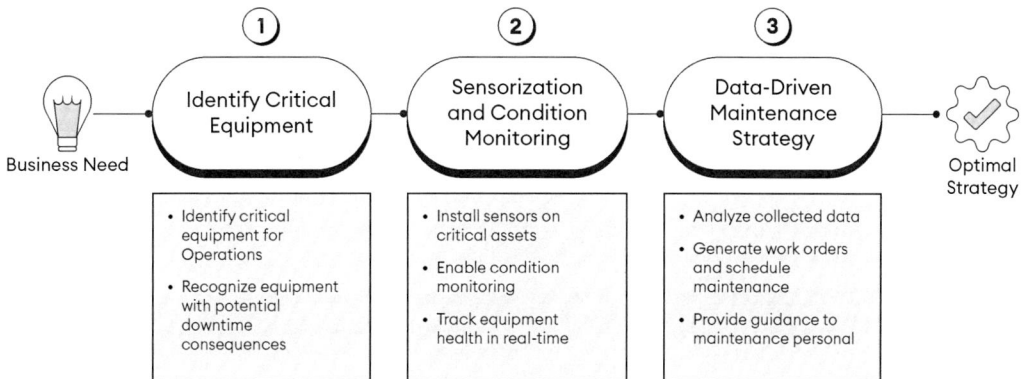

Figure 7.1: Steps required for an optimal maintenance strategy

Figure 7.1 illustrates a three-step process for implementing predictive maintenance. Starting with identifying critical equipment and recognizing potential downtime consequences, moving on to sensorization and condition monitoring with real-time health tracking, and culminating in a data-driven maintenance strategy that analyzes collected data, generates work orders, schedules maintenance, and provides guidance to personnel, ultimately leading to an optimal maintenance strategy that reduces costs and increases revenue.

Optimal maintenance strategy

An optimal maintenance strategy isn't a one-size-fits-all solution. It's about choosing the right blend of approaches based on your specific equipment and operational needs. These approaches range from highly complex and expensive at one end to simpler, more affordable options at the other:

- **Reactive maintenance**: This is the most basic approach in which maintenance is performed after a machine fails. While simple, it can lead to unexpected downtime and higher repair costs.

- **Preventive maintenance**: This is a proactive approach that involves scheduling maintenance tasks based on predetermined time intervals or usage metrics. This helps prevent breakdowns but can be inefficient as machine conditions can vary. Thresholds for these tasks may need to be adjusted due to factors such as aging equipment, changes in processes, or different materials being used.

- **Condition-based maintenance (CBM)**: This approach continuously monitors the health of the machine through sensors and data analysis. Maintenance is then triggered based on the actual condition of the equipment rather than a set schedule. This is more efficient than preventive maintenance as it avoids unnecessary maintenance. Threshold-based alerting systems are often used with CBM.

- **Predictive maintenance**: This is the most advanced approach, using data analytics to predict potential equipment failures before they occur, which allows for proactive maintenance and minimizes downtime. Predictive maintenance requires significant upfront investment in sensors and data analysis tools.

Predictive maintenance uses data analysis to identify problems in machines before they fail. This allows organizations to schedule maintenance at the optimal time, maximizing machine reliability and efficiency.

Here's how predictive maintenance can benefit manufacturing operations, according to Deloitte [1]:

- **3–5%** Reduction in new equipment costs
- **5–20%** increase in labor productivity
- **15–20%** reduction in facility downtime
- **10–30%** reduction in inventory levels
- **5–20%** reduction in carrying costs

Predictive maintenance is constantly evolving. We've moved beyond basic threshold-based monitoring to advanced techniques such as machine learning models. These models not only predict failures but also diagnose the root cause and contributory factors, allowing for targeted repairs.

The latest trend in predictive maintenance is automated strategy creation. This involves using AI to predict equipment breakdowns based on a combination of quantitative and qualitative factors, but also to generate repair plans, ensuring the right fixes are made at the right time. Automated strategy creation requires substantial investment in R&D, along with deep industry knowledge, access to relevant data, and practical operational experience. The question is, can GenAI help?

Current state and challenges

The answer is yes, GenAI can help. But there are challenges at each stage of implementation that organizations must consider. Each stage presents a key question and unique challenges, demonstrating the technical and operational hurdles organizations face in predictive maintenance deployment.

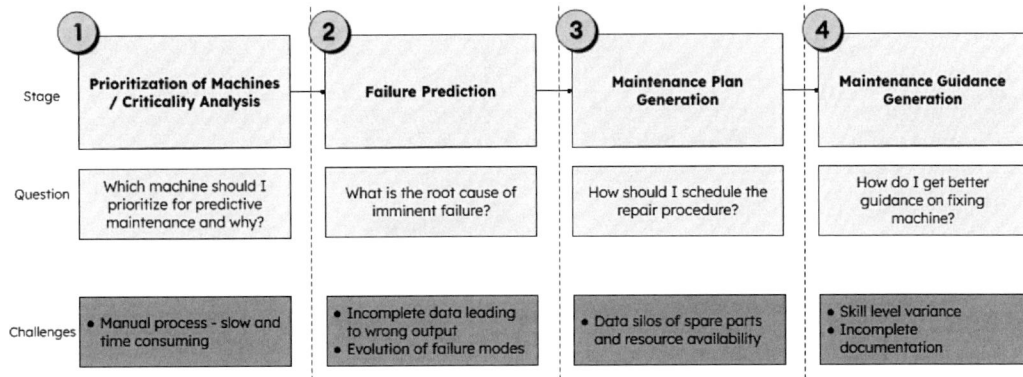

Figure 7.2: Different challenges seen at each stage of predictive maintenance deployment

Figure 7.2 outlines the four-stage predictive maintenance implementation process, showing the key question and associated challenges for each phase. What's particularly noteworthy is how the complexity and data requirements evolve across stages, from the manual, time-consuming machine prioritization process in stage 1, to the technical challenges of insufficient training data and evolving failure modes in stage 2, to the integration complexities and skill gaps in stages 3 and 4. This progression reveals why many organizations struggle with predictive maintenance implementation: each stage presents distinct technical and operational hurdles that must be systematically addressed. The figure also illustrates why a holistic, AI-driven approach becomes essential; traditional methods simply cannot handle the multifaceted nature of these interconnected challenges effectively.

Now, let's envision a factory containing both automated and manual machines. Let's call it **Gear Transmission Systems Ltd**, whose primary output is gearboxes. Within this factory, we have an array of equipment: cutting machines, milling machines, measurement devices, and more. As its general manager, you are tasked with managing the budget allocated for maintenance processes and improving strategies. One pressing question you must address is: *"Which machines should take priority for the predictive maintenance projects, and why?"* This involves consulting with the maintenance managers and leaders and conducting quantitative analyses, a rather manual process.

Once you've identified the machines, the next step is to install sensors and train the machine learning model. However, two major challenges arise. First, you lack sufficient *run to failure* data to effectively train the model. Secondly, machine health deteriorates over time, leading to evolving failure modes with the age of the machine.

Assuming you manage to overcome these hurdles, the next phase involves maintenance scheduling and execution. You're faced with a myriad of data silos, including inventory data and resource availability data, which need to be integrated to formulate a comprehensive repair plan. Furthermore, it's essential to ensure that operators are adept at addressing minor machine issues to reduce reliance on external experts and forestall more critical failures. While complex issues may still require OEM or **system integrator** (**SI**) support, internal troubleshooting capabilities are invaluable. Therefore, developing easy-to-follow documentation tailored to the skill levels of our staff is important.

As *Figure 7.3* demonstrates, different data is required to solve the listed challenges:

- **Prioritization of machines/criticality analysis**: At this stage, we require both structured and unstructured data. We need previous machine failure data as well as expert analysis and opinion on which machines to prioritize for predictive maintenance and why.
- **Failure prediction**: This stage involves structured data such as sensor data and maintenance logs to identify the root cause of imminent failure.
- **Maintenance plan and guidance generation**: In both of these stages, we deal with both structured and unstructured data. The objective is to combine this data to generate an optimal repair plan and operator guidance.

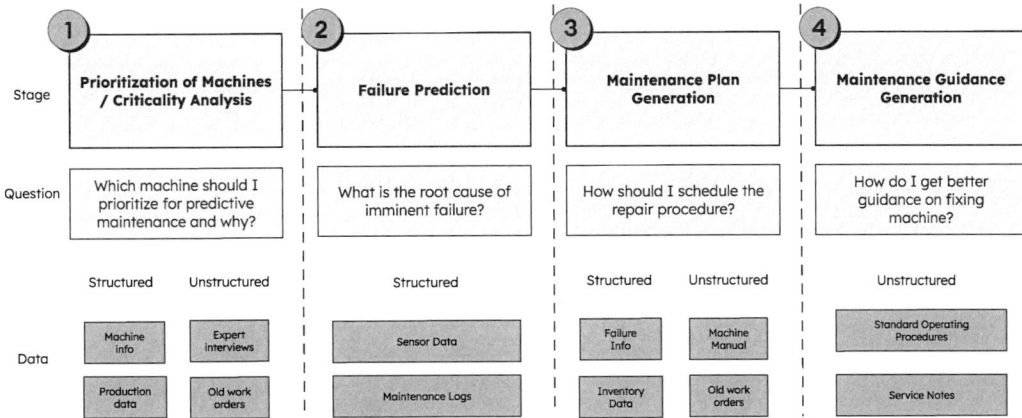

Figure 7.3: Different data requirements at each stage

This diagram shows the specific data needs of each stage of predictive maintenance implementation. Stage 1 requires both structured data (machine info, production data) and unstructured data (expert interviews, old work orders) for machine prioritization. Stage 2 uses structured data (sensor data, maintenance logs) for failure prediction. Stages 3 and 4 combine structured data (failure info, inventory data) with unstructured data (machine manuals, old work orders, standard operating procedures, service notes) to generate maintenance plans and operator guidance.

These varied data requirements across the predictive maintenance lifecycle reveal a fundamental challenge: traditional approaches struggle to integrate the diverse mix of structured sensor data, historical records, and unstructured expert knowledge needed for effective decision-making. This integration complexity sets the stage for exploring how AI and modern data platforms can transform these traditionally siloed processes into collaborative, intelligent systems.

How AI and MongoDB help

MongoDB Atlas is a multi-cloud developer data platform designed to accelerate and simplify how developers work with data. By using MongoDB Atlas, developers can power end-to-end value chain optimization with AI/ML, advanced analytics, and real-time data processing for innovative mobile, edge, and IoT applications.

To address the data integration challenges we've identified, we'll explore how MongoDB Atlas enables each stage of the predictive maintenance journey: first, transforming machine prioritization from manual analysis to AI-driven insights; second, implementing real-time failure prediction systems; third, generating comprehensive repair plans that combine multiple data sources; and finally, creating intelligent maintenance guidance that adapts to real-world conditions and multilingual inputs.

Stage 1: Machine prioritization

Current machine prioritization for predictive maintenance relies heavily on manual analysis. Factory personnel gather historical and current machine data on losses due to breakdowns. This data is then reviewed alongside the experience of maintenance managers and leaders. Based on this combined analysis, a roadmap for the predictive maintenance project is recommended, highlighting which machines should be prioritized.

However, this approach has limitations. A reliance on manual analysis can be time-consuming and may not always capture the full picture of the maintenance project due to the limited use of quantitative data sources. Additionally, inconsistencies in interpretation can lead to an overdependence on institutional knowledge, which in turn can result in potentially false or inaccurate analyses that impact the project's **return on investment (ROI)**.

With the arrival of GenAI, things have changed. A GenAI-based machine prioritization tool can be created to reduce the time manufacturing experts spend on manual analysis and to decrease the risk of poor investments. To leverage AI, experts need a data store capable of saving and operationalizing structured and unstructured data. This data store enables them to perform semantic searches and to provide the right context to the LLM, ensuring it generates responses based on factory data without hallucinating. Such a system can result in positive business outcomes. *Figure 7.4* shows how the system would look with MongoDB Atlas as the AI data store.

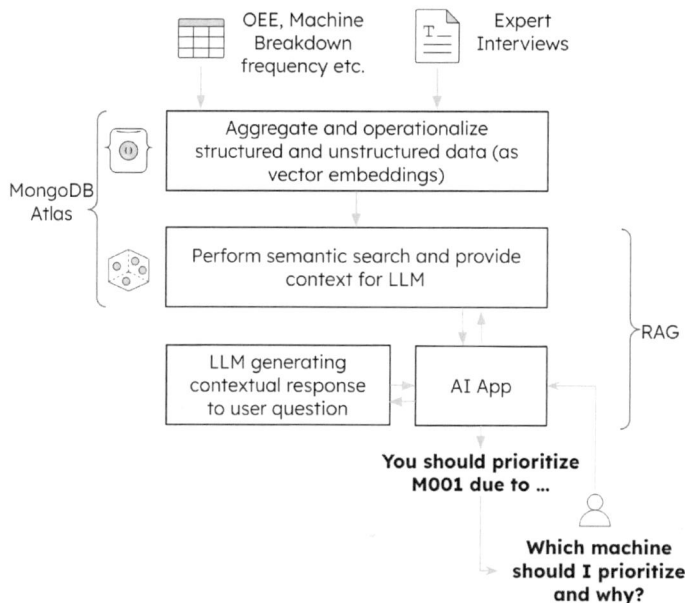

Figure 7.4: GenAI-powered machine prioritization

This AI-powered approach combines structured data (**overall equipment effectiveness (OEE)**, machine breakdown frequency) with unstructured expert knowledge (interviews, reports) through vector embeddings. The system uses MongoDB Atlas Vector Search to find relevant context and feeds this information to LLMs via **retrieval-augmented generation (RAG)** methodology. When maintenance managers ask "Which machine should I prioritize and why?", the system can recommend specific machines such as M001 or M002 based on a comprehensive analysis of criticality, maintenance costs, and operational impact. AI applications such as LangChain, LlamaIndex, or custom-built maintenance management interfaces can trigger Atlas Vector Search to retrieve contextual information and generate these data-driven recommendations.

Stage 2: Failure prediction

Now that we've discussed prioritizing equipment, let's move on to failure prediction. MongoDB Atlas provides all the necessary building blocks and tools to implement failure prediction. By providing a unified view of operational data, real-time processing capabilities, integrated monitoring and alerting, and seamless compatibility with machine learning tools, MongoDB Atlas enables organizations to optimize machine performance and minimize downtime.

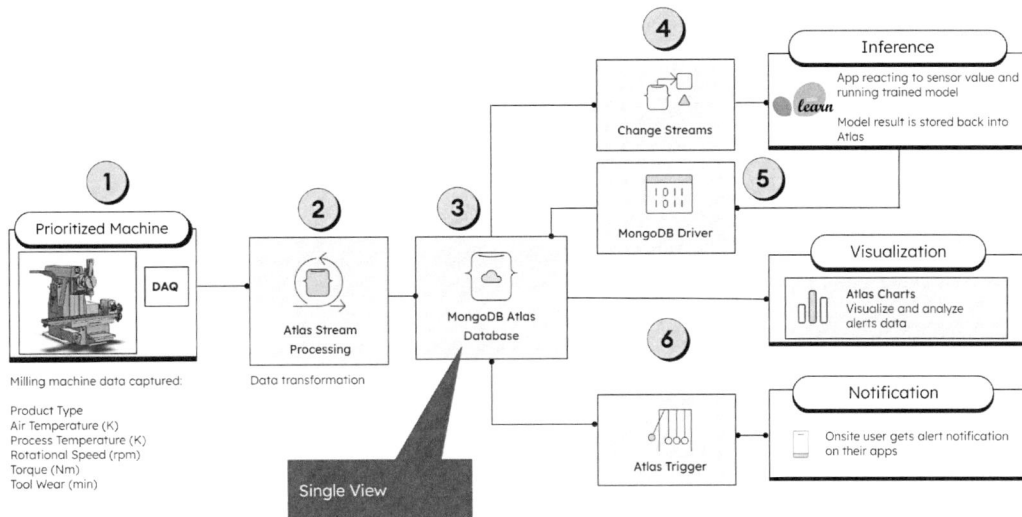

Figure 7.5: Smart milling machine uses real-time data to predict failures

Figure 7.5 shows a six-step failure prediction workflow using MongoDB Atlas. It begins with prioritized machine data capture, including milling specifications and sensor readings, followed by data transformation through Atlas Stream Processing. The transformed data is stored in MongoDB Atlas with a unified view. Change streams then trigger inference processes, and operational analysis is performed using visualization through Atlas Charts. Finally, Atlas Triggers enable automated notifications to alert users of potential failures, creating a comprehensive real-time predictive maintenance system.

As seen in the preceding figure, we have our prioritized machine, which is a milling machine with attached sensors that collect data such as air temperature, rotational speed, torque, and tool wear. This data is processed through Atlas Stream Processing, enabling the processing of streams of complex data using the same data model and Query API used in Atlas databases. Atlas Stream Processing enables developers to build aggregation pipelines to continuously operate on streaming data without the delays inherent to batch processing. Results can be continuously published to MongoDB Atlas or a Kafka topic. This allows data transformation and enrichment before it even lands in the database.

Once the data is in MongoDB, another application can react to sensor values and run a trained model designed to predict failures. The model results can be stored back in Atlas between the inference and visualization stages. These results can then be visualized using Atlas Charts. Finally, Atlas Triggers and Functions can be used to push notifications to on-site users. This establishes an end-to-end system for failure prediction.

Maritime fleet predictive maintenance in practice

Ceto has revolutionized maritime operations by partnering with MongoDB to integrate AI with real-time data collected from thousands of sensors across customer fleets. This implementation allows Ceto to predict and pre-empt potential mechanical failures, streamline operations, and manage risks proactively.

Ceto's core thesis is that vessel sensor data can reveal how close a ship is to a mechanical breakdown and, by extension, an insurance claim. By applying advanced filtering and real-time analysis to vessel sensor readings, Ceto is keeping crews safer at sea while providing more appropriate insurance policies and pricing.

Ceto is now processing over three billion data points per year. MongoDB's architecture provided Ceto with several key features crucial for their operations, including scalability for managing increasing data volumes and time series collections for advanced data compression. As Ben Harrison, CTO of Ceto, notes: *"MongoDB's time series collections have revolutionized how we manage and utilize data from our fleet. The ability to process and analyze data in real time has significantly enhanced our predictive maintenance capabilities."*

Learn more at https://mdb.link/leading-maritime-technology-company.

Stage 3: Repair plan generators

Having identified the nature of the equipment failures, the implementation of a comprehensive repair strategy becomes paramount. First, we have to generate a maintenance work order. This order should include repair instructions, spare parts needed, a schedule, and resource availability information. In this case, both structured and unstructured data are involved. The repair instructions will come from the machine manual. For this process, MongoDB Atlas acts as the operational data layer, seamlessly integrating structured and unstructured data.

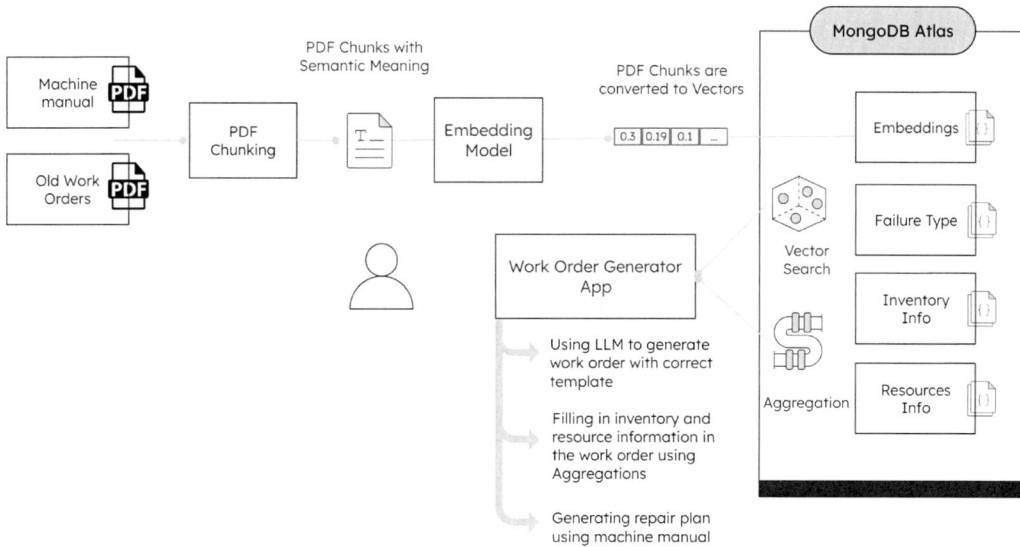

Figure 7.6: MongoDB Atlas as the operational data layer for structured and unstructured data

MongoDB Atlas serves as the central operational data layer for repair plan generation, combining machine manuals and old work orders (processed through PDF chunking and embedding) with structured data, including failure types, inventory info, and resource information. A Work Order Generator app uses LLMs and aggregation frameworks to generate comprehensive work orders with correct templates, schedule information, and repair plans, leveraging both vector search capabilities and structured data integration.

Figure 7.6 shows the process of work order generation using GenAI. First, we extract information chunks from a milling machine manual and old work orders stored in PDF files and convert them into vectors. These embeddings are then stored in MongoDB Atlas. MongoDB's versatility enables the storage of structured and unstructured data within the same database. Leveraging Atlas Vector Search and aggregation pipelines, we can integrate this data to feed into an LLM powering a Work

Order Generator application. The LLM analyzes the data to generate the appropriate work order and template, drawing from past examples. It populates inventory and resource details using aggregation techniques and structured data. Finally, it generates a repair plan similar to the old work orders. What sets this approach apart is the ability to use the same MongoDB database to store structured data such as failure types, spare parts inventory, and resource information. By employing the aggregation framework to extract relevant information from structured data and vector search to glean insights from vectors, the LLM within the Work Order Generator application gains contextual understanding.

This application seamlessly utilizes the LLM to generate work orders with the correct template, filling in inventory and resource details through aggregations, and ultimately creating repair plans based on machine manuals. This application can run inside a central maintenance management system.

Stage 4: Maintenance guidance generation

So, we come to the last step: How can we use GenAI to enhance the operator or technician guidance to maintain the machine? The challenge here is that maintenance scenarios often involve multilingual documentation, evolving service notes, and the need to integrate new insights with existing repair procedures in real time.

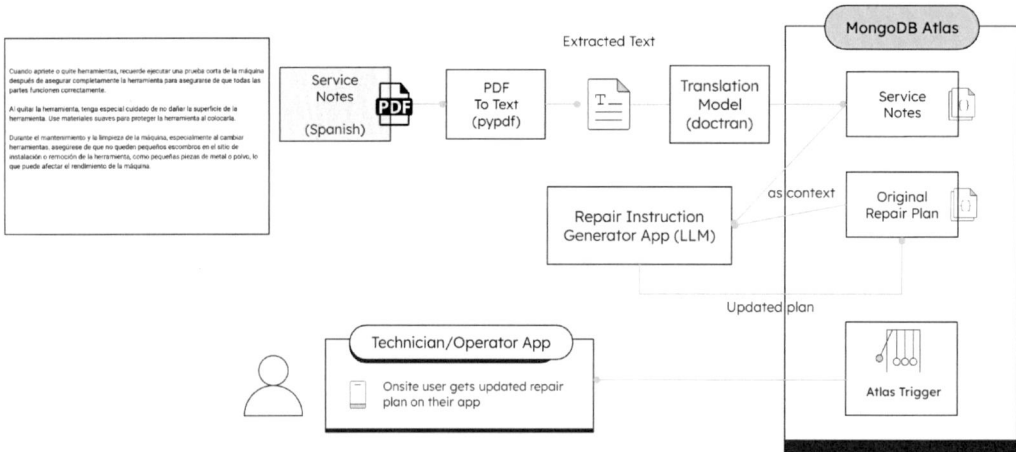

Figure 7.7: Using the RAG approach for operator work instructions

Figure 7.7 illustrates how MongoDB Atlas enables maintenance guidance generation through a RAG approach. Service notes in multiple languages are processed through PDF-to-text conversion and translation models, then stored in MongoDB Atlas alongside original repair plans. A Repair Instruction Generator app using LLMs creates updated repair plans by combining translated service notes with existing repair instructions, which are then delivered to technicians/operators through a dedicated app and triggered via Atlas Triggers for real-time updates.

Let's walk through an example scenario here. The repair plan was generated in the last step. Now, the **computerized maintenance management system (CMMS)** has found some service notes uploaded to the platform by another technician, but they're written in another language (let's say Spanish). We can use the RAG architecture again to intelligently merge these service notes with the repair instructions generated in the previous step.

We first need to extract text from the PDF, translate it into English, since our other data is in English, and then provide the service notes as well as the repair plan to the LLM as context. So, we have the original plan from the previous steps, and we combine it integrally using the LLM with the service notes obtained in this step.

> **Note**
>
> We're not performing vector search here. Once the plan is updated, we can publish notifications down to the technician's application via Atlas Triggers and Functions.

In summary, we are essentially integrating AI and GenAI apps to implement an end-to-end predictive maintenance strategy. This comprehensive approach demonstrates how the four stages work together (from intelligent machine prioritization through failure prediction, repair planning, and finally adaptive maintenance guidance), creating a unified system that transforms traditional reactive maintenance into a proactive, data-driven operation.

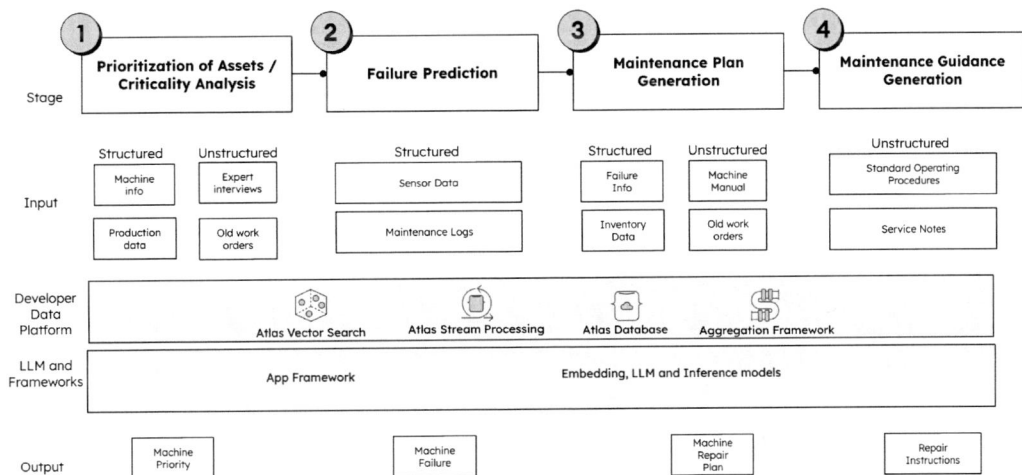

Figure 7.8: Model chaining with unified data store

Figure 7.8 shows an end-to-end predictive maintenance strategy using MongoDB Atlas as the unified data platform across four stages. Each stage processes both structured and unstructured data inputs through the MongoDB Atlas developer platform (featuring Atlas Vector Search, Stream Processing, Database, and Aggregation Framework), combined with LLM and foundation/AI frameworks to produce specific outputs at each stage: machine priority, failure types, repair plans, and repair instructions.

Our input consisted of a combination of structured and unstructured data. We leveraged the various services offered by the MongoDB Atlas developer data platform, including Atlas Vector Search, Atlas Stream Processing, and, of course, the MongoDB database and aggregation framework. These features enabled us to provide the right context to the LLM and the appropriate data to the AI model. Ultimately, we obtained the desired output at each stage, ranging from machine prioritization, failure type identification, and repair plan formulation to instruction generation.

You can learn more about how AI is being used in renewable energy by leveraging MongoDB Atlas Vector Search to drive efficiency through real-time audio diagnostics here: `https://www.mongodb.com/solutions/solutions-library/real-time-audio-based-ai-diagnostics`

Multi-agent collaboration system

In addition to advancing predictive maintenance strategies through RAG architectures, agentic systems are emerging as the next frontier in GenAI applications. These systems consist of one or more AI agents that collaborate to deliver value, often interacting with each other in the same or external systems. Designed to engage with humans for feedback and review after executing steps, these systems adapt their behavior based on the context provided by the outputs of other agents and human inputs.

In predictive maintenance, a multi-agent system can assign one agent to analyze machine data for early detection of mechanical issues, while another optimizes resource allocation of materials and labor. What's more, different agents can use specialized models for specific tasks. For instance, one transcribes videos, while another employs natural language processing to answer questions.

In this setting, MongoDB serves as the memory provider for agentic systems. Conversation histories and vector embeddings are stored using MongoDB's flexible document model. Atlas Vector Search enables semantic search on stored embeddings, while sharding capabilities provide horizontal scaling without sacrificing performance. Up next, we explore how to develop a three-agent collaboration system to optimize machine performance.

Optimizing a production environment

In manufacturing operations, leveraging multi-agent collaboration for predictive maintenance can significantly boost operational efficiency. For instance, consider a production environment where three distinct agents (predictive maintenance, process optimization, and quality assurance) collaborate in real time to refine machine operations and maintain the factory at peak performance.

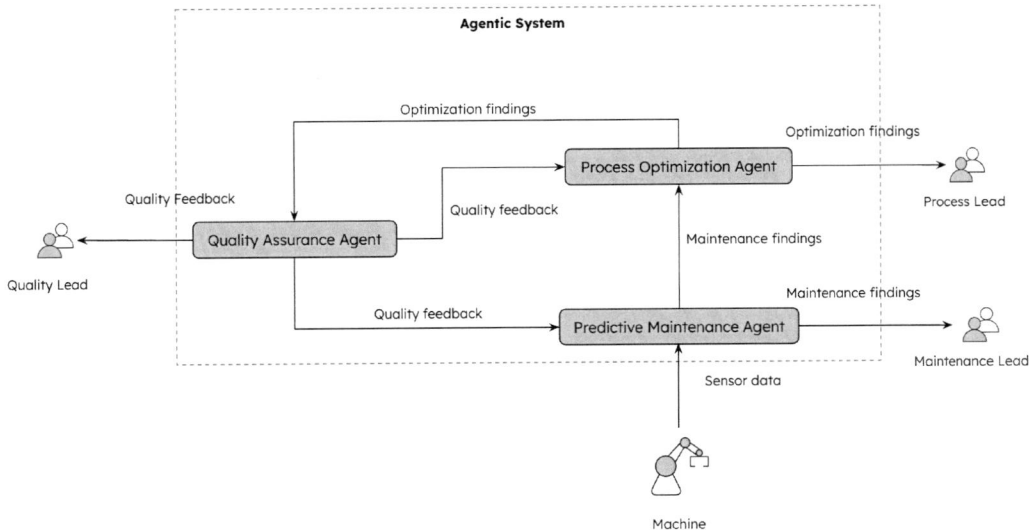

Figure 7.9: Multi-agent system for production optimization

Figure 7.9 shows a collaborative agentic system where three specialized AI agents work together to optimize manufacturing operations. The **Quality Assurance Agent** receives quality feedback and shares it with the **Process Optimization Agent**, which handles optimization findings and maintenance findings. The **Predictive Maintenance Agent** monitors sensor data from machines and exchanges maintenance findings with the Process Optimization Agent, creating a coordinated approach to maintain peak factory performance through real-time collaboration between predictive maintenance, process optimization, and quality assurance functions.

In this setup, the Predictive Maintenance Agent is focused on machinery maintenance. Its main tasks are to monitor equipment health by analyzing sensor data generated from the machines. It predicts machine failures and recommends maintenance actions to extend machinery lifespan and prevent downtime as much as possible.

Complementing this role, the Process Optimization Agent is designed to enhance production efficiency by analyzing and adjusting production parameters, such as speed and vibration, to eliminate bottlenecks and maintain product quality. This agent incorporates feedback from the other agents to decide which parameters to tune. For example, if the Predictive Maintenance Agent detects rising temperatures in a milling machine, the Process Optimization Agent can adjust the cutting speed.

Finally, the Quality Assurance Agent evaluates product quality by analyzing optimized production parameters and assessing their impact on the product. It also provides feedback to the other two agents. The three agents continuously share feedback with one another, storing this information as short-term memory in the MongoDB Atlas database, while vector embeddings and sensor data are kept as long-term memory.

With its flexible document model, robust security, comprehensive data governance features, and horizontal scalability, MongoDB serves as an exceptional memory provider for developing AI-driven agent systems.

AI workflow automation company transforms business operations with MongoDB Atlas

A leading workflow automation company faced the challenge of building personalized and dynamic AI agents to handle repetitive tasks in strategic business roles. To address this, they leveraged MongoDB Atlas, which unified their operational, analytical, and GenAI data services, thereby simplifying the development of intelligent applications.

With MongoDB Atlas, the company's AI agents enabled new work modes with fewer resources, allowing businesses to automate complex workflows while maintaining human oversight and collaboration. Their platform demonstrates how AI agents can be made more accessible and capable of continuous learning, enabling multiple stakeholders to collaboratively modify and optimize AI-generated content for improved business outcomes.

This example has been anonymized for editorial clarity. To learn more, see: https://mdb.link/ai-workflow-company-agents.

Knowledge management and preservation

The workflow automation example demonstrates how AI agents can transform business operations, but it also reveals a fundamental dependency: these intelligent systems are only as effective as the knowledge they can access and leverage. While multi-agent systems excel at coordinating real-time decisions and optimizing operations, they require a deep foundation of institutional knowledge to make truly informed decisions. This brings us to another transformative application of AI in manufacturing: the preservation and operationalization of decades of accumulated expertise.

Traditional knowledge management approaches often rely on documentation, training programs, and mentorship. However, these methods face significant limitations:

- Documentation is often incomplete, outdated, or difficult to access when needed
- Training programs may not capture the nuanced expertise developed through years of experience
- Mentorship depends on the availability of experienced personnel and can be inconsistent

These limitations become particularly acute as the manufacturing workforce ages and experienced personnel retire, taking with them invaluable knowledge that could enhance the decision-making capabilities of the AI systems we've been discussing. The solution lies in transforming this tribal knowledge into AI-accessible formats that can feed directly into the predictive maintenance and multi-agent systems we've explored.

The challenge of institutional knowledge and AI-powered solutions

To understand why this knowledge preservation is so critical, consider what happens when a veteran maintenance technician who has worked with a particular machine for decades suddenly retires. Manufacturing organizations often rely heavily on this institutional knowledge: the unwritten information, skills, and practices known by experienced workers but not formally documented. This knowledge typically includes troubleshooting techniques for specific equipment issues, optimal machine settings for different materials or conditions, quality inspection insights based on subtle visual or auditory cues, and process adjustments to accommodate environmental variables.

When experienced workers retire or leave the organization, this valuable knowledge can be lost, leading to decreased efficiency, quality issues, and increased training costs for new employees. More critically, this knowledge gap limits the effectiveness of AI systems like those we've discussed.

Predictive maintenance algorithms become less accurate without understanding the subtle operational nuances that experienced workers instinctively know, and multi-agent systems cannot optimize processes they don't fully comprehend.

AI-powered knowledge management systems address this challenge by capturing and indexing valuable worker knowledge, including both textual and unstructured information. By creating semantic vectors from documents, manuals, and notes, manufacturers can eliminate the traditional task of locating and transferring knowledge from data silos. This approach enables users to perform cross-system searches using natural language queries, facilitating seamless access to information across different platforms.

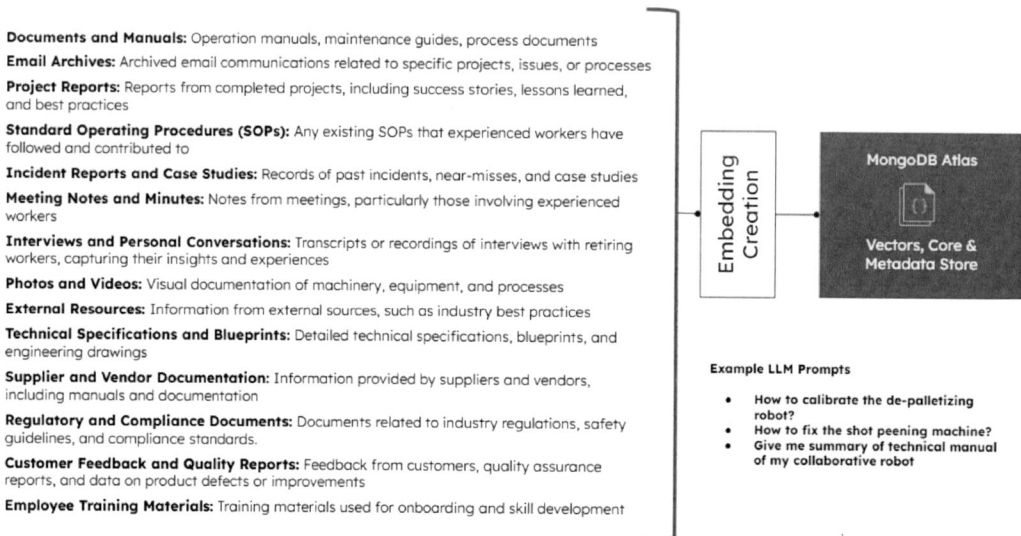

Documents and Manuals: Operation manuals, maintenance guides, process documents

Email Archives: Archived email communications related to specific projects, issues, or processes

Project Reports: Reports from completed projects, including success stories, lessons learned, and best practices

Standard Operating Procedures (SOPs): Any existing SOPs that experienced workers have followed and contributed to

Incident Reports and Case Studies: Records of past incidents, near-misses, and case studies

Meeting Notes and Minutes: Notes from meetings, particularly those involving experienced workers

Interviews and Personal Conversations: Transcripts or recordings of interviews with retiring workers, capturing their insights and experiences

Photos and Videos: Visual documentation of machinery, equipment, and processes

External Resources: Information from external sources, such as industry best practices

Technical Specifications and Blueprints: Detailed technical specifications, blueprints, and engineering drawings

Supplier and Vendor Documentation: Information provided by suppliers and vendors, including manuals and documentation

Regulatory and Compliance Documents: Documents related to industry regulations, safety guidelines, and compliance standards.

Customer Feedback and Quality Reports: Feedback from customers, quality assurance reports, and data on product defects or improvements

Employee Training Materials: Training materials used for onboarding and skill development

Embedding Creation

MongoDB Atlas

Vectors, Core & Metadata Store

Example LLM Prompts

- How to calibrate the de-palletizing robot?
- How to fix the shot peening machine?
- Give me summary of technical manual of my collaborative robot

Figure 7.10: Knowledge sources and storage architecture

Figure 7.10 illustrates how this comprehensive approach works in practice. The system aggregates diverse organizational knowledge sources, from operational documentation and historical records to expert insights, regulatory information, and training materials. Rather than simply cataloging information, the architecture creates intelligent connections between different types of knowledge. For example, when a maintenance technician encounters unusual equipment behavior, the system can instantly connect that observation to relevant troubleshooting procedures, historical incident reports, expert insights from recorded interviews, and regulatory requirements, all through natural language queries. All content flows into MongoDB Atlas as vectors, core data, and metadata, creating a unified knowledge repository that transforms isolated pieces of information into a comprehensive knowledge network, enhancing both human decision-making and AI system performance.

Real-time knowledge application

Having established how institutional knowledge can be captured and structured, the next critical step is making this knowledge instantly accessible when and where it's needed most. The knowledge management architecture processes shop floor requests through an intelligent pipeline, as shown in *Figure 7.11*. This real-time application represents the culmination of our knowledge preservation efforts, transforming static information into dynamic, actionable guidance that can enhance the multi-agent systems and predictive maintenance workflows we explored earlier.

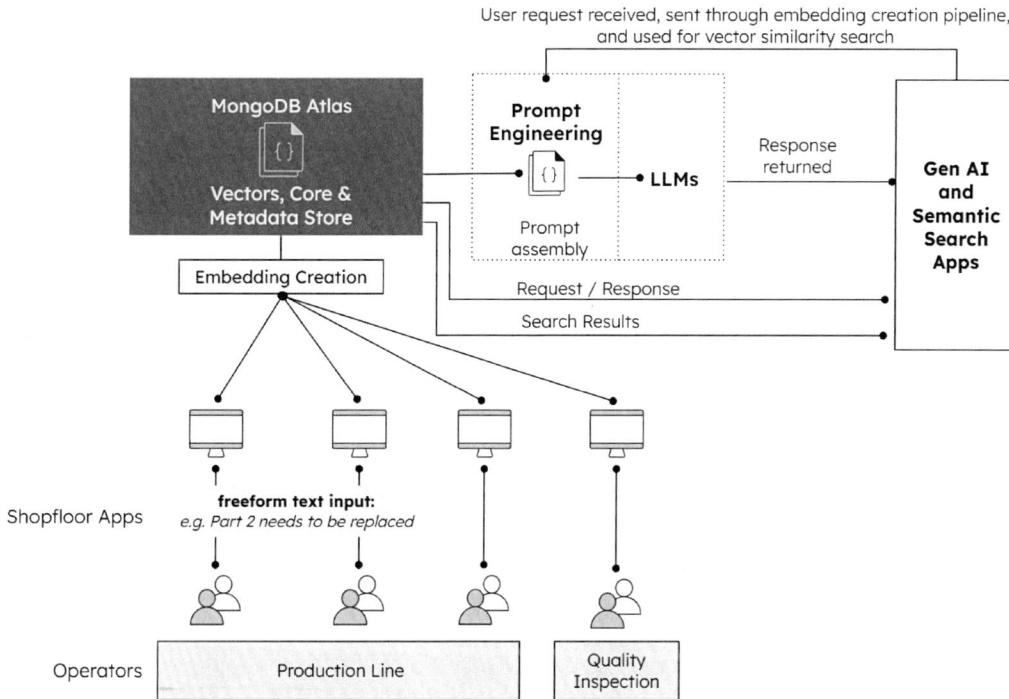

Figure 7.11: Knowledge management architecture

When operators input their observations and issues through shop floor applications, the system does the following:

- **Processes input**: User requests are sent through the embedding creation pipeline
- **Semantic search**: MongoDB Atlas Vector Search identifies relevant knowledge using semantic similarity
- **Contextual assembly**: The prompt engineering system combines search results with the current context
- **Intelligent response**: LLMs generate actionable guidance based on organizational knowledge
- **Continuous learning**: New interactions enhance the knowledge base for future queries

This architecture enables instant access to institutional knowledge, whether operators need troubleshooting guidance, process optimization tips, or regulatory compliance information. More importantly, it creates a feedback loop where the knowledge repository continuously grows and improves, ensuring that the insights generated today become the institutional knowledge that will guide tomorrow's AI systems and human operators.

> **Major European energy company makes terabytes of subsurface unstructured data actionable with MongoDB Atlas**
>
> Based in Italy, this global energy company has more than 30,000 employees across 69 countries. Its operations vary from exploring and drilling for natural gas and oil to cogenerating electricity, renewables, biorefining, and chemical production.
>
> The company partnered with MongoDB Consulting for training and to support the migration of workloads into MongoDB Atlas. The organization wanted to move to a managed service with a seamless user experience and easy-to-use interface for developers.
>
> With MongoDB Atlas, the company's users can quickly find data spanning multiple years and geographies to identify trends and analyze models. MongoDB Atlas Search also assists by filtering out irrelevant documents. The team also integrated AI and machine learning models with the platform to make it even easier to identify patterns.
>
> This example has been anonymized for editorial clarity. To learn more, see: `https://mdb.link/european-energy-company-insights`.

Hyper-personalized in-cabin experiences

While knowledge management addresses how manufacturing organizations preserve and leverage institutional expertise, another domain where AI is transforming user experiences lies in the automotive industry. The applications we've explored, from predictive maintenance to knowledge management, demonstrate AI's power to enhance operational efficiency through intelligent data integration. Now we'll turn to a consumer-facing application that showcases how these same principles of contextual understanding and personalized assistance are revolutionizing the way drivers interact with their vehicles.

The automotive industry is undergoing rapid transformation with electric vehicles, autonomous driving, and advanced safety features. These advancements have created a growing demand for more sophisticated and intelligent in-car systems that can provide personalized experiences for drivers and passengers alike. Voice assistants have become a standard feature in modern vehicles, but today's implementations are often limited to basic functions such as navigation, in-vehicle controls, and phone calls.

According to recent research by SoundHound AI, 83% of drivers planning to buy a car in the next 12 months would select one with AI features over one without. Additionally, 79% of drivers across Europe indicate they would use voice GenAI capabilities in their vehicles[2]. These statistics highlight the significant market readiness for next-generation in-cabin experiences powered by advanced AI technologies.

The current voice assistants found in vehicles face several limitations. While most vehicles come equipped with these systems, and drivers use them regularly, they're often frustrating due to their limited capabilities. Many of these systems can only respond to specific commands in predetermined ways, creating a rigid user experience that fails to adapt to individual preferences or situational contexts.

Challenges and AI-powered solutions for in-car voice assistants

The advancement of in-car voice assistants faces dual challenges from both driver needs and automaker constraints. Drivers have clear expectations of in-vehicle voice technologies: personalized experiences that understand their preferences and provide customized interactions tailored to their specific needs, intuitive use that requires no extensive learning periods, and advanced features that enhance their driving experience while maintaining simplicity.

Meanwhile, automotive manufacturers and technology providers face their own set of challenges. Development costs are substantial, as building intelligent in-cabin systems requires specialized expertise in AI, natural language processing, and automotive integration. Time-to-market pressure forces companies to quickly launch scalable solutions that meet rapidly evolving customer expectations while keeping pace with competitors. Additionally, automakers seek unique, branded experiences to stand out in an increasingly commoditized market while navigating regulatory constraints.

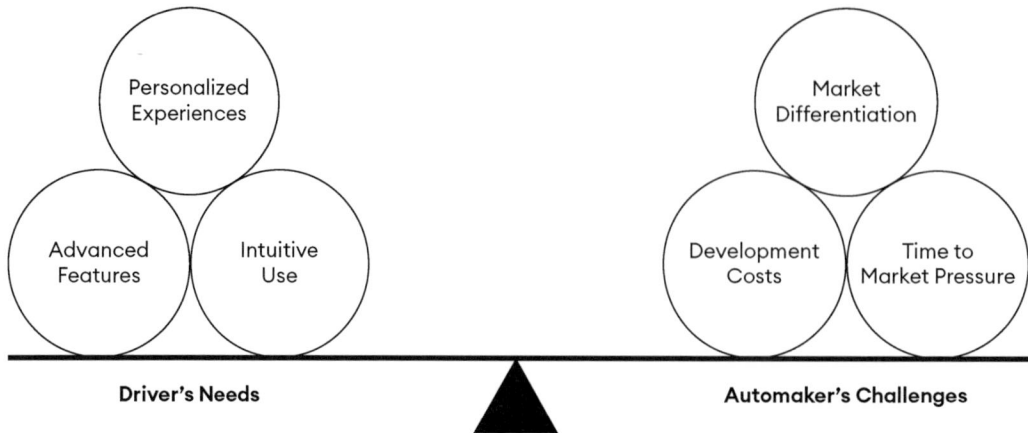

Figure 7.12: Balancing driver needs and automaker challenges in voice assistant development

This diagram illustrates the tension between driver expectations and automotive industry constraints in developing advanced voice assistants. The key to resolving this tension lies in leveraging GenAI technologies that can simultaneously address driver demands for sophisticated, personalized experiences while providing automakers with scalable, cost-effective solutions that accelerate time-to-market.

GenAI: transforming in-car assistants

GenAI offers a solution to these competing demands by fundamentally transforming how voice assistants function, moving from basic command-response patterns to dynamic, interactive experiences that satisfy both driver expectations and automaker requirements. These advanced assistants can do the following:

1. Understand natural language and conversational context

2. Provide personalized responses based on user preferences and history

3. Access relevant information sources to deliver accurate and helpful answers

4. Adapt to different driving scenarios and environmental conditions

Rather than requiring specific command phrases or following rigid scripts, GenAI-powered voice assistants can engage in more natural dialogue with users. This enables more intuitive interactions and reduces the cognitive burden on drivers, allowing them to focus more on the road while still accessing the information and functions they need.

Solution architecture: MongoDB Atlas and Google Cloud integration

Having established the transformative potential of GenAI for in-car assistants, the next critical question becomes: how do we actually implement these capabilities? To address these challenges and opportunities, technical architecture combining Google Cloud Platform and MongoDB Atlas provides the foundation for next-generation in-car voice assistants.

> **Note**
>
> While this solution highlights cloud components, effective in-car assistants require hybrid architectures. Key functions must be available onboard for offline operation, with lightweight versions of cloud capabilities embedded in the vehicle. As automotive processing power and connectivity improve, this balance of onboard and cloud capabilities will become increasingly critical to assistant performance.

Figure 7.13 shows a hybrid cloud and onboard solution for next-generation automotive voice assistants. The Google Cloud side handles data ingestion (document AI, embeddings generation), serving (speech-to-text, text-to-speech, Vertex AI), and MongoDB Atlas integration (vector search, change streams, user data). The onboard system manages frontend/dashboard functions, backend assistant workflow, inference requests, and vehicle signals through the PowerSync SDK, enabling both cloud-connected and offline voice assistant capabilities with seamless data synchronization.

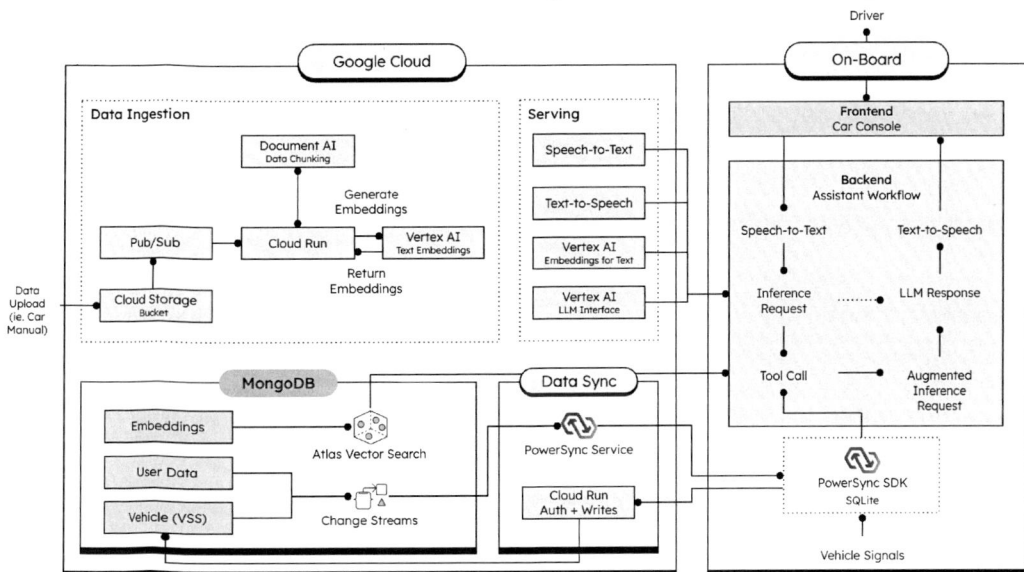

Figure 7.13: Google Cloud and MongoDB Atlas integration for in-car voice assistants

This solution integrates several key components:

1. **Speech APIs:** Google Cloud's comprehensive speech technology handles both speech-to-text transcription of driver commands and natural text-to-speech conversion for responses, functioning reliably even in challenging acoustic environments such as moving vehicles.

2. **Vector search for context retrieval:** MongoDB Atlas Vector Search retrieves relevant sections of the car manual and other contextual information based on semantic understanding rather than simple keyword matching.

3. **LLM integration:** The retrieved context is then fed into an LLM through Google's Vertex AI, enabling the assistant to generate accurate, context-aware responses that directly address the user's query.

4. **Onboard integration:** The system connects seamlessly with the vehicle's existing interface systems through a dedicated backend that manages the assistant workflow. This integration provides access to real-time vehicle signal data, allowing the assistant to understand the car's current status (running/stopped), speed, diagnostic information, and other telemetry, enabling more contextual responses and proactive assistance based on the vehicle's condition.

This architecture addresses several critical challenges in implementing advanced in-car voice assistants. The system achieves contextual understanding through multiple data access methods: vector search retrieves information specific to the vehicle model and query, while direct integration with vehicle systems provides real-time access to operational signals and **diagnostic trouble codes (DTCs)**, enabling responses informed by both documentation and the vehicle's actual state. Additionally, the system learns from user interactions to improve relevance over time, building increasingly personalized experiences that adapt to individual driver preferences and usage patterns.

Advanced agentic architecture: MongoDB Atlas and Google Cloud integration

While the initial implementation focuses on enhancing voice interactions with improved context and accuracy, the architecture shown in *Figure 7.14* is designed to support more sophisticated agentic systems.

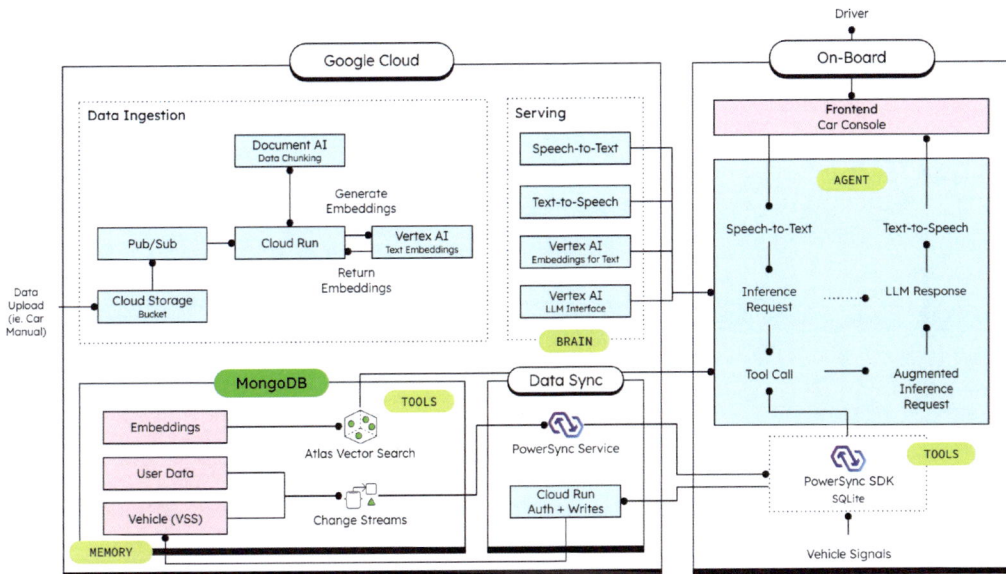

Figure 7.14: Google Cloud and MongoDB Atlas architecture with AI agent integration

This architecture builds upon the previous solution by adding AI agent capabilities and tool integration. The agentic approach organizes the system into four core components:

- **Agent:** The central orchestrator that coordinates the overall interaction flow and maintains coherence across multiple exchanges.

- **Brain:** The language model capabilities and reasoning functions that generate responses and make decisions.

- **Tools:** The various capabilities the agent can leverage, including vector search, database access, and vehicle system controls.

- **Memory:** Short-term conversation context and long-term user preferences that maintain continuity across interactions.

This foundation can be expanded to incorporate additional capabilities in future iterations. Real-time data access to traffic, weather, and point-of-interest information will enable more informed routing and travel recommendations. Personalized recommendations based on driver preferences and habits will create increasingly tailored experiences, while multi-step reasoning for complex tasks such as trip planning or vehicle diagnostics will handle sophisticated user requests that require coordinated actions across multiple systems. Integration with smart home systems and other connected devices will extend the vehicle's role as part of a broader connected ecosystem, enabling seamless transitions between home, vehicle, and workplace environments.

RAG implementation challenges for vehicle manuals

While the architectures we've explored provide the technical foundation for intelligent voice assistants, one of the most critical components involves accessing and processing vehicle-specific documentation, which presents unique implementation challenges that can make or break the system's effectiveness. A critical aspect of the system is effectively managing the complex technical documentation required for accurate vehicle-specific responses. Car manuals present unique challenges for traditional RAG implementations. Traditional chunking methods often fragment technical documentation into isolated pieces, losing critical context in the process. This is particularly problematic with automotive manuals, which contain deeply interconnected information including procedures, warnings, specifications, and diagrams.

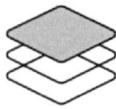

Fragmentation

Current RAG implementations fragment technical documentation into isolated pieces

Linkages

Technical manuals contain deeply interconnected information (procedures, warnings, specifications)

Risks

Without context preservation, retrieval produces technically incomplete or unsafe answers

Chunks!

Chunks are the **foundation** of RAG - their quality determines the quality of responses

Figure 7.15: RAG implementation challenges for vehicle manuals

This diagram illustrates three key challenges in implementing RAG systems for automotive technical documentation:

- **Hierarchical structure**: Car manuals have a deep hierarchical organization with titles, headings, subheadings, and content sections that create natural relationships between information

- **Specialized content**: These manuals include safety warnings, step-by-step procedures, technical specifications, part numbers, and diagnostic codes that must be preserved intact

- **Relationship preservation**: Many sections reference other parts of the manual or contain illustrations that apply to multiple procedures, creating a complex web of interdependencies

To address these challenges, advanced chunking strategies are necessary that go beyond simple text segmentation. Structure-aware chunking approaches respect document structure boundaries and keep related content together, preventing fragmentation of critical information.

Content recognition techniques use pattern recognition to identify and tag specialized content such as warnings or procedural steps to ensure they remain intact during the chunking process. Finally, relationship management systems maintain next/previous chunk references to enable sequential navigation, while related chunk identification preserves cross-references for content with similar context, ensuring that interconnected information remains accessible even when distributed across multiple chunks.

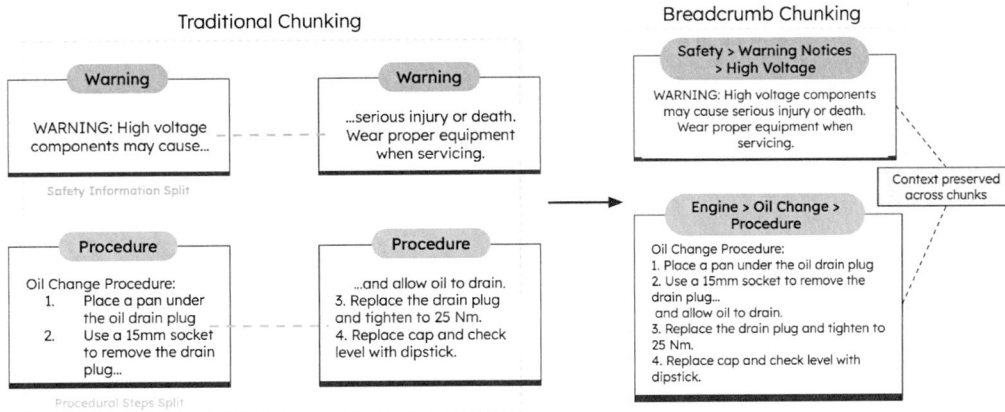

Figure 7.16: Chunking strategies: traditional versus breadcrumb chunking

This diagram compares traditional chunking methods (left side) that fragment warnings and procedures into isolated pieces, losing critical safety information, with breadcrumb chunking (right side) that maintains document structure and context. The *breadcrumb* method of chunking preserves context by maintaining hierarchical paths (e.g., **Engine > Oil Change > Procedure**) and keeping semantically related content together. This ensures that when a driver asks about a maintenance procedure, the assistant can access not only the specific steps but also relevant warnings, specifications, and related information.

Google Cloud and MongoDB: Better together

The solution leverages the complementary strengths of Google Cloud and MongoDB Atlas to deliver a robust, scalable platform for in-car voice assistants.

Google Cloud contributes the following:

- **AI leadership**: Cutting-edge tools for GenAI and machine learning optimized for voice applications
- **Integrated AI and cloud platform**: End-to-end integration for speech recognition, real-time processing, and cloud scalability

- **Scalable infrastructure:** Reliable cloud services ensuring smooth performance even with demanding data volumes
- **Developer tools:** Robust tools for the integration and scaling of AI features, accelerating development

MongoDB complements these capabilities with the following:

- **Document-oriented data model:** Flexible schema design that can handle complex requirements at any scale
- **Vector store at scale:** Superior capabilities for storing operational, metadata, and vector data together efficiently
- **Automotive industry presence:** Trusted by top auto manufacturers with experience in scaling and optimizing data solutions
- **Accelerated development:** The fully managed MongoDB Atlas platform streamlines development and reduces operational complexity

This partnership enables automotive manufacturers to rapidly deploy sophisticated in-cabin experiences that differentiate their vehicles while maintaining the reliability and performance expected in automotive applications.

Strategic advantages of AI-integrated in-cabin systems

Hyper-personalized in-cabin experiences represent more than just a technological upgrade; they provide strategic advantages for automotive manufacturers in an increasingly competitive market. By leveraging advanced AI capabilities, particularly GenAI for conversational interactions and agentic AI for proactive assistance, manufacturers can create distinctive user experiences that build brand loyalty and differentiation.

The integration of these technologies with flexible, scalable data platforms enables automotive companies to develop more intuitive and responsive interfaces that reduce cognitive load while driving, creates personalized experiences that adapt to individual driver preferences and habits, enhances safety by providing contextually relevant information when and how it's needed, and differentiates vehicles through unique AI-powered features in a competitive market.

As the automotive industry continues to evolve toward software-defined vehicles, these AI-powered in-cabin experience platforms will become increasingly essential competitive advantages, transforming how drivers and passengers interact with their vehicles and redefining expectations for the driving experience.

Learn more about this use case at the following links:

- GitHub repository with code examples and implementation details: `https://github.com/mongodb-industry-solutions/genai-in-car-voice-assistant`

- In-depth technical blog post: `https://www.mongodb.com/company/blog/innovation/how-mongodb-google-cloud-power-future-of-in-car-assistants`

Fleet management and optimization

Fleet operations represent a critical component of manufacturing and logistics enterprises, directly impacting operational efficiency, customer satisfaction, and profitability. As organizations navigate the complexities of global supply chains and increasing customer demands for speed and reliability, traditional fleet management approaches are giving way to AI-driven systems that can dynamically optimize routes, maintenance schedules, and resource allocation in real time. Fleet operation optimization through AI delivers significant efficiency gains and cost reductions. By leveraging advanced technologies, particularly agentic AI for autonomous decision-making, organizations can achieve unprecedented levels of fleet performance while reducing operational costs, enhancing driver safety, and improving customer service levels.

Scheduler agent for fleet operations

The integration of agentic AI into fleet management represents a paradigm shift in how logistics operations are orchestrated. Unlike traditional systems that rely on static rules and human intervention, agentic AI systems can autonomously process complex inputs, reason through multiple constraints, and make optimal decisions that balance competing priorities.

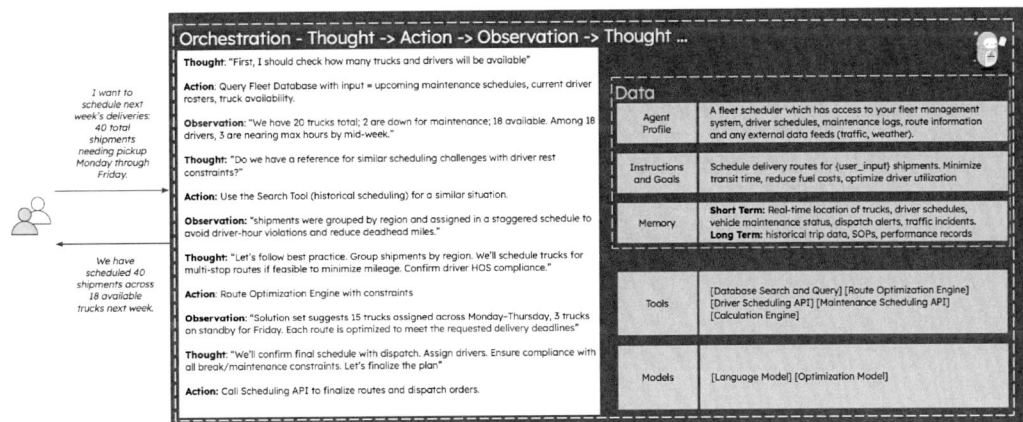

Figure 7.17: AI fleet scheduler agent: orchestration and decision-making process

This diagram shows how an AI scheduler agent for fleet operations follows a Thought → Action → Observation → Thought orchestration pattern to manage complex logistics decisions. The scheduler agent is driven by user requests and guided by both short-term context and long-term data stored in MongoDB Atlas. It orchestrates interactions with various services such as route planning, maintenance scheduling, and driver scheduling to produce a feasible delivery task schedule.

When a fleet manager inputs a request such as "I want to schedule next week's deliveries: 40 total shipments needing pickup Monday through Friday", the agent activates a sophisticated orchestration process. The system first checks available resources (trucks and drivers), identifies constraints (maintenance schedules, driver hours), searches historical data for similar scheduling challenges, and applies best practices such as regional grouping and staggered scheduling to avoid violations. The agent then uses route optimization engines with constraints, generates optimized delivery schedules, and finalizes routes through scheduling APIs. This entire process demonstrates the agent's ability to think through complex logistics problems, take informed actions based on multiple data sources, observe results, and iteratively refine its approach until reaching an optimal solution. This agentic approach integrates multiple tools, data sources, and objectives within a single coherent decision-making framework, enabling significantly more sophisticated scheduling than traditional methods.

Logical and physical architecture

Having demonstrated how the agentic AI system makes intelligent scheduling decisions, we'll now examine the technical architecture that enables this sophisticated orchestration. The implementation of the fleet scheduling agent follows a modular architecture that separates concerns while enabling seamless integration across components.

Figure 7.18 illustrates the logical flow of the fleet scheduling system, showing how a user request of "Schedule 40 shipments next week" flows through the orchestration and reasoning logic that interprets requests using the ReAct framework and LLM interactions. The system executes tasks via API calls to route optimization, driver scheduling, and maintenance APIs, while connecting to MongoDB Atlas through the MongoDB driver for database queries and vector search capabilities, ultimately returning results such as "We have scheduled 40 shipments across 18 available trucks next week" to the user interface.

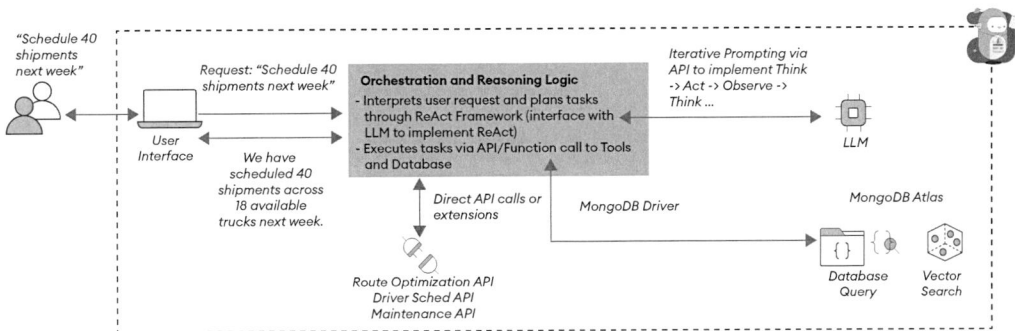

Figure 7.18: Logical architecture

At the logical level, the architecture consists of the following:

1. **User interface**: Provides an intuitive interface for fleet managers to input scheduling requests and view results.

2. **Orchestration and reasoning logic**: Interprets user requests and plans tasks using the ReAct framework, then executes those tasks via API or function calls to tools and database. ReAct enables AI to cycle through thinking, acting, and observing results.

3. **LLM**: Provides iterative prompting via API to implement the Think → Act → Observe → Think pattern.

4. **MongoDB driver**: Connects the orchestration service to MongoDB Atlas.

5. **Tools**: Including Database Query, Vector Search, and specialized APIs for Route Optimization, Driver Scheduling, and Maintenance Scheduling.

6. **MongoDB Atlas**: Provides database query and vector search capabilities.

The physical implementation builds on this logical architecture. *Figure 7.19* shows the physical implementation of the fleet scheduling system within a corporate cloud network. Users interact through an API gateway that connects to containerized microservices, including the fleet scheduling agent (with orchestration and reasoning logic), route optimization microservice, driver scheduling microservice, and maintenance scheduling microservice. The system connects via private links to both an LLM enterprise server and MongoDB Atlas hosted on a public cloud, which provides database query and vector search capabilities, ensuring secure and scalable fleet management operations.

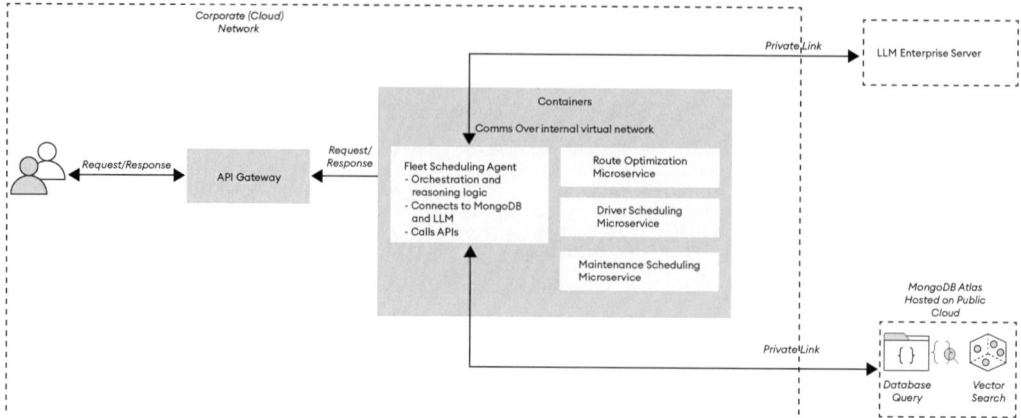

Figure 7.19: Physical architecture

This architecture provides a scalable, maintainable foundation for implementing advanced fleet management capabilities while ensuring that the sophisticated decision-making processes we've explored can be deployed reliably in enterprise environments.

MongoDB for fleet scheduler

Having established the technical architecture for our agentic fleet management system, we'll now turn to a critical foundation element: how the system stores and manages the complex data structures that enable intelligent decision-making. A critical aspect of the fleet management system is its data model, which must accommodate the diverse information types required for effective decision making. MongoDB's document model provides an ideal foundation for representing the complex, hierarchical data structures involved in fleet operations.

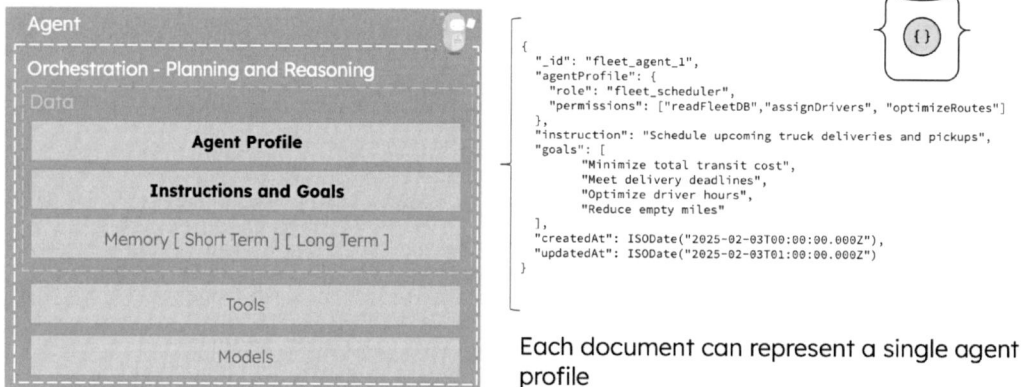

Figure 7.20: MongoDB for fleet scheduler

The agent-based fleet scheduling system operates through a modular architecture where each component serves a specific purpose in the decision-making process. *Figure 7.20* illustrates how MongoDB's document model supports this architecture by organizing agent data into distinct but interconnected components. The agent profile establishes the core identity and operational parameters, while instructions and goals provide the decision-making framework. The memory system distinguishes between short-term operational context and long-term historical knowledge, enabling the agent to learn from past experiences while maintaining awareness of current conditions. The tools component provides access to specialized capabilities such as database queries and vector search, while the models component manages the AI capabilities that power the agent's reasoning processes. This modular approach allows each component to be independently managed while maintaining seamless integration across the entire system.

Agent profile and instructions

The agent profile document defines the core identity and operating parameters of the fleet scheduler:

```
{
  "_id": "fleet_agent_1",
  "agentProfile": {
  "role": "fleet_scheduler",
  "permissions": ["readFleetDB","assignDrivers", "optimizeRoutes"]
  },
  "instruction": "Schedule upcoming truck deliveries and pickups",
  "goals": [
    "Minimize total transit cost",
    "Meet delivery deadlines",
    "Optimize driver hours",
    "Reduce empty miles"
  ],
  "createdAt": ISODate("2025-02-03T00:00:00.000Z"),
  "updatedAt": ISODate("2025-02-03T01:00:00.000Z")
}
```

This document encapsulates the agent's operational mandate, establishing clear parameters for its decision-making processes.

Short-term and long-term memory

The agent's memory architecture distinguishes between ephemeral operational data and persistent knowledge. *Figure 7.21* illustrates how AI agents manage short-term memory by storing discrete interactions or ephemeral state data in MongoDB documents. The agent architecture shows memory as a distinct component alongside agent profile, instructions and goals, tools, and models. Each short-term memory document captures specific operational data such as trip IDs, driver assignments, route status, and estimated arrival times, enabling the agent to maintain context about current fleet operations while distinguishing between temporary operational data and persistent knowledge.

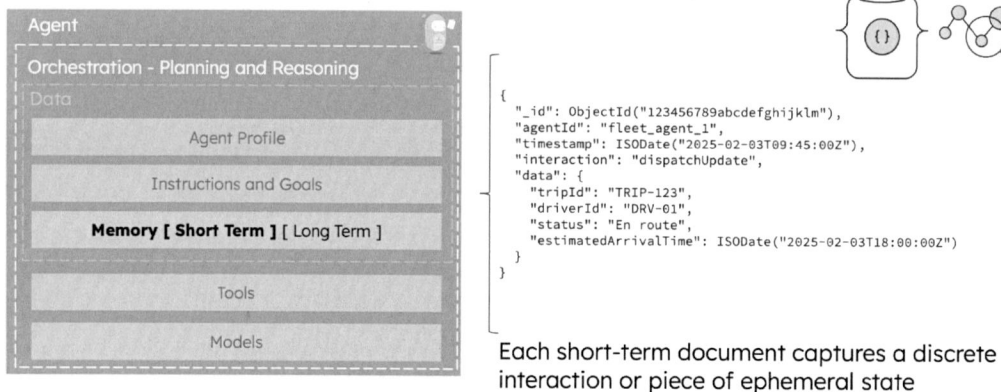

Figure 7.21: Short-term memory in agents

Short-term memory captures discrete interactions or pieces of ephemeral state:

```
{
  "_id": ObjectId("123456789abcdefghijklm"),
  "agentId": "fleet_agent_1",
  "timestamp": ISODate("2025-02-03T09:45:00Z"),
  "interaction": "dispatchUpdate",
  "data": {
    "tripId": "TRIP-123",
    "driverId": "DRV-01",
    "status": "En route",
    "estimatedArrivalTime": ISODate("2025-02-03T18:00:00Z")
  }
}
```

Long-term memory stores route planning information that can be queried by parameters such as date range. This diagram shows how AI agents store persistent route planning information in long-term memory that can be queried by parameters such as date range or route plan ID. The long-term memory document contains comprehensive fleet operation data, including route plan identifiers, date ranges, total shipments, and historical issues encountered (such as weather delays and driver hour requirements), enabling agents to learn from past experiences and make informed decisions based on historical fleet management patterns and outcomes.

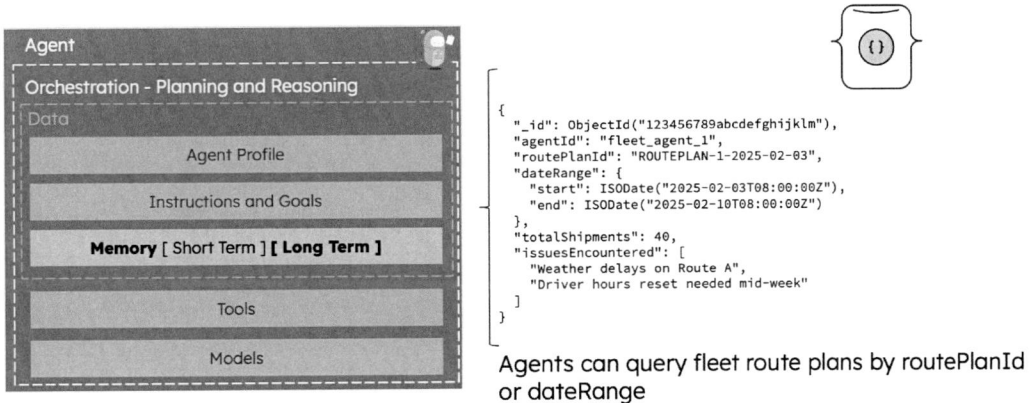

Figure 7.22: Long-term memory in agents

```
{
  "_id": ObjectId("123456789abcdefghijklm"),
  "agentId": "fleet_agent_1",
  "routePlanId": "ROUTEPLAN-1-2025-02-03",
  "dateRange": {
    "start": ISODate("2025-02-03T08:00:00Z"),
    "end": ISODate("2025-02-10T08:00:00Z")
  },
  "totalShipments": 40,
  "issuesEncountered": [
    "Weather delays on Route A",
    "Driver hours reset needed mid-week"
  ]
}
```

The agent leverages MongoDB's tools, including the database Query API, Vector Search, and full text search, to access this information efficiently. *Figure 7.23* illustrates how these agents leverage MongoDB's comprehensive toolkit for data access and reasoning. The agent architecture shows the **Tools** component as a key element alongside **Agent Profile**, **Instructions and Goals**, **Memory**, and **Models**. The three primary MongoDB tools available to agents are the database Query API for structured data retrieval, Vector Search for semantic similarity matching, and full text search for document-based queries, providing agents with multiple powerful methods to access and analyze information efficiently during decision-making processes.

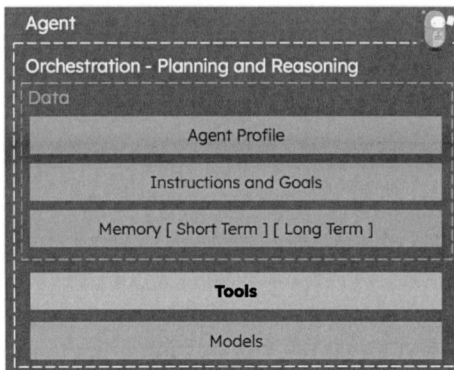

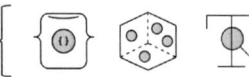

Database query API, Vector and Full Text Search are all powerful tools at the agent disposal

Figure 7.23: Powerful tools for agent reasoning

Connected fleet incident advisor

Building on the foundational agent architecture we've explored, we can extend these concepts to create specialized systems that address specific fleet management challenges. The connected fleet incident advisor represents a practical application of the agentic principles we've discussed, demonstrating how AI-powered systems can provide real-time diagnostic support and build organizational knowledge over time.

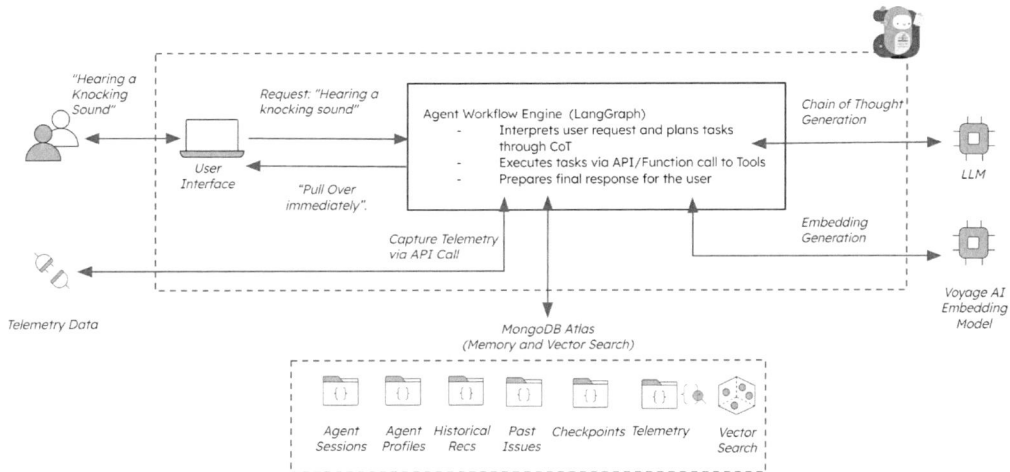

Figure 7.24: Connected fleet incident advisor

This diagram shows a comprehensive AI-powered connected fleet advisor system built using MongoDB Atlas, Voyage AI, OpenAI, and LangGraph. The system processes driver complaints or fleet manager queries, captures telemetry data via API calls, and uses an agent workflow engine (LangGraph) to interpret requests, plan tasks, execute functions, and prepare responses. The architecture integrates with MongoDB Atlas for memory and vector search capabilities, storing agent sessions, profiles, alerts, issues, checkpoints, and telemetry data, while utilizing LLMs and embedding generation to provide intelligent fleet incident management and diagnostic recommendations.

Incident advisor architecture

This system is built using MongoDB Atlas, Voyage AI, OpenAI, and LangGraph, creating an integrated workflow that processes driver complaints or fleet manager queries, analyzes vehicle telemetry data, generates a chain-of-thought reasoning process, and delivers diagnostic recommendations.

When a driver reports an issue such as "Hearing a knocking sound", the system does the following:

1. Receives the complaint through the user interface.
2. Processes the request through the agent workflow engine (LangGraph).
3. Generates a chain-of-thought reasoning process.
4. Captures telemetry data via an API call.
5. Performs vector search in MongoDB Atlas to identify similar past incidents.
6. Formulates a recommendation based on the analysis.

The physical architecture implements this workflow as follows:

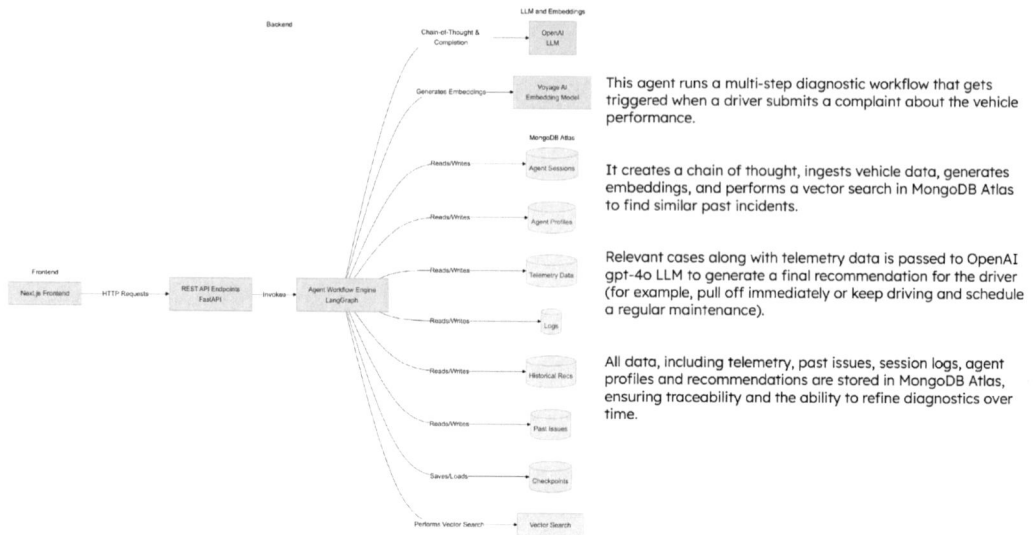

Figure 7.25: Fleet advisor physical architecture

This diagram shows the physical implementation of the connected fleet incident advisor workflow, illustrating how driver complaints trigger a multi-step diagnostic process.

The system's components are organized into the following:

1. **Frontend**: A Next.js-based interface for drivers and fleet managers

2. **Backend**: REST API endpoints with FastAPI and an agent workflow engine powered by LangGraph

3. **AI services**: OpenAI LLM for chain-of-thought reasoning and recommendations, and Voyage AI embedding model for generating vector representations

4. **Data store**: MongoDB Atlas for storing agent sessions, profiles, telemetry data, historical recommendations, issue logs, and vector search functionality

This architecture enables a detailed sequence of operations:

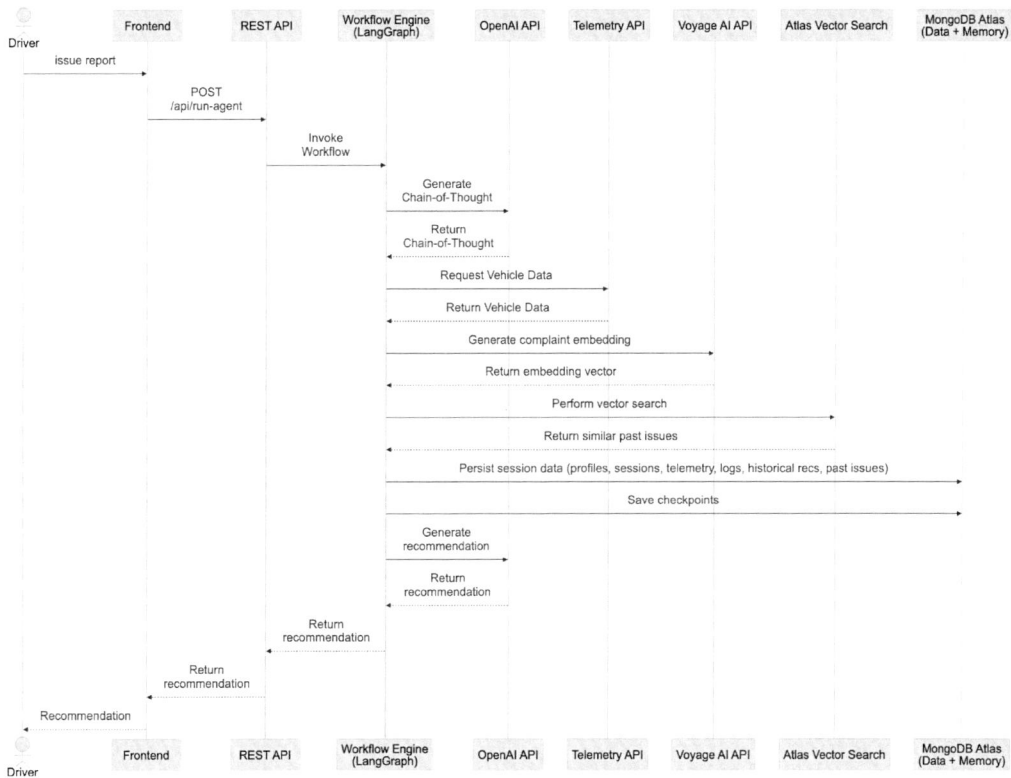

Figure 7.26: Fleet advisor sequence diagram

This sequence diagram shows the detailed operational flow of the connected fleet incident advisor system.

The sequence of operations flows from the driver reporting an issue through multiple processing stages:

1. Issue report submission through the frontend.
2. API processing and workflow invocation.
3. Chain-of-thought generation for diagnostic reasoning.
4. Vehicle data retrieval and analysis.
5. Embedding generation and vector search for similar past incidents.
6. Data persistence of session information.
7. Recommendation generation and delivery to the driver.

This approach provides not only immediate assistance to drivers but also builds a knowledge base of issues and solutions that improves over time.

Data types and storage

The incident advisor system manages multiple data types, each serving a specific purpose in the diagnostic workflow:

Data type	Description	Example in MongoDB

Agent profile	This contains the identity of the agent. It includes instructions, goals, and constraints.	`{`
		`    "_id": "67c20cf886f35bcb8c71e53c",`
		`    "agent_id": "default_agent",`
		`    "profile": "Default Agent Profile",`
		`    "instructions": "Follow diagnostic procedures meticulously.",`
		`    "rules": "Ensure safety; validate sensor data; document all steps.",`
		`    "goals": "Provide accurate diagnostics and actionable recommendations."`
		`}`

Short-term memory	This holds temporary, contextual information, such as recent data inputs or ongoing interactions, that the agent uses in real-time. For example, short-term memory could store sensor data from the last few hours of vehicle activity
	
	In certain agentic AI frameworks such as LangGraph, short term memory is implemented through a checkpointer. The checkpointer stores intermediate states of the agent's actions and/or reasoning. This memory allows the agent to seamlessly pause and resume operations.
		Telemetry data stored in time series collections
		
		`{`
		`    "_id": "67cb23ee370eb8f40c9bf677",`
		`    "timestamp": "2025-02-19T13:00:00",`
		`    "vin":"5TFUW5F13CX228552",`
		`    "engine_temperature": "90",`
		`    "oil_pressure": "35",`
		`    "avg_fuel_consumption": "8.5",`
		`    "thread_id": "thread_20250307_125027"`
		`}`

Long-term memory	This is where the agent stores accumulated knowledge over time. This may include patterns, trends, logs and historical recommendations, and decisions.	**Historical issues with connected vehicles vectorized and stored in MongoDB**
		
		`{`
		`    "_id": "67ca173679c7c286f44f4a24",`
		`    "issue": "Engine knocking when turning",`
		`    "recommendation": "Inspect spark plugs and engine oil.",`
		`    "embedding": [`
		`        -0.021414414048194885,`
		`        -0.0031116530299186707,`
		`        0.014275052584707737,`
		`        -0.030444633215665817,`
		`        0.018614845350384712,`
		`        0.06425976008176804,`
		`        0.0060801152139902115,`
		`        -0.012883528135716915,`
		`        -0.007000760640949011,`
		`        -0.04991862177848816,`
		`        ...`
		`    ]`
		`}`

Table 7.1: Data types and storage structure for fleet incident advisor

This table illustrates how the incident advisor system manages different data types in MongoDB, showing three key categories: **Agent Profile** (containing agent identity, instructions, goals, and constraints for diagnostic procedures), **Short-Term Memory** (storing temporary contextual information such as recent telemetry data in time series collections, including vehicle metrics such as engine temperature and fuel consumption), and **Long-Term Memory** (accumulating historical knowledge including patterns, trends, and vectorized historical issues with recommendations, such as engine knocking problems with embedded vector representations for similarity matching).

Agent Profile contains the identity of the agent, including instructions, goals, and constraints:

```
{
  "_id": "67c20cf886f35bcb8c71e53c",
  "agent_id": "default_agent",
  "profile": "Default Agent Profile",
  "instructions": "Follow diagnostic procedures meticulously.",
  "rules": "Ensure safety; validate sensor data; document all steps.",
  "goals": "Provide accurate diagnostics and actionable recommendations."
}
```

Short-Term Memory holds temporary, contextual information, such as telemetry data:

```
{
  "_id": "67cb23ee370eb8f40c9bf677",
  "timestamp": "2025-02-19T13:00:00",
  "vin":"5TFUW5F13CX228552",
  "engine_temperature": "90",
  "oil_pressure": "35",
  "avg_fuel_consumption": "8.5",
  "thread_id": "thread_20250307_125027"
}
```

Long-Term Memory stores accumulated knowledge of historical issues and recommendations:

```
json
{
  "_id": "67ca173679c7c286f44f4a24",
  "issue": "Engine knocking when turning",
  "recommendation": "Inspect spark plugs and engine oil.",
  "embedding": [
    -0.021414414048194885,
```

```
    -0.0031116530299186707,
    0.014275052584707737,
    // Additional vector dimensions...
  ]
}
```

This unified data approach allows all fleet management information to be modeled within a single database, providing the flexible foundation needed for intelligent, adaptive fleet operations.

Advantages of MongoDB for fleet management

Having explored the technical architecture and implementation details of agentic fleet management systems, it's important to understand why MongoDB Atlas serves as an ideal foundation for these sophisticated applications. The platform offers several key advantages that directly enable the advanced capabilities we've demonstrated throughout our fleet management examples.

MongoDB's document data model provides the flexibility essential for handling complex, hierarchical data structures such as vehicle telemetry, route plans, and driver schedules, while its vector search capabilities enable the semantic search functionality we've seen in incident diagnosis and route optimization. Time series collections efficiently store and process the temporal data that powers predictive analytics, and fine-grained security controls ensure appropriate data access across different stakeholders in the fleet ecosystem. For specialized applications such as the incident advisor, best-in-class embedding models with Voyage AI deliver high-quality vector representations for semantic matching and analysis.

These technical capabilities translate directly into strategic advantages for organizations implementing AI-integrated fleet systems. By leveraging advanced AI capabilities, particularly agentic AI for autonomous decision-making and GenAI for diagnostic analysis, organizations can achieve new levels of operational excellence while balancing costs, service levels, and sustainability goals. The integration enables organizations to optimize route planning and vehicle utilization, reduce fuel consumption and emissions, improve driver safety and compliance with regulations, enhance maintenance scheduling and vehicle uptime, deliver superior customer service through reliable delivery performance, and build organizational knowledge of operational patterns and incident resolution.

As manufacturing and logistics continue to evolve toward Industry 5.0, these AI-powered fleet management approaches will become increasingly essential for maintaining competitive advantage in global markets, demonstrating how sophisticated data platforms enable the transformation from traditional fleet management to intelligent, adaptive systems.

Learn more about this use case at the following links:

- Complete implementation guide for building agentic AI fleet management systems: `https://www.mongodb.com/solutions/solutions-library/fleet-agents`

- In-depth technical blog post on next-generation mobility solutions: `https://www.mongodb.com/blog/post/next-generation-mobility-solutions-agentic-ai-mongodb-atlas`

The expanding role of AI in manufacturing

The applications we've explored throughout this chapter represent just the beginning of AI's transformative impact on manufacturing operations. AI is revolutionizing manufacturing by creating intelligent, adaptive systems that optimize operations across the entire production ecosystem. From transforming supply chains with GenAI to enabling predictive maintenance through multi-agent collaboration, these technologies are delivering measurable improvements in efficiency, quality, and cost reduction. A few examples have shown how a modern and intelligent database such as MongoDB Atlas provides the flexible data platform needed to implement these AI solutions at scale, connecting data from production equipment, inventory systems, and even connected vehicles to create a comprehensive digital manufacturing environment.

The manufacturing industry is witnessing a surge in AI agent deployments that leverage capabilities such as deep reasoning, context management, and human-like decision-making to solve complex operational challenges:

- **Supply chain orchestration**: AI agents enable multi-step supplier coordination, from placing orders to tracking shipments and updating delivery timelines, resulting in reduced delays and enhanced efficiency in day-to-day operations.

- **Quality inspection reports**: AI agents compile, format, and file repetitive inspection data, flag anomalies, and even suggest corrective actions, thus freeing human operators from repetitive tasks while ensuring product standards are met with precision through computer vision technology. With historical data tracking, they also help identify recurring issues and guide continuous improvement initiatives.

- **Production re-optimization**: When disruptions occur (machine failure, labor shortage, or late supply of parts), AI agents dynamically re-plan schedules by analyzing time series data from sensors installed on production lines and contextual information from ERP and MES. They can simulate multiple re-routing scenarios, select the most efficient one, and implement changes autonomously. This leads to improved asset utilization, reduced idle time, and lower scrap rates, enabling just-in-time manufacturing even under volatile conditions.

- **Connected fleet incident manager:** In environments where products or materials are transported using autonomous or semi-autonomous fleets, AI agents manage the full lifecycle of incident response. They collect telemetry and diagnostic data from vehicles, cross-reference historical maintenance records, and trigger automated workflows for repair scheduling and part ordering. Additionally, they notify human operators and customers in real time, offering transparency and minimizing service disruptions.

- **Maintenance optimization:** Manufacturers can utilize AI-driven predictive analytics to offer proactive maintenance support and personalized assistance to the workforce, enhancing equipment uptime and operational efficiency within the production environment.

For more information and resources, visit the *MongoDB for Manufacturing and Mobility* page at `https://www.mongodb.com/solutions/industries/manufacturing`.

Summary

As we've seen in the previous chapter and this one, AI is revolutionizing manufacturing by creating intelligent, adaptive systems that optimize operations across the entire production ecosystem. From transforming supply chains with GenAI to enabling predictive maintenance through multi-agent collaboration, these technologies are delivering measurable improvements in efficiency, quality, and cost reduction. The examples we've explored demonstrate how modern and intelligent data platforms provide the flexible foundation needed to implement these AI solutions at scale, connecting data from production equipment, inventory systems, and even connected vehicles to create a comprehensive digital manufacturing environment.

The manufacturing industry is witnessing a surge in AI agent deployments that leverage capabilities such as deep reasoning, context management, and human-like decision-making to solve complex operational challenges. Supply chain orchestration through AI agents enables multi-step supplier coordination, while quality inspection systems automatically compile and format inspection data, flag anomalies, and suggest corrective actions. Production re-optimization agents dynamically re-plan schedules when disruptions occur, and connected fleet incident managers handle the full lifecycle of incident response for autonomous fleets. Additionally, we explored how knowledge management systems preserve institutional expertise through AI-powered assistance, and how hyper-personalized in-cabin experiences are transforming automotive interactions through sophisticated voice assistants and RAG implementations for vehicle manuals.

These applications demonstrate how manufacturers can utilize AI-driven predictive analytics to offer proactive maintenance support and personalized assistance to the workforce, enhancing equipment uptime and operational efficiency within the production environment. The integration of agentic AI with flexible data platforms enables organizations to achieve unprecedented levels of operational excellence while reducing costs and improving safety. In the next chapter, we will continue to explore how AI is transforming the telecommunications and media industries.

References

1. *Predictive Maintenance; Deloite's approach*: https://www.deloitte.com/content/dam/assets-zone3/us/en/docs/services/consulting/2024/us-predictive-maintenance.pdf

2. *Research Finds 79% Of Drivers Across Europe Would Use Voice Generative AI Capabilities In Their Vehicles*: https://www.soundhound.com/newsroom/press-releases/research-finds-79-of-drivers-across-europe-would-use-voice-generative-ai-capabilities-in-their-vehicles/

8
AI-Driven Strategies for Media and Telecommunication Industries

In a world drowning in content but starving for relevance, the telecommunication and media industries face a paradoxical challenge. While global telecom spending continues to rise into the trillions, media leaders report alarming declines in social referral traffic, with platform-driven visits plummeting dramatically. Meanwhile, AI adoption is accelerating at a breakneck pace, with the AI market in telecommunications projected to grow at an astonishing rate, transforming how these industries operate at their core.

This isn't just another technology cycle; it's a fundamental reinvention of how we connect, consume, and communicate. For telecom operators and media companies, the stakes couldn't be higher: those who master AI-driven personalization are seeing billion-dollar returns (Netflix generates $1 billion annually from AI recommendations alone) [1], while those clinging to traditional models watch their audiences and revenues evaporate.

In this chapter, you will learn about:

- The architecture of content personalization systems that use behavior analytics and vector search to deliver tailored recommendations and increase conversion rates
- The transformation of information retrieval into conversational, context-aware interactions through **search generative experiences** (**SGE**) to reduce bounce rates and boost engagement
- Agentic AI Ops frameworks that automate telecom workflows, enable predictive maintenance, and potentially boost revenue

- AI-powered fraud detection systems that process millions of events in real time, reducing losses through pattern recognition and risk profiling
- Automation strategies that streamline content workflows through AI-driven processes, adaptive formatting, and conversational interfaces to cut manual work and improve engagement

Evolving landscape of media and telecommunication

In recent years, the media industry has faced serious challenges, from adapting to digital platforms and on-demand consumption to monetizing digital content and competing with tech giants and new media upstarts. Adding to these challenges is the rise in digital content, which has saturated the media market and made it more difficult to capture and retain audience attention.

As a result, media organizations are continually being pushed to reevaluate their strategies and explore new pathways to success. A global industry survey of over 326 digital leaders [2] highlighted several trends they must address in the coming years, including the following:

- **Declining referral traffic**: Around three-quarters (74%) of survey respondents are concerned about a potential decline in referral traffic from search engines as AI overviews are implemented. Aggregate Facebook traffic to news and media properties has fallen by two-thirds (67%) in the last two years, while traffic from X (formerly Twitter) is down by half (50%). The platform owners' intent is clear: to retain user traffic within their own ecosystems.
- **Prioritizing platform strategies**: Publishers are focusing on platforms like ChatGPT and Perplexity while maintaining interest in video networks such as YouTube, TikTok, and Instagram.
- **Focusing on innovation**: There is a strong emphasis on developing new products to engage audiences, with around four in ten (42%) planning offerings aimed at young people, and between a quarter and a third exploring audio (26%) or video (30%) products and services.

AI supports media organizations to overcome these changes by improving content research, production, and distribution. For instance, AI can summarize key points from multiple articles, making research more efficient. You can also leverage LLMs to draft new content based on specified themes, streamlining production. Additionally, AI enables content customization for diverse audiences, such as tailoring materials for young readers or foreign language speakers. It also enhances user experiences by personalizing content recommendations and interactions, a capability famously demonstrated by Netflix.

In particular, AI-powered tools such as SGE and AI-driven chatbots are expected to provide faster, more intuitive access to information, significantly reshaping how users interact with content. SGE refers to the integration of GenAI into search engines, enabling them to produce conversational, synthesized responses to user queries instead of simply displaying a list of links. This approach can reduce the need to click through to external websites, potentially altering traditional traffic patterns. As a result, these innovations are not only shifting audience behavior and financial dynamics across the industry but also presenting publishers with new opportunities to diversify their revenue streams.

Let's now shift focus to the challenges and opportunities in the telecommunication industry, which operates in a landscape of tight profit margins and growing pressure on connectivity services. As digital transformation accelerates, telecom operators must continuously redefine their business models and service offerings, with AI emerging as a transformative force reshaping the entire industry.

With offerings such as voice, data, and internet access being largely homogeneous and low-margin, telecom companies need to differentiate and diversify their revenue streams to create value and stand out in the market. The industry continues to experience significant growth globally, with investments reaching into the trillions of dollars as operators expand infrastructure and develop new service capabilities.

As digital natives disrupt traditional business models with agile and innovative approaches, established companies are competing not only among themselves but also with newcomers to deliver enhanced customer experiences and adapt to evolving consumer demands. For instance, Starlink's satellite internet service bypasses traditional broadband infrastructure entirely, offers competitive pricing that undercuts traditional satellite providers while delivering superior performance, and is rapidly growing by serving rural and remote areas that traditional telecom companies have largely ignored due to high infrastructure deployment costs [3].

To thrive in an environment where advanced connectivity is increasingly expected, telecom operators must prioritize cost efficiency in their **operations support systems (OSS)** and **business support systems (BSS)**. OSS refers to systems used to manage network infrastructure, such as service provisioning and fault management, while BSS handles customer-facing activities like billing, order management, and customer relationship management. By optimizing these systems, operators can elevate customer service standards and enhance overall customer experiences— critical steps to securing market share and gaining a competitive edge.

To implement these changes, AI helps telecom operators adopt innovative solutions to navigate the digital landscape. According to **Neuralt**, *"AI is not just an add-on technology but a driving force that is reshaping how telecom companies operate, provide services, and improve customer experiences"* [4]. For example, it provides automated processes for network operations, optimization mechanisms for network management, and prompt detection of suspicious data usage patterns for revenue protection and fraud prevention.

Capgemini's research highlights that *"Agentic AI is emerging as the next frontier in telco innovation, enabling systems that can make decisions and solve complex problems with minimal human oversight. This new level of autonomy is helping companies to dramatically increase operational efficiency and realize the promise of self-optimizing networks"* [5].

Altogether, leading companies in the media and telecommunication industry are using AI to optimize their operations, safeguard their businesses, and drive innovation.

Content discovery and personalization

Media organizations, from streaming services to online publications, are expected to offer a degree of content personalization. Viewers seek personalized content recommendations based on their interests.

Leveraging AI can significantly improve suggestions for the next best article to read or show to stream. The most powerful content personalization systems track user behavior in real time, such as the content searched, the time spent before the next click happened, and the categories explored by the user. These parameters allow personalization systems to increase engagement by presenting related content, or, as an alternative, display new content that helps users discover different media types and check their interest in consuming them.

To bring the right content to the right people at the right time, a content personalization system needs to maintain multiple information facets, which lay the foundation for proper suggestions. With modern document databases such as MongoDB and its flexible data model, all this information can be easily managed.

Additionally, developing with a JSON-based content layer is much faster, more intuitive, and less error-prone compared to handling relational tables. Moreover, this approach combines vectorized content with operational data. Vector search capabilities allow for creating advanced content suggestion systems that power semantic searches, going beyond basic keyword or attribute matching.

Content suggestions and personalization platform

By drawing on user data, behavior analytics, and the multi-dimensional vectorization of media content, modern data platforms improve end user experiences. Media organizations can now suggest content that aligns closely with individual preferences and past interactions.

Advanced data platforms enhance a content personalization strategy by incorporating advanced user experience features, as illustrated in *Figure 8.1*. These features include personalized recommendations, content summarization, keyword extraction, and automatic insight generation, making the system more dynamic and user-focused:

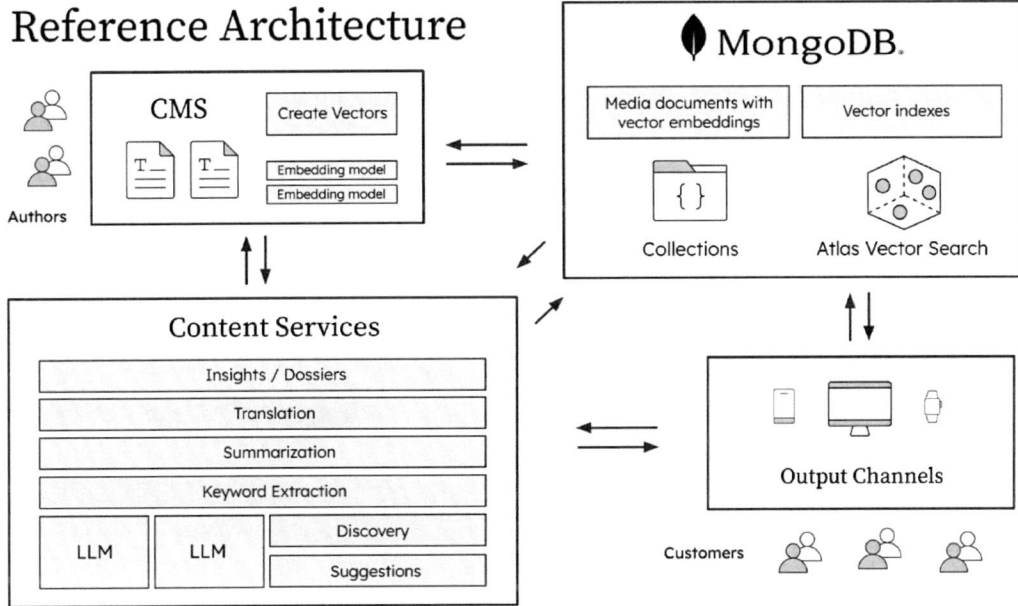

Figure 8.1: Reference architecture for creating personalized user experiences in MongoDB with Atlas Vector Search

This diagram illustrates a comprehensive content personalization platform where authors create content through a CMS that uses Voyage AI to generate vector embeddings and stores media documents in MongoDB with Atlas Vector Search capabilities. The system includes content services powered by LLMs for insights, translation, summarization, keyword extraction, discovery, and suggestions. All components integrate through MongoDB collections and vector indexes to deliver hyper-personalized content recommendations across multiple output channels (mobile, web, and tablet) to customers, creating dynamic experiences through the advanced capabilities of the MongoDB data platform.

Content suggestions and personalization

Media platforms can suggest content aligned with individual preferences and past interactions by referencing user data, behavior analytics, and vectorization of media items. This mechanism enhances user engagement and increases the likelihood of converting free users into paying subscribers. For this solution, vectors are sometimes embedded directly in documents.

Furthermore, built-in scalability and resilience are advantageous when handling vector search operations. Organizations can scale their MongoDB database vertically or horizontally, and even choose to scale search nodes independently from operational database nodes, adapting to specific load scenarios in a cost-efficient way.

Content summarization and reformatting

Beyond suggesting which content to show users, media platforms can also adapt how that content is presented using the same user data and behavioral insights. For example:

- **Device-specific formatting**: A recommended article might be automatically reformatted as bullet points for mobile users, while desktop users see the full text.
- **Personalized summaries**: Users who typically read quickly receive condensed versions, while others get detailed explanations.
- **Format adaptation**: Based on consumption patterns, the same recommended content could be delivered as text for some users, audio for others, or video summaries.
- **Channel optimization**: When sharing content across different platforms, the system automatically creates shortened versions with key highlights for social media while providing comprehensive coverage through other channels.

This approach leverages the same user preference data and behavioral analytics used for content recommendations to determine the optimal format and length for each individual, further improving engagement by matching both what people want to read and how they prefer to consume it.

Keyword and entity extraction

Media platforms can draw essential information from content through advanced keyword and entity extraction, enabling users to find new content they like quickly and with minimum fuss. Keywords are fundamental to how content is indexed and found in search engines, and they significantly influence the **search engine optimization (SEO)** performance of digital content. With the help of the underlying LLM, media platforms can automatically extract a greater range of keywords with high sophistication, further improving the quality of the metadata used for search.

Automatic creation of insights and summaries

Media platforms such as online news or sports services can automatically generate comprehensive insights and summaries by analyzing multiple pieces of related content within their own archives or from external sources. For example, a news platform can create summaries that synthesize information from several related news stories about the same event, while sports platforms can generate comprehensive overviews by combining match reports, player statistics, and expert commentary.

This feature is particularly valuable for users interested in deep dives into specific topics or events, as it can surface related content that might otherwise have been hard to find, or generate a daily news summary, saving time by providing all the content they want in a digestible form. This is achieved using one or more LLMs to generate natural language output, enhancing the accessibility of information from multiple source materials.

Altogether, AI-powered personalization stands out as an important tool for publishers. By using AI to deliver tailored content and automate back-end processes, publishers can better address the decline in traditional referrals and build stronger, more direct relationships with their audiences.

Search generative experiences (SGEs)

With the rise of AI capturing the public's attention, it is clear that a basic search box returning a list of plain links is no longer enough for users. SGEs represent a transformative shift in how media and content industries approach interactions with user information requests (search). SGEs utilize AI to generate search results that are not just links to existing content, but comprehensive, natural language responses tailored to actual user intent. These immediate and concise answers help media platforms keep users engaged longer, reduce bounce rates, and increase the likelihood of deeper content interaction.

Using modern data platforms with built-in vector search capabilities at the core of an SGE solution (see *Figure 8.2*), organizations can develop robust **retrieval-augmented generation** (**RAG**) systems. These systems enhance LLMs by providing extra information that serves as context for the prompt, generating more accurate, relevant, and interesting responses.

The versatility of SGE systems opens up a wide range of use cases, including intelligent research tools, smart conversational interfaces, and gamified learning experiences. Tailoring these solutions to industry needs unlocks new opportunities for innovation, monetization, and engagement.

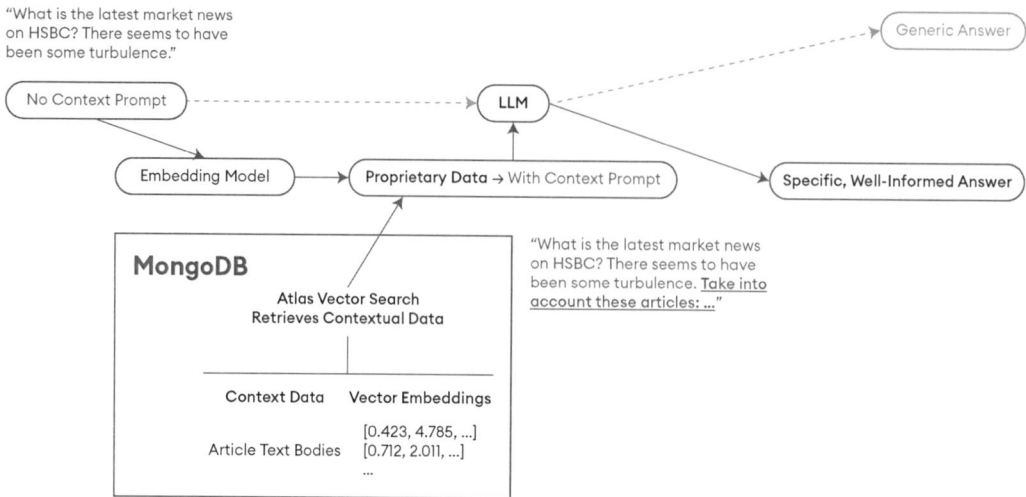

Figure 8.2: Reference architecture for creating an SGE

This diagram illustrates how an SGE transforms traditional search by using AI to generate comprehensive, natural language responses rather than just a list of links. The architecture shows how a user query about HSBC market news flows through an embedding model, such as Voyage AI, to MongoDB's Atlas Vector Search, which retrieves contextual data from article text bodies and vector embeddings. This proprietary data enhances the LLM prompt, enabling it to generate specific, well-informed answers instead of generic responses and demonstrating the shift from simple information retrieval to intelligent, context-aware content generation.

Smart conversational interfaces

If talking to your toaster or fridge about your breakfast plans still sounds like science fiction, welcome to the future. Smart conversational interfaces enable seamless data access in everyday life through devices such as smartwatches, wearables, and cars. This new opportunity for interaction creates novel ways to engage users through intuitive experiences that feel natural and comfortable.

According to Bernard Marr, a world-renowned futurist, influencer, and thought leader in business and technology, *"2025 will bring further widespread adoption of generative AI across the telecom industry, and without a doubt, one of the most prominent use cases will be customer experience transformation"* [6]. This includes hyper-personalized services and AI chatbots taking on increasingly sophisticated customer interactions.

Gamified learning experiences

Educational technology platforms are leveraging AI to create more engaging learning experiences, similar to popular apps like Duolingo. These systems use AI algorithms to continuously monitor student performance and adapt content difficulty in real time, creating personalized learning paths that offer:

- **Adaptive content delivery**: Adjust difficulty and provide personalized explanations when users make mistakes, helping them understand concepts better

- **Intelligent feedback systems**: Provide contextual hints and explanations powered by AI when users struggle with specific topics

- **Progress optimization**: Use behavioral data to identify optimal study schedules and content types for individual learners

For media companies, this represents a significant opportunity to expand into the growing educational content market, with digital storytelling and interactive learning experiencing substantial growth.

Service assurance

Moving from media applications back to telecommunications infrastructure, providers need to deliver high quality network services with performance levels that meet customer expectations and **service-level agreements (SLAs)**. Key aspects of service assurance include performance monitoring, **quality-of-service (QoS)** management, and predictive analytics to anticipate potential service degradation or network failures. With the increasing complexity of telecommunications networks and the growing expectations of customers for always-on services, a new bar has been set for service assurance, which is requiring companies to invest heavily in solutions that can automate these processes just to try and maintain a competitive edge.

Service assurance has been revolutionized by AI through several key capabilities:

- **Predictive maintenance**: Machine learning analyzes patterns to predict network failures, enabling preemptive maintenance and reducing downtime

- **Root cause analysis**: AI identifies the underlying causes of network issues, improving troubleshooting effectiveness

- **Network optimization**: AI evaluates log data to find improvement opportunities, reducing operational costs and optimizing performance in real time

Together, these capabilities demonstrate how AI is transforming network reliability and operational efficiency.

Agentic AIOps for network management

Building on the AI-powered insights from service assurance systems, Agentic AI Ops takes automation a step further by enabling autonomous decision-making and actions. While traditional AI systems provide recommendations, agentic AI can independently execute solutions without waiting for human approval.

Agentic AI Ops frameworks help **communication service providers (CSPs)** deploy AI-powered systems that can autonomously:

- **Execute corrective actions**: Automatically reconfigure routers for load management during network congestion
- **Make real-time decisions**: Determine and deploy appropriate responses to network issues as they occur
- **Call APIs directly**: Interface with network infrastructure to implement changes immediately
- **Manage workflows**: Coordinate complex operational processes with minimal human intervention

For example, when these systems detect network latency issues, they don't just alert operators, they can automatically redistribute traffic loads, adjust routing protocols, or scale resources in real time to maintain optimal performance.

These autonomous capabilities enable CSPs to manage complex workflows with minimal human intervention, accelerating the deployment of new services and potentially boosting annual revenue by up to 5% [7].

Building AI-powered network systems for telecommunications

With modern data platforms, telecommunication providers can build customized network management applications that integrate semantic search with generative text responses, as outlined in the following diagram.

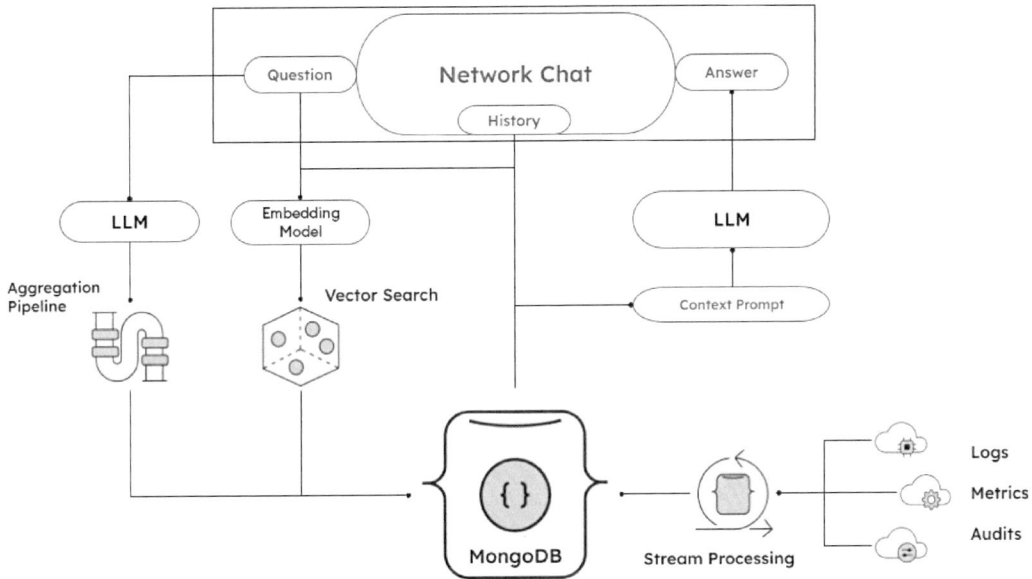

Figure 8.3: Reference architecture to create a network chatbot with MongoDB

This diagram shows how telecommunications providers can build AI-powered network chatbots using MongoDB as the core data platform. The architecture integrates three main components: data ingestion through aggregation pipelines and vector search capabilities; question analysis, where user queries are converted to embeddings to find relevant network data and generate appropriate database queries using embedding models and LLMs for context prompts; and natural language output generation. The system processes network chat interactions (questions, answers, history), while MongoDB handles data storage and stream processing, with outputs including logs, metrics, and audits for comprehensive network system management and customer support.

First, network managers capture log entries and telemetry events, storing details such as IP addresses, geographic information, request paths, timestamps, router logs, and sensor data. Using Atlas Stream Processing, data can be collected and enriched in real time, providing a complete view of network activity.

RAG Architecture

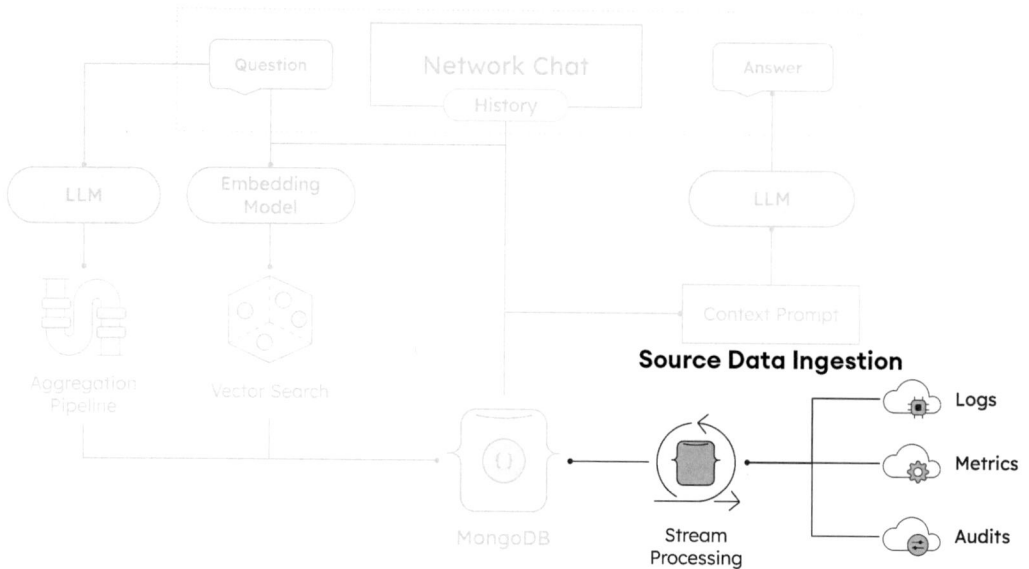

Figure 8.4: Data ingestion with Atlas Stream Processing

This diagram illustrates the RAG architecture for network chatbots, showing how source data can be ingested and enriched using Atlas Stream Processing.

RAG Architecture

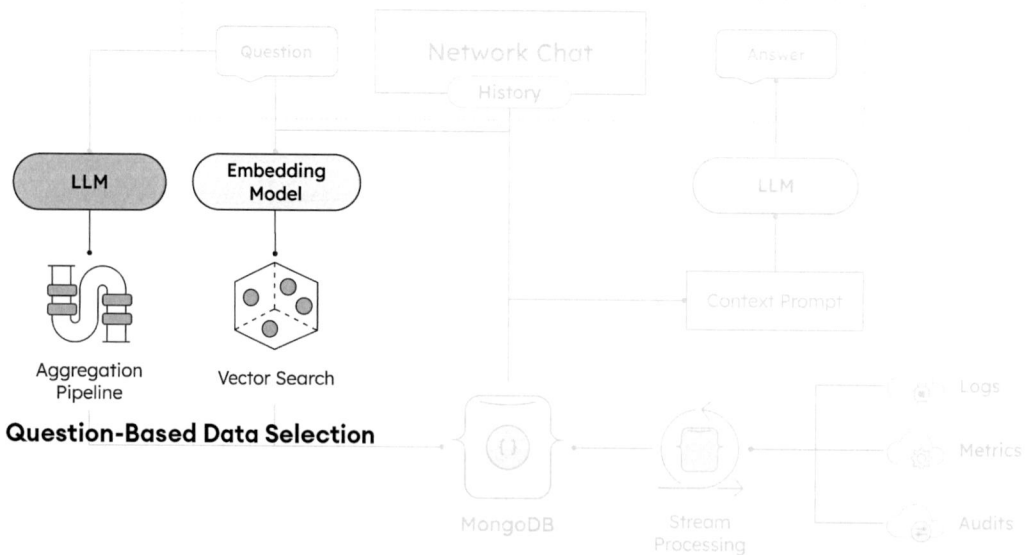

Figure 8.5: Question-based data selection with the MongoDB aggregation pipeline and Atlas Vector Search

This diagram demonstrates how the RAG system processes natural language queries from network managers, for example, "What's causing the client's video streaming issue in Toronto?".

The LLM first creates aggregation pipelines for structured data retrieval, while an embedding model performs semantic vector search to find contextually relevant information.

Once the system identifies the relevant data, a subsequent LLM translates this information into a natural language explanation for the user. During this process, the LLM analyzes the retrieved data to detect patterns and anomalies, enabling precise identification of root cause candidates and supporting informed decision-making. For example, it might uncover that an overloaded local CDN node, along with high requests from older routers, is causing the problem.

RAG Architecture

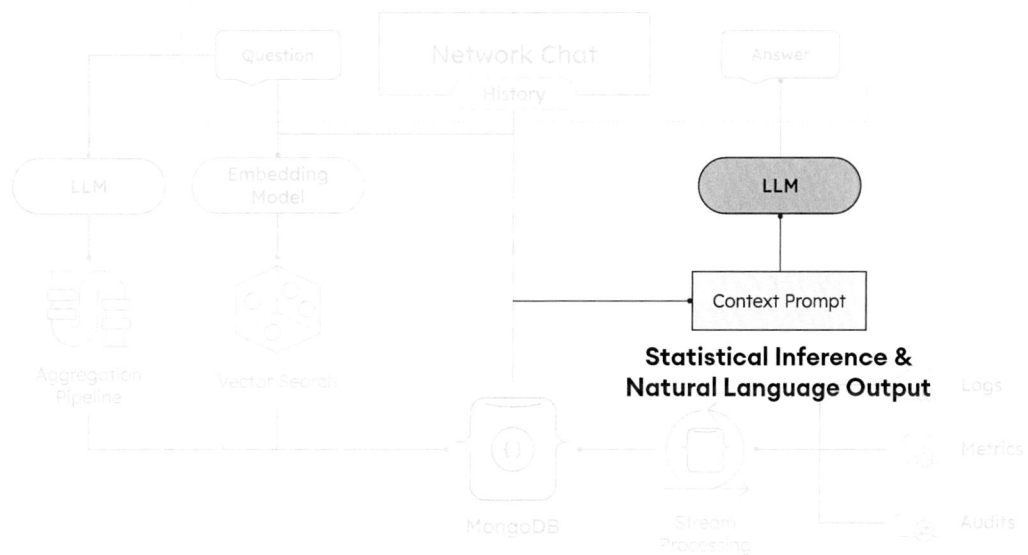

Figure 8.6: Inference and natural language output

This diagram shows the final stage of the RAG architecture. Through context prompting, the LLM performs statistical inference and pattern detection on the selected data, translating network metrics into natural language explanations and actionable insights.

The next era of AI-powered operations

This use case highlights how agentic AIOps and modern data platforms complement each other to transform network management through the following:

- **Schema flexibility**: Document-based models effortlessly store logs, performance metrics, and user feedback in a single, consistent environment

- **Real-time performance**: With horizontal scaling, you can ingest the massive volumes of data generated by network logs and user requests at any hour of the day

- **Vector search integration**: By embedding textual data (such as logs, user complaints, or FAQs) and storing those vectors in the database, you enable instant retrieval of semantically relevant content, making it easy for an LLM to find what it needs

- **LLMs building aggregation pipelines**: LLMs can generate aggregation pipelines to examine numeric data with ease, while a second pass to the LLM composes a final summary that merges both numeric and textual analysis

Adopting this end-to-end workflow saves time and effort while enabling scalability across your organization. It streamlines tasks such as analyzing traffic spikes in specific regions, diagnosing security incidents, and managing peak periods. By combining modern data platforms such as MongoDB Atlas, LLMs, and RAG architecture, telecommunication providers can transform network operations into conversational, automated, and intelligent systems.

Fraud detection and prevention

Telecom providers today are utilizing an array of techniques for detecting and preventing fraud, constantly adjusting to the dynamic nature of fraud in this space. Routine activities for detecting fraud include tracking unusual call trends and data usage, along with safeguarding against SIM swap incidents, a method frequently used for identity theft. To prevent fraud, strategies are applied at various levels, starting with stringent verification for new customers, during SIM swaps, or for significant transactions, taking into account each customer's risk profile. These measures are vital to mitigate fraud's harmful effects, such as financial losses, reputational damage, regulatory fines, and security risks that threaten network integrity.

Machine learning offers telecommunication companies a powerful tool to enhance their fraud detection capabilities by training models on data, such as **call detail records** (**CDRs**). Moreover, these algorithms can assess the individual risk profile of each customer, tailoring detection strategies to their specific patterns of use, as outlined in *Figure 8.7*.

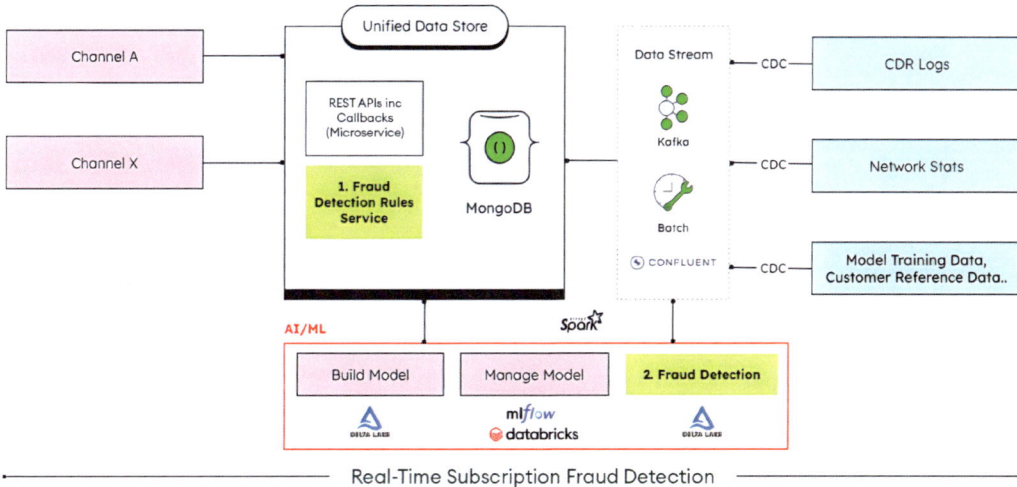

Figure 8.7: Machine learning-driven fraud detection system

This architectural diagram illustrates a comprehensive fraud detection system that processes data from multiple telecommunications channels (**Channel A** and **Channel X**) through a unified data store such as MongoDB Atlas.

Machine learning models can adapt over time, learning from new data and emerging fraud tactics, enabling real-time detection and the automation of fraud prevention measures, which speeds up response times.

To deal with fraud successfully, a multitude of data dimensions need to be considered. With reaction time being a critical factor in preventing the worst outcomes, the solution must support fast decisions. By vectorizing the data with an appropriate ML model, normal (healthy) business can be defined, and deviations from the norm identified. In addition to vector search, MongoDB's query APIs support stream processing, allowing for enrichment and filtering of data in real time.

Real-time fraud detection at scale with MongoDB

One of the customers utilizing MongoDB for its anti-fraud strategy is a leading U.S. telecommunication provider. The company selected MongoDB for its ability to ingest and store rapidly changing data. MongoDB Atlas also exceeds the provider's key requirements for performance, availability, and security. The fraud prevention platform now operates over 50 different AI models, utilizes more than 1,200 features, stores 30 TB of data, and processes up to 20 million events daily. Events are processed in under 200 milliseconds, enabling real-time fraud detection and prevention. As a result, fraud, particularly iPhone-related fraud, which was previously a $1 billion problem, has been reduced by over 80%.

This example has been anonymized for editorial clarity. To learn more, see: `https://www.youtube.com/watch?v=gRw5xYAsz4U`.

The expanding role of AI in media and telecommunication

AI is reshaping the media and telecommunication industries by enabling smarter, faster, and more personalized content, while enabling operational agility and innovation. From AI-augmented content discovery to network automation, the integration of intelligent systems has become a critical business requirement. However, AI's transformative potential in these industries extends far beyond these core domains.

AI is also driving innovation through differential pricing strategies, backend automation, and legacy modernization efforts. These use cases further exemplify how AI is enhancing operational efficiency and transforming processes for telecom and media providers. By leveraging emerging technologies that prioritize autonomous decision-making and continuous optimization, businesses are able to adapt to an ever-changing marketplace.

Differential pricing

For media and telecommunication organizations, AI-powered applications can gather insights into what customers are willing to spend on content or a service by conducting A/B tests and analyzing the data with an ML algorithm.

With this information, organizations can adopt dynamic pricing models instead of sticking to a standard price list, thereby increasing the overall revenue and expanding the paying customer base.

Video search and clipping

With the new embedding models of **Voyage AI** [8], which became part of MongoDB in 2025, it is possible to create multimodal embeddings to deliver fundamentally new search experiences for videos. You can use natural language to describe which video sequence you want to watch (for example, "Show me Mario Götze shooting the winning goal at the FIFA world cup final in 2014") and the system will be able to find the right video, including the offset within the video where the requested action takes place, providing a clip back to the user.

How a global telecom leader accelerated developer velocity

A leading telecommunication provider revolutionized its software development by adopting a **telco-as-a-service (TaaS)** model with MongoDB Atlas. This strategic move to serverless computing accelerated secure app delivery, reduced costs, and empowered developers to deploy code faster, enhancing both innovation and customer experience.

This example has been anonymized for editorial clarity. To learn more, see: `https://mdb.link/new-developer-speed-and-dexterity`.

For more information and resources, visit the *MongoDB for Media and Entertainment* page at `https://www.mongodb.com/solutions/industries/media-and-entertainment` and *MongoDB for Telecommunications* page at `https://www.mongodb.com/solutions/industries/telecommunications`.

Summary

In this chapter, we've explored how AI is revolutionizing the media and telecommunication industries through personalized content experiences, SGE, enhanced network management, and fraud prevention. These AI-driven strategies are improving operational efficiency while fundamentally transforming how these industries engage with customers and deliver services.

Modern data platforms such as MongoDB provide the flexible, scalable foundation needed to support these AI initiatives, enabling organizations to store diverse data types, perform vector searches, and integrate with LLMs for natural language processing. The combination of AI capabilities with data infrastructure is helping media and telecommunication companies overcome some of the biggest industry challenges, from declining referral traffic to ever tightening profit margins, while creating amazing new opportunities for innovation.

The next chapter will explore how AI is transforming the retail industry. We'll delve into how retailers are leveraging AI for personalized shopping experiences, inventory optimization, demand forecasting, and seamless omnichannel integration to meet evolving consumer expectations in an increasingly competitive marketplace.

References

1. *50 NEW Artificial Intelligence Statistics*: `https://explodingtopics.com/blog/ai-statistics`

2. *Journalism, media, and technology trends and predictions 2025*: `https://reutersinstitute.politics.ox.ac.uk/journalism-media-and-technology-trends-and-predictions-2025`

3. *Starlink and the Disruption of the $2.18 Trillion Telecom Industry: A Strategic Bet for the Future of Connectivity:* `https://www.ainvest.com/news/starlink-disruption-2-18-trillion-telecom-industry-strategic-bet-future-connectivity-2508/`

4. *Telecom Consumer Shift: A New Era of Expectations*: `https://www.neuralt.com/news-insights/ai-next-frontier-in-telecom-what-to-expect-in-2025`

5. *What's next for telecoms: 7 key trends and takeaways from MWC 2025*: `https://www.capgemini.com/in-en/insights/expert-perspectives/whats-next-for-telecoms-7-key-trends-and-takeaways-from-mwc-2025/`

6. *9 Critical Telecom Trends In 2025: What Industry Leaders Need to Know*: `https://bernardmarr.com/9-critical-telecom-trends-in-2025-what-industry-leaders-need-to-know/`

7. *Nokia: Achieving next-level network autonomy (research report)*: `https://onestore.nokia.com/asset/214230?_gl=1*qmnhb0*_ga*MTU4NTI3MTAxMy4xNzM5ODI4OTY3*_ga_D6GE5QF247*MTczOTgyODk2Ni4xLjAuMTczOTgyODk2OS4wLjAuMA`

8. Voyage AI: `https://www.voyageai.com`

9

Cognigy's Voice and Chatbots in the Time of Agentic AI

While the previous chapter explored how AI-driven strategies are revolutionizing content discovery and operational efficiency across media and telecommunications industries, a key implementation of these AI capabilities lies in direct customer communication, where intelligent agents are transforming every interaction into an opportunity for personalized, contextual engagement.

The landscape of customer communication has undergone a fundamental transformation. We're moving from rigid, script-driven interactions of traditional call centers to dynamic, intelligent conversations enabled by modern AI agents. Yet behind every AI success story lies a critical truth: we still witness embarrassing chatbot blunders, frustrating hallucinations, and infamous incidents such as the bot that sold a truck for a dollar. These failures expose a hard reality: AI alone cannot deliver reliable business value at scale without high-quality data foundations.

The partnership between Cognigy and MongoDB represents a ground-up approach to next-generation customer communication, where agentic AI that plans, reasons, and acts autonomously meets the data architecture needed to succeed at enterprise scale.

By the end of this chapter, you will have a clear understanding of the following:

- The fundamental shift from rule-based chatbots to goal-oriented agentic AI and how Cognigy enables this transformation
- Why high-quality, real-time data serves as the lifeblood of agentic AI systems, and how data mastery directly translates to personalization capabilities
- The critical performance requirements for modern AI agents, including real-time access to inventory systems, CRMs, and operational platforms

- How businesses can scale excellence rather than mistakes by building AI workforce capabilities
- The comprehensive approach to intelligent personalization that combines long-term customer memory with real-time context

As we embark on this exploration of comprehensive approaches for communication, we'll discover how the convergence of advanced AI capabilities and robust data architecture creates opportunities for businesses to reimagine customer engagement entirely, moving beyond the limitations of traditional contact centers toward a future where many interactions can be intelligent, personalized, and valuable.

The evolution from rule-based to goal-oriented AI

The landscape of customer communication has undergone a fundamental transformation in recent years. Modern AI agents can now understand context, reason through complex scenarios, and adapt their responses in real time rather than following predetermined pathways. This evolution represents more than just a technological upgrade; it embodies a shift in how businesses can engage with their customers, moving from reactive, rule-based responses to proactive, contextually aware assistance that anticipates needs and delivers personalized solutions in real-time.

To see this evolution in action, consider the following case.

Case study: How a Tier-1 airline responded to crisis

On March 7, 2024, Germany faced a perfect storm of transportation chaos. Airport security staff walked off the job at Frankfurt, one of the world's busiest international hubs, while a Tier 1 airline's 25,000 ground staff launched a coordinated strike across German airports [1]. Traditional call centers would have buckled under the pressure, leaving hundreds of thousands of stranded passengers waiting hours for assistance.

Instead, something remarkable happened. During the peak of the crisis, the leading airline's AI agents, powered by Cognigy's platform, handled up to 10,000 incoming interactions per minute over a 48-hour period, a volume that would have completely overwhelmed traditional operations. These agents seamlessly processed rebooking and refunds end-to-end, maintaining service quality even under extreme pressure, while human agents were redirected to handle the most complex cases.

This wasn't just a technology success story; it was a preview of how intelligent communication systems can transform crisis response from reactive damage control into proactive customer care. But behind this transformation lies a critical truth that separates genuine AI success from expensive failures: *the quality of the data foundation.*

The limitations that held us back

Traditional chatbots and **interactive voice response** (**IVR**) systems have long been a source of frustration in customer experience, representing the many issues that concern consumers about automated interactions. These systems were inherently static and rule-based, following rigid decision trees that couldn't adapt in real time and consistently left customers frustrated with scripted, impersonal answers that failed to address their actual needs.

The core problem with these legacy systems wasn't just their inflexibility; it was their complete inability to understand context, learn from interactions, or make intelligent decisions based on the unique circumstances of each customer encounter. Because traditional systems were confined to preconfigured flows and predetermined response patterns, there was no real-time reasoning and dynamic decision-making capabilities.

The agentic AI breakthrough

Cognigy's agentic AI represents a significant shift away from these limitations, embodying a substantially different philosophy about how AI should interact with customers. Unlike older bots that simply execute predetermined scripts, AI agents built with Cognigy possess sophisticated capabilities that enable them to function more like intelligent human agents than traditional automation systems.

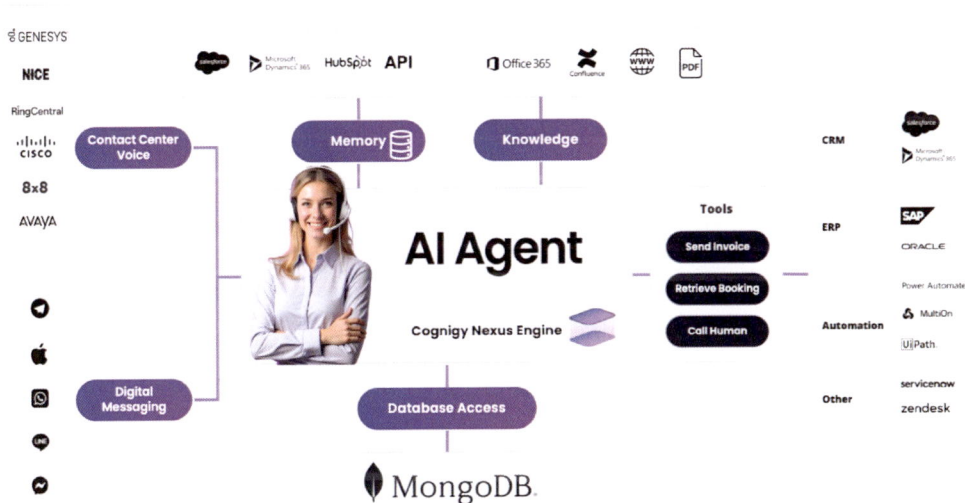

Figure 9.1: Cognigy's agentic AI architecture with MongoDB integration

Figure 9.1 illustrates how Cognigy's AI agents operate within a comprehensive enterprise ecosystem. At the center, the AI agent, powered by the Cognigy Nexus Engine, connects multiple communication channels (contact center voice and digital messaging) with enterprise systems across CRM, ERP, and automation platforms. The agent accesses unified memory and knowledge repositories while leveraging MongoDB's database capabilities for real-time data processing. This architecture enables seamless integration with existing enterprise tools, including Salesforce, Microsoft Dynamics 365, SAP, Oracle, and various automation platforms, demonstrating how agentic AI transforms isolated chatbots into intelligent workforce members that can act across an organization's entire technology stack.

The transformation begins with contextual understanding through real-time data and memory capabilities. Cognigy's AI agents don't just process the current interaction in isolation; they maintain comprehensive awareness of the customer's history, preferences, previous interactions, and current context. This memory extends beyond simple data retrieval to include an understanding of emotional context, communication preferences, and the broader business relationship between the customer and the organization.

Additionally, Cognigy's agents can make autonomous decisions based on reasoning rather than rigid scripts. This capability represents a significant departure from rule-based systems, enabling agents to evaluate complex situations, weigh multiple factors, and determine the most appropriate course of action based on the specific circumstances of each interaction.

The platform's ability to use tools such as APIs, CRMs, and even on-device sensors to act dynamically creates considerable opportunities for real-time problem-solving. Rather than being limited to information retrieval and scripted responses, Cognigy's agents can actually take actions on behalf of customers, processing refunds, rebooking flights, updating account information, or coordinating with other systems to resolve complex issues.

Why data is the lifeblood of agentic AI

The difference between genuine personalization and mere tokenism lies not in the sophistication of the AI models themselves, but in the quality, completeness, and accessibility of the data that powers those models. Without fast access to complete, high-quality data, there is no personalization beyond the basic `"Hi [first.name]"` greeting that has become synonymous with shallow automation.

The scope of modern data requirements

Whether an AI agent is checking flight statuses for stranded travelers, resolving complex insurance claims with multiple stakeholders, or booking rental cars with specific customer preferences and constraints, these agents depend on immediate access to diverse data sources that paint a complete picture of the customer's situation and needs.

Historical interactions form the foundation of contextual understanding, enabling agents to recognize patterns in customer behavior, understand communication preferences, and avoid repeating previous mistakes or frustrations. Purchase and service history provide important insights into customer value, preferences, and life cycle stage, enabling agents to make appropriate recommendations and prioritize service levels accordingly.

Customer preferences extend beyond simple demographic data to include communication style preferences, channel preferences, timing preferences, and even emotional context that might affect how interactions should be handled. Location and device context add another layer of personalization opportunity, enabling agents to provide location-specific information, understand the customer's current situation and constraints, and optimize interactions for the device and channel being used.

MongoDB's role in enabling real-time intelligence

This is where the partnership between Cognigy and MongoDB becomes particularly effective. MongoDB's document-oriented data model with flexible schema capabilities (meaning fields can be added dynamically without predefined table structures, unlike traditional relational databases that require fixed schemas) and real-time capabilities enable Cognigy's agents to access and process diverse data sources efficiently, while maintaining the performance characteristics necessary for real-time customer interactions.

The combination creates a foundation where comprehensive personalization becomes not just possible, but practical and scalable across large customer bases and complex interaction scenarios.

Real-world application: transforming retail customer experience

Consider a practical retail scenario that demonstrates this real-time intelligence in action. When a customer contacts a retailer's support through WhatsApp asking about their delivery date, the interaction triggers a sophisticated data orchestration process that showcases the power of the Cognigy-MongoDB partnership, as shown in *Figure 9.2*.

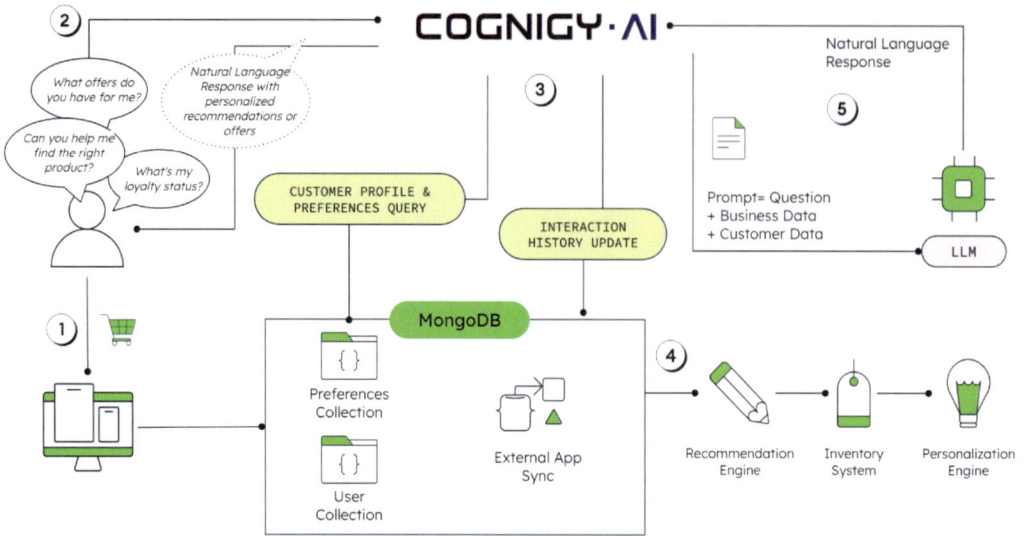

Figure 9.2: Real-time data integration in action

This diagram illustrates how Cognigy's AI agents seamlessly integrate with MongoDB to deliver personalized customer experiences. The flow shows a customer's journey from initial purchase (**1**) through conversational inquiry (**2**), real-time data retrieval and processing (**3**), automated system synchronization (**4**), and intelligent response generation (**5**), demonstrating how every interaction leverages live business data for maximum relevance and accuracy.

The customer's inquiry travels through Cognigy's **contact center as a service (CCaaS)** platform, which immediately queries MongoDB to retrieve both user profile data and real-time order information. MongoDB's flexible document structure allows the system to store diverse data types from customer preferences and purchase history to current order status and delivery logistics, all within unified collections that can be accessed instantly.

As Cognigy's AI agent processes the customer's natural language query, it combines this real-time business data with the customer's question to create a comprehensive prompt for the **large language model (LLM)**. The LLM then generates a personalized, contextually aware response that not only answers the delivery question but can also proactively update order information or suggest related services.

What makes this particularly powerful is MongoDB's change streams and triggers functionality. When the AI agent updates delivery information during the conversation, perhaps rescheduling a delivery appointment, MongoDB automatically synchronizes this data with other systems in the customer journey, including inventory management and delivery providers. This ensures that every touchpoint in the customer's experience reflects the most current information without manual intervention.

The technical foundation for seamless integration

MongoDB's real-time capabilities ensure that AI agents aren't operating on stale data; they're interacting with customers using the latest information and context, even during peak demand periods when traditional systems might struggle with latency or availability issues. This architectural approach transforms customer service from reactive problem-solving to proactive relationship building, where each interaction becomes an opportunity to strengthen customer loyalty through personalized, accurate, and timely assistance.

The combination creates a foundation where comprehensive personalization becomes not just possible but also practical and scalable across large customer bases and complex interaction scenarios.

Real-time performance in critical moments

In the high-stakes world of customer service, speed isn't just a competitive advantage; it's often the difference between customer retention and defection, between successful problem resolution and escalating frustration. Modern AI agents need real-time access to inventory systems, CRMs, order management platforms, and reservation tools at the exact moment of interaction.

When systems are pushed to their limits

The true test of an AI-powered customer service system comes not during normal operating conditions but during crisis situations that push every component to its limits. The March 2024 German airport strikes created exactly such a scenario, overwhelming contact centers across the aviation industry as thousands of passengers simultaneously sought rebooking, refunds, and alternative travel arrangements.

During this crisis, the Tier 1 airline's AI agents maintained service continuity even as traditional call centers struggled to cope with the sudden surge in customer inquiries. This performance stands as a testament not just to the capabilities of Cognigy's AI agents but to the critical importance of having instant access to data across multiple systems at hyper speed.

The complexity behind simple requests

However, the need for speed and data quality isn't limited to rare disruptive events. Consider the seemingly simple customer inquiry, *When will my package arrive?*. This everyday question requires a complex sequence of real-time data operations that must be completed in seconds, not minutes, to meet customer expectations and maintain service quality.

The system must first identify the user through authentication processes, access past order data, query logistics systems for real-time status, process information from multiple shipping providers, generate human-like responses using LLMs, and log the interaction for future reference. All of this complex orchestration needs to happen in seconds to maintain the illusion of effortless service.

According to HubSpot research, 90% of customers expect an immediate response when they contact customer service, and companies that meet this benchmark see significantly higher retention and satisfaction rates [2]. Quick access to data doesn't just make AI faster; it makes it trustworthy, actionable, and customer-centric in ways that build lasting business relationships.

Scaling excellence, not mistakes

The era of human-first and phone-centric contact centers has reached its inevitable conclusion, marking the end of an operational model that has become unsustainable in the modern business environment. The traditional approach of manually scaling customer service operations through hiring more agents, who organizations struggle to retain for extended periods, represents a costly and inefficient strategy that cannot keep pace with growing customer expectations.

The mathematics of transformation

The mathematics of manual scaling reveals the inherent problems with traditional contact center models. As customer bases grow and interaction volumes increase, organizations face exponential increases in staffing costs, training requirements, and operational complexity. The challenge becomes even more acute when considering the high turnover rates that plague the customer service industry.

In the AI-first era, the goal has clearly shifted from simply handling customer inquiries to delivering the same or better service quality at significantly lower cost while simultaneously improving customer satisfaction and business outcomes. Cognigy's AI agents represent a solution to this challenge, offering a path toward sustainable, scalable customer service that improves rather than degrades as volume increases.

Demonstrated results across industries

The transformation that Cognigy enables goes beyond simple automation to encompass a complete reimagining of what customer service can accomplish. Rather than viewing customer interactions as cost centers to be minimized, AI-first organizations can treat every customer touchpoint as an opportunity to build relationships, gather insights, and create value.

Use Case	Channel	KPI	Impact
Sportswear and Apparel	Chat + Voice	Deflection rate	25%
Insurance	Chat + Voice	ID&V	95%
Insurance	Chat + Voice	AHT reduction	27%
Industrial Technology and Mobility Solutions	Chat + Voice	Deflection rate	76%
Energy Utilities	Chat + Voice	Deflection rate	63%
Airlines	Chat	Deflection rate	70%
Apparel and Luxury Goods	Chat	Deflection rate	43%
Home Healthcare Services	Voice	AHT reduction	50-80%
Home Healthcare Services	Voice	Deflection rate	35%
Airlines	Chat + Voice	Deflection rate	80%
Online Optics and Eyewear	Chat + Voice	ID&V	70%
Online Optics and Eyewear	Chat + Voice	AHT reduction	10%
Online Optics and Eyewear	Chat + Voice	Deflection rate	50%
Telecommunications	Chat	Response time decrease	95%
Robotic Process Automation (RPA)	Chat	Deflection rate	26%
Employee Wellbeing Solutions	Chat + Voice	Deflection rate	43%

Table 9.1: AI-driven customer service performance results across industries

This table demonstrates the measurable impact of AI-powered customer service solutions across diverse industries and use cases. The data shows significant improvements in **key performance indicators (KPIs)**, including deflection rates ranging from 25% to 95%, substantial reductions in **average handle time (AHT)**, **identification and verification (ID&V)**, and enhanced operational metrics such as decreases in response time and gains in agent efficiency.

The evidence for this transformation can be seen in the consistent results that Cognigy has delivered across industries and use cases. Organizations implementing Cognigy's agentic AI approach report meaningful changes in their operational efficiency, cost structure, and competitive positioning. The ability to handle complex customer interactions autonomously while maintaining high-quality, personalization standards creates opportunities for businesses to scale their customer service capabilities without proportional increases in human resources.

The foundation for sustainable growth

Backed by MongoDB's high-performance, flexible schema database architecture, Cognigy agents operate with enterprise-grade speed, flexibility, and reliability that can scale to handle massive interaction volumes without degradation in performance or service quality. MongoDB's real-time capabilities ensure that AI agents aren't just pulling yesterday's data they're interacting with customers using the latest information and context, even during peak demand periods when traditional systems might struggle with latency or availability issues.

Personalization isn't magic, it's data mastery

True personalization represents far more than the simple name recognition that has characterized most customer service automation efforts to date. While basic systems might greet customers with `"Hello, [name]"` or reference their account number, genuine personalization requires a sophisticated understanding of customer context, preferences, behavior patterns, and current needs that goes well beyond surface-level data retrieval.

The architecture of intelligent personalization

Cognigy AI agents achieve this deeper level of personalization by leveraging comprehensive data to access customer order history, preferences, and behavioral insights instantly, enabling them to tailor every single response based not just on the user's past interactions, but on the evolving context of the current interaction as well.

True personalization operates across multiple interaction layers simultaneously. Beyond delivering relevant information, it involves calibrating communication style to match customer expectations, selecting optimal channels based on context, and adjusting the pace of service delivery to align with individual urgency levels and technical comfort zones.

AI achieves this nuanced personalization by integrating both long-term memory, such as detailed user profiles, comprehensive purchase history, and documented preferences, with short-term context, which includes the current query or issue, the customer's emotional state, the channel they've chosen for communication, and any external factors that might be influencing their needs or constraints.

The technical foundation for personalization excellence

MongoDB's flexible data model plays a crucial role in enabling this sophisticated personalization by allowing Cognigy to ingest and unify diverse data sources without the constraints of rigid schema requirements that characterize traditional database approaches. This flexibility supports seamless cross-channel experiences that truly listen to the user and their needs rather than simply regurgitating standardized replies that ignore individual context and preferences.

The relationship between data capabilities and AI outcomes can be understood through the systematic way that different types of data enable specific AI capabilities, which, in turn, drive measurable business outcomes.

Function of data	AI capability	Outcome
Customer profiles	Segmentation and context understanding	Relevant, personalized interactions
Real-time access	Dynamic engagement and tool integration	Fast, responsive service
High-quality data	Accurate responses and decision-making	Trust and satisfaction
Predictive behavior modeling	Proactive recommendations and alerts	Increased conversion and loyalty
Centralized data architecture	Unified CX across all channels	Seamless omnichannel journeys

Table 9.2: How data powers agentic AI

The familiar adage *garbage in, garbage out* has never been more relevant or consequential than in the context of AI-powered customer service systems. Nowhere is this principle more starkly demonstrated than in our everyday experiences with AI systems that provide confident-sounding but completely incorrect responses based on flawed or incomplete training data.

The stakes of accuracy

In customer service contexts, where trust and accuracy are paramount, poor data quality doesn't just lead to minor inconveniences; it leads to poor, biased, or flat-out incorrect responses that can destroy customer relationships and damage brand reputation. The consequences of poor data quality in customer service AI extend far beyond simple factual errors.

When AI agents provide incorrect information about product availability, pricing, or policies, customers may make decisions based on that information that lead to disappointment, financial loss, or missed opportunities. When AI systems exhibit bias based on incomplete or skewed training data, they may provide different levels of service to different customer segments, creating legal and ethical issues that can have serious business consequences.

The comprehensive requirements for AI excellence

High-quality, accurate, current, and complete data serves as a critical requirement for delivering relevant, human-like responses that customers can trust and act upon. This data quality requirement encompasses multiple dimensions that must all be maintained simultaneously to ensure reliable AI performance:

- **Accuracy** ensures that the information provided to customers reflects reality and can be relied upon for decision-making
- **Currency** ensures that information reflects the most recent state of systems and processes
- **Completeness** ensures that AI agents have access to all relevant information needed to provide comprehensive assistance
- **Consistency** ensures that information provided through AI channels aligns with information available through other channels and systems

In short, without high-quality data across all dimensions, even the most advanced AI will fall short. But when these foundations are in place, agentic AI doesn't just respond, it builds trust, drives action, and delivers experiences that feel genuinely human.

Governance and compliance framework

With Cognigy, enterprises get not only intelligent agents capable of sophisticated reasoning and decision-making but also governed, compliant AI systems with comprehensive features designed to protect sensitive information and ensure regulatory compliance. These features include **personally identifiable information** (**PII**) redaction capabilities that automatically identify and protect PII, role-based access controls that ensure only authorized personnel can access sensitive data, and end-to-end encryption that protects information throughout the entire interaction life cycle.

These governance and compliance capabilities meet strict regulatory standards across multiple industries and jurisdictions, enabling organizations to deploy AI-powered customer service with confidence that they're meeting their legal and ethical obligations.

Summary

The shift from rule-based chatbots to intelligent agentic AI represents a substantial technological advancement reflecting a comprehensive rethinking of customer communication capabilities when structured data foundations integrate with advanced AI systems. Throughout this chapter, we've examined how the collaboration between Cognigy and MongoDB establishes the infrastructure for this advancement, enabling organizations to transcend traditional contact center constraints toward operational models where each customer interaction becomes an opportunity for tailored, intelligent engagement.

The analysis demonstrates that effective AI agents require robust data architectures, and organizations that master this integration will maintain competitive advantages in demanding, customer-focused markets.

The following chapter will examine how these principles of intelligent data utilization and agentic AI are transforming retail operations from customer experience to operational efficiency. We'll analyze how contemporary retailers are integrating intelligence throughout their operations, from AI-enhanced search that processes customer intent beyond keyword matching, to individualized marketing and content systems that generate dynamic, customized experiences at scale.

References

1. *New Lufthansa Ground Staff Strikes On Thursday & Friday, March 7th-9th*: `https://loyaltylobby.com/2024/03/04/new-lufthansa-ground-staff-strikes-on-thursday-friday-march-7th-9th/`

2. *The Top 5 Most Important Customer Service Standards, According to Consumers*: `https://blog.hubspot.com/service/customer-service-standards`

10

Harnessing AI to Transform the Retail Industry

Retail has changed. It's no longer about reacting to what customers want. Leading retailers now understand that to win, they must anticipate their customers' every need and personalize every single interaction. AI is the essential technology making this possible. To create this predictive and hyper-personalized future, retailers need to integrate AI into their solutions right now.

Until now, the retail industry has thrived on its ability to understand and respond to customer needs. But in today's connected, experience-driven world, that's no longer enough. The modern customer journey is fragmented, fast-moving, and deeply personal. Retailers must now do more than react; they must predict, adapt, and engage with intelligence and precision across every touchpoint.

AI is not just an emerging trend in this landscape; it is the engine powering the next era of retail. From product discovery to fulfillment, from content creation to customer support, AI is transforming how retailers operate, innovate, and compete. Yet, as many IT decision-makers know, leveraging AI in meaningful, scalable ways is often easier said than done. Success requires more than plugging in a model; it demands a data-first approach, integrated platforms, real-time responsiveness, and architectures capable of evolving with the business.

In this chapter, you will learn about the following:

- Semantic search powered by vector search is transforming product discovery and customer engagement through real-time, intent-driven experiences
- Personalized marketing and content generation leverage GenAI and **retrieval-augmented generation (RAG)** to create dynamic, scalable customer experiences across all channels

- Demand forecasting and predictive analytics use AI to shift from reactive to proactive planning, optimizing inventory and supply chain management
- Digitizing in-store interactions bridges the gap between online and offline retail through intelligent data capture and real-time personalization
- Conversational and agentic chatbots are revolutionizing customer service with autonomous, adaptive, and context-aware interactions
- Companies across the retail industry are achieving measurable business results through intelligent, data-driven AI implementations
- MongoDB's unified database provides the flexible and scalable infrastructure needed to support AI-powered retail workloads
- Agentic AI is emerging as the next frontier, enabling proactive, autonomous systems that continuously optimize retail operations
- Modern retailers are expanding AI applications into loss prevention, merchandising execution, workforce orchestration, and sustainability optimization

Semantic search powered by vector search

A customer journey often begins with viewing an item on display, which can quickly shift between a physical store and an online one. In today's competitive online retail landscape, the traditional search bar has transformed from a mere functional tool into a sophisticated engine taking customer intent and turning it into revenue. Successful retailers are now leveraging the real-time operational data they have on customer journeys and enriching it with AI to create intelligent, **search generative experiences (SGE)**. This evolution, driven by innovations such as vector search, empowers them to understand customer intent, surface highly relevant results, and deliver proactive, personalized interactions that boost sales.

As online shopping becomes more competitive and customer expectations rise, traditional search capabilities no longer suffice. This section explores how search, once a functional tool, has become a powerful driver of customer engagement and revenue. We'll dive into how modern retailers are evolving their search infrastructure by integrating real-time analytics, AI, and operational data to deliver intelligent, adaptive search experiences. These advancements, including semantic vector search, allow retailers to surface more relevant results, understand customer intent, and create proactive, intent-aware interactions.

Transforming retail search

As customers navigate this increasingly personalized retail landscape, their journey often begins with the crucial interaction of search. While retailers strive to offer a differentiated buying experience by leveraging vast amounts of customer data, the effectiveness of this personalization hinges on how accurately and swiftly search results can be tailored. Traditionally, achieving this involved complex data warehousing and AI models to segment customers. However, the future of retail search lies in even more dynamic and real-time personalization to truly guide the customer through their unique buying journey.

However, the world of search is not limited to just finding the one item the customer is interested in. Retailers are given the opportunity to rank those results in a way that will give the customer multiple compelling options. Traditionally, decisions on how to rank search results in a personalized way were made by segmenting customers through data acquisition from various operational systems, moving it all into a data warehouse, and then running it through various machine learning algorithms. Typically, this would run in a batch mode (every 24, 48, or even 72 hours or a few days), and the next time a customer logged in, they would have a personalized experience. It did not, however, capture the customer's true desire in real time.

Modern retailers are now enhancing their search results with real-time data and AI-driven analytics. By incorporating data from shopping carts, customer clickstream, and trending purchase activity, retailers can deliver product recommendations that are highly relevant and perfectly aligned with customer intent. This leads to higher conversion rates, better cross-selling opportunities, and the ability to capitalize on emerging trends as they develop rather than days later.

Also, in the age of GenAI, retailers are beginning to shift from keyword-based search to prompt-based interactions that mimic natural conversations. Customers can now express their needs in plain language, such as, "I need a gift for my dad who loves hiking", and receive curated results instantly. This approach unlocks deeper personalization by interpreting intent rather than just matching terms. It also allows retailers to surface relevant products more intuitively, even when customers aren't sure what to search for. Prompt-based search marks a significant step forward in delivering smarter, more human-like digital shopping experiences.

Visual search represents another transformative capability, allowing customers to upload photos of items they want to find or discover similar products. A customer can snap a picture of a friend's jacket or a piece of furniture they saw in a magazine and instantly find matching or similar items in the retailer's catalog. This technology uses computer vision and AI to analyze visual features such as color, pattern, texture, and style, then matches them against product images. Visual search eliminates the challenge of describing complex visual attributes in words and opens up discovery opportunities that traditional text-based search simply cannot provide.

Beyond personalization, retailers strategically influence search rankings to meet business objectives. Search results are increasingly weighted by factors such as inventory levels, profit margins, and promotional campaigns. A retailer might boost products that are overstocked to clear warehouse space, or prioritize higher-margin items to improve profitability. Sponsored product placements allow brands to pay for prominent positioning in relevant searches, creating an additional revenue stream. This business-intelligent ranking ensures that search serves both customer needs and commercial goals, balancing relevance with operational realities such as stock levels and seasonal inventory management.

Building a unified customer view

The first step in truly understanding the customer is to build a customer operational data store that consolidates data from across the organization: support, e-commerce transactions, in-store interactions, wish lists, reviews, and more. Flexible document-based database architecture enables bringing data of different types and formats together into one document to get a clear view of the customer in one place. A customer record store is just that, a single document with all the customer's history in it, not a multitude of tables with data spread across different rows. As the retailer captures more data points about the customer, they can easily add fields without the need for downtime due to schema changes. Data is stored in exactly the way that it needs to be consumed.

Then comes the ability to run analytics in real time, rather than retroactively in another separate system. As an example, MongoDB's architecture allows for workload isolation, meaning operational workloads (the customer's actions on the e-commerce site) and the analytical or AI workload (calculating what the next best offer should be) can be run simultaneously without one interrupting the other. Retailers can build dynamic ranking by using the MongoDB aggregation framework for advanced analytical queries or triggering an AI model in real time to give an answer that can be embedded into the search ranking.

The benefit of an all-in-one platform is huge, as instead of having to update your search indexing to incorporate your AI augmentation, MongoDB has search built in. This whole flow can be completed in one data platform automatically; as your data is being enriched with AI results, the search indexing will sync to match.

As discussed in *Chapter 2, What Sets GenAI, RAG, and Agentic AI Apart*, vector search enables semantic understanding by finding content with proximity to a user's query in vector space. In retail applications, this means when a customer searches for "comfortable running shoes", the system returns products ranked by similarity scores indicating how closely they match the query's intent, potentially including athletic sneakers, performance footwear, or sports shoes, even if those exact terms weren't used in product descriptions.

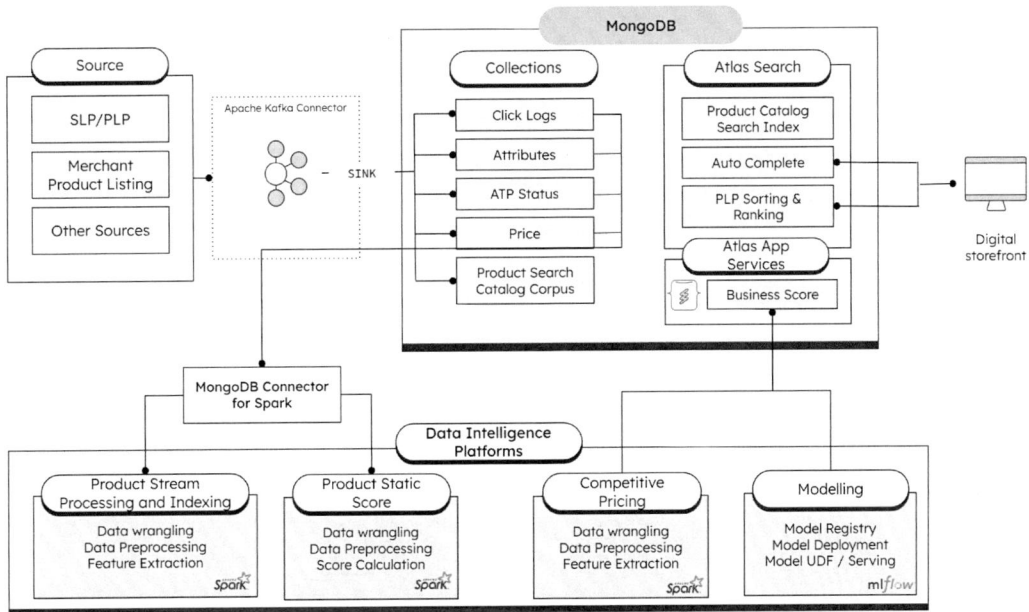

Figure 10.1: MongoDB Atlas architecture for a unified customer view with AI-enhanced search and analytics

This architecture diagram shows how MongoDB Atlas creates a unified customer view by integrating multiple data sources into a single platform. The system combines traditional database operations with vector search capabilities, enabling real-time analytics, semantic search, and personalized recommendations. Key components include data ingestion from various sources, MongoDB's flexible document storage, Atlas Vector Search for semantic matching, and downstream analytics for product intelligence and competitive analysis.

Vector search technology in retail provides notable economic benefits. Industry research suggests that customers who engage with personalized search results are 2–3 times more likely to convert [1].

Evolving from reactive to proactive

Applying the agentic AI principles from *Chapter 2, What Sets GenAI, RAG, and Agentic AI Apart*, to retail search, these systems continuously monitor customer behavior, evaluate changing trends, and autonomously refine ranking strategies or initiate promotional workflows without human intervention. This addresses the reactive nature of most current search implementations, where even real-time models wait for explicit input rather than driving initiatives autonomously. By closing this gap, agentic AI empowers retailers to deliver adaptive, context-aware experiences at scale.

For the end customer, this results in a far more intuitive and satisfying shopping experience. Instead of just surfacing relevant products, agentic AI ensures that search results evolve with the customer's journey in real time, not only suggesting similar products but orchestrating bundles, reordering reminders, or offers based on inferred intent. This moves the experience from passive recommendation to intelligent assistance, driving increased customer satisfaction, loyalty, and, ultimately, conversion rates.

> **How a global food delivery platform tackled inventory challenges**
>
> An example of a company transforming real-time customer engagement with AI is a leading global food delivery platform. Faced with the challenge of perishable inventory frequently going out of stock, this company developed an item replacement tool that provides personalized product alternatives in real time. Powered by advanced AI models and live inventory data, the solution ensures customers always find a suitable option, reducing cart abandonment and preserving revenue. Built on a modern data infrastructure, the tool is already being piloted in the Middle East, where it's expected to increase monthly gross merchandise value. By accelerating AI innovation, this food delivery platform is not only improving customer satisfaction but also future-proofing its operations for scalable, intelligent growth.
>
> This example has been anonymized for editorial clarity. To learn more, see: `https://mdb.link/food-delivery-platform-ai-innovation`.

Personalized marketing and content generation

Today's retail environment is defined by a diverse digital landscape, where social media, email, websites, and mobile apps serve as crucial consumer touchpoints. However, the true challenge lies in tailoring personalized content that resonates uniquely across each of these distinct channels. What engages a consumer on social media might differ significantly from what captures their attention in an email or prompts action within a mobile app. As customer expectations for relevant and dynamic experiences grow, generic campaigns are no longer effective.

Retailers require scalable solutions to craft deeply personalized interactions that drive engagement, cultivate loyalty, and convert interest into tangible results. This section explores how advanced technologies, particularly generative and agentic AI, are empowering retailers to achieve this sophisticated level of channel-specific personalization. AI plays a pivotal role in creating these personalization features by generating diverse content variations, from personalized subject lines for emails to dynamic layouts for mobile apps. For testing, AI-powered A/B testing and multivariate analysis can rapidly evaluate the effectiveness of different personalization strategies across channels, identifying optimal approaches. Finally, in deployment, AI systems can automatically trigger and deliver personalized content via email, SMS, and in-app notifications, ensuring timely and relevant communication based on real-time customer behavior and preferences.

We will examine how **large language models (LLMs)**, vector databases, and real-time data processing enable personalized content creation at unprecedented scale and speed. By leveraging tools such as modern databases (for example, MongoDB) and RAG, retailers can integrate customer preferences, behavior, and product availability directly into marketing workflows. Further, we introduce agentic AI, which empowers marketing systems to self-optimize campaigns in real time, responding to customer signals and continuously adapting to improve outcomes. Together, these innovations are redefining how marketing content is produced, delivered, and refined.

Meeting the content demands of modern retail with GenAI

GenAI can now create a vast array of content, including personalized advertising copy, product descriptions in multiple languages, and diverse visual assets such as lifestyle photography and graphics. This integration into retail workflows streamlines the entire content generation process, drastically reducing the manual effort traditionally required for copywriting, editing, and visual production. For instance, GenAI can automatically adapt product literature to reflect specific brand tones of voice for different locales and generate relevant product images for varied audiences. This accelerates the time to market for new products and campaigns, allowing retailers to keep pace with rapidly changing consumer-buying patterns and product catalogs. By automating content creation, GenAI frees up human teams to focus on strategic initiatives, enhancing overall marketing efficiency and effectiveness.

In retail, advertising and marketing materials are vital to capturing a customer's interest and driving toward a purchase. The advent of social media has created many more touchpoints to reach customers: Instagram, Facebook, email outreach, newsletters, and promotional banners on sites. This creates both opportunities for retailers and challenges around the volume of content generation required, which can be effectively addressed by adopting GenAI.

Customer-buying patterns, constantly updating the product catalog, and inventory availability are critical components of retail operations. Along with this, there is also the task of ensuring that the product literature is in the right tone of voice to reflect the brand in multiple languages. The product images need to be relevant to the audience in the locale. Traditionally, this required a huge amount of labor in copywriting and editing, photography of different models, and the generation of visuals and graphics.

The retailer must also understand in real time what the impact of campaigns is so that they can quickly redirect their marketing spend and strategy to reflect what is working. In an industry where marketing and branding are critical business activities, retailers need as much insight into their customers as possible so they can reach them with the right message at the right time.

Companies will take advantage of the sharp rise in consumer touchpoints to personalize and reach the growing population of consumers who use digital channels to discover, consider, and purchase products. 65% of consumers research products online, and 30% buy online. These numbers have doubled over the past three to four years. This creates an enormous need for brands to target online consumers with personalized content, an opportunity enabled by GenAI's lower content creation costs [2].

Accelerating personalized content with GenAI and LLMs

GenAI is a catalyst for innovation across the retail industry, from personalization in the fashion industry to streamlining back-office operations. Through RAG with LLMs, fashion retailers can now create individualized marketing materials, newsletters, social media posts, and email outreach tailored to each customer in seconds. This extends to generating unique visuals, graphics, and even photo-realistic images by leveraging existing customer data. This automation significantly reduces the manual effort previously required for campaign creation and drastically shortens the time to market for new collections and promotions.

In back-office operations, GenAI can quickly and easily analyze campaign effectiveness, providing actionable insights that drive intelligent, strategic decisions regarding inventory management, supply chain optimization, and customer relationship management. This ability to rapidly synthesize complex data into clear recommendations empowers fashion brands to make more informed choices, ultimately improving efficiency and profitability.

The key to creating content that is personalized to the customer and the brand is leveraging the vast amount of data that retailers have in-house to provide an LLM with context. One compelling example of this data-driven personalization in action comes from the beauty industry.

> **Fueling innovation in beauty retail with MongoDB Atlas**
>
> A leading global beauty retailer accelerated its digital transformation through an internal tech accelerator, building high-performance applications that support complex real-time analytics to guide better business decisions. Faced with limitations in their previous NoSQL database, particularly around latency and code complexity, the team migrated to MongoDB Atlas on Google Cloud. This shift dramatically improved backend performance and developer agility, reducing latency from seconds to milliseconds and enabling faster innovation. The simplified architecture empowered product teams to iterate rapidly and scale efficiently, aligning with their mission to deliver personalized and inclusive beauty experiences powered by technology.
>
> This example has been anonymized for editorial clarity. To learn more, see: `https://mdb.link/leader-in-beauty-digital-transformation`.

Leveraging modern databases for scalable, AI-driven marketing

Achieving this level of personalized content creation at scale requires a robust data infrastructure that can seamlessly integrate customer data with AI models. In MongoDB, the Apache Spark Connector allows for model training of LLMs so that prompts such as `"create a personalized newsletter for each customer suggesting an item based on what is on offer and their previous purchases"` can use data, images, and tonal or language references to create outreach.

With integrated platform approaches such as MongoDB, as new items or visuals are added to the product catalog, change streams can trigger the vectorization of new data, making the process seamless. Training models with internal data provides retailers with an invaluable resource for effectively reaching their audience.

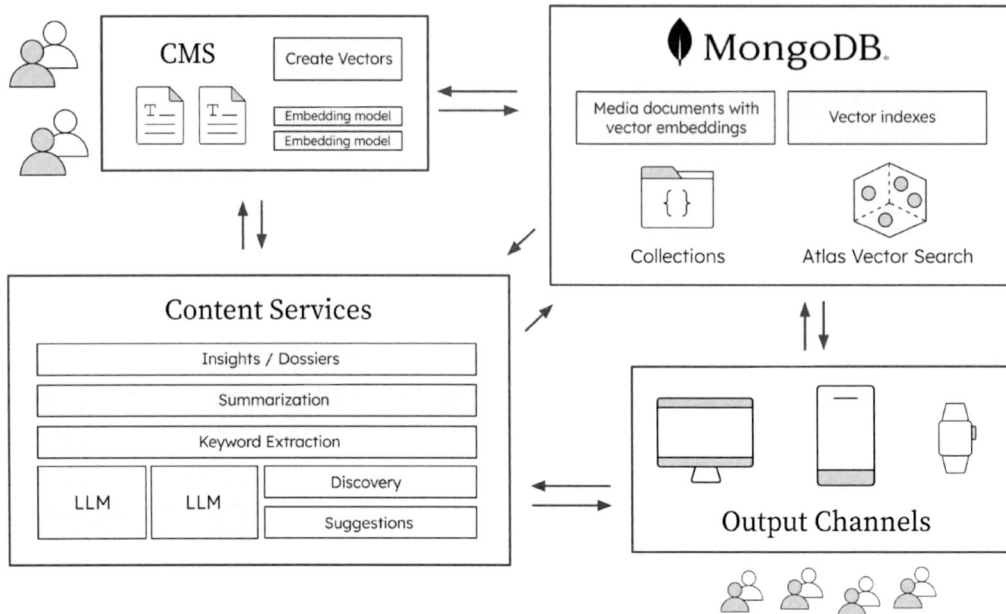

Figure 10.2: AI-powered personalization architecture

The preceding figure shows a reference architecture highlighting where MongoDB can be leveraged to achieve AI-powered personalization. By leveraging user data and the multi-dimensional vectorization of media content, MongoDB Atlas can be applied to multiple AI use cases. This allows for the utilization of media channels to more effectively improve end user experiences.

By doing so, retailers can suggest content that aligns more closely with individual preferences and past interactions. This not only enhances user engagement but also increases the likelihood of converting free users into paying subscribers.

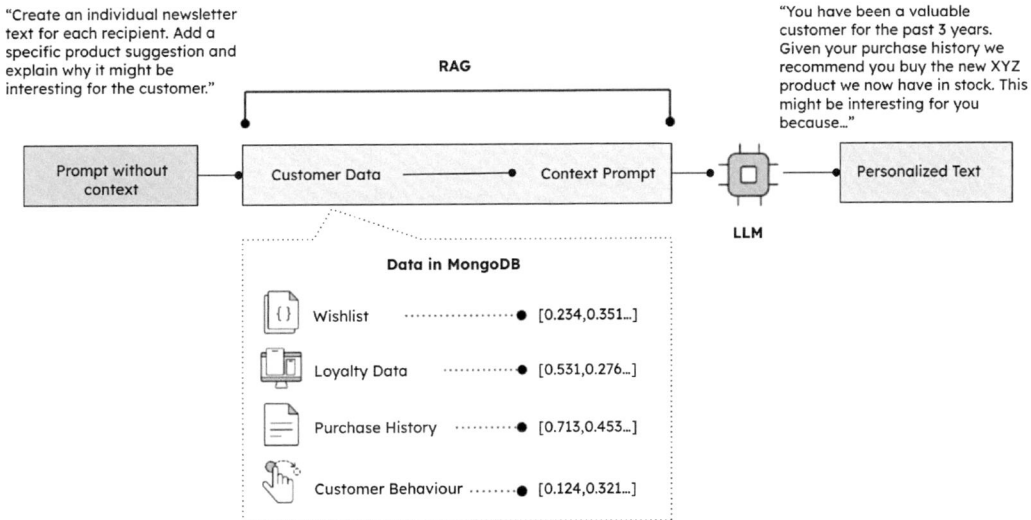

"Create an individual newsletter text for each recipient. Add a specific product suggestion and explain why it might be interesting for the customer."

RAG

"You have been a valuable customer for the past 3 years. Given your purchase history we recommend you buy the new XYZ product we now have in stock. This might be interesting for you because..."

| Prompt without context | Customer Data | Context Prompt | | Personalized Text |

LLM

Data in MongoDB

{ } Wishlist .... ● [0.234,0.351...]

Loyalty Data .... ● [0.531,0.276...]

Purchase History .... ● [0.713,0.453...]

Customer Behaviour .... ● [0.124,0.321...]

Figure 10.3: RAG-based personalized newsletter generation using MongoDB customer data

This workflow demonstrates how customer data (wishlist, loyalty data, purchase history, and customer behavior) is ingested into MongoDB. This raw data is transformed and vectorized using embedding models. Each vector represents a numerical representation of the customer's attributes and interactions, capturing their preferences, past purchases, and browsing behavior. These vectors are stored in a vector database within MongoDB, enabling efficient similarity searches. When a user prompt for newsletter content is received (e.g., "Generate a personalized newsletter for a customer interested in outdoor gear"), the RAG system springs into action. First, the user's prompt is vectorized. This prompt vector is then used to query the MongoDB vector database to retrieve the most relevant customer data vectors. For example, if the prompt is about outdoor gear, the system would retrieve customer profiles and their historical data related to outdoor product purchases, wishlists for camping equipment, or browsing behavior for hiking boots. This retrieved customer data, which is highly specific and contextual to the individual, forms the basis of the *context*.

The extracted customer context, along with the initial user prompt, is then fed into an LLM. The LLM leverages this rich, personalized context to generate highly relevant and tailored newsletter content. For instance, if the retrieved customer data indicates a past purchase of a specific brand of hiking boots, the LLM can generate a newsletter that highlights new arrivals from that brand, accessories that complement the boots, or upcoming sales on similar outdoor gear. This process enables retailers to create customized marketing communications at scale, moving beyond generic campaigns to deliver truly personalized experiences that resonate with each customer. The LLM's ability to understand and synthesize information from the context ensures that the generated content is not only personalized but also coherent and engaging, ultimately driving higher customer engagement and conversion rates.

How agentic AI is revolutionizing adaptive marketing in retail

Agentic AI takes this a step further by introducing autonomous systems that not only generate personalized content but also monitor, evaluate, and adjust marketing campaigns in real time based on customer engagement signals. These intelligent agents can assess which messages are resonating with different audience segments and dynamically adjust the tone, format, channel, and timing to maximize performance without human intervention.

The biggest challenge in content marketing is the lag between content deployment and response. Typically, marketing teams have to wait for analytics, interpret the data, and then manually adjust their campaigns. Agentic AI collapses that loop, continuously optimizing outreach in real time, completely eliminating that delay.

For the end customer, this results in content that feels truly relevant and timely; offers arrive when they're most needed, in a tone that resonates, and through their preferred communication channels. For retailers, it means improved return on marketing spend, increased conversion rates, and less reliance on static campaigns that may lose impact over time. With agentic AI, personalized marketing evolves from being a static process based on historical insights to a dynamic system that intelligently adapts to consumer behavior in the moment.

Demand forecasting and predictive analytics

Accurate demand forecasting is a critical differentiator between operational efficiency and costly missteps. As consumer expectations rise and supply chains grow increasingly complex, the ability to predict demand with precision can significantly impact a retailer's profitability, inventory management, and customer satisfaction. This section explores how AI-powered demand forecasting and predictive analytics are helping retailers shift from reactive to proactive planning. With the support of vast historical data and real-time inputs, businesses can generate forecasts that inform smarter purchasing, replenishment, and promotional decisions.

We'll cover the evolution from traditional machine learning models to cutting-edge techniques such as GenAI and agentic AI. The section will examine how modern forecasting approaches integrate contextual signals, such as seasonality, economic shifts, and behavioral patterns, to increase accuracy. You'll learn how RAG enhances data relevance, and how agentic AI goes even further by automating adjustments and actions in real time. Together, these innovations equip retailers to meet demand efficiently while minimizing waste and maximizing customer satisfaction.

AI-driven demand forecasting for smarter inventory and supply chain management

Retailers typically predict demand by either building their own applications with traditional machine learning or by purchasing specialized forecasting products. While homegrown systems can be effective, they come with several challenges:

- **Significant infrastructure requirements**: Homegrown systems demand substantial infrastructure for both data storage and processing, as well as for **machine learning operations (MLOps)**. This implies a need for considerable hardware, software, and networking resources.

- **Dedicated technical expertise**: The development, management, and maintenance of these systems necessitate specialized technical knowledge. This can be a challenge in terms of finding and retaining skilled professionals.

- **Constant care and maintenance**: These systems require constant care to ensure optimal performance and provide value to businesses. This leads to an ongoing demand for monitoring, troubleshooting, updates, and general upkeep, which can be resource-intensive and time-consuming.

Subsequently, feature engineering is there to extract seasonality, promotions, impact, and general economic indicators. A RAG model can be incorporated to improve demand forecasting predictions and reduce the possibility of hallucinations. The same datasets could be utilized from historical data to train and fine-tune the model for improved accuracy.

Such efforts lead to the following business benefits:

- Precision in demand forecasting
- Optimized product/supply planning
- Accuracy in inventory management
- Enhanced customer satisfaction

How GenAI is reshaping predictive analytics in retail

Traditional AI is used in demand forecasting and predictive analytics in retail by integrating data from diverse sources, such as sales transactions, social media, and weather patterns, leading to highly accurate and timely forecasts.

GenAI, unlike traditional machine learning, can create novel data, such as realistic images, text, and audio, rather than just analyzing existing data for predictions. This capability enables applications such as content creation, synthetic data generation for training, and personalized experiences, extending beyond the analytical and predictive limitations of traditional machine learning.

GenAI can significantly enhance product design and development by rapidly generating novel design iterations, simulating performance under various conditions, and optimizing for specific criteria. This accelerates the prototyping phase, reduces the need for costly physical mock-ups, and allows for the exploration of a wider range of creative solutions, ultimately leading to more innovative and market-ready products.

MongoDB for Predictive Analytics

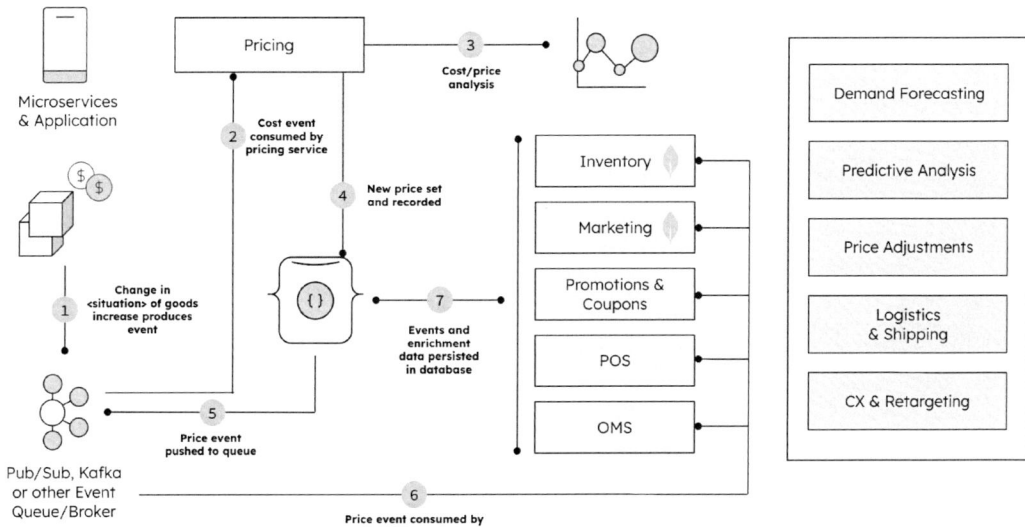

Figure 10.4: An illustration of a price-change scenario where fuel costs have risen, which leads to a rise in shipping costs and, in turn, pricing

Let's break down the steps mentioned in the image:

- [1] This produces events about the cost increase and places them in the message stream, where the event queue makes them available. All microservices are listening for such messages.

- [2–4] The pricing microservice consumes the event, analyzes it against existing data, and further conveys the new pricing into the message stream.

- [5–6] The database pushes those messages to the event queue, which makes them available to all consumers listening for messages. Microservices directly impacted by pricing changes, such as those that manage inventory, marketing, promotions, coupons, **point of sale (POS)**, and the e-commerce provider's **order management system (OMS)**, consume the price change events and update their individual databases accordingly.

- [7] The centralized database aggregates and persists events, enriches event streams with data from other sources, including historical data, and provides a central repository for multiple event streams.

Transforming predictive analytics with agentic AI in retail

A powerful next step in this evolution is the use of agentic AI, which goes beyond static prediction to actively monitor, adapt, and act upon forecasting outputs in real time. Agentic AI introduces autonomous agents that constantly evaluate forecast accuracy, market shifts, and supply chain disruptions, then adjust pricing, replenishment orders, and promotional strategies without requiring human prompts. The challenge this addresses is the lag between insight and execution in traditional systems, where forecasts are generated but often manually acted upon, creating delays that reduce their effectiveness.

By automating the response loop, agentic AI reduces that gap dramatically. For the end customer, this results in a better shopping experience, products are more likely to be in stock, pricing is more dynamic and responsive to actual demand, and promotions are better timed and targeted. For retailers, it means fewer lost sales, less waste, and a supply chain that's truly responsive to real-world dynamics. Agentic AI transforms demand forecasting from a decision-support tool into an intelligent operational engine.

Agentic AI, unlike traditional predictive analytics systems that often operate on static models and predefined rules, excels by dynamically adapting and learning from ongoing interactions and a wider array of real-time signals. This allows for significantly more nuanced and accurate predictions.

Consider a retail scenario: a customer browses a new clothing line online. A traditional system might recommend similar items based on past purchases or general popularity. However, an agentic AI system would not only consider historical data but also actively observe the customer's current behavior on the website – how long they linger on certain product images, items they add to their cart and then remove, their mouse movements, and even their scrolling speed. If the customer repeatedly views items in a particular color or fabric type, the agentic AI could instantly adjust its recommendations, prioritizing new arrivals or accessories that perfectly match that preference. It could even detect hesitation and offer a targeted discount on a specific item they're contemplating, all in real time. This dynamic, responsive approach goes far beyond what a static model can achieve.

Agentic AI systems in retail can listen to a diverse range of signals, including the following:

- **Behavioral signals:** Clickstream data, time spent on pages, scroll depth, search queries, items added to/removed from cart, product views, and interactions with promotions
- **Contextual signals:** Time of day, day of week, location (if permissible), device type, and previous interactions with the brand

- **External signals:** Weather patterns, local events, social media trends, news headlines, and competitor promotions (where data is accessible and ethical)
- **Implicit signals:** Hesitation in browsing, repeated viewing of specific product attributes, and changes in browsing patterns

By continuously analyzing these multifaceted signals, agentic AI can build a more comprehensive and real-time understanding of customer intent, leading to more effective predictive analytics and personalized experiences.

Digitizing in-store interactions with intelligence

As digital transformation accelerates across retail, one area with great potential is the in-store experience. While online channels have long captured customer signals for personalized engagement, physical retail remains fragmented, with customer behavior often going unrecorded or siloed. This creates a critical gap in the omnichannel customer journey, especially when consumers increasingly expect the same personalized, real-time experiences in store as they receive online.

GenAI is reshaping how retailers interpret customer intent in digital environments, transforming basic search and segmentation into conversational recommendations and real-time personalization. The same technologies, when paired with digitized in-store interactions such as digital receipts, can bring this intelligence into physical retail. By turning traditionally analog events, such as POS transactions, into structured, analyzable data, retailers can gain a holistic understanding of the customer, personalize recommendations, and drive loyalty through meaningful, data-driven engagement.

As an example of the potential this transformation has, a study made by Bain & Company found that *"consumer product company leaders outperform laggards on digital intent and resource allocation and have superior technology investments representing around 2X faster growing tech budget over the past five years which represents around 30% higher budget for digital change and transformation (as a percentage of revenue)"* [2].

From paper to insight: Digital receipts as a data catalyst

The traditional receipt, once a static and disposable artifact, is becoming one of the most valuable assets in modern retail. When digitized, receipts provide a structured, high-fidelity record of in-store transactions, capturing details such as items purchased, pricing, discounts applied, payment method, location, and customer identifiers. Unlike traditional batch-based loyalty systems, which take a significant amount of time just to be able to glean the intelligence from transactions, digital receipts offer immediate, granular insights into customer preferences and intent.

For example, when a customer purchases athletic shoes and a hydration pack in-store, a digital receipt instantly feeds this context into a unified customer data platform. GenAI can use this input to recommend complementary items, such as performance socks or a running app subscription, via email, an app, or even digital signage the next time they visit.

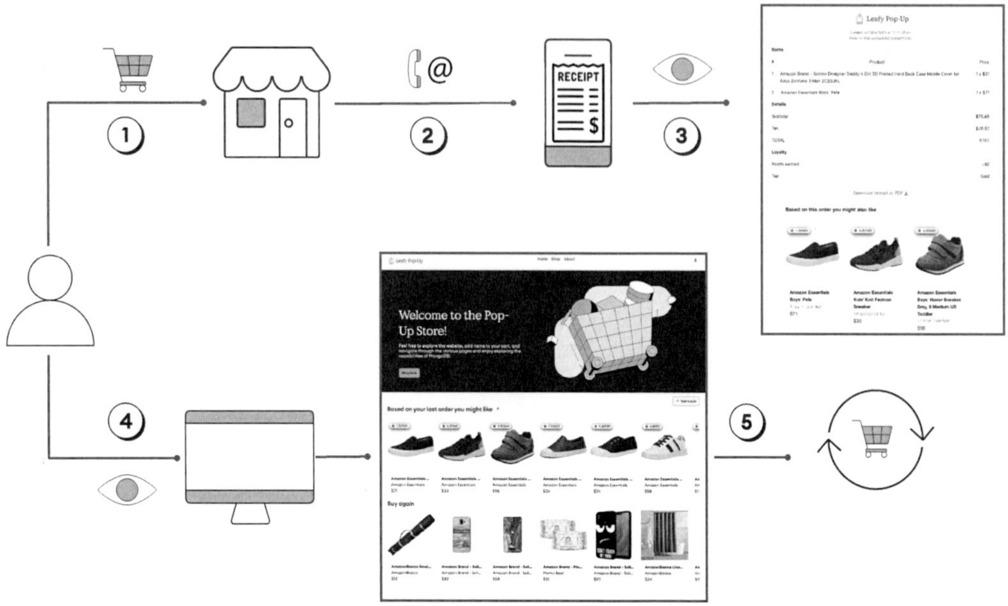

Figure 10.5: Digital receipt customer journey: From purchase to personalized recommendations.

This workflow diagram shows how digital receipts transform the customer experience through five key steps:

1. Customer makes an in-store purchase.
2. They receive a digital receipt via email or SMS.
3. They verify the purchase through a mobile app.
4. The customer accesses purchase history and receives AI-generated personalized product recommendations.
5. They can repurchase items directly through the app.

The process demonstrates how digital receipts serve as a data catalyst for creating seamless omnichannel retail experiences.

Flexible document databases such as MongoDB are ideal for storing these types of dynamic, multi-format data records. With schema flexibility and native support for complex, nested documents, retailers can evolve receipt structures over time, incorporate new metadata fields, and query insights instantly, without downtime or refactoring legacy tables.

> **How a supermarket digitized in-store receipts to drive personalization and cut costs**
>
> An example of a company evolving into store digitization is a major European supermarket chain. The retailer used MongoDB Atlas to digitize in-store receipts within their mobile app, giving customers real-time and historical purchase visibility. This data now powers personalized recommendations and promotions. The unified data approach improved customer experience, boosted developer efficiency, and enabled faster innovation. As a result, this retailer achieved 25% annual cost savings. This sets the stage for more advanced, AI-driven engagement, such as predictive inventory management, personalized marketing campaigns based on real-time behavior, and intelligent customer service chatbots.
>
> This example has been anonymized for editorial clarity. To learn more, see: `https://mdb.link/innovation-largest-netherlands-supermarket`.

Building a real-time omnichannel customer profile

Digital receipts do more than just digitize purchases; they connect offline behavior with online identity. By linking each in-store transaction to a unified customer ID, retailers can construct a comprehensive profile of behavior across all touchpoints: what a customer browsed online, what they tried in-store, what they returned, what discounts influenced their choices, and more.

Retailers using MongoDB can merge real-time data from store systems, mobile apps, web portals, loyalty programs, and customer service channels into a single operational data layer. This enables immediate personalization logic: if a customer recently bought cold-weather gear in store, they can be presented with recommendations for accessories or local-weather-based promotions the next time they open the app or receive a follow-up email.

This approach shifts personalization from reactive, channel-specific campaigns to a proactive, real-time engagement strategy, one that responds to the customer's evolving context and preferences, regardless of where the interaction originated.

Personalization at the point of sale

Digitized in-store interactions also open the door to real-time personalization within the store. For example, a returning customer enters a store, and the associate, using a mobile POS or customer insights app, can view recent purchases, the loyalty tier, and relevant product suggestions based on their last visit. If the customer bought espresso beans and a grinder, for example, the associate could recommend a cleaning kit or a premium blend from the same brand.

These recommendations are increasingly powered by GenAI systems trained on customer journey data. The key enabler is infrastructure: MongoDB's ability to support operational and analytical workloads side by side allows AI models to access the freshest transactional data without delay or duplication. Whether building custom vector embeddings for product recommendations or generating smart receipts enriched with curated offers, MongoDB provides the data agility and performance needed to deliver personalized retail at scale.

Agentic AI: From insights to intelligent action

While GenAI enables responsive, contextual personalization, the next step is agentic AI, systems that not only interpret customer behavior but act on it autonomously. Instead of waiting for input, agentic systems observe patterns, anticipate customer needs, and orchestrate experiences across channels to meet business goals such as retention, upsell, or conversion.

In the context of digitized in-store interactions, agentic AI might automatically identify that a customer regularly buys baby care products and initiate a smart subscription offer. It might notice a drop in store visits from a previously loyal customer and deploy a personalized reactivation campaign. These actions require more than static rules; they require real-time orchestration of workflows, data, and AI-driven reasoning.

By consolidating data on a platform such as MongoDB, which supports intelligent triggers, event-driven architectures, and real-time analytics, retailers can lay the foundation for agentic AI systems that evolve with the customer, across physical and digital channels alike.

Conversational and agentic chatbots

In today's digitally connected retail environment, customers expect immediate, personalized, and seamless interactions with brands. Conversational chatbots, especially those powered by generative and agentic AI, are meeting these expectations and reshaping how retailers deliver customer support, drive product discovery, and build brand loyalty. This section delves into the rise of conversational AI in retail, examining how chatbots are being used not only to improve customer service but also to enhance marketing effectiveness, drive operational efficiency, and unlock deeper insights through intelligent data processing. The section also introduces advanced architectures and technologies, such as RAG and vector search, to show how chatbots are becoming smarter, faster, and more relevant with every interaction.

Building on the growing use of conversational AI, it's essential to understand the evolving needs of today's retail customers. Shoppers now demand not only fast responses but also deeply personalized experiences that reflect their preferences, history, and context. Agentic chatbots, with their ability to retain memory, reason through complex queries, and take proactive actions, empower enterprises to deliver these elevated customer experiences. For instance, a chatbot embedded with RAG can instantly retrieve a customer's past purchases and recommend complementary items based on real-time inventory. Similarly, an agentic support bot can detect frustration signals in a conversation and autonomously escalate to a human agent or offer a tailored discount, turning potential churn into loyalty. By intelligently curating content and dynamically adjusting their responses, these advanced chatbots help retailers move from transactional service to empathetic, value-driven engagement. They can remember interactions and act logically, enabling this. These advanced chatbots, by intelligently selecting information and adapting in real time, help retailers build empathetic and valuable customer relationships instead of just processing transactions.

As we explore these innovations, we will look at how conversational agents are evolving from scripted responders to dynamic, autonomous entities that adapt in real time. The section covers the transformative potential of agentic AI, an emerging approach that enables chatbots to optimize their behavior based on live customer feedback without human intervention. This shift addresses the limitations of reactive systems and lays the foundation for a new era of proactive, context-aware digital engagement. Through architecture examples, use cases, and business impact stories, you will gain a comprehensive understanding of how conversational AI is becoming a strategic differentiator in retail.

How GenAI chatbots are revolutionizing retail engagement

Conversational chatbots powered by GenAI are revolutionizing the retail industry by enhancing customer service. These chatbots can handle a wide range of customer inquiries, from product recommendations to order tracking, providing instant and accurate responses. This reduces wait times and improves the overall customer experience, leading to higher satisfaction and increased loyalty. Additionally, chatbots can operate on real-time data 24/7, ensuring customers receive support at any time, which is especially beneficial for global retailers. Recent studies in the United States reveal that AI-powered chatbots can boost online sales by nearly 4% year over year [3], reinforcing the notion that AI is not just a trend but a lasting driver of growth in retail.

Beyond customer service, AI chatbots are also transforming marketing and sales strategies in retail. They can analyze customer data to personalize shopping experiences, offering tailored recommendations and promotions based on individual preferences and behavior. This personalization helps retailers boost conversion rates and increase sales. Moreover, chatbots can engage customers through various digital channels, including social media, websites, and messaging apps, broadening the reach and effectiveness of marketing campaigns.

Operational efficiency is another area where AI chatbots are making a significant impact. By automating routine tasks such as answering FAQs, managing inventory inquiries, and processing returns, chatbots free up employees to focus on more complex and value-added activities. This not only reduces operational costs but also improves accuracy and consistency in service delivery. Furthermore, the data collected by chatbots can provide valuable insights into customer preferences and behavior, helping retailers refine their strategies and improve their offerings.

Across both digital savvy and non-savvy users, 50–60% have shown a high preference to move to conversational journeys for day-to-day use cases across verticals [4].

Powering intelligent conversations with search and AI

The following is a chatbot RAG architecture example. This chatbot is built using the RAG architecture. RAG augments the knowledge of LLMs by retrieving relevant information for users' queries and using that information in the LLM-generated response. MongoDB's public documentation is used as the information source for chatbot-generated answers.

To retrieve relevant information based on user queries, MongoDB Atlas Vector Search is utilized. In this example, OpenAI is being used in tandem with Vector Search to generate answers to the customer questions. Using data from private data sources and enhanced by the LLMs, the data is augmented, given context, and then returned to the user. The Azure OpenAI embeddings API is used to convert MongoDB documentation and user queries into vector embeddings to help find the most relevant content for queries using Atlas Vector Search.

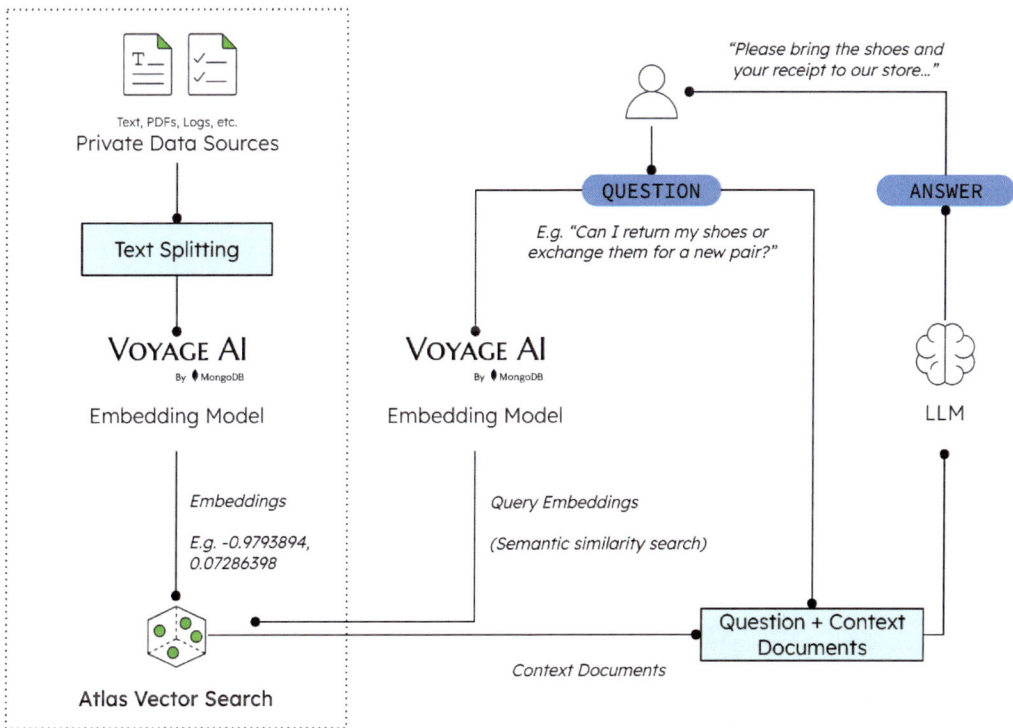

Figure 10.6: Data flow example for a chatbot RAG architecture

AI is revolutionizing the way retailers enhance their competitive edge by providing deeper insights into customer behavior and optimizing profit margins through smart decision-making processes. By incorporating both traditional AI and GenAI, retailers can harness the benefits of enhanced and semantic search powered by vector search, create targeted marketing content based on current market trends, effectively utilize predictive analytics for demand forecasting, employ conversational chatbots, and significantly elevate the overall customer experience.

From scripted to smart: Transforming retail chatbots with agentic AI

Agentic AI takes chatbot capabilities a step further by introducing autonomous agents that can continuously learn from customer interactions and optimize their behavior in real time. Unlike traditional chatbots that follow scripted paths or rely solely on pre-trained models, agentic AI can independently monitor engagement signals, adjust tone and messaging, escalate issues when needed, and even decide the best time and channel to engage a customer, all without requiring human intervention. The primary challenge this addresses is the reactive nature of conventional chatbot workflows, where improvements often rely on post-analysis and manual reprogramming. Agentic systems collapse that lag, allowing chatbots to evolve with each interaction.

For end customers, this translates to a service that feels genuinely intuitive and adaptive. Rather than receiving templated responses, users interact with bots that understand context, personalize the conversation dynamically, and act with proactive intelligence, delivering offers, answers, or support just when it's needed most. Retailers benefit from this continuous optimization loop through improved engagement, higher conversion rates, and stronger brand trust, all while reducing operational overhead. As agentic AI matures, conversational journeys in retail will become increasingly human-like, making digital customer experiences more relevant, responsive, and effective than ever before.

The expanding role of AI in retail

The power of AI in retail goes far beyond search, personalization, and forecasting. It's now transforming the core of store operations, from security and workforce management to sustainability.

The expanding role of AI in retail is exemplified by emerging agentic technologies that move beyond insight generation to autonomous action and continuous optimization.

A study by McKinsey states: *"Over the next three years, 92 percent of companies plan to increase their AI investments. But while nearly all companies are investing in AI, only 1 percent of leaders call their companies 'mature' on the deployment spectrum"* [5].

Proactive loss prevention, AI-driven merchandising, self-healing store operations, dynamic workforce orchestration, and real-time sustainability optimization illustrate how AI is evolving from a supportive tool to an active partner in retail management. By shifting from reactive to proactive and from isolated automation to integrated, context-aware intelligence, retailers are unlocking new efficiencies, reducing risk, and enhancing both employee and customer experiences. This final section delves into these cutting-edge applications, showcasing how AI's role continues to grow, empowering retailers to lead confidently in an ever-changing marketplace.

Proactive loss prevention

AI is shifting retail security from reactive people-led monitoring to proactive intervention. Modern computer vision systems, combined with agentic AI, now analyze video feeds in real time to detect suspicious behavior patterns, such as product concealment, item switching, or repeat offenders. These models don't just flag anomalies; they initiate workflows such as notifying staff or adjusting exit gate protocols. Retailers are seeing a measurable impact in shrink reduction and improved asset protection without increasing human oversight.

AI-driven merchandising execution

Agentic AI is optimizing planogram compliance and promotional execution by continuously comparing shelf data with expected layouts. Leveraging images from in-store cameras or associates' mobile devices, these systems auto-identify misplacements, out-of-stock scenarios, or incorrect signage. Instead of surfacing alerts alone, the AI suggests specific actions, such as reordering, restocking, or flagging vendor issues, enabling faster corrective measures and more consistent shopper experiences across locations.

Self-healing store operations

With intelligent edge infrastructure powered by AI, stores are gaining the ability to self-heal. From frozen kiosks to malfunctioning POS systems, agentic AI monitors performance telemetry and initiates real-time diagnostics and remediation. In many cases, it can auto-resolve issues, restarting services, adjusting configurations, or isolating faults, without waiting for IT intervention. This autonomous operations layer enhances uptime and ensures smoother customer experiences on the floor.

Dynamic workforce orchestration

Retail labor scheduling has long struggled to balance staffing levels with demand surges and employee preferences. Agentic AI now enables adaptive workforce orchestration by continuously learning from store traffic, weather patterns, local events, and individual productivity trends. These systems don't just forecast labor needs; they propose and even implement optimal shift plans, notify employees, and make trade-offs aligned with business goals. This leads to better coverage, higher associate satisfaction, and more agile operations.

Real-time sustainability optimization

Retailers are under pressure to cut carbon emissions and reduce waste without sacrificing performance. Agentic AI supports these efforts by tracking energy usage, refrigeration efficiency, and packaging waste in real time. This technology can autonomously adjust systems such as lighting, HVAC, or cold-chain settings, and it flags inefficiencies before they become costly. Some systems can even optimize delivery routes to meet sustainability goals. These continuous, incremental optimizations lead to significant environmental and financial benefits.

For more information and resources, visit the MongoDB for Retail page at `https://www.mongodb.com/solutions/industries/retail`.

Summary

This chapter has explored the comprehensive transformation of retail through AI, demonstrating how modern retailers are leveraging AI to create smarter, faster, and more personalized customer experiences while driving operational excellence. From AI-augmented search that moves beyond keyword matching to intent-driven, conversational product discovery, to personalized marketing that generates dynamic content at scale using GenAI and RAG, we've seen how retailers are fundamentally reimagining customer engagement. The integration of demand forecasting with predictive analytics enables proactive inventory management and supply chain optimization, while the digitization of in-store interactions through technologies such as digital receipts bridges the critical gap between online and offline experiences. Advanced conversational chatbots powered by agentic AI are revolutionizing customer service by providing autonomous, context-aware assistance that continuously learns and adapts to customer needs.

The emergence of agentic AI represents the next frontier in retail transformation, moving beyond reactive systems to proactive, goal-driven intelligence that operates autonomously across multiple domains. We've witnessed how companies across the retail industry are achieving measurable business results through intelligent data-driven implementations. The expanding role of AI now encompasses proactive loss prevention, AI-driven merchandising execution, self-healing store operations, dynamic workforce orchestration, and real-time sustainability optimization. These advancements collectively demonstrate that AI in retail has evolved from a supportive tool to an active partner in business management, driving efficiency, reducing costs, and elevating customer experiences while enabling retailers to lead confidently in an increasingly competitive marketplace.

In the next chapter, on financial services, we'll explore how financial institutions are evolving beyond predictive analytics to deploy autonomous, agentic AI systems that can independently perceive, reason, and act within defined parameters. This transformation encompasses everything from GenAI revolutionizing regulatory compliance and document analysis to the creation of *digital relationship managers* and *virtual compliance officers* that proactively monitor markets and engage with clients in real time while meeting the sector's rigorous security and explainability requirements.

References

1. *5 Search Trends in Ecommerce You Need to Know in 2025*: https://searchanise.io/blog/site-search-trends/

2. *Capturing the Future of Digital in Consumer Products*: https://www.bain.com/insights/capturing-the-future-of-digital-in-consumer-products/

3. *AI-influenced shopping boosts online holiday sales, Salesforce data shows*: https://www.reuters.com/business/retail-consumer/ai-influenced-shopping-boosts-online-holiday-sales-salesforce-data-shows-2025-01-06/

4. *Win with Conversations*: https://www.bain.com/insights/win-with-conversations/

5. *Superagency in the workplace: Empowering people to unlock AI's full potential*: https://www.mckinsey.com/capabilities/mckinsey-digital/our-insights/superagency-in-the-workplace-empowering-people-to-unlock-ais-full-potential-at-work

11

Financial Services and the Next Wave of AI

In today's rapidly evolving financial landscape, AI has emerged as the cornerstone of modern banking transformation. As financial institutions worldwide race to embrace AI technologies, a new paradigm is taking shape, one where intelligent systems evolve from simple prediction to autonomous action, revolutionizing everything from customer experience to risk management across the financial services value chain.

This chapter explores how AI is transforming financial services and creating unprecedented opportunities for efficiency, personalization, and innovation.

By the end of this chapter, you will understand the following:

- How **generative AI (GenAI)** is transforming key use cases in banking
- The ways AI is enhancing customer experiences through intelligent, conversational interactions
- Advanced approaches to financial crime prevention and regulatory compliance using AI
- Real-world examples of operational data stores that can also serve as AI feature stores, powering both prediction and generation
- How domain-specific embeddings are revolutionizing search, compliance, and contextual analysis in finance
- Design principles and reference architectures for building and deploying agentic AI, balancing innovation, security, and regulatory trust

The evolution of AI in finance

AI's journey in finance began with predictive analytics: leveraging historical and real-time data to assess credit risk, flag fraud, forecast market shifts, and predict customer churn. These use cases remain foundational, delivering critical business value and driving operational efficiency. Financial institutions need robust, real-time feature stores enabling scalable access to the rich, governed data that predictive models require to optimize decisions and outcomes.

The arrival of GenAI expanded the field. With **large language models (LLMs)** and **retrieval-augmented generation (RAG)**, financial institutions are now automating and enhancing tasks once considered too complex: generating policy documents, responding to regulatory queries, summarizing large compliance filings, and powering conversational banking for clients and employees alike. GenAI uplevels intelligence from *"what might happen"* to *"let me generate, synthesize, and explain,"* unlocking even more value from both structured and unstructured data.

Today, we stand at the threshold of the next major advance: agentic AI. Unlike predictive and generative approaches that support decision-making or content creation, agentic AI delivers autonomous, goal-driven agents that can perceive, reason, and act within defined parameters. Think of agentic AI as the *digital relationship manager* or *virtual compliance officer* proactively monitoring markets, adapting to regulatory changes, managing workflows, and engaging with clients in real time, all while continuously learning and improving.

This evolution from predictive AI to GenAI to agentic AI demands a data platform that is both flexible and powerful:

- For **predictive AI**, financial institutions need robust, real-time feature stores, where machine learning features are stored, versioned, and accessed seamlessly
- For **GenAI**, they require integration of structured data and unstructured data, spanning transaction records, documents, emails, images, voice recordings, video content, and domain-specific knowledge bases to accelerate language models, Vector Search, and context retrieval
- For **agentic AI**, a unified substrate and operational agility are essential for agents to perceive the world, remember context, make informed decisions, and act with confidence

In financial services, these AI waves are not isolated; they build upon one another. Leaders continue to rely on robust predictive models, amplified by generative automation, orchestrated by agentic systems that adapt and govern in real time. Modern and intelligent databases such as MongoDB, with their flexible architecture and deep integration capabilities, such as MongoDB's integration with Voyage AI, offer best-in-class embedding models and rerankers and are uniquely positioned to support this hybrid landscape.

The power of finance-specific embeddings

In financial services, precision, context, and explainability are essential. Whether analyzing regulatory disclosures, automating compliance workflows, or engaging clients with intelligent assistants, AI systems must interpret complex language and domain-specific constructs with a high degree of accuracy. General-purpose LLMs, trained broadly across internet content, often struggle with the specialized terminology, abbreviations, and structured formats that define the financial world.

Domain-specific embeddings, particularly those tuned for finance, are a foundational solution to this challenge. These embeddings are designed to capture the semantics, patterns, and regulatory context unique to the industry, enabling AI models to do the following:

- **Accurately interpret financial documents**, from earnings calls and filings to contracts and risk reports
- **Surface relevant insights** using RAG or semantic search, improving accuracy and reducing hallucinations
- **Support explainability**, making outputs more auditable and compliant with regulatory expectations
- **Deliver just-in-time intelligence**, drawing on domain knowledge instantly to guide decision-making

Recent developments in this space, such as Voyage AI's `voyage-finance-2` embeddings, demonstrate how domain-tuned models outperform general-purpose alternatives in finance-specific tasks. Benchmark results have shown significantly improved relevance in information retrieval and question-answering over financial texts.

These finance-specific embeddings allow developers to build AI applications that are not only more context aware but also more aligned with the rigorous standards of the financial industry.

As financial institutions adopt GenAI and agentic AI, *embedding domain knowledge directly into model representations will be critical* to building systems that are intelligent, trustworthy, and operationally resilient.

Learn more about Voyages AI's finance embeddings in this blog post: `https://blog.voyageai.com/2024/06/03/domain-specific-embeddings-finance-edition-voyage-finance-2/`.

Transforming credit applications with AI

The same AI progression from predictive AI to GenAI to agentic AI is profoundly reshaping how credit applications are assessed, processed, and scored. Traditionally, credit scoring was based on rigid rules and limited historical data, often excluding individuals with thin or no credit files. Predictive AI began to address these limitations by using machine learning to forecast loan defaults based on historical patterns in credit behavior.

As the industry moved toward alternative credit scoring, AI models started incorporating non-traditional data sources such as rental history, utility payments, and digital footprints, offering a broader and more inclusive view of creditworthiness. This shift enabled lenders to assess risk with greater nuance and serve previously overlooked segments.

Today, GenAI and agentic AI are driving the next leap forward, creating a more adaptive, intelligent, and inclusive credit ecosystem:

- GenAI enhances data understanding and synthesis, making it possible to extract and structure information from unstructured sources such as bank statements, income proofs, or email correspondence. It can also generate human-readable explanations of complex decisions and create synthetic data that fills gaps in limited datasets, offering a more holistic view of financial behavior.

- Agentic AI brings autonomous, goal-driven capabilities that allow systems to manage entire credit workflows, automating document collection, verifying identity, adapting scoring logic in response to regulation changes, and even guiding applicants through the process interactively and intelligently.

This progression delivers benefits across several dimensions:

- **Adaptability**: AI models continuously learn and evolve in response to changing economic conditions and consumer behaviors. This ensures credit scoring systems remain accurate, responsive, and relevant in dynamic financial environments.

- **Fraud detection**: AI detects anomalies and suspicious activity in real time by analyzing patterns across applications and transaction histories.

- **Predictive analysis**: Machine learning techniques uncover correlations and indicators of credit risk from vast, complex datasets, going beyond what rule-based systems can detect.

- **Behavioral scoring**: For individuals lacking credit history, AI can generate dynamic risk assessments based on real-time financial behavior and spending habits.

- **Transparency in declinations**: AI can help explain why a credit application was denied, moving beyond binary decisions to offer actionable, human-readable feedback.

Despite the clear benefits, **transparency and explainability** remain common concerns, particularly among financial institutions subject to regulatory scrutiny. The complexity of deep learning models has historically made it difficult to explain decisions to consumers and regulators. Fortunately, advancements in **explainable AI (XAI)**, including techniques such as **SHapley Additive exPlanations (SHAP)** values and **Local Interpretable Model-agnostic Explanations (LIME)** plots, now provide visibility into how models arrive at their conclusions, helping demystify the *black box* and restore trust in AI-driven decisions.

Moreover, GenAI can complement these techniques by generating natural language explanations for credit outcomes, further bridging the gap between complex model logic and human understanding.

Building a smarter credit system with MongoDB

Supporting this evolution requires a modern, flexible data platform. MongoDB, with its document-based data model and developer-friendly architecture, is ideally suited to power AI-driven credit workflows.

Key advantages include the following:

- **Simplified data capture and processing**: By leveraging JSON for online application forms, institutions can streamline data ingestion, reduce redundancy, and improve processing speed. The document model excels at managing diverse data types, such as personal, financial, and employment, without sacrificing structure.

- **AI-enhanced credit scoring**: With MongoDB's developer data platform, a unified suite of data services built around a cloud-native database, financial institutions can build a 360-degree view of each customer by combining structured, semi-structured, and unstructured data sources.

- **Transparent declinations with LLMs**: LLMs integrated with MongoDB can interpret the outputs of complex machine learning models such as XGBoost. Instead of issuing vague or templated rejections, LLMs can generate personalized, understandable explanations that improve customer experience and aid compliance.

For example, the credit decision pipeline illustrated in *Figure 11.1* is used for predicting delinquency probability and credit scoring. This pipeline involves several key stages: data collection, processing, risk profile generation, model development, data transformation, and decision collection.

The outcome of the credit scoring could mean an approval or declination of the credit application. Understanding the reasons behind a decline is especially vital for both regulatory compliance and customer experience. LLMs, integrated with platforms such as MongoDB, can enhance explainability. For instance, LLMs can interpret the outputs of complex models such as XGBoost to generate clear, human-readable explanations for why an application was declined, moving beyond simple templated messages that only convey the final status.

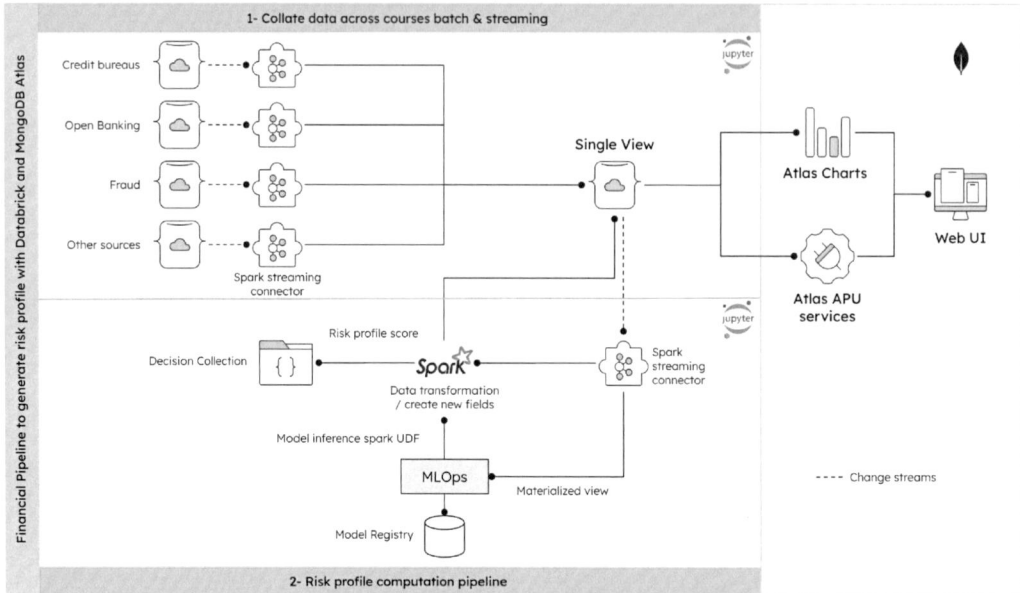

Figure 11.1: Architecture of the data processing pipeline for predicting the probability of delinquency and credit scoring

This diagram illustrates the end-to-end data processing pipeline for credit risk assessment, showing how customer data flows through the collection, processing, risk profiling, model development, and decision-making stages to produce accurate delinquency predictions. In *Figure 11.2*, you can see the architecture explaining credit scoring using an LLM.

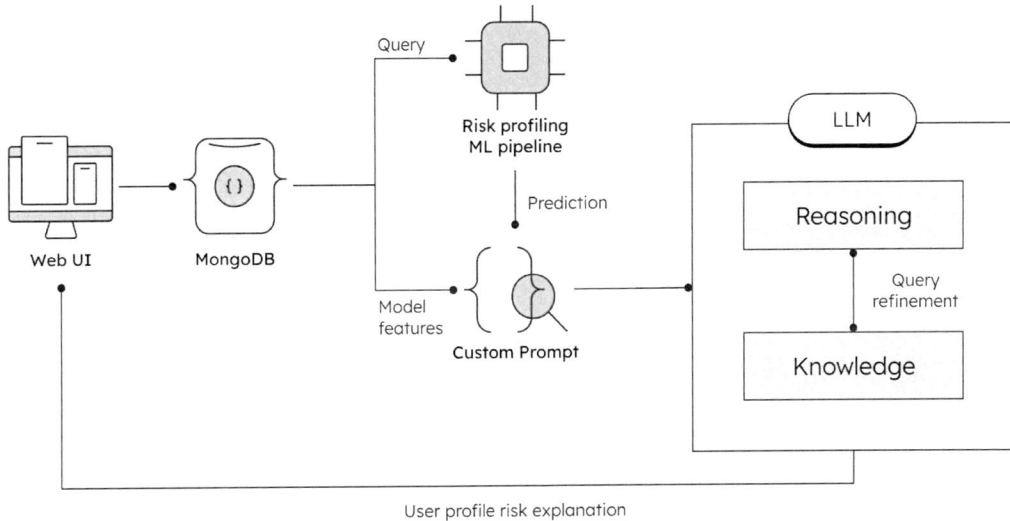

Figure 11.2: Architecture of the credit application declination

This visualization demonstrates how LLMs can be integrated into credit decision systems to provide clear, understandable explanations for application declinations, improving transparency and customer experience. In cases where a credit application is declined, the interaction should not end with a rejection. Instead, it presents a valuable opportunity for institutions to retain engagement by offering personalized, alternative credit products that better align with the applicant's financial profile.

Traditional recommendation engines typically rely on static rule-based systems or collaborative filtering models, which may lack the flexibility to respond to nuanced customer needs or evolving product offerings. These systems often struggle to contextualize why an applicant was declined and what viable alternatives exist. GenAI changes this dynamic entirely.

By leveraging customer data, credit scoring outcomes, and real-time product availability, GenAI models can function as intelligent recommendation engines, proactively suggesting suitable alternatives tailored to an applicant's risk profile, income, credit behavior, and preferences. For example, if a personal loan application is declined due to insufficient credit history, a GenAI model might recommend a more basic credit card with lower fees without premium features, a small installment loan with lenient terms, and/or a financial literacy product to build creditworthiness.

In addition to generating product matches, LLMs can explain why a particular alternative is being offered, improving transparency and building trust. This level of personalization and clarity was previously difficult to achieve with conventional recommendation systems.

The following architecture demonstrates how GenAI can be integrated into a credit decisioning pipeline, not just to assess risk but to provide *next-best-action recommendations* that keep customers engaged, informed, and supported through their financial journey:

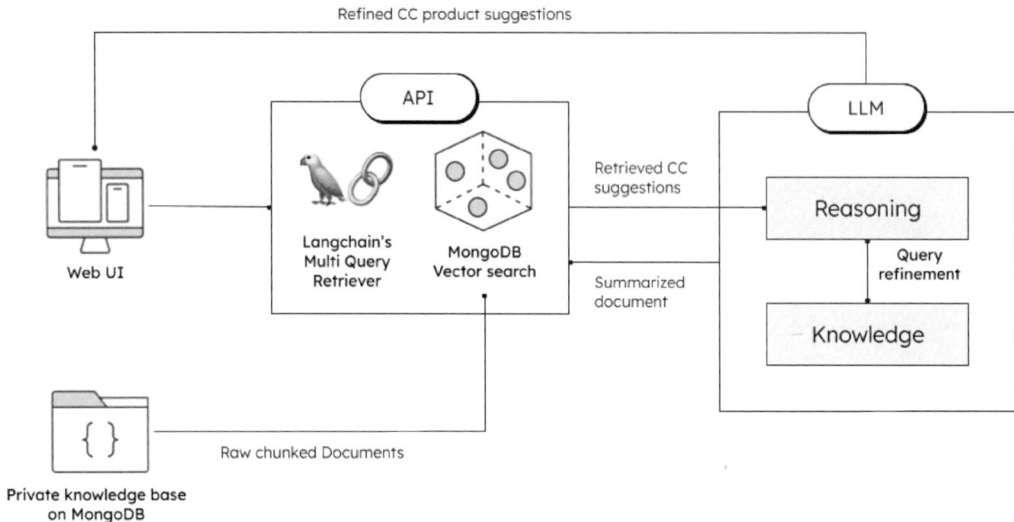

Figure 11.3: Architecture of the alternative credit product recommendations

Figure 11.3 illustrates the comprehensive architecture of an alternative credit product recommendation system. It shows how user interactions through the web UI trigger API calls, leveraging LangChain's MultiQueryRetriever and MongoDB Vector Search to process raw chunked documents from a private knowledge base on MongoDB. It retrieves relevant credit card suggestions and summarized documents, which are then fed into an LLM-powered reasoning engine for query refinement and knowledge processing. Ultimately, refined credit card product suggestions are delivered through an intelligent system that combines vector-based document retrieval, multi-query processing, and LLM reasoning to provide personalized financial product recommendations.

Learn how the convergence of alternative data, AI, and GenAI is reshaping the foundations of credit scoring at https://www.mongodb.com/docs/atlas/architecture/current/solutions-library/credit-card-application-with-generative-ai/.

Base39's AI-powered credit analysis

Besides the use of alternative data, predictive AI, and GenAI, agentic AI is also now being applied in the credit decision domain. One such firm is Base39. Base39 is a financial technology provider based in São Paulo, Brazil. Its core offerings are centered on providing advanced services for credit and risk analysis. Base39 was established to disrupt credit analysis by harnessing the power of AI with MongoDB Atlas Vector Search and Amazon Bedrock.

Base39 realized that existing credit analysis produces financial decisions that are insufficiently comprehensive, primarily due to data scarcity. Essential data, such as income verification, employment history, and credit score, represent a fraction of the information required. Furthermore, gathering and selecting these data points is heavily reliant on subjective processes. This complex and highly manual process can extend over several days and yield inaccurate and incomplete results.

While predictive machine learning algorithms are designed to handle basic scoring, the combined efforts with GenAI enhance data feeding, result interpretation, and *what-if* analyses. GenAI streamlines the updating of model parameters by analyzing historical data patterns. This eliminates the need for manual updates in spreadsheets or configurations. The LLM serves as a smart assistant for risk analysts, delivering recommendations and guiding the analyst to select the most pertinent data sources and fields for each loan scenario.

"MongoDB underpins the data layer, providing flexible schema support, vector search for LLM context, and a managed deployment model that aligns with Base39's developer-first philosophy."

— **Bruno Nunes, CEO, Base39**

MongoDB Atlas is the core component behind Base39's feature store. A feature store is a tool or system used in machine learning to store, manage, and serve data known as *features*. Features are individual measurable properties or characteristics used in machine learning models to make predictions. MongoDB's native search capabilities over both structured (enriched financial) and unstructured (behavioral) data via Atlas Vector Search make it critical for the assessment process.

With Atlas Vector Search, Base39 was able to accelerate feature retrieval and dynamically update their machine learning models. This flexibility is critical for making real-time adjustments to credit policies. By using the data retrieved by Vector Search, Base39 can augment the LLM's recommendations with domain-specific context, thereby increasing their reliability and accuracy for risk assessors. This avoids manually sifting through numerous documents or configuration files. Last but not least, one of the cutting-edge innovations and key differentiators of Base39's solution lies in the autonomy achieved through its agentic AI approach. Base39's model can perceive, reason, and act based on data. It employs a **chain-of-thought (CoT)** methodology, a reasoning method where AI breaks down complex problems into sequential steps. This enables the required autonomy for analyzing information and making decisions tailored to the particular individual loan's content. This enables the collection of credit information to be dynamic and hyper-personalized without having to prescribe many rules like in traditional rule-based AI automation systems (which, anyway, cannot exhaustively decide what information needs to be collected from the credit applicants). This agentic AI approach opens up infinite potential for more accurate and comprehensive credit profiles and eventual credit decisions. Learn more about the Base39 story at `https://www.mongodb.com/solutions/customer-case-studies/base39`.

While AI transforms customer-facing credit decisions, it is equally revolutionary in how banks manage internal knowledge and operations.

Revolutionizing enterprise knowledge management in banking with GenAI

Efficient access to and utilization of enterprise knowledge are paramount. Internal employees across various departments rely on vast amounts of information, ranging from policies and procedures to regulatory guidelines and product details. Traditional **enterprise knowledge management (EKM)** systems often fall short in providing seamless and intuitive access to this information. GenAI presents a transformative opportunity to revolutionize EKM within banks, empowering employees with intelligent tools that significantly enhance productivity and decision-making.

Challenges of traditional EKM systems in banking

Traditional EKM systems have played a central role in organizing information within banks, but they are increasingly challenged by evolving business and regulatory demands. These systems often struggle to deliver accurate, timely, and contextually relevant information, suffering from several limitations:

- **Information silos**: Knowledge can be fragmented across disparate systems and departments, making it difficult for employees to find a holistic view of a particular topic
- **Complex search interfaces**: Keyword-based search often yields irrelevant results, requiring employees to spend significant time sifting through documents to find the information they need
- **Outdated or difficult-to-understand content**: Policies and procedures can be lengthy, complex, and not easily digestible, hindering quick comprehension and application
- **Lack of contextual awareness**: Traditional systems often fail to understand the specific context of an employee's query, leading to generic and unhelpful responses
- **High maintenance overhead**: Keeping knowledge bases up to date and relevant requires significant manual effort

These limitations hinder operational efficiency and compliance. Overcoming these challenges necessitates the adoption of more advanced, context-aware EKM solutions.

How GenAI is transforming EKM systems in banking

GenAI offers powerful capabilities to overcome these limitations and create more effective and user-friendly EKM systems for internal bank employees. Many banks have begun implementing GenAI chatbots, often first consolidating data into a central enterprise knowledge repository to power their new generation of intelligent knowledge management applications.

Here are some of the key features often implemented in such services:

- **Natural language querying and conversational search**: GenAI enables employees to ask questions in natural language, just as they would to a colleague. The AI can understand the intent behind the query and provide precise and relevant answers, significantly reducing search time and frustration.
- **Intelligent document summarization**: GenAI can automatically summarize lengthy policies, procedures, and regulatory documents, providing employees with concise overviews and key takeaways. This allows for quicker understanding and application of critical information.

- **Contextualized information retrieval:** By understanding the user's role, their department, and the context of their query, GenAI can provide more tailored and relevant information, avoiding generic responses.

- **Dynamic knowledge generation:** GenAI can synthesize information from multiple sources to answer complex questions that might not be explicitly addressed in a single document. This allows employees to get comprehensive answers to nuanced queries.

- **Personalized knowledge recommendations:** Based on an employee's past queries and their role, GenAI systems can proactively recommend relevant knowledge and updates, ensuring they stay informed about critical information.

- **Automated knowledge base updates:** GenAI can assist in keeping knowledge bases up to date by identifying outdated information and suggesting revisions based on new regulations or internal policy changes, reducing manual maintenance.

- **Enhanced knowledge sharing and collaboration:** GenAI can facilitate internal knowledge sharing by identifying subject matter experts based on employee queries and connecting them for direct collaboration. It can also summarize key discussion points from internal forums and meetings, making knowledge more accessible.

These capabilities not only improve operational efficiency but also strengthen compliance and decision-making across the organization. As banks continue to adopt GenAI-powered EKM systems, they are laying the groundwork for more agile, informed, and collaborative knowledge ecosystems that evolve alongside regulatory and business demands.

Use cases of GenAI for internal EKM systems in banks

Several practical use cases highlight how banks are leveraging or can leverage GenAI for internal EKM:

- **Compliance and regulatory inquiries:** Employees can quickly get answers to complex regulatory questions by asking in natural language, with the GenAI system synthesizing information from various compliance documents

- **Product knowledge support:** Front-office staff can rapidly access detailed information about banking products and services to answer customer inquiries accurately and efficiently

- **Internal policy and procedure guidance:** Employees can easily understand and navigate internal policies and procedures through natural language queries and summaries

- **IT support and troubleshooting**: Internal IT teams can leverage GenAI to quickly find solutions to technical issues by querying knowledge bases and documentation using natural language

- **Onboarding and training**: New employees can quickly get up to speed by asking questions about internal processes and accessing relevant training materials through a GenAI-powered EKM system

- **Risk management insights**: Risk analysts can leverage GenAI to synthesize information from various risk reports and identify emerging trends and potential issues

These use cases demonstrate how GenAI-powered EKM can streamline access to critical information, reduce operational bottlenecks, and enhance employee productivity, ultimately enabling banks to respond more quickly and effectively to both internal needs and external demands.

Architectural considerations for GenAI-powered EKM systems

Implementing GenAI for EKM in a banking environment requires careful architectural design with a focus on integration, security, and scalability. A critical aspect of this design is the data platform consideration, as the effectiveness of GenAI heavily relies on the ability to store, manage, and efficiently retrieve diverse types of enterprise knowledge. Key considerations include the following:

- **Integration with existing knowledge infrastructure**: The GenAI system must seamlessly integrate with the bank's existing systems. This often involves building connectors and APIs to access information from disparate systems. A central operational data store can consolidate data from various sources, providing a unified view for the GenAI system.

- **Data platform selection**: Choosing the right data platform is fundamental. Modern databases capable of handling structured, semi-structured, and unstructured data, as well as supporting advanced indexing and search capabilities, are essential. Document-oriented storage excels at managing diverse enterprise knowledge assets. This multimodal approach proves crucial for effective GenAI applications.

- **Secure data access and governance**: Given the highly sensitive nature of banking data, robust security measures are paramount. Features including access controls and encryption ensure data protection and compliance.

- **Choice of GenAI models and platforms**: Banks need to choose appropriate LLMs and the underlying infrastructure (cloud or on-premises). The architecture should allow for easy integration with these models.

- **RAG**: To ensure that GenAI responses are accurate and grounded in the bank's specific knowledge, implementing RAG is crucial. Integrated search and Vector Search capabilities are particularly well suited to support RAG implementations, efficiently storing, indexing, and retrieving diverse data types, including text content and their corresponding vector embeddings for semantic similarity searches, ensuring that GenAI has context for its responses.

- **Scalability and performance**: The EKM system must handle a large volume of queries. Auto-scaling features ensure scalability and low-latency responses, meeting peak demand.

- **Monitoring and explainability**: Implementing robust monitoring of the GenAI system's performance and accuracy is essential. Storing logs and metadata about queries and responses aids in analysis and explainability.

- **UI and workflow integration**: The GenAI-powered EKM system should have an intuitive UI and be integrated into existing workflows. A flexible data model allows for easy adaptation to changing requirements and seamless integration.

By addressing these considerations holistically, banks can create a GenAI-powered EKM architecture that not only meets stringent security and compliance requirements but also delivers measurable gains in efficiency, knowledge accessibility, and decision-making quality.

An Asian bank's GenAI chatbot implementation

One of the progressive banks in Asia implemented a GenAI chatbot for an internal application to enhance the operational efficacy of the staff. The chatbot offers features such as content generation, text summarization, and language translation, helping employees improve work efficiency. It also assists in retrieving regulations, procedures, business contacts, application forms, and documents, saving employees significant time on information searches.

The bank's technology leadership openly acknowledges that developing effective GenAI applications presents unique hurdles, foremost among them being the art and science of prompt engineering – crafting the instructions given to the AI model. The quality of the AI's output is highly dependent on the clarity and specificity of these prompts. Recognizing this, the bank is actively evolving its application development culture. They strategically adjust the responsibility, encouraging business users, those with deep domain knowledge, to become *champions* in the GenAI development life cycle, particularly in refining and adjusting prompts. This marks a departure from conventional software development, where IT typically handles the bulk of the technical implementation.

To facilitate this cultural shift, the bank has instituted internal GenAI training programs aimed at equipping business personnel with essential prompt engineering skills. This organizational adaptation aims to bridge the gap between technical capability and business needs, ensuring GenAI tools and applications are maximally relevant and effective by directly incorporating user expertise into the fine-tuning process. The bank is also exploring automated prompt enhancement techniques to further streamline this process.

Furthermore, the bank understands the internal chatbot does not exist in isolation but is part of a broader, interconnected ecosystem of AI applications within the banking group and its subsidiaries. While serving a distinct internal purpose, it shares the underlying GenAI technology push and potentially leverages common data infrastructure with initiatives in other areas.

The following figure shows the knowledge workflow:

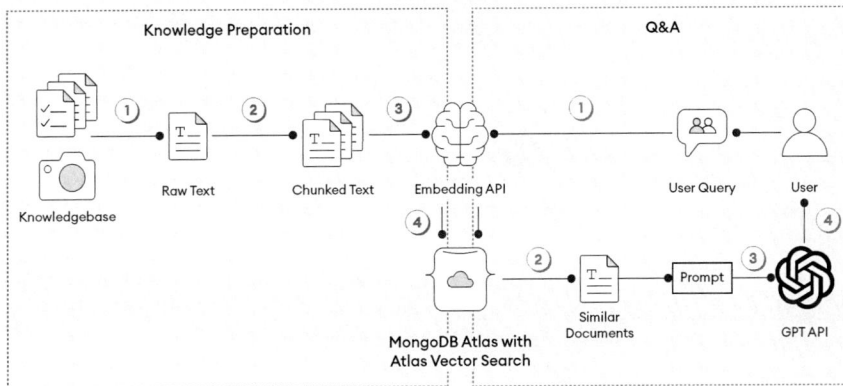

Figure 11.4: RAG knowledge system workflow

This diagram illustrates the seamless flow of information between various components in an AI-powered customer support system, showing how user queries are processed through Vector Search, enriched with context, and transformed into natural language responses.

The impact of GenAI on EKM systems

The integration of GenAI into EKM systems promises significant benefits for banks:

- **Increased employee productivity**: Faster and easier access to knowledge empowers employees to perform their tasks more efficiently

- **Improved decision-making**: Access to comprehensive and contextualized information enables employees to make more informed and timely decisions
- **Enhanced employee experience**: User-friendly GenAI-powered EKM systems can reduce frustration and improve job satisfaction by making it easier for employees to find the information they need
- **Reduced errors and improved compliance**: Accurate and readily available knowledge of policies and regulations can help reduce errors and ensure better compliance
- **Faster onboarding and training**: New hires can become productive more quickly with intelligent access to training materials and internal knowledge
- **Better knowledge retention**: GenAI systems can help preserve institutional knowledge by making it easily accessible and searchable, even as employees leave or roles change

While these internal applications of GenAI are transforming how banks operate behind the scenes, the technology is equally revolutionary in customer-facing applications, reshaping how financial institutions interact with and serve their clients.

Better digital banking experiences through AI-driven interactions

This shift toward customer-centric AI is creating more intuitive, personalized, and intelligent banking experiences. To meet rising expectations, banks are adopting AI-powered platforms built on LLMs and smart automation. This transformation requires a flexible, scalable data foundation essential for modern AI-driven banking.

Elevating customer experience with GenAI

GenAI introduces advanced capabilities such as intelligent chatbots and virtual assistants, enabling banks to provide real-time, context-aware support. These AI-driven tools can interpret complex customer inquiries, access relevant information, and deliver concise, personalized responses instantly. This not only enhances customer satisfaction but also streamlines operations by reducing reliance on traditional customer service channels.

Beyond assistance, GenAI also enables proactive banking. AI systems can surface insights derived from transaction data, usage trends, and behavioral analytics to recommend personalized financial products, notify users about unusual activity, or guide them through life events such as buying a home or saving for education. Rather than simply reacting to queries, banks can now anticipate customer needs, offering a seamless and value-rich experience.

Incorporating GenAI into banking workflows fundamentally changes how financial services are delivered. Customers engage with their bank through natural conversation rather than rigid forms or dropdowns. Instead of reading through dense policy documents, they receive AI-generated summaries and explanations tailored to their questions. The bank becomes a true financial partner, available 24/7, scalable, and intelligent.

AI-powered digital banking data foundations

Implementing AI in modern banking requires more than powerful models; it demands a flexible, real-time data foundation. A document-based architecture is ideal for managing complex banking data such as customer profiles, transaction histories, account behaviors, and unstructured content such as FAQs or policy documents, all in one place. This unified model allows AI systems to access rich, contextual information instantly, driving more accurate, personalized, and responsive customer experiences.

Modern data platforms such as MongoDB also support advanced AI patterns such as RAG, allowing banking assistants to instantly retrieve relevant documents and generate precise answers tailored to customer queries, whether it's explaining mortgage terms or flagging a suspicious charge.

Additionally, robust aggregation frameworks let smart agents analyze real-time account activity, spending trends, or loan balances in combination with historical data, enabling proactive insights and decision support. Security and compliance are essential, with features such as encryption, fine-grained access controls, and auditing being critical for any AI handling sensitive personal financial data.

With seamless integration into modern AI ecosystems and support for event-driven architectures, the right data platform empowers banks to automate workflows, personalize engagement at scale, and bring intelligent services to market faster, making it a core enabler of AI-powered digital banking.

Reference solution architecture for AI-powered customer support

To enable these capabilities, a reference architecture designed to enhance customer interactions using GenAI is essential. At the core of this architecture is MongoDB, serving as the centralized platform for storing and accessing both structured and unstructured data.

The process begins with data ingestion and transformation, where policy documents, frequently asked questions, product information, and other text-heavy resources are processed using **natural language processing (NLP)** techniques. NLP uses computational methods to analyze and understand human language, extracting meaning, structure, and context from unstructured text. These documents are broken into smaller segments and converted into vector embeddings. Both the original text and the embeddings are stored in MongoDB, leveraging its vector search capabilities for efficient retrieval.

When a new interaction occurs, whether initiated by voice, chatbot, or form input, the user query is vectorized in the same way. The application then performs a semantic similarity search across stored vectors, retrieving the most relevant content aligned with the user's intent. This approach enables accurate, context-aware responses that improve both efficiency and customer satisfaction.

Figure 11.5 illustrates the end-to-end flow of an AI-powered customer support system.

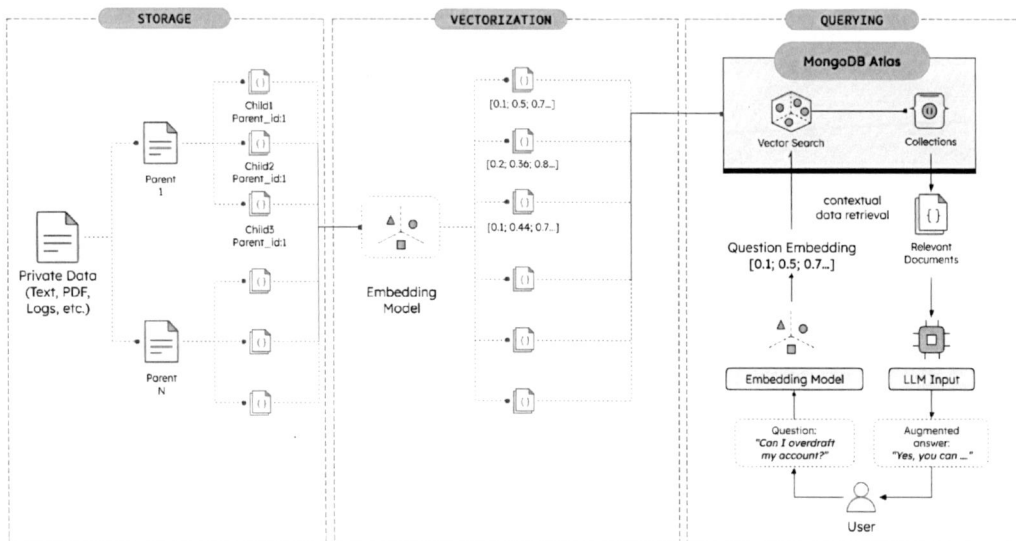

Figure 11.5: Process and component interactions from AI-powered customer support

The diagram shows how user queries are processed, enriched with contextual data, and transformed into personalized responses through the integration of Vector Search, language models, and operational data. These retrieved documents, enriched with additional context from operational data (such as account history or eligibility criteria), are passed into a language model that generates a natural language response.

This architecture relies heavily on real-time access to multiple forms of data. For example, transaction metadata, user profiles, and behavioral signals are all stored in MongoDB and can be aggregated as needed. By using Atlas Triggers, the system can also react dynamically. For instance, if a customer asks about an overdraft, the system could trigger a lookup of current balances and payment schedules before responding.

This modular architecture is designed to integrate with the broader AI stack, including LLM orchestration frameworks (such as LangChain or LlamaIndex), and deployment environments that manage AI models and workflows. MongoDB sits at the intersection of all these layers, enabling both the storage and the dynamic retrieval of the high-value data that AI agents depend on.

As banks enhance customer interactions through AI, they must simultaneously strengthen their defenses against increasingly sophisticated financial crimes.

AI-enhanced financial crime mitigation and compliance

AI is transforming risk and compliance in financial services through real-time fraud detection, automated regulatory interpretation, and smarter decision-making. MongoDB provides the flexible, scalable data foundation these AI systems rely on, especially for handling diverse data in **know your customer (KYC)** and **anti-money laundering (AML)** processes, from documents to voice and images. As fincrime grows more sophisticated and regulations become increasingly complex, AI and cutting-edge data platforms are enabling institutions to stay ahead, turning risk into resilience and compliance into a competitive advantage.

Fincrime has evolved dramatically in recent years, with criminals leveraging advanced technologies and exploiting vulnerabilities in digital systems. Traditional detection methods that rely on static rules and predefined thresholds struggle to keep pace with these sophisticated schemes. At the same time, regulatory requirements continue to expand, creating significant compliance burdens for financial institutions. The costs of inadequate fincrime prevention are substantial, encompassing monetary losses, regulatory penalties, reputational damage, and diminished customer trust. To address these challenges, institutions need adaptive solutions capable of responding to emerging threats while maintaining operational efficiency.

Strengthening financial crime mitigation with AI

In general terms, **fincrime** represents a comprehensive collection of policies, controls, analytics, and investigations to prevent, detect, report, and recover from any criminal activity that could not only harm customers, but, even more critically, damage financial institutions' reputation. Thus, it is considered a major operational risk that needs to be addressed accordingly.

Among the different potential threats, the most common are fraud management (asset loss), AML (asset origins), sanction compliance (asset legality), and all the operational risks mainly due to weak governance, antiquated screening, lack of process controls, or poor data quality and validation. All of these threats could be substantially augmented and become undetectable by sophisticated techniques in cyberspace, making manual checks futile. Therefore, cyber-threats must be encountered by the equivalent modern technologies, making AI the perfect fit as the right solution to optimize fincrime mitigation technical capabilities.

Emerging trends redefining the future of AI in compliance

AI, especially GenAI, is emerging as a vital tool in helping organizations shift from reactive risk mitigation to proactive governance. At the core of this transformation are flexible data platforms designed to support real-time, AI-driven decision-making at scale. For instance, traditional fraud detection systems rely on static rules and predefined thresholds. These are increasingly ineffective against modern fraud techniques, which are fast, adaptive, and often hidden within legitimate activity. AI enhances risk management by learning from historical and real-time data, detecting anomalies, and identifying patterns of suspicious behavior.

GenAI goes further by enabling scenario modeling and synthetic fraud simulations, helping organizations test hypotheses and uncover previously unknown threat vectors. AI-driven systems can detect not just individual fraudulent actions but coordinated, multi-channel fraud networks. By integrating with modern data platforms such as MongoDB, these systems gain access to a unified, contextualized view of data across sources, enhancing detection and decision accuracy.

Enabling all these AI capabilities requires a data platform that can not only store vast historical and real-time transaction data but also efficiently serve this data to various AI models, from predictive anomaly detectors to generative models for simulation, often in real time or near-real time. By having a modern data platform, financial institutions can unlock smart capabilities such as the following:

- **XAI:** As regulatory scrutiny increases, financial institutions need AI systems that can explain their decisions. XAI approaches provide transparency into how AI models reach conclusions, satisfying regulatory requirements for accountability while maintaining detection accuracy. Leading data platforms support this explainability by preserving the relationships between data points and decisions.

- **Proactive risk sensing:** Rather than just responding to known patterns, advanced AI systems can anticipate emerging risks by analyzing subtle changes in behavior and market conditions. This forward-looking approach requires a flexible data foundation that can integrate diverse signals and support real-time analytics.

- **Federated learning for collaborative defense:** Financial institutions are exploring federated learning techniques that allow them to collectively train fraud detection models without sharing sensitive customer data. This collaborative approach strengthens the entire financial ecosystem while preserving privacy and confidentiality. Modern data platforms with sophisticated security features are essential for implementing these sophisticated approaches.

Together, these capabilities position financial institutions to stay ahead of evolving threats, meet regulatory demands with confidence, and transform compliance from a defensive necessity into a strategic advantage.

AI for regulatory intelligence and policy automation

The primary goal of fincrime prevention is to stop criminal activity while ensuring regulatory compliance. GenAI is transforming this space by creating powerful new capabilities for detecting and preventing fincrime:

- **Synthetic fraud datasets:** GenAI can create synthetic datasets of fraudulent transactions that mimic novel attack patterns not yet observed in the wild. This allows financial institutions to train their detection systems proactively, preparing for emerging threats before they materialize in actual attacks.

- **Adversarial testing:** By simulating sophisticated fraud attempts, GenAI helps institutions identify vulnerabilities in their existing controls. These simulations can model complex, multi-channel attacks that traditional testing methods might miss.

- **Anomaly generation:** Rather than waiting for rare fraud events to occur naturally, GenAI can produce realistic anomalies that help improve detection models, particularly for low-frequency but high-impact fraud scenarios.

AI also helps institutions interpret regulations, translate them into internal policies, and monitor ongoing adherence. GenAI can read and summarize legal texts, extract obligations, and suggest enforcement policies. Intelligent autonomous agents, that is, AI-powered systems that can perceive their environment, make decisions, and take actions to achieve specific goals, continuously validate operational activities against regulatory requirements, flagging noncompliant behavior in real time.

With modern data platforms as the underlying foundation, compliance systems benefit from real-time access to critical data: customer profiles, transactions, communications, and audit logs. The document model of platforms such as MongoDB allows organizations to store regulatory interpretations, compliance rules, and contextual metadata in a format that is easily searchable and traceable, enabling efficient, automated compliance checks and auditable reporting.

MongoDB's role in KYC and AML

AI is transforming risk and compliance in financial services through real-time fraud detection, automated regulatory interpretation, and smarter decision-making. Modern data platforms such as MongoDB provide the flexible, scalable data foundation these AI systems rely on, especially for handling diverse data in KYC and AML, from documents to voice and images.

MongoDB enables financial institutions to ingest and store unstructured data such as scanned IDs, biometric information, and customer support voice logs alongside structured data such as transactions and account histories. This allows AI models to perform deeper, multimodal analysis. For example, GenAI can transcribe and analyze voice interactions for suspicious intent, or detect document forgeries using image data.

MongoDB Atlas further enhances this by offering built-in capabilities such as full-text search, Vector Search (for similarity matching), and integration with machine learning pipelines. With these features, institutions can compare customer-submitted documents to known fraud patterns, run facial recognition or voiceprint validation, and perform semantic searches across customer interactions, enabling a much richer KYC/AML risk assessment process.

An AI-first approach to risk and compliance begins with a dynamic, single-customer view, as shown in *Figure 11.6*. MongoDB Atlas ingests structured and unstructured data from internal systems, customer touchpoints, and external sources, which is then processed by AI models to detect potential fraud or compliance violations based on learned behaviors and regulatory logic. Diverse data sources, including structured transaction data, unstructured documents, and external datasets, are integrated into a unified profile, enabling comprehensive risk assessment and personalized service delivery.

Converged Data Store for KYC

Evolving business regulations demands continuous checks

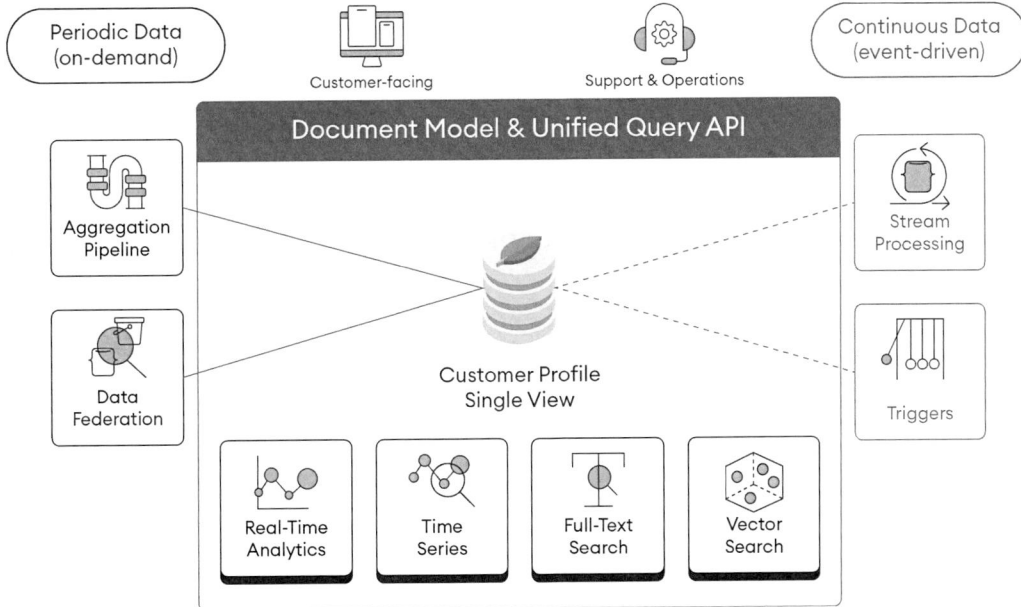

Figure 11.6: Converged data store for building a dynamic customer profile

Once this single view is built, it can be combined with additional unstructured data, such as sanction watchlists and AML policies, along with transactional data, for comprehensive analysis. The flexibility of MongoDB's document model enables this multimodal database approach. After the data is converged into a complete dataset, MongoDB's Vector Search can identify similar vector representations of known suspicious activities, as shown in *Figure 11.7*. This ensures that only high-likelihood fraudulent transactions are flagged for review, reducing false positives while maintaining detection accuracy.

Real-time Screening
Comprehensive Analysis

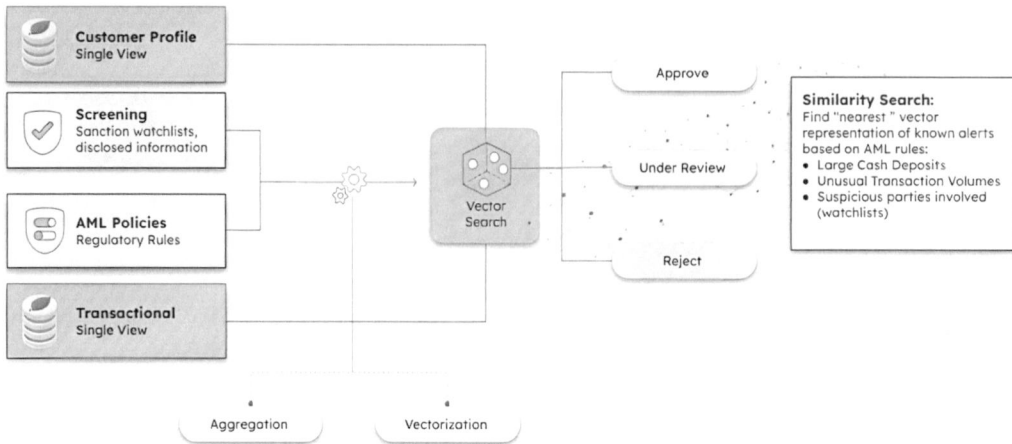

Figure 11.7: Real-time transaction screening using Vector Search

Vector Search plays a critical role in real-time transaction screening, enabling the comparison of incoming transactions against established patterns of suspicious activity. By leveraging this approach, financial institutions can significantly reduce false positives, improve detection accuracy, and respond faster to potential threats.

Strategic business benefits

The implementation of AI-driven real-time transaction screening and Vector Search capabilities can deliver the following measurable strategic capabilities for financial institutions:

- **Better fraud detection**: AI models powered by MongoDB's real-time data access can catch subtle fraud signals across large datasets, reducing false positives and speeding response times.

- **Improved compliance**: Automated interpretation and enforcement of regulations reduce manual overhead and audit risks.

- **Enhanced KYC/AML**: The ability to store and analyze unstructured customer data enriches identity verification and risk scoring.

- **Increased agility**: IT departments can rapidly adapt to new regulatory mandates or emerging fraud typologies, as MongoDB's flexible schema supports iterative development and quick deployment of new data models and AI-driven rules without lengthy database redesign cycles.

- **Operational efficiency**: AI automation and integrated data workflows free human teams to focus on high-value tasks.

- **Regulatory trust**: By providing a unified data platform with comprehensive audit trails for AI-driven decisions, IT decision-makers can help their institutions more effectively demonstrate robust controls and accountability to regulators, fostering greater trust and potentially reducing scrutiny.

As fincrime continues to evolve, AI-powered prevention systems will become increasingly sophisticated. Comprehensive techniques such as federated learning, which allows models to be trained across multiple institutions without sharing sensitive data, promise to enhance detection capabilities while preserving privacy and confidentiality.

Autonomous intelligent agents represent the next frontier, with systems that can proactively hunt for suspicious patterns, adapt defenses in real time, and even predict emerging threats before they materialize. These systems will require robust data platforms that can handle complex, interconnected data and support real-time decision-making at scale.

By investing in AI-powered fincrime prevention built on flexible, scalable data platforms such as MongoDB, financial institutions can stay ahead of evolving threats while reducing operational costs and maintaining regulatory compliance.

Beyond traditional risk management, AI is also transforming how institutions approach environmental and social responsibility.

Multimodal and AI-driven ESG analysis

The profound impact of **environmental, social, and governance** (**ESG**) principles is evident, driven by regulatory changes, especially in Europe, compelling financial institutions to integrate ESG into investment and lending decisions. Regulations such as the EU **Sustainable Finance Disclosure Regulation** (**SFDR**) and the EU Taxonomy Regulation are examples of such directives that require financial institutions to consider environmental sustainability in their operations and investment products. Investors' demand for sustainable options has surged, leading to increased ESG-focused funds. The regulatory and commercial requirements, in turn, drive banks to also improve their green lending practices. This shift is strategic for financial institutions, attracting clients, managing risks, and creating long-term value.

However, financial institutions face many challenges in managing different aspects of improving their ESG analysis. The key challenges include defining and aligning standards and processes, and managing the flood of rapidly changing and varied data to be included for ESG analysis purposes.

AI can help to address these key challenges in not only an automatic but also an adaptive manner via techniques such as machine learning. Financial institutions and ESG solution providers have already used AI to extract insights from corporate reports, social media, and environmental data, improving the accuracy and depth of ESG analysis. As the market demands a more sustainable and equitable society, predictive AI combined with GenAI can also help to reduce bias in lending to create a fairer and more inclusive financing while improving the predictive powers. The power of AI can help facilitate the development of sophisticated sustainability models and strategies, marking a leap forward in integrating ESG into broader financial and corporate practices.

Under the broader umbrella of ESG, environmental and climate risk is a key challenge for financial and non-financial institutions alike. With climate change accelerating at an unprecedented rate, millions of assets are at risk. Institutions will need intelligent climate data analytics to manage the climate risk and find better risk-adjusted opportunities.

Ambee's climate data platform

Ambee, a fast-growing climate tech start-up based in India, is making waves in the world of environmental data with its mission to create a sustainable future. With over 1 million daily active users, Ambee provides proprietary climate and environmental data-as-a-service to empower governments, healthcare organizations, and private companies to make informed decisions about their policies and business strategies.

MongoDB Atlas has been at the core of Ambee's database architecture, supporting their AI and machine learning models. The firm leveraged MongoDB Atlas to manage its extensive and diverse environmental datasets. Processing approximately 4 terabytes of data daily from over 800,000 sensors and 11 Earth observation satellites, Ambee faced challenges in scaling and ensuring rapid API responses. By adopting MongoDB Atlas, the company centralized its data storage, which streamlined data access and reduced the need for complex joins across multiple tables. This transition enabled Ambee to scale from handling 60,000 API calls per month in 2020 to approximately 790 million by 2023, all while improving API response times from 2 seconds to under 300 milliseconds.

Ambee's data provides users with precise environmental insights within a <1 Km² radius. To achieve this high level of accuracy and granularity, Ambee required a platform capable to not only support a large volume of data but also to be able to support extensive geospatial needs. MongoDB Atlas perfectly fits their requirements due to its rapid geospatial querying capabilities. For instance, with MongoDB, they can query the nearest location to a given coordinate within 20 milliseconds, even with millions of geospatial data points.

The performance, scalability, and multimodal capabilities of MongoDB Atlas support Ambee's AI-driven services, such as forecasting forest fires and providing real-time air quality and pollen data. Additionally, MongoDB Atlas Search facilitates text search functionalities, including partial, wildcard, and autocomplete searches, enhancing the platform's ability to deliver precise information swiftly.

MongoDB's role in ESG data management

MongoDB's dynamic architecture revolutionizes ESG data management, handling semi-structured and unstructured data. Its flexible schema nature allows the adaptation of data models as ESG strategies evolve. Advanced text search capabilities efficiently analyze vast semi-structured data for informed ESG reporting. Support for Vector Search enriches ESG analysis with multimedia content insights.

Incorporating LLMs enhances MongoDB's capacity to process ESG textual content, automating sentiment extraction, summarization, and trend identification. Combining LLMs with vector data management capabilities, GenAI applications can be created to interpret the complex and evolving sustainability taxonomy and guide the investment and financing processes in a compliant manner. This AI-driven approach, supported by MongoDB's robust data management, offers a sophisticated means of analyzing extensive narrative data in ESG reporting.

Furthermore, MongoDB supports geospatial and network graph analytics, providing a powerful combination of analytics to identify the physical risks associated with climate change (e.g., floods or wildfires) to assets financed by banks or investment firms and for assessing supply chain impacts of the climate risks. The risk analytics can then enable targeted strategies for risk mitigation and supply chain resilience.

With the evolution of agentic AI, new sustainability use cases are emerging. For example, agentic AI applications can serve as intelligent copilots for relationship managers during green loan origination, ensuring ESG compliance and eligibility in real time. Agentic AI can continuously monitor ESG disclosures and external media to detect greenwashing, autonomously trigger risk alerts, and recommend mitigation steps for compliance teams. In supply chain management, agentic AI agents can proactively map climate vulnerabilities of suppliers, simulate disruption scenarios, and orchestrate automated resilience measures, driving more sustainable procurement and operations.

Leveraging the out-of-box, rich, multimodal capabilities and integrated AI tooling, MongoDB's data platform is an ideal foundation for advancing the use of AI to agentic AI applications, as it can serve as a real-time operational and analytical data store for ingesting, storing, and organizing all relevant ESG, regulatory, and contextual data that agentic AI agents require to make informed, autonomous decisions. By seamlessly integrating with AI models and supporting real-time event processing, MongoDB enables agentic AI to monitor ESG risks, trigger alerts, and orchestrate workflows across lending, compliance, or supply chain modules, all using operational ESG data.

AI-driven ESG policy and regulatory compliance

AI can play a transformative role in ESG policy analysis and regulatory interpretation by automating the ingestion, understanding, and synthesis of complex and frequently changing regulations across jurisdictions. Utilizing advanced NLP and machine learning models, AI can rapidly analyze lengthy regulatory texts, accurately extract key requirements, and compare them against an organization's current policies and practices. This enables compliance teams to quickly identify gaps, overlaps, or potential violations, and receive actionable recommendations for policy updates. AI-powered tools can also track regulatory changes in real time, generating concise summaries and alerting relevant stakeholders to new obligations or opportunities, significantly reducing manual effort and the risk of oversight.

Agentic AI systems can autonomously monitor multiple regulatory jurisdictions, proactively initiate reviews or policy updates when new ESG requirements are detected, orchestrate internal workflows for cross-departmental compliance, and even assist in drafting initial responses or disclosures to regulators.

For example, in a real-time use case, agentic AI can continuously scan official publications from international regulators and, upon detecting a newly issued ESG rule, automatically update internal policy documents, create tailored action items for compliance teams, and trigger notifications for impacted business units, all within minutes of the regulation's release. However, recognizing the importance of institutional control and accountability, many organizations can implement a *man-in-the-loop* approach, where AI-driven recommendations, updates, and action items are routed to human experts for review and approval before any final decisions or public disclosures are made. This ensures that while AI brings speed and consistency to ESG policy processes, critical judgments and final controls remain in the hands of experienced professionals. For global financial institutions navigating an ever-evolving ESG regulatory landscape, both traditional and agentic AI-driven policy analysis, combined with human oversight, offer a scalable and consistent way to maintain compliance, optimize reporting, and confidently pursue sustainability objectives.

MongoDB's value extends beyond ESG data management, accelerating productivity for developers and data science teams. Its intuitive data model, analytical tools, and AI integrations streamline the development and deployment of data-driven applications, making MongoDB pivotal for organizations advancing their ESG agendas efficiently.

Figure 11.8 represents an enterprise ESG solution architecture with the boxes labeled with a leaf where MongoDB can be deployed to support the ESG data analytics services.

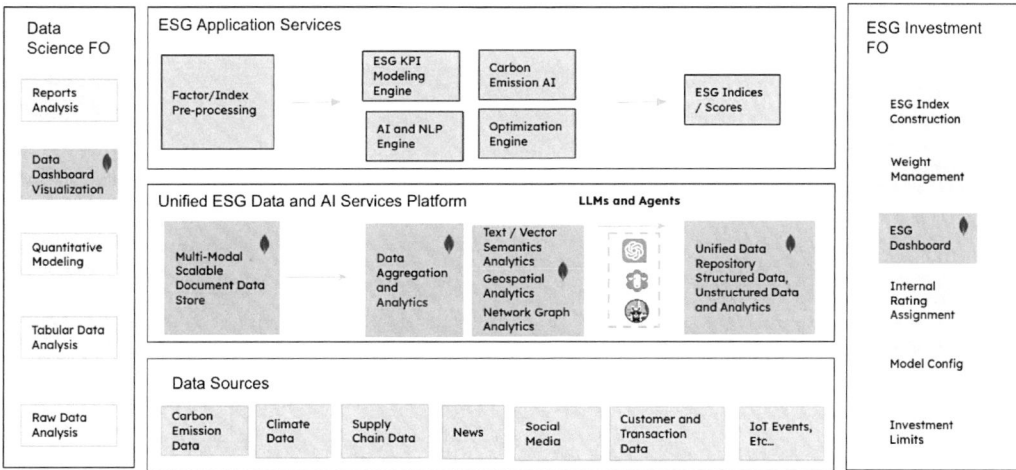

Figure 11.8: Blueprint for enterprise ESG solution architecture using MongoDB

This illustrates a complete ESG solution architecture, highlighting the integration points where MongoDB can be deployed to support data collection, analysis, and reporting across ESG domains.

Straight-through payments processing powered by AI

The payments sector is undergoing rapid transformation. As corporate clients demand faster, smarter, and more efficient services, financial institutions are turning to AI to enable real-time, data-driven decision-making and automation. Central to unlocking these benefits is not just AI itself, but the foundational technology that supports it, most notably, flexible, scalable, and high-performance data infrastructure such as MongoDB.

This section explores how **straight-through payment processing (STP)**, the seamless, end-to-end execution of payment transactions without manual intervention, is being revolutionized by AI, and how MongoDB provides a critical backbone for this transformation.

Business outlook

The payments industry stands at the cusp of a profound transformation, driven by AI. With the rise of real-time transactions, digital banking expectations, and complex compliance requirements, banks and financial institutions are under increasing pressure to deliver more intelligent, automated, and personalized services. AI is no longer just an innovation initiative; it's becoming a business imperative.

Several forces are converging to make AI a cornerstone of modern payments processing:

- **Customer expectations**: Both retail and corporate customers now demand real-time insights, seamless payment experiences, and predictive services such as cash flow forecasting or anomaly alerts.

- **Operational complexity**: Traditional manual workflows in payment reconciliation, fraud checks, and routing are increasingly untenable due to growing transaction volumes.

- **Competitive pressures**: Fintech disruptors and digital-native banks are leveraging AI to differentiate themselves. Traditional banks risk falling behind if they don't evolve quickly.

- **Regulatory demands**: Regulations such as PSD2, ISO 20022, and real-time payment schemes (e.g., RTP, FedNow) require financial institutions to modernize infrastructure and data workflows, which aligns well with AI's data-hungry nature.

In corporate banking, AI adoption is particularly strategic. According to Celent's research, 73% of corporate banks reported clear revenue opportunities from investments in advanced analytics. On the other hand, 30% of banks increasing their investment in payments technology have ranked AI as a high priority [1].

This emphasis is not only on incremental efficiencies but also on new business models and monetizable value-added services, such as real-time financial dashboards, automated forecasting, and smart liquidity tools.

The role of GenAI

The emergence of GenAI and LLMs has added new dimensions to AI's role in payments:

- **Natural language interfaces**: Clients can now query payment data conversationally ("What are my outstanding receivables over $10,000 this quarter?"), transforming the user experience

- **Code generation and testing**: GenAI tools enhance developer productivity, allowing for faster creation of payment processing logic, validations, and compliance checks

- **Data summarization and reporting**: LLMs can synthesize vast volumes of transaction data into insights, summaries, or regulatory reports, reducing reliance on manual data handling

However, the application of GenAI introduces challenges in data security, explainability, and regulatory compliance, especially when handling sensitive financial information, making data architecture and governance critical enablers.

The future of payments is NOW
The combination of all needs stresses existing data handling

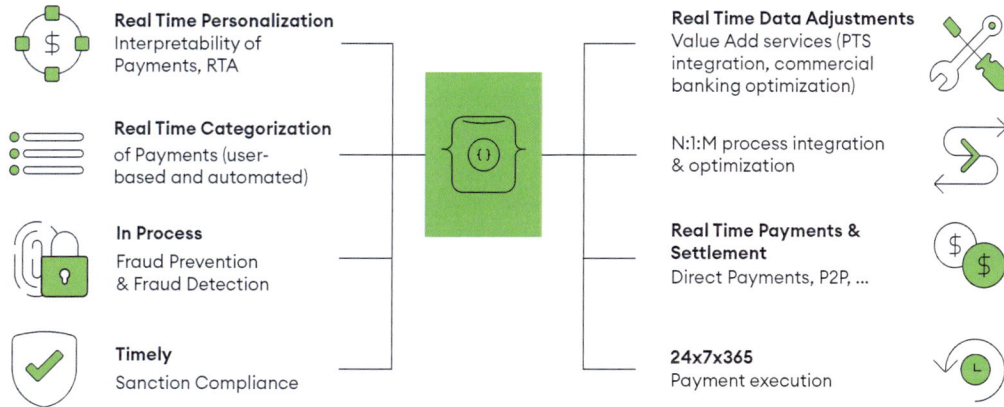

Real Time Personalization
Interpretability of
Payments, RTA

Real Time Categorization
of Payments (user-
based and automated)

In Process
Fraud Prevention
& Fraud Detection

Timely
Sanction Compliance

Real Time Data Adjustments
Value Add services (PTS
integration, commercial
banking optimization)

N:1:M process integration
& optimization

**Real Time Payments &
Settlement**
Direct Payments, P2P, ...

24x7x365
Payment execution

Figure 11.9: Payments key drivers

This diagram illustrates the foundational architecture of modern real-time payment systems, showing how the central processing core manages comprehensive payment workflows by integrating input capabilities such as real-time personalization, automated categorization, fraud prevention, and compliance monitoring with output services including data adjustments, process integration, payment settlement, and 24/7 execution to enable seamless, secure, and continuous payment processing with real-time operational capabilities.

The success of AI in payments depends fundamentally on a robust data infrastructure. AI models are only as good as the data they are trained on, and the insights they produce are only as trustworthy as the systems that manage that data. This is where MongoDB plays a pivotal role:

- **Unified data layer**: MongoDB enables organizations to unify disparate data sources (payment messages, account data, customer profiles, and logs) into a single view, structured and ready for analytics or machine learning pipelines

- **Real-time analytics and AI readiness**: Its ability to support streaming, time-series, and high-volume transactional workloads ensures AI applications are responsive and scalable

- **Modern developer experience**: MongoDB's rich developer ecosystem, integrating with Python, Spark, TensorFlow, and vector databases, makes it ideal for building and iterating on AI-driven features

With a unified, scalable, and AI-ready data foundation, MongoDB empowers payment providers to harness AI with speed, accuracy, and confidence, driving innovation while ensuring trust in every transaction.

Despite the promise, integrating AI into STP presents significant data challenges:

- **Volume and variety**: Payment systems process millions of transactions in diverse formats and from disparate sources
- **Real-time processing**: Many AI applications depend on streaming or near-real-time data processing
- **Data quality and normalization**: Legacy formats and inconsistent data structures hinder model performance
- **Auditability and governance**: AI, especially GenAI, requires transparent data handling for regulatory compliance

These challenges demand a database platform that's agile and scalable and handles structured, semi-structured, and unstructured data. MongoDB delivers unique capabilities tailored for AI-driven STP systems:

- **Flexible data modeling**: MongoDB's document-oriented model allows for the seamless integration of diverse financial data sources, such as transaction histories, invoices, and market data, into a unified format. This flexibility is crucial for accurate cash flow forecasting, or for supporting several payment schemas, including ISO 20022, facilitating intelligent routing decisions.
- **High-performance queries**: The database's indexing and aggregation capabilities allow for swift analysis of transaction patterns, aiding in the detection of fraudulent activities.
- **Secure data handling**: Features such as encryption at rest and in transit, along with role-based access control, ensure sensitive financial data is protected during analysis.
- **Data validation**: Built-in schema validation helps in identifying and correcting anomalies in payment data, reducing the need for manual intervention.
- **Real-time data processing**: With features such as change streams and time-series collections, MongoDB enables real-time tracking and analysis of financial transactions, facilitating timely insights into cash positions.
- **Integration with analytics tools**: MongoDB's compatibility with tools such as Apache Spark and its own aggregation framework supports complex analytical queries necessary for forecasting models.

- **Operational resilience**: MongoDB's replication and sharding capabilities ensure high availability and scalability, which are essential for processing and rerouting payments efficiently.

- **Multi-cloud and hybrid readiness**: MongoDB Atlas, the fully managed cloud platform, enables banks to run AI workloads across on-premises, public cloud, or hybrid environments, which is critical for compliance and data residency needs in global banking.

The ultimate goal is to accelerate development and AI-adoption while enabling real-time analytics as a key technological enabler for modern payments processing.

The road ahead

As the payments industry enters a new phase of digitization, the fusion of AI and scalable data infrastructure will define future leaders. STP is no longer a technical aspiration; it is a strategic imperative. MongoDB empowers banks to realize this vision by making it easy to manage, analyze, and act on payments data in real time. By investing in flexible data architectures and AI-enabling technologies today, banks will not only enhance their current offerings but also lay the foundation for continuous innovation tomorrow.

Capital markets

The capital markets sector faces unique challenges in managing vast amounts of diverse data in a fast-paced, high-stakes environment. Modern financial institutions require flexible and scalable data platforms that can address the demands of data-intensive trading operations. Effective data architecture enables the integration of real-time market trends, alternative data sources, regulatory information, and customer profiles while facilitating seamless connections across various functions in the capital markets business.

AI can address several financial services industry challenges, including the following:

- **Risk management:** Improves resilience to market volatility through real-time monitoring, adaptive decision-making, and automated risk mitigation, thereby reducing human error.

- **Data analytics:** Enhances data processing by seamlessly ingesting unstructured inputs such as news sentiment and social media data, harnessing GenAI and RAG solutions for deeper analytics and more precise insights.

- **Regulatory compliance:** Streamlines operations by automating reporting, detecting anomalies, preventing fraud, and improving auditability.

- **Customer service:** Improves human-AI collaboration to optimize customer service with AI assistants, while automating workflows to make financial institutions more agile, responsive, and cost-efficient.

Modern data platforms with robust high-performance data ingestion, real-time analytics, advanced security, and support for time-series data strengthen financial services organizations' ability to unlock actionable insights and drive smarter decision-making. AI capabilities and Vector Search technologies enable capital markets to adapt to evolving market conditions, changes in regulatory requirements, and client needs. Whether it's transforming market data management, enhancing trading strategies, optimizing risk management, or streamlining compliance reporting, the right data architecture provides the agility to innovate and excel in a rapidly changing financial services landscape.

Reimagining investment portfolio management with agentic AI

Risk management in capital markets is becoming increasingly complex and data-driven, presenting significant challenges for investment portfolio managers. The need to process vast amounts of diverse data, from real-time market data to unstructured social media data, demands a level of flexibility and scalability that traditional systems struggle to keep up with.

AI agents, a type of AI that can operate autonomously and take actions based on goals and real-world interactions, are set to transform how investment portfolios are managed [2]. According to Gartner, 33% of enterprise software applications will include agentic AI by 2028, up from less than 1% in 2024. At least 15% of day-to-day work decisions are made autonomously through AI agents [3]. The right data architecture can support these AI agents to effectively transform the landscape of investment portfolio management. By leveraging the combination of LLMs, RAG, and advanced Vector Search capabilities, AI agents can analyze vast financial datasets, detect patterns, and adapt in real time to changing conditions dynamically. This advanced intelligence elevates decision-making and empowers portfolio managers to enhance portfolio performance, manage market risks more effectively, and perform precise assets impact analysis.

Intelligent investment portfolio management

Investment portfolio management is the process of selecting, balancing, and monitoring a mix of financial assets such as stocks, bonds, commodities, and derivatives to achieve a higher **return on investment (ROI)** while managing risk effectively and proactively. It involves thoughtful asset allocation, diversification to mitigate market volatility, continuous monitoring of market conditions, and the performance of underlying assets to stay aligned with investment objectives.

To stay relevant today, investment portfolio management requires the integration of diverse, unstructured alternative data, such as financial news, social media sentiment, and macroeconomic indicators, alongside structured market data such as price movements, trading volumes, indexes, spreads, and historical execution records. This complex data integration presents a new level of sophistication in portfolio analytics, as outlined in *Figure 11.10*. It requires a flexible, scalable, unified data platform that can efficiently store, retrieve, and manage such diverse datasets, and pave the way for building next-gen portfolio management solutions.

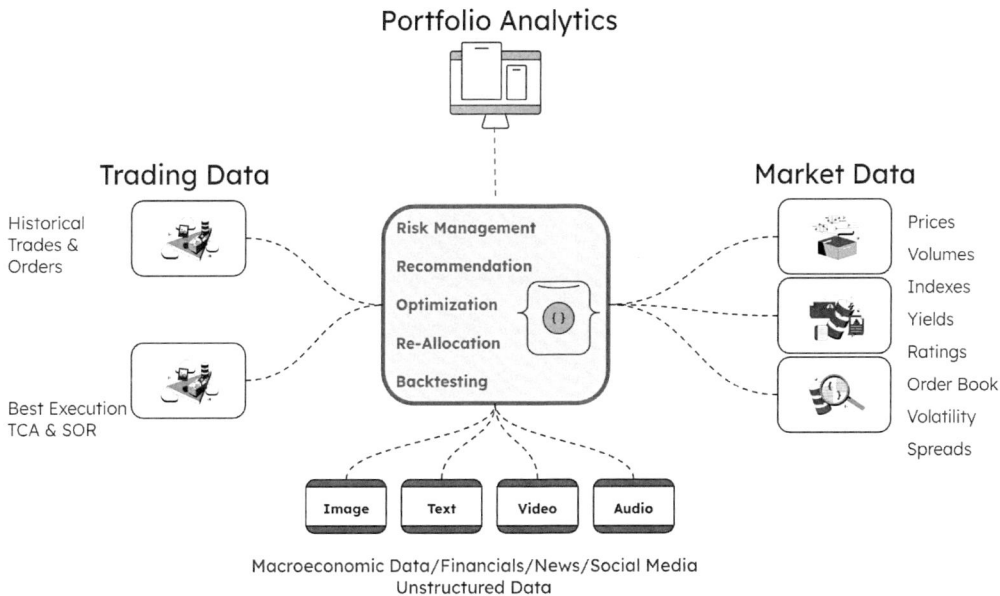

Figure 11.10: Investment portfolio analysis

This diagram illustrates the comprehensive architecture of modern investment portfolio analysis systems, showing how the central analytics engine integrates diverse data inputs including trading data (historical trades, orders, and best execution metrics), market data (prices, volumes, indexes, yields, ratings, order book data, volatility, and spreads), and unstructured macroeconomic data from multiple formats (image, text, video, and audio) to deliver core portfolio management functions, including risk management, recommendation generation, optimization, reallocation, and backtesting capabilities that enable intelligent decision-making and proactive market risk mitigation through MongoDB's flexible schema for accelerated data ingestion across various sources.

Incorporating MongoDB's flexible schema accelerates data ingestion across various data sources, such as real-time market feeds, historical performance records, and risk metrics. New portfolio management solutions, enabled with the alternative data, support more intelligent decision-making and proactive market risk mitigation. This paradigm shift realizes deeper insights, enhances alpha generation, and refines asset reallocation with greater precision, underscoring the critical role of data in intelligent portfolio management.

How MongoDB unlocks AI-powered portfolio management

AI-powered portfolio asset allocation has become a desirable characteristic of modern investment strategies. By leveraging AI-based portfolio analysis, portfolio managers gain access to advanced tools that provide insights tailored to specific financial objectives and risk tolerances. This approach optimizes portfolio construction by recommending an alternate mix of assets ranging from equities and bonds to **Exchange Traded Funds (ETF's)** and emerging opportunities while continuously assessing the evolving market conditions.

The following figure illustrates a proposed workflow for AI-powered investment portfolio management that brings diverse market data, including stock price, **volatility index (VIX)**, and macroeconomic inductors such as GDP, interest rate, and unemployment rate, into an AI analysis layer to generate actionable and more intelligent insights:

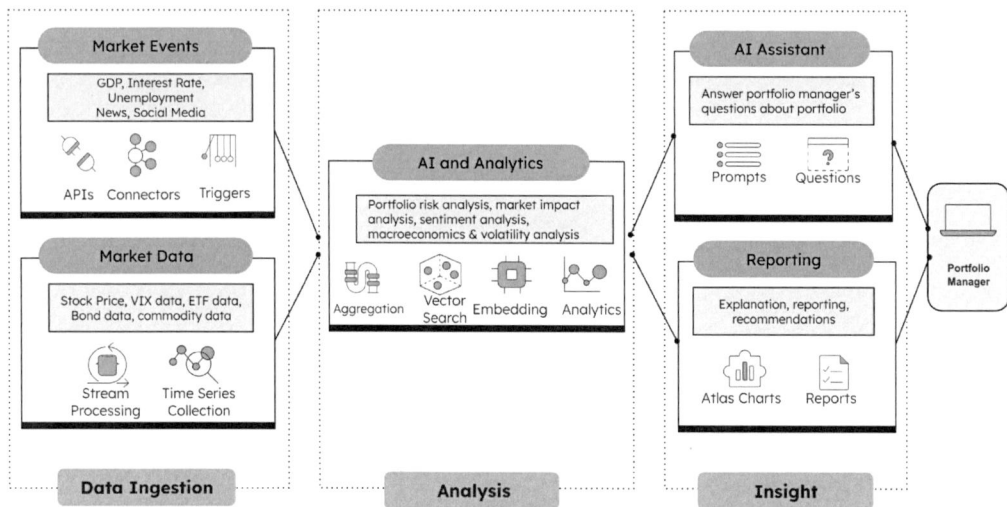

Figure 11.11: AI-powered portfolio management workflow

This diagram illustrates the end-to-end architecture of AI-powered investment portfolio management systems. It shows a three-stage workflow that starts with processing data ingestion from market events (such as GDP, interest rates, unemployment, news, and social media through APIs, connectors, and triggers) and market data, such as stock prices, VIX, ETF, bonds, and commodity data via stream processing and time-series collection. It then feeds into centralized AI and analytics capabilities (such as portfolio risk analysis, market impact analysis, sentiment analysis, macroeconomics, and volatility analysis using aggregation, Vector Search, embedding, and analytics). Finally, it delivers actionable insights through AI assistants (such as answering portfolio manager questions via prompts and queries) and comprehensive reporting (explanations and recommendations through Atlas Charts and reports) to enable intelligent, data-driven investment decision-making for portfolio managers.

MongoDB's versatile document model unlocks a more intuitive way for the storage and retrieval of structured, semi-structured, and unstructured data. This is aligned with the way developers structure the objects inside the applications.

In capital markets, time series are often used to store time-based trading data and market data. MongoDB time-series collections are optimal for analyzing data over time. They are designed to efficiently ingest large volumes of market data with high performance and dynamic scalability. Discovering insights and patterns from MongoDB time-series collections is easier and more efficient due to faster underlying ingestion and retrieval mechanisms.

By taking advantage of MongoDB Atlas Charts' business intelligence dashboard and evaluating advanced AI-generated investment insights, portfolio managers gain access to sophisticated capabilities that integrate high-dimensional insights derived from diverse datasets, revealing new patterns that can lead to enhanced decision-making for alpha generation and higher portfolio performance.

MongoDB Atlas Vector Search plays a critical role in the analysis of market news sentiment by enabling the context-aware retrieval of related news articles. Traditional keyword-based searches often fail to capture semantic relationships between news stories, while Vector Search, powered by embeddings, allows for a more contextual understanding of how different articles relate to a stock sentiment. The following capabilities power a more context-aware and accurate approach to market news sentiment analysis:

- **Storing news as vectors**: When stock-related news is ingested, each news article is vectorized as a high-dimensional numerical representation using an embedding model. These embeddings encapsulate the meaning and context of the text, rather than just individual words. The raw news articles are embedded and stored in MongoDB as vectors.

- **Finding related news**: Vector Search is used to find news articles based on similarity algorithms, even if they don't contain the exact same stock information. This helps in identifying patterns and trends across multiple news articles based on contextual similarity.

- **Enhancing sentiment calculation**: Instead of relying on a single news sentiment, a final sentiment score is aggregated from multiple related news articles with similar and relevant content. This prevents one individual outlier news article from influencing the result and provides a more holistic view of market news sentiment.

MongoDB Atlas Vector Search transforms market news sentiment analysis by going beyond simple keywords to capture deeper context and connections, empowering smarter, more reliable insights for better investment decisions.

Intelligent investment portfolio management with AI agents

AI agents are positioned to revolutionize portfolio management by shifting from rule-based to adaptive, context-aware, and AI-powered decision-making. AI-enabled portfolio management applications continuously learn, adapt, and optimize investment strategies more proactively and effectively. The future isn't about AI replacing portfolio managers, but rather humans and AI working together to create more intelligent, adaptive, and risk-aware portfolios. Portfolio managers who leverage AI gain a competitive edge and deeper insights to significantly enhance portfolio performance.

The solution illustrated in *Figure 11.12* includes a data ingestion application, three AI agents, and a market insight application that work in harmony to create a more intelligent, insights-driven approach to portfolio management.

The data ingestion app continuously collects market data, storing it in MongoDB as time series or standard collections. The datasets ingested include the following:

- **Market data:** Collects and processes real-time market data, including prices, volumes, trade activity, and VIX
- **Market news:** Captures and extracts market and stock-related news. News data is vectorized and stored in MongoDB
- **Market indicators:** Retrieves key macroeconomic financial indicators, such as GDP, interest rate, and unemployment rate

The market analysis agent and market news agent have AI analytical workflows. They run based on a daily schedule in a fully automated fashion, producing the expected output and storing it in MongoDB. The market assistant agent has a more dynamic workflow and is designed to play the role of assistant to the portfolio manager. It works based on prompt engineering and agentic decision-making. The market assistant agent is capable of responding to questions about asset reallocation and market risks based on current market conditions and brings the new AI-powered insights to portfolio managers.

Each agent plays a distinct role in the overall workflow to produce intelligent insights:

- **Market analysis agent:** Analyzes market trends, volatility, and patterns to generate insights related to the risk of portfolio assets
- **Market news agent:** Assesses the news sentiment for each of the assets by analyzing news that directly and indirectly can impact the portfolio performance. This agent is empowered by MongoDB Vector Search

- **Market assistant agent:** On demand and through a prompt, answers the portfolio manager's questions about market trends, risk exposure, and portfolio allocation by using data sources and insights that other agents create

The market insight application is a visualization layer that provides charts, dashboards, and reports for portfolio managers, with a series of actionable investment insights from the outputs created by AI agents. This information is generated based on a predetermined daily schedule automatically and presented to portfolio managers.

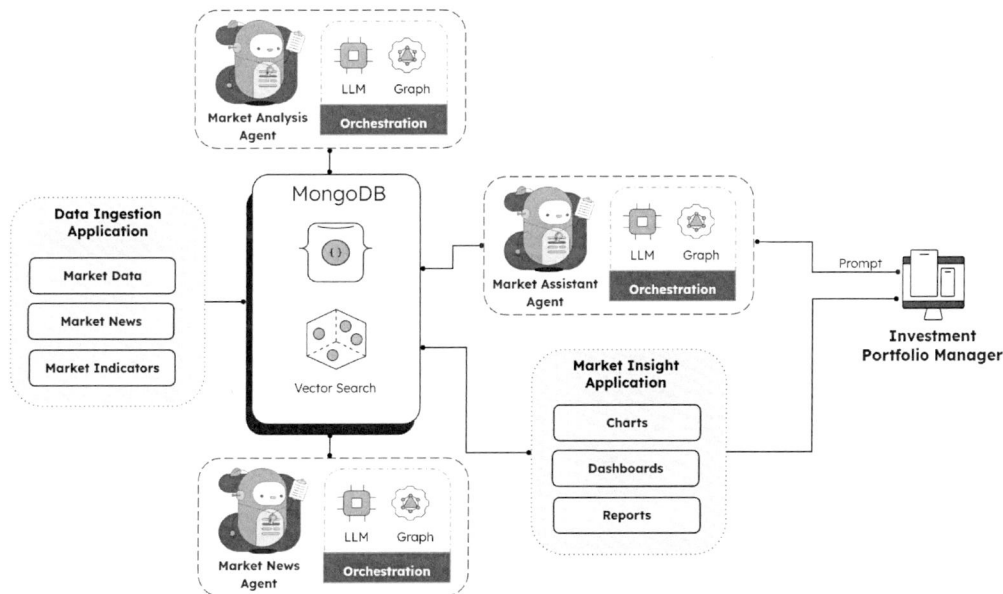

Figure 11.12: Investment portfolio management powered by MongoDB AI agents

As illustrated here, the investment portfolio management is powered by MongoDB AI agents, showing how specialized AI agents (market analysis agent, market assistant agent, and market news agent) leverage LLM and graph orchestration capabilities to process data from the data ingestion application (market data, news, and indicators) through MongoDB's Vector Search functionality, enabling seamless integration with the market insight application (charts, dashboards, and reports) to deliver intelligent, prompt-driven responses to investment portfolio managers through a unified AI-powered ecosystem that combines real-time data processing, advanced analytics, and conversational interfaces for enhanced investment decision-making.

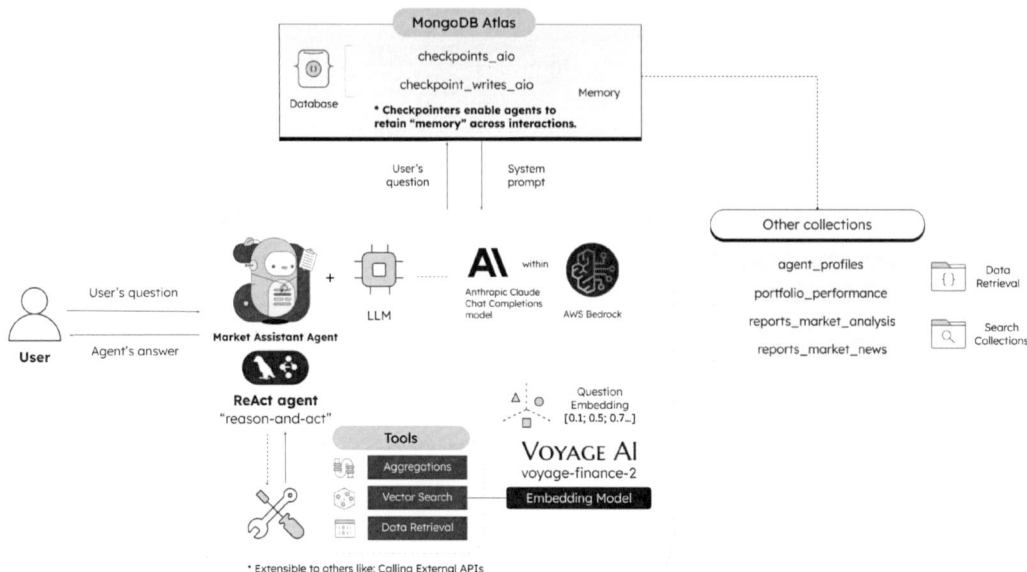

Figure 11.13: Market assistant ReAct agent architecture

AI agents enable portfolio managers to take an intelligent and risk-based approach by analyzing the impact of market conditions on the portfolio and its investment goals. The AI agents capitalize on MongoDB's powerful capabilities, including the aggregation framework and Vector Search, combined with embedding and GenAI models to perform intelligent analysis and deliver insightful portfolio recommendations.

For more details on AI agents, see *Chapter 2, What Sets GenAI, RAG, and Agentic AI Apart.*

The expanding role of AI in financial services

As we close this section, it's clear that AI is a powerful force reshaping the future of financial services, and MongoDB is enabling the AI transformation journey. AI success is a function of the right data architecture, scalability, quality, accessibility, and agility. MongoDB's flexible document model, Vector Search, and comprehensive developer data platform provide the backbone for AI applications. The AI shift from experimentation to enterprise adoption requires a strategic rethink of how data, models, and decisions flow through the organization. Whether you're driving innovation, managing risk, or building next-generation customer experiences, the financial institutions that lead over the next decade won't just adopt AI; they will embed it into every decision, every product, and every client interaction.

With the rise of agentic AI, financial services institutions have great potential to redefine how to manage risk more intelligently, optimize complex workflows, and deliver hyper-personalized client experiences. As autonomous AI agents advance, they offer the potential to transform decision-making from reactive to proactive, combined with reasoning and actions, moving beyond merely a data response into a deeper understanding of cause and effect, empowering financial institutions with greater precision and smarter solutions. As we look ahead, those who effectively harness the potential of AI will be best positioned to lead in this rapidly evolving financial services landscape, setting a new standard for agility, innovation, and customer trust.

The following are additional examples of how AI is transforming financial services:

- **Advanced customer behavior and KYC analytics**: Vector Search enables sophisticated customer profiling by correlating behavioral patterns with unstructured data sources, including emails, social media activity, and transaction narratives. This provides deeper insights into customer risk profiles and enables more accurate identity verification processes.

- **Intelligent market research**: AI systems can rapidly synthesize market intelligence by searching across vast repositories of research reports, earnings calls, regulatory filings, and news sources. Semantic similarity enables analysts to discover non-obvious connections and emerging trends across different market segments and geographies.

- **Large document intelligence for regulatory filings**: AI-powered document processing transforms how financial institutions handle complex regulatory submissions. Systems can automatically extract, validate, and cross-reference data across hundreds of pages of regulatory documents, ensuring compliance while reducing manual review time from weeks to hours.

- **AI-powered financial application code generation**: Development teams leverage AI to accelerate the creation of financial applications by generating compliant code snippets, API integrations, and regulatory validation logic. This enables the faster deployment of new financial products while maintaining strict security and compliance standards.

- **Retail banking dynamic product pricing**: AI-powered real-time pricing enables banks to instantly adjust fees and rebates based on market conditions, service costs, and customer behavior. By analyzing live data, AI can optimize pricing for competitiveness, profitability, and responsiveness, ensuring agility in dynamic payment environments.

- **Treasury liquidity and cash flow forecasting**: Dynamic cash positioning using AI-enabled dashboards provides real-time cash flow visibility and prediction. By leveraging AI in scenario analysis and modeling various economic conditions, banks can proactively adjust funding strategies.

- **Payment smart routing**: AI-enabled payment smart routing leverages dynamic decision-making and continuous learning to intelligently optimize every transaction in real time. AI analyzes several conditions, fees, exchange rates, and historical patterns to proactively select the most efficient and cost-effective routes. As payment ecosystems become more complex and global, smarter AI-driven routing is essential to navigate shifting regulations, rising transaction volumes, and increasing demand for speed, cost efficiency, and reliability.

These emerging applications demonstrate how AI continues to push the boundaries of what's possible in financial services, enabling institutions to operate with greater intelligence, efficiency, and customer focus than ever before.

For more information and resources, visit the *MongoDB for Financial Services* page at: `https://www.mongodb.com/solutions/industries/financial-services`.

Summary

In this chapter, we've explored the transformative impact of AI on the financial services industry, tracing its evolution from predictive analytics to GenAI and now to agentic AI. We've seen how these technologies are revolutionizing EKM, customer experiences, fincrime prevention, ESG analysis, credit applications, and payments processing.

The financial services industry stands at a pivotal moment where AI is not just enhancing existing processes but fundamentally reimagining how financial institutions operate and deliver value. From intelligent chatbots that provide personalized customer support to sophisticated fraud detection systems that can anticipate new attack vectors, AI is enabling unprecedented levels of efficiency, personalization, and security.

Looking ahead, the continued evolution of agentic AI promises even more profound changes, with autonomous systems that can perceive, reason, and act within defined parameters. These intelligent agents will increasingly serve as digital relationship managers, virtual compliance officers, and automated risk analysts, working alongside human experts to drive better outcomes for financial institutions and their customers.

Key to this transformation is the underlying data infrastructure. Modern, flexible data platforms such as MongoDB provide the foundation that AI systems need to access, analyze, and act on diverse data in real time. The integration of domain-specific intelligence, such as finance-specialized embedding models, further enhances the accuracy and relevance of AI applications in this highly regulated industry.

As we've seen through various case studies, from Asia Bank's GenAI chatbot to Ambee's climate data platform to Base39's credit analysis solution, financial institutions that embrace AI and build on robust data foundations are gaining significant competitive advantages. They're able to make better decisions faster, provide more personalized customer experiences, and navigate complex regulatory landscapes with greater confidence.

As we move into the next chapter, on insurance, we'll see how many of these same AI technologies and approaches are being applied to transform another critical sector of the financial services industry, with its own unique challenges and opportunities.

References

1. *Celent Report: Harnessing the Benefits of AI in Payments*: https://www.mongodb.com/resources/solutions/use-cases/celent-report-harnessing-the-benefits-of-ai-in-payments

2. *Demystifying AI Agents: A Guide for Beginners*: https://www.mongodb.com/resources/basics/artificial-intelligence/ai-agents

3. *Intelligent Agents in AI Really Can Work Alone. Here's How.*: https://www.gartner.com/en/articles/intelligent-agent-in-ai

12

RegData, MongoDB, and Voyage AI: Semantic Data Protection in FSI

AI has become an increasingly important part of modern banking transformation. However, as the **financial services industry (FSI)** worldwide embraces AI technologies, it faces a critical challenge: how to leverage AI *without compromising* the privacy, compliance, and control requirements that define the financial industry.

This chapter explores how MongoDB, RegData, and Voyage AI have formed a powerful alliance to address this challenge through semantic data protection, a sophisticated methodology that allows financial institutions to preserve the quality and utility of AI outputs while enforcing rigorous data security standards. It also supports the secure deployment of AI agents, which are increasingly acting autonomously on regulated information across complex financial workflows. Together, these technologies offer an integrated solution tailored to the high-security, high-stakes demands of AI in financial services.

By the end of this chapter, you will understand the following:

- Why traditional protection methods such as encryption and masking fall short in AI-driven financial services
- How semantic data protection preserves meaning, context, and format while without exposing sensitive data
- The core components of a secure AI architecture for financial institutions, from tokenization to prompt decoration
- How domain-specific embeddings improve both protection and performance in financial AI applications

- Secure deployment patterns for AI agents, including **Model Context Protocol (MCP)** and hybrid cloud strategies

- Compliance strategies aligned to frameworks such as GDPR, FINMA, and the EU AI Act

The data protection dilemma in financial AI

Financial institutions sit at the intersection of two powerful but seemingly contradictory forces: the drive to innovate with AI and the mandate to protect sensitive data. Banks and financial services companies possess vast repositories of highly regulated information, from **personally identifiable information (PII)**, which includes data such as names, addresses, and social security numbers that can identify an individual, to **client identifying data (CID)**, which refers to any information that can be used to identify a specific client or customer, and transaction histories. This data represents both their greatest asset for AI innovation and their greatest vulnerability. If mishandled, it can enable fraud, privacy violations, or costly regulatory penalties. If locked down too tightly, it becomes unusable for innovation.

Traditional approaches to data security, such as complete encryption, data masking, and restricted access, often render data unusable for AI applications or significantly diminish the quality of AI outputs. When financial institutions attempt to leverage cloud-based AI services, they face additional challenges as sensitive data may leave their controlled environments, exposing them to regulatory violations and security risks.

This dilemma has created a significant barrier to AI adoption in financial services. According to industry research, many financial institutions cite data security and compliance concerns as major obstacles to implementing advanced AI solutions. The consequences are substantial: limited innovation, competitive disadvantage, and an inability to deliver the personalized, intelligent services that customers increasingly expect.

Traditional data protection methods fall short in AI contexts for several key reasons:

- **Loss of context:** Masking or encryption strips away the semantic relationships and context that AI models need to generate meaningful outputs. A fraud-detection system, for instance, can no longer see spending patterns that flag suspicious behavior.

- **Binary approach:** Traditional methods often take an all-or-nothing approach; either data is fully accessible or completely restricted, with no middle ground for AI processing. For example, either every analyst sees a customer's full SSN, or no one does, and neither works for AI processing.

- **Static protection:** Fixed rules for data protection cannot adapt to the dynamic, contextual nature of AI interactions and use cases. Consider a rule that works during training but fails when the model encounters novel inputs in production.

- **Diminished utility**: Heavy-handed protection techniques significantly reduce the quality and relevance of AI outputs. In such cases, insights become so generic that they no longer help relationship managers or product teams.

These shortcomings explain why legacy approaches are incompatible with the needs of financial AI and point to the necessity of a new paradigm: semantic data protection.

Understanding the MongoDB, RegData, and Voyage AI approach to semantic data protection

The integration of MongoDB, RegData, and Voyage AI represents a paradigm shift in how financial institutions can secure sensitive information while preserving AI functionality. Unlike traditional approaches that focus solely on hiding or restricting data, this combined solution preserves the meaning, context, and format of information while replacing the sensitive values themselves.

MongoDB provides a flexible, scalable data foundation with its document model and Atlas Vector Search capabilities. RegData contributes its advanced protection methodology and compliance expertise. Voyage AI (acquired by MongoDB) supplies domain-specific embeddings that understand financial terminology and concepts. Together, they create a comprehensive approach to addressing the unique challenges of AI security in financial services. This alliance makes AI adoption practical, not theoretical, for banks under regulatory scrutiny.

What is semantic data protection?

Semantic data protection safeguards the *meaning* and *context* of information rather than just its raw values or surface format. While traditional data protection methods (such as encryption, masking, and access control) often focus on securing data values or formats, semantic data protection looks deeper. It replaces sensitive values in ways that preserve format, relationships, and regulatory context so that AI systems remain useful without exposing real identities.

The core principles of semantic data protection include the following:

- **Semantic protection**: The protection keeps the semantic or the original data. A phone number is replaced by another phone number; a city name is replaced by another city name.
- **Contextual semantic protection**: Protection depends on the meaning and usage of data, not just its type or label. For example, a phone number may be treated differently depending on whether it's personal, business-related, or public. The name of a city may be replaced by the name of a city of the same jurisdiction, where the same type of laws will apply.

Beyond these foundational approaches, semantic data protection incorporates several additional sophisticated capabilities. Data classification and controls are determined by semantic sensitivity rather than simple data types, ensuring that protection levels match the actual risk and importance of the information. The system leverages semantic models such as ontologies, taxonomies, or knowledge graphs to define data relationships and meanings, enabling consistent policy enforcement across complex data ecosystems. Furthermore, data governance becomes truly contextual, with usage rules that dynamically adapt based on the contextual meaning of data, user roles, intended use cases, and applicable regulatory frameworks such as GDPR, FINMA, or HIPAA.

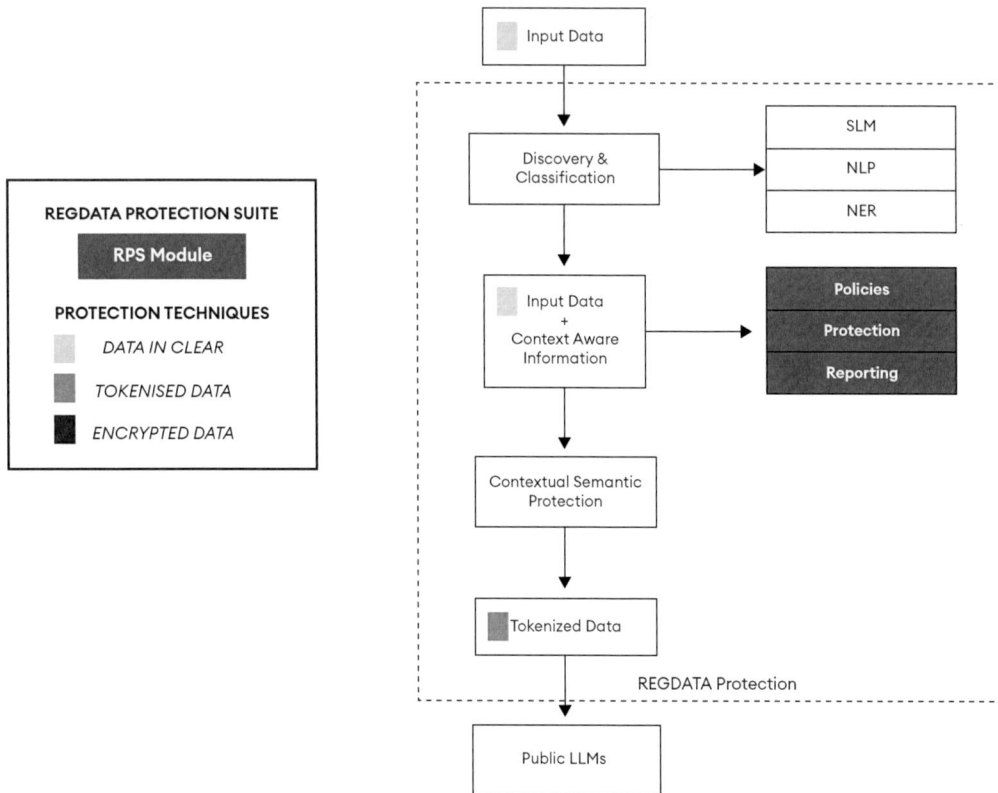

Figure 12.1: Semantic data protection framework architecture and data flow

This diagram illustrates the key components of a semantic data protection framework, showing how data flows through discovery, classification, protection, and secure processing stages while maintaining semantic integrity. It demonstrates how sensitive information is transformed while preserving context and format, enabling AI systems to process protected data without compromising security or output quality.

The **Discovery & Classification** module analyzes the input data to identify any sensitive information, classifies it appropriately, and understands the context and scope of the query. Based on these findings, the data protection module applies the most suitable protection technique to safeguard the sensitive data, ensuring that the chosen method aligns with the classification and contextual understanding provided by the discovery and classification module. The data protection module is responsible for protecting the sensitive data contained in the input. Based on the classification and context identified by the **Discovery & Classification** module, the most appropriate technique is chosen to protect the sensitive data.

RegData supports techniques that preserve the format or type of information (e.g., tokens matching **International Bank Account Number** (**IBAN**) format and checksum, or replacing a city name with another from the same country). With added semantic logic, it can now choose the technique based on an understanding of the information. The output is tokenized data that can be processed by public LLMs without revealing PII.

Key techniques in semantic data protection

Semantic data protection in financial services relies on advanced techniques designed to safeguard sensitive information while preserving its utility. Let's take a closer look at these techniques.

Format-preserving tokenization

One such method is *format-preserving tokenization*, which replaces sensitive data with surrogate tokens that maintain the same format (length, character classes, patterns) as the original. For example, an IBAN number such as **CH93 0076 2011 6238 5295 7** might be replaced with **CH93 [BANK_TOKEN_001]**, where the token preserves the format while obscuring the actual account details. This technique is particularly valuable for financial data such as account numbers, credit card numbers, IBANs and routing codes, and transaction IDs.

Contextual semantic protection

Another powerful approach is *Contextual Semantic Protection*, which maps real entities into consistent pseudonyms that carry the same type and role in the data. For instance, let's focus on a relocation application. This application contains location information about people: where they are moving from and where they are moving to. If we are only interested in hiding the locations, then semantic protection is enough. We would replace the names of the cities with other random city names, or with names of cities in the same country as the destination country.

But if we are interested in providing advice or in estimating the cost of relocation, including the living costs, as well as local taxes that will apply in the target location, then a random pseudonym will fail to provide the advice. This is where contextual semantic protection comes in. The name of the target city will be pseudonymized to the name of another city where the same rules or taxes will apply.

For instance, the question: *What would be the increase in taxes if John Smith moved to Zurich?* might get pseudonymized to *What would be the increase in taxes if Marcus Reed moved to Elsau?* In this transformation, semantics are preserved. *Marcus Reed* remains clearly identifiable as a person (individual customer). Elsau is a legitimate city name, and the tax rules in Elsau are consistent with the rules in Zurich.

We could also think about banking transfers, where we could pseudonymize the IBAN values, with a format-preserving scheme. In contextual semantic protection, we would choose target pseudonymized IBANs that are consistent with some company rules. For example, an IBAN of a given European country would be replaced by the **IBAN of another European country**, while a US IBAN would be replaced by **another US IBAN**.

For instance, all client names might be replaced with consistent pseudonyms that preserve their identity as people while hiding their actual identities.

By maintaining a consistent relationship between the data to protect, we are allowing AI models to generate meaningful insights without exposing real identities.

Semantic partitioning with token classes

This technique classifies tokens into semantic buckets (PII, client identifiers, financial, location, etc.) and tokenizes each category with its own namespace. Here are some examples:

- [PII_001] for PII
- [CID_017] for CID
- [FIN_042] for financial information

Semantic partitioning with token classes allows for granular protection policies based on data type and context, while still enabling AI models to understand the semantic role of each token.

Deterministic tokens

Deterministic tokenization ensures that the same input always produces the same token (e.g., Alice always maps to the same token). This consistency is crucial for multi-step reasoning or dialogue, where the model must recognize references across interactions. For example, if a client asks about "my UBS account" in one message and then refers to it as that account in a follow-up, deterministic tokens ensure the AI understands both references resolve to the same entity, preserving continuity.

Building a comprehensive semantic protection architecture

Effective semantic data protection extends beyond individual techniques; it requires a holistic architecture that integrates with all components of a financial institution's AI ecosystem. The MongoDB, RegData, and Voyage AI alliance has pioneered this comprehensive approach, developing an end-to-end architecture that addresses the full spectrum of security and compliance challenges. This section outlines the key components of this integrated semantic protection framework.

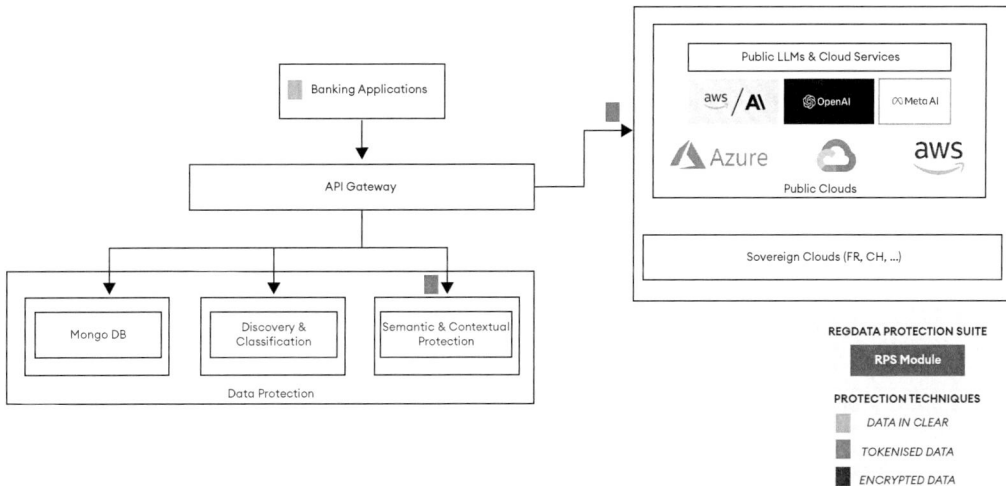

Figure 12.2: End-to-end semantic protection architecture

This diagram shows the complete flow of data through a semantically protected AI system, from initial data ingestion through processing by cloud AI services to secure output rendering. The visualization highlights integration points between bank systems, protection layers, API gateways, and cloud services, demonstrating how sensitive data remains protected throughout the entire lifecycle.

Input data can be of multiple types and can come from different sources, such as files, databases, applications, and audio files. Calls to public LLMs are generally done via API calls through an API gateway. The API gateway ensures that the PII is protected before being sent to public LLMs. So, the gateway uses protection services to classify and protect the sensitive data. The data protection module replaces the sensitive fields with tokenized data before being sent to the LLMs.

MongoDB as the foundation with RegData's data security platform

MongoDB is the foundational data platform for this integrated solution, with RegData's **Data Security Platform (DSP)** providing the specialized protection layer. This combination offers the following:

- **Unified data storage**: MongoDB's flexible document model stores structured, semi-structured, and unstructured data in a single platform, eliminating silos and simplifying architecture
- **Discovery and classification**: RegData's automated identification of sensitive data within unstructured content uses advanced techniques such as NLP and **Named Entity Recognition (NER)**, a technology that identifies and categorizes specific entities in text
- **Scalable performance**: MongoDB's distributed architecture ensures the solution can handle financial data at any scale, from thousands to billions of records
- **Protection technique selection**: Intelligent application of the most appropriate protection method based on data type and context
- **Token vault management:** Secure storage of the mapping between original values and their tokenized representations
- **Policy enforcement:** Consistent application of protection policies across all AI interactions

Together, MongoDB and RegData provide a resilient and intelligent backbone for financial services, enabling institutions to unify their data, enforce robust protection policies, and accelerate AI adoption without sacrificing security.

API gateway with MongoDB and RegData's prompt decoration

The integrated solution features an API gateway that acts as an intelligent AI-aware secure middleware (intermediary software that connects different applications) between financial applications and AI models. MongoDB provides the data infrastructure, while RegData contributes prompt decoration capabilities:

- **MongoDB Atlas as the data hub**: Serves as the central repository for all data flowing through the API gateway, ensuring consistency and persistence

- **Prompt decoration**: RegData's wrapper layer modifies, annotates, or enhances prompts (instructions given to AI models) before they're sent to AI models

- **Normalization**: Standardizes the format of semantic tokens and wrappers to ensure consistent processing

- **Protection application**: Applies all required protection techniques before sending requests to cloud-based AI models

- **MCP**: A standardized framework that defines how context (relevant information about the conversation or task) is passed between user sessions, AI models, and backend systems

By combining MongoDB's centralized data infrastructure with RegData's intelligent prompt handling, the solution creates a secure, AI-ready bridge between financial systems and models, streamlining interactions while safeguarding sensitive content at every step.

Protected vector search with MongoDB Atlas and Voyage AI

MongoDB Atlas Vector Search, combined with RegData's protection techniques and Voyage AI's domain-specific embeddings, creates a powerful protected search capability essential for RAG in financial AI applications:

- **MongoDB Atlas Vector Search**: Provides the infrastructure for storing and querying billions of vectors with sub-second performance

- **Voyage AI's financial embeddings**: Generate domain-specific vector representations that understand financial terminology and concepts

- **RegData's tokenized embeddings**: Store vector embeddings (numerical representations of text that capture semantic meaning) of documents and data in tokenized form

- **Semantic preservation**: Ensures vector similarity remains valid even when surface text is masked

- **Contextual recall**: Allows AI to *remember* that [ADDR_42] is semantically similar to other addresses without exposing the actual address

This integrated approach delivers high-performance, privacy-preserving vector search tailored for financial contexts, allowing AI systems to retrieve nuanced, domain-aware insights while keeping all sensitive details under wraps.

Secure output rendering

The final component ensures that protected data is only revealed in appropriate contexts:

- **Token remapping:** On authorized devices or within secure environments, tokens are mapped back to their original values
- **Contextual authorization:** Access to original values is granted based on user role, location, and purpose
- **Audit logging:** All access to original values is logged for compliance and security monitoring

This final safeguard ensures that sensitive information is revealed only when conditions are met, maintaining compliance and trust while giving authorized users access to the data they need; nothing more, nothing less.

Domain-specific intelligence for enhanced security and performance

While semantic protection provides the foundation for secure AI in financial services, domain-specific intelligence takes both security and performance to the next level. As explored in detail in *Chapter 11, Financial Services and the Next Wave of AI*, financial services involve specialized language, complex regulations, and nuanced concepts that general-purpose AI models often struggle to interpret accurately.

Leveraging financial-specific embeddings for enhanced protection

The MongoDB, RegData, and Voyage AI integration builds upon the domain-specific embedding capabilities detailed in *Chapter 11*. By incorporating Voyage AI's financial-specialized embedding models, the semantic protection framework gains several key advantages:

- **Enhanced detection accuracy:** Financial embeddings better identify sensitive information that requires protection, improving the precision of RegData's classification systems
- **Contextual protection:** Domain-specific understanding enables more nuanced protection decisions based on financial context rather than simple pattern matching
- **Improved retrieval quality:** When combined with MongoDB Atlas Vector Search, financial embeddings ensure that protected searches maintain relevance and accuracy

This approach delivers significant performance improvements over general-purpose models, particularly for compliance-related tasks and sensitive data identification. It ensures that semantic protection is not only secure but also maintains the high-quality, contextually relevant outputs that financial institutions require for effective AI applications. The combination of RegData's protection techniques with financial-specific intelligence creates a comprehensive solution that addresses both security and performance requirements in the demanding financial services environment.

Real-world innovation: interactive banking

To illustrate how the integrated MongoDB, RegData, and Voyage AI solution works in practice, let's examine a use case scenario of a private bank offering a digital GenAI-powered chat assistant for its **ultra-high-net-worth** (**UHNW**) clients. This implementation showcases the power of combining MongoDB's data platform, **RegData's Protection Suite** (**RPS**), and Voyage AI's domain-specific embeddings to enable secure yet effective AI interactions in a highly regulated environment.

The bank's UHNW clients use the AI banking assistant for various tasks:

- Checking account balances and transaction histories
- Requesting transfers (e.g., *Transfer 300K CHF to my lawyer*)
- Receiving market alerts and investment insights
- Reviewing portfolio performance and asset allocations
- Scheduling meetings with relationship managers

These interactions involve highly sensitive data: account numbers, transaction histories, personal identifiers, and behavioral patterns. Processing this data through cloud-based GenAI models risks exposing it to third-party platforms, potentially violating regulations and compromising client confidentiality. How can we then leverage public GenAI services or LLM models while protecting highly sensitive data?

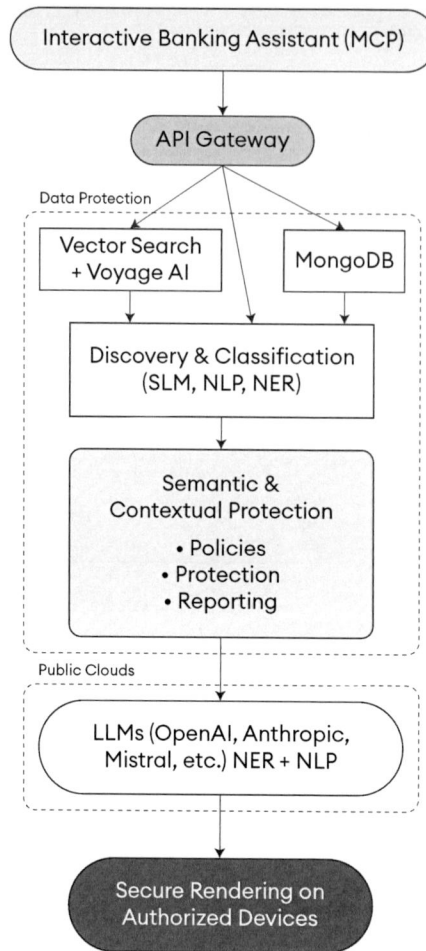

Figure 12.3: Interactive banking system workflow and user interface components

This diagram illustrates the comprehensive architecture of a semantically protected banking assistant, showing how client queries are processed through multiple protection layers before reaching AI models. The system integrates MongoDB's data platform with Voyage AI's domain-specific embeddings and RPS to deliver both semantic and contextual protection.

The architecture demonstrates how semantic protection maintains data meaning and format (replacing sensitive values with semantically equivalent tokens), while contextual protection adapts security measures based on data usage, user roles, and regulatory requirements. Client queries flow through the API gateway to the **Discovery & Classification** layer (utilizing SLM, NLP, and NER technologies), then through the **Semantic & Contextual Protection** module with its integrated policies, protection mechanisms, and reporting capabilities.

Protected data is then processed by public cloud LLMs, with responses securely rendered, showing original values only on authorized devices. The visualization highlights the end-to-end protection of sensitive financial information throughout the entire conversation flow, ensuring regulatory compliance while maintaining the quality and utility of AI-powered banking interactions.

Here's how the MongoDB, RegData, and Voyage AI integration enables secure yet effective AI interactions:

- **Data Discovery & Classification:** When a client says *Transfer 200K CHF to Pierre*, the system uses RegData AI-powered PII identification and Voyage AI's financial-specific models to identify *Pierre* as PII and *200K CHF* as financial information requiring protection.

- **Semantic data protection with RegData:** Before sending the details to the GenAI model, **RegData Protection Suite (RPS)** applies the following:

  - **Semantic-preserving protection:** *What are the fees, and conditions, if I want to transfer 200K CHF to this IBAN CH93 0076 2011 6238 5295 7?* becomes *What are the fees, and conditions, if I want to transfer 200K CHF to CH2008770435380216999?*

  - **Contextual semantic protection:** *Provide me with the list of all the transactions on my UBS account* becomes *Provide me with the list of all the transactions on my Bank_CH account*

  - **Deterministic tokens:** *Pierre* always maps to *Jacques* and *IBAN CH2008770435380216999* always maps to CH93 0076 2011 6238 5295 7, across all interactions

- **Prompt decoration with MCP:** The prompt decorator ensures the GenAI model receives only protected tokens, and treats them accordingly, while preserving their semantic meaning through MCP.

- **Protected vector search with MongoDB Atlas:** When the client asks *What did I spend on philanthropic activities last month?*, the system uses Voyage AI to convert the protected query into a vector (a mathematical representation of text). MongoDB Atlas Vector Search finds similar content in tokenized transaction data, and RegData ensures only protected data is retrieved without exposing actual transaction details.

- **Secure output rendering:** On the client's authorized device, the app re-maps tokens to real values (e.g., Jacques → Pierre). The client sees natural, fluent responses with their actual data, while the AI model only processed protected tokens.

This integrated MongoDB, RegData, and Voyage AI implementation delivers significant benefits:

- **Regulatory compliance:** Meets requirements of FINMA (the Swiss Financial Market Supervisory Authority), GDPR, and other regulations by never exposing sensitive data to third-party AI providers
- **Enhanced user experience:** Clients receive personalized, context-aware responses despite the underlying protection
- **Operational efficiency:** Relationship managers focus on high-value activities while the AI handles routine inquiries
- **Scalable security:** MongoDB's distributed architecture, combined with RegData's protection, ensures the solution can scale to handle growing AI use cases without compromising data protection
- **Superior relevance:** Voyage AI's domain-specific embeddings ensure responses are highly relevant to financial contexts

These core capabilities form the foundation, whereas advanced techniques can build on them to unlock even greater possibilities.

Building the future with advanced techniques and emerging standards

As financial institutions continue to advance their AI capabilities, several emerging techniques and standards are shaping the future of semantic data protection.

MCP

MCP represents a significant advancement in standardizing how context is managed across AI interactions. As will be detailed extensively in *Chapter 19, Outlook: Beyond Today's AI*, MCP is transforming how AI applications are built and integrated, moving beyond the previous approach of creating one-off tools for each integration.

MCP provides several key advantages for semantic data protection systems:

- **Standardized context management:** A consistent framework for passing context between user sessions, AI models, AI agents, and backend systems
- **Enhanced interoperability:** Elimination of data silos by standardizing AI model interactions with business applications
- **Reduced cloud processing time:** More efficient context handling reduces the time sensitive data spends in cloud environments

In the context of the MongoDB, RegData, and Voyage AI alliance, MCP enables more seamless integration of protection workflows with AI agents and external systems. This standardization is particularly valuable for financial institutions that need to maintain context across complex, multi-step AI interactions while ensuring data protection remains consistent throughout.

As you'll discover, MongoDB's MCP server exemplifies this integration potential, enabling AI agents to directly interact with MongoDB databases while respecting existing access controls, a critical capability for maintaining semantic protection in agentic AI environments.

Hybrid protection strategies

Establishing hybrid cloud approaches can enhance both security and performance by enabling secure data processing across private and public cloud environments. Through intelligent data orchestration and the selective exposure of protected data, a hybrid cloud architecture ensures that sensitive information remains secure while still supporting advanced analytics and AI workloads. RegData further strengthens this approach with support for both hybrid and multi-cloud deployments, allowing organizations to choose the infrastructure that best meets their operational and compliance needs.

Within this architecture, multi-layer protection plays a key role by incorporating structured and unstructured documents, as well as knowledge graphs, into a unified ecosystem framework. This integration ensures that all forms of data are consistently protected and accessible for authorized use. The result is a system that systematically safeguards sensitive information while enabling AI capabilities across diverse environments, delivering both enhanced security and flexible deployment options.

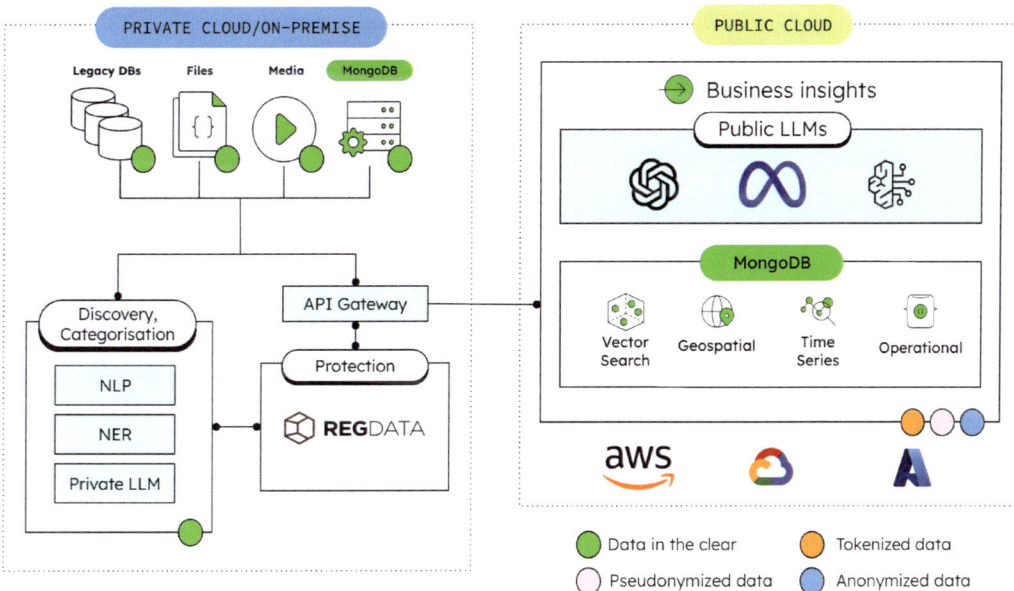

Figure 12.4: Hybrid cloud architecture for secure financial AI

This diagram illustrates a hybrid cloud architecture that enables secure financial AI processing across private/on-premises and public cloud environments. The visualization shows how sensitive data remains protected in private cloud/on-premises infrastructure (including legacy databases, files, and media) while leveraging powerful public cloud AI services through RegData protection layers. The API gateway ensures that only semantically protected data (tokenized, pseudonymized, or anonymized) crosses into public cloud environments, where MongoDB provides unified data orchestration and public LLMs deliver advanced AI capabilities. This hybrid approach maximizes both security compliance and AI performance by keeping sensitive data secure while accessing cutting-edge cloud AI services through comprehensive data protection throughout the entire process.

Compliance and regulatory considerations

Financial institutions must navigate complex regulatory requirements when implementing AI with semantic data protection. This section outlines key considerations and best practices.

Regulatory framework alignment

Semantic protection architectures must align with the complex regulatory landscape and frameworks detailed in *Chapter 4, Trustworthy AI, Compliance, and Data Governance*. As discussed in that chapter's analysis of navigating regulatory requirements across different industries and jurisdictions, organizations must address multiple overlapping regulatory frameworks, such as the following:

- **GDPR**: Ensures proper handling of personal data with principles such as data minimization and purpose limitation[1]
- **FINMA**: Addresses Swiss financial regulatory requirements for data security and client confidentiality[2]
- **MAS**: Complies with Monetary Authority of Singapore guidelines for AI governance and data protection[3]
- **EU AI Act**: Meets European Union requirements for AI risk management, transparency, and accountability in high-risk AI applications[4]
- **ECB**: Meets European Central Bank standards for operational resilience and data security[5]

The semantic protection approach directly supports trustworthy AI principles, particularly transparency, accountability, and robust data governance, by ensuring that sensitive data protection is maintained even while enabling AI explainability and regulatory compliance. This alignment demonstrates how technical solutions can operationalize the ethical and regulatory frameworks that are essential for responsible AI implementation.

Auditability and explainability

Regulatory compliance requires comprehensive audit capabilities, including detailed access logging that records who accessed specific data, when the access occurred, and for what purpose. It also demands protection verification to provide evidence that sensitive data was properly safeguarded throughout AI processing. In addition, decision traceability is essential, ensuring clear audit trails that document how AI-generated recommendations were produced.

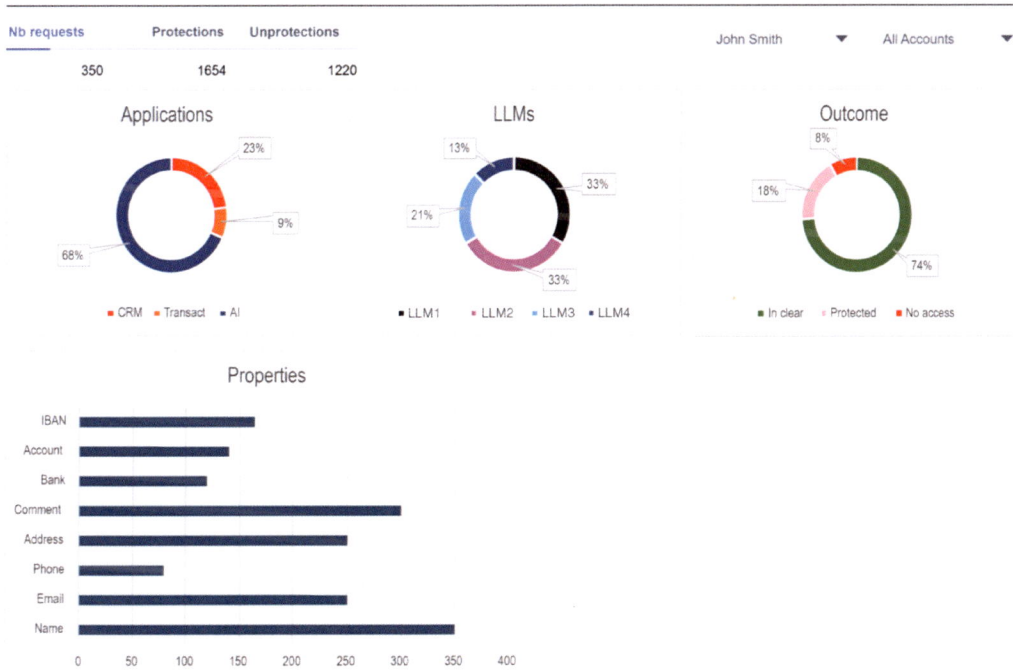

Figure 12.5: Sensitive data consumption, per user

This dashboard visualization shows how financial institutions can monitor and demonstrate compliance with various regulatory requirements across their AI systems. The interface displays key metrics, including protection coverage, access logs, and compliance status across different regulations and data types.

The dashboard shows how a given user got access to sensitive data. This could be when consuming internal applications such as a CRM or a transactional tool, or data sent to LLMs.

It is then possible to know in what LLM this sensitive data was used, and the outcome in the response: how many times the user got access to the data in full, how many times they got no access, or how may times they got access to protected data only. In this screenshot, we can also see the type of sensitive data the user consumed (**Name**, **Email**, **IBAN**, (free text) comments, and more).

This dashboard is made possible because RegData monitors all the requests to access sensitive data, as well as how RegData responds to these requests. It is then possible to build custom reports demonstrating sound usage of the sensitive data, as well as the secure use of the sensitive data in external or public LLMs.

Summary

This chapter showed how the MongoDB, RegData, and Voyage AI alliance addresses the critical challenge facing financial institutions: leveraging AI capabilities while maintaining rigorous data protection and regulatory compliance. You were introduced to the concept of semantic data protection, which goes beyond traditional encryption and masking approaches that render data unusable for AI applications. Semantic data protection preserves the meaning, context, and format of information while removing or replacing the sensitive values themselves, enabling AI models to generate meaningful outputs without compromising security.

However, semantic protection alone is insufficient for high-quality AI outputs in financial applications. The chapter emphasized that contextual semantic protection is essential to deliver meaningful AI responses. While basic semantic protection simply replaces sensitive data with semantically equivalent alternatives (a phone number with another phone number, a city name with another city name), contextual semantic protection adapts based on the meaning and usage context to maintain analytical relevance. For example, in a relocation application, contextual semantic protection would replace a target city with another city where the same tax rules and regulations apply, enabling AI to provide accurate advice about living costs and local taxes while maintaining privacy. This sophisticated approach, combined with MongoDB's unified data platform, RegData's protection techniques, and Voyage AI's domain-specific embeddings, creates an integrated solution that addresses both security and performance requirements in the demanding financial services environment.

In the next chapter, we will explore how GenAI copilots can transform wealth management by addressing the fundamental catch-22 of scaling personalized client relationships without compromising service quality. We'll examine how AI-powered assistance can shift relationship managers from administrative tasks to high-value client interactions while delivering significant revenue improvements through intelligent automation.

References

1. What you need to know about the 7 principles of GDPR: `https://usercentrics.com/knowledge-hub/principles-of-gdpr/`

2. FINMA: Making Sense of Client Identifying Data (CID): `https://bigid.com/blog/finma-making-sense-of-client-identifying-data-cid/`

3. Navigating AI Model Risks: Key Insights from MAS Guidelines: `https://www.coriniumintelligence.com/content/navigating-ai-model-risks-key-insights-from-the-mas-guidelines`

4. Everything You Need To Know (So Far) About The EU AI Act: `https://www.isms.online/iso-42001/everything-you-need-to-know-so-far-about-the-eu-ai-act/`

5. Digital Operational Resilience Act (DORA): `https://www.eiopa.europa.eu/digital-operational-resilience-act-dora_en`

13

Driving Client Success in Banking with GenAI Copilots

The wealth management industry stands at a crossroads. While relationship managers have traditionally been the cornerstone of personalized financial services, they now face an unprecedented challenge: how to scale intimate, high-touch client relationships without compromising the quality of service that drives customer loyalty and business growth. Companies such as QuantumBlack, AI by McKinsey, have been tracking this change and what it means for business and technology leaders.

The banking sector's digital transformation has accelerated dramatically over recent decades, moving from branch-based interactions to omnichannel experiences that meet customers wherever they are. Customer expectations for immediate, personalized service have never been higher, while regulatory pressures and competitive forces demand greater efficiency and broader reach. This evolution has created both opportunity and tension; banks must serve more clients across wider geographic areas while maintaining the personal touch that differentiates premium wealth management services.

But there remains a core challenge: human relationship managers can only manage so many meaningful client relationships effectively. The traditional model relies heavily on personal memory, manual research, and one-to-one interactions that simply don't scale. As client portfolios grow and market complexity increases, relationship managers find themselves spending more time on administrative tasks and less time adding genuine value to client relationships.

By the end of this chapter, you will understand the following:

- How the catch-22 of wealth relationship management creates an opportunity for AI transformation

- Why traditional relationship management relies heavily on manual effort and personal memory, limiting scalability

- How GenAI copilots can transform relationship manager productivity from 20–30% client interaction time to over 70%

- The technical architecture that powers real-time AI recommendations and automated follow-up generation

- How to implement four essential AI factory pipelines for production-grade GenAI applications

- Why guardrails against hallucinations and compliance frameworks are critical for financial services

- Real-world use cases across call center analysis, virtual agent support, and fraud detection

- How to build organizational adoption through strategic infrastructure planning and user engagement

- The business impact of GenAI implementation: 10–25% revenue uplift per relationship manager and 5–15% increase in active customers managed

The catch-22 of wealth relationship management

Wealth management relationship managers have long served as the personalized bridge between high-net-worth clients and financial institutions. They provide their elite clientele with white-glove service: personalized financial advice, investment recommendations, fiscal planning services, and more. But they also face unprecedented pressure to increase the number of clients under their management.

This dual mandate places relationship managers in a catch-22 situation. On the one hand, banking institutions require scalability and revenue growth. On the other hand, the human capacity for high-touch relationship management cannot scale without sacrificing service quality.

Traditional wealth management relies heavily on the relationship manager's personal memory and manual effort. For example, they personally assess portfolio positions, risks, and opportunities, manually contact their clients, manually research relevant news and market updates, gather insights ad hoc during conversations, and rely on broad and generalized ideas and strategies rather than personalized ones.

QuantumBlack, AI by McKinsey's extensive work with clients has revealed that relationship managers typically spend only 20–30% of their time interacting with customers while 70–80% of their time is spent on research, preparation, and paperwork. This represents a massive opportunity for transformation through AI.

Scaling a successful relationship management GenAI copilot

GenAI copilots are transforming how relationship managers work, allowing them to bring in and manage more clients without compromising (and often improving) the quality of service. The GenAI copilot sits on the relationship manager's desktop, tunes in to client calls, and leverages the bank's vast data repositories from a wide variety of sources to provide hyper-personalized real-time recommendations, next-step actions, and upsell opportunities.

For example, a GenAI copilot powered by advanced AI solutions such as MongoDB and Iguazio—an AI platform company acquired by QuantumBlack, AI by McKinsey—helps relationship managers identify investments aligned with a client's portfolio. The copilot also proactively shares relevant research, conducts sentiment analysis based on the client's wording, tone of voice, and context, determines and classifies intent to identify potential opportunities, and even highlights relevant life events that trigger recommendations for additional banking products (such as opening a new student account for the client's child, based on the fact that they've just turned 18).

Banking Relationship Manager Co-Pilot Flow

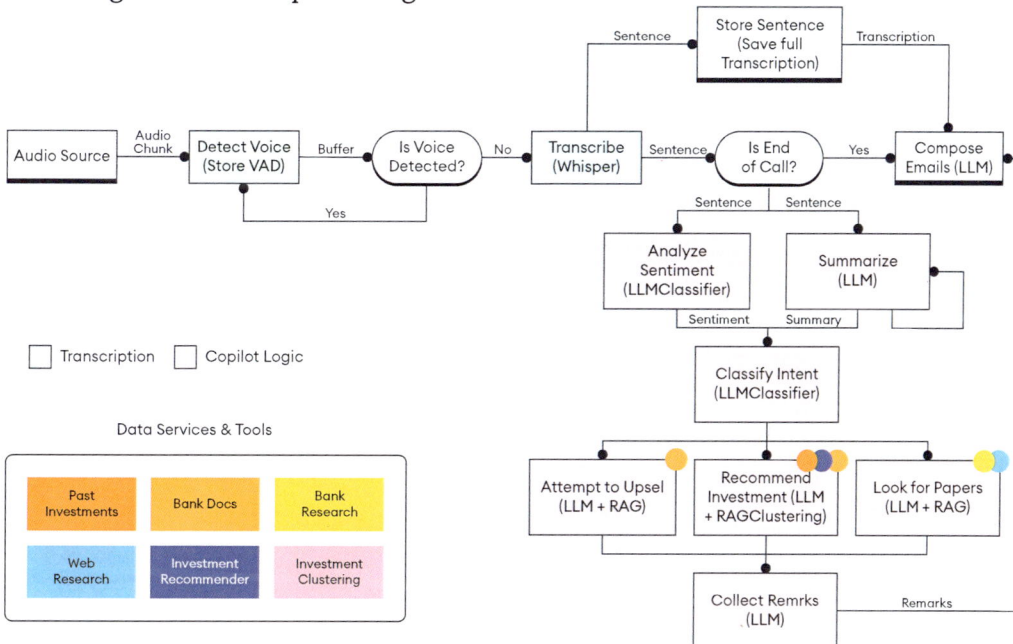

Figure 13.1: Real-time GenAI copilot workflow: from voice detection to automated follow-up

This flowchart demonstrates the end-to-end operational workflow of a banking relationship manager GenAI copilot during live client interactions. The process begins with audio source detection using **voice activity detection (VAD)**, followed by real-time transcription via Whisper technology. The system then analyzes sentiment and classifies client intent using LLM-powered **natural language processing (NLP)**. Based on this analysis, the copilot accesses multiple data sources, including past investments, bank documentation, research databases, and investment clustering algorithms, to generate three types of intelligent recommendations: upsell opportunities using LLM and **retrieval-augmented generation (RAG)**, personalized investment suggestions through RAG and clustering, and relevant research papers via LLM and RAG. This workflow illustrates how AI orchestrates complex data processing and decision-making in real time to enhance relationship manager effectiveness.

All these insights are presented to the relationship manager, who can decide whether or not to share them with the client in real time. After the call, the copilot automatically generates a personalized email summarizing the call, along with any additional documents needed based on the discussion that was held, enabling the relationship manager to simply check, edit, and send the documents with the click of a button.

By automatically providing these insights to relationship managers, the GenAI copilot frees the manager from preparation time, allowing them to allocate more of their day to value-generating interactions with clients. Based on our work with clients, we observed that the numbers can shift dramatically, going from 20–30% of their time spent with clients to over 70%. The result is a potential uplift of 10–25% in revenue per relationship manager and an increase of 5–15% in active customers managed.

How the relationship management GenAI copilot works under the hood

The GenAI copilot application operates by drawing on a wide range of the bank's data sources, including structured databases such as MongoDB Atlas as a unified data platform, containing historical and real-time data. It continuously ingests internal and external data from call recordings, past interactions across emails, chats, and texts, social media activity, public news, and the client's portfolio and transaction history to build and maintain a dynamic customer profile.

The bank's knowledge base, accumulated over time, includes details such as family status, life events, sentiment history, loan and credit activity, risk profile, and shopping preferences, which are integrated from internal and external data sources and interactions. Banking-specific data, such as product information, policies, and operational systems, is also integrated.

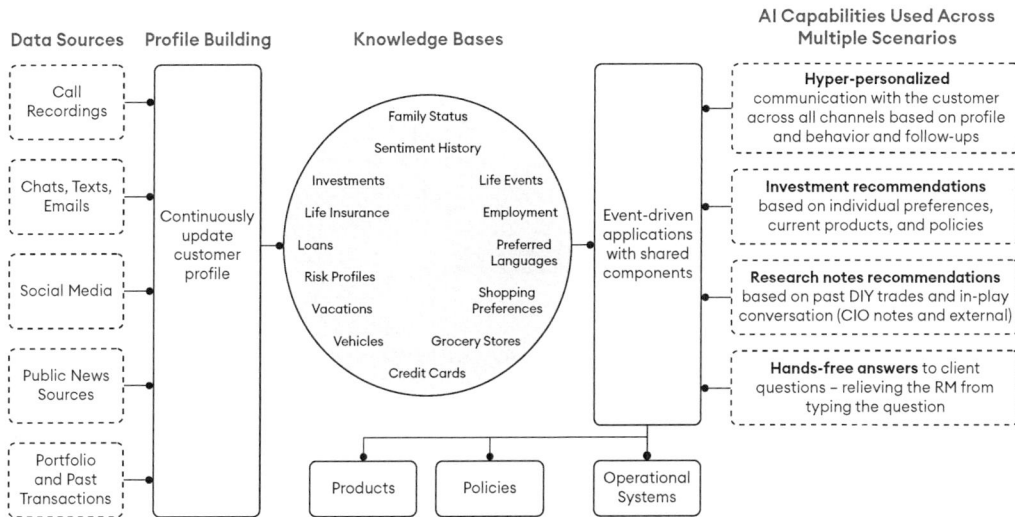

Figure 13.2: AI-powered client intelligence architecture: from data sources to personalized banking experiences

This diagram illustrates how GenAI copilots transform diverse data sources into intelligent client insights through a comprehensive profile-building system. On the left, multiple data streams, including call recordings, communications, social media, public news, and transaction history, feed into a centralized profile-building engine. The system creates rich knowledge bases encompassing family status, financial preferences, risk profiles, and behavioral patterns. These insights power event-driven applications that deliver four core AI capabilities: hyper-personalized communication across all channels, investment recommendations tailored to individual preferences and current products, research notes based on past interactions and market intelligence, and hands-free answers to client questions that relieve relationship managers from routine inquiries. This architecture demonstrates how modern banking AI systems unify structured and unstructured data to enable real-time, contextual client engagement at scale.

All of this information flows into event-driven applications and real-time pipelines. This data is leveraged by the GenAI copilot in real time to recommend strategies to the human agent. The output for the relationship manager is hyper-personalized communication, customized investment ideas, relevant research notes, and answers to client queries.

The AI workflows that support this architecture are designed to process the voice from client calls in real time with AI, provide relationship managers with insights and suggestions, and automate follow-ups based on the conversation taking place in real time.

What does it take to productize AI applications such as the GenAI copilot for relationship managers? This is where the GenAI factory comes in.

GenAI factory: Powering copilots, agents, and GenAI apps

An AI architecture that supports the use of the copilot at scale is based on four pipelines:

- Data pipelines for processing the raw data (eliminating risks, improving quality, encoding, and so on).

- Application pipelines for processing incoming requests, enriching with data from MongoDB's unified data platform supporting structured, unstructured, and vector data, running the agent logic, and applying various guardrails and monitoring tasks.

- Development and CI/CD pipelines for fine-tuning and validating models, testing the application to detect accuracy risk challenges, and automatically deploying the application.

- A governance and monitoring system for collecting application and data telemetry to identify resource usage, application performance, risks, and so on. The monitoring data can be used to further improve the application performance.

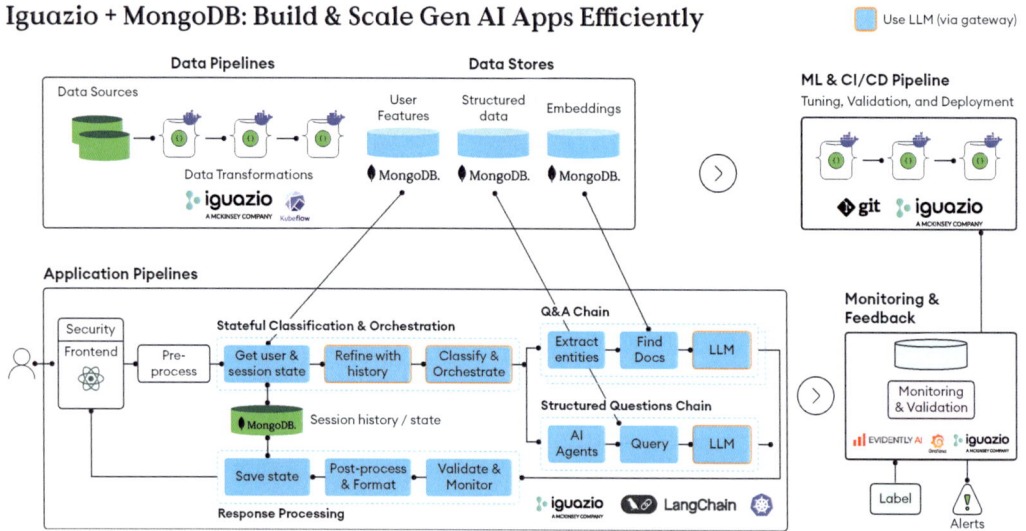

Figure 13.3: Iguazio and MongoDB's integrated AI factory architecture for production-scale GenAI applications

This comprehensive architecture diagram illustrates how Iguazio's AI factory platform integrates with MongoDB to deliver enterprise-grade GenAI applications at scale. The system encompasses four critical operational layers: **data pipelines** that transform raw data sources through Iguazio's processing capabilities into MongoDB's unified data platform that handles user features, structured data, and vector embeddings within a single system; **application pipelines** featuring stateful classification and orchestration with security controls, Q&A chains for entity extraction and document retrieval, and structured question chains powered by AI agents; an **ML and CI/CD pipeline** providing automated tuning, validation, and deployment through Git and Iguazio workflows; and comprehensive **monitoring and feedback** systems with real-time validation and alert capabilities. The architecture demonstrates how MongoDB's converged data store approach eliminates the complexity of managing multiple database technologies by supporting structured, unstructured, and vector data types natively within one platform, while Iguazio orchestrates the complex AI workflows, session management, and response processing required for production financial services applications. This integrated approach enables the pipeline orchestration, scalability, and governance capabilities essential for **financial services industry** (**FSI**) compliance while maintaining the performance and reliability demanded by banking operations.

In addition, the AI factory should support both on-premises and hybrid implementations, and enable simple migration from one environment to the other, to address the financial sector's stringent regulatory, data privacy, and security requirements and to enable flexibility in a very dynamic world. On-premises deployments offer full control over sensitive data and infrastructure, which is required for meeting compliance mandates such as GDPR or the EU AI Act. At the same time, hybrid models enable banks to leverage the scalability and innovation of cloud-based AI, while retaining sensitive workloads on-premises.

How the AI factory addresses FSI engineering needs

By implementing an AI factory, banks, insurance companies, and other financial institutions can benefit in a number of ways.

One of the chief benefits is that users gain access to pipeline orchestration with minimal engineering. The factory simplifies the development and management of end-to-end robust and repeatable workflows across four pipelines: data, application, development, and LiveOps. This is done in a simple and resilient manner without requiring significant engineering efforts.

The AI factory also increases the options for scalable and rapid deployment. The factory enables building and deploying models at enterprise scale, across millions of banking customers, global regions, and teams, in a streamlined manner and without friction or cost inefficiencies on cloud, on-premises, or hybrid environments. By combining with databases such as MongoDB, for example, large volumes of data and complex data transformations can be handled with ease, while maintaining high levels of performance and ensuring reliability and accuracy.

Unification of data from multiple sources also becomes more viable. GenAI applications involve multiple types of data, such as geospatial, graphs, tables, and vectors. Each data type requires considerations such as security, scalability, and metadata management. This creates data management complexity. An AI factory combined with MongoDB's unified platform can handle all data types, structured, unstructured, and vector data, in a single solution. This ensures consistency, faster performance, and significantly less overhead.

The versatility of the factories is also a huge benefit. Once built, the factory can be adapted to multiple use cases without the overhead or challenges of rebuilding. If any changes are needed, the architecture is modular, and components can be easily swapped or replaced without having to re-architect entirely.

GPU and compute optimization become easier to manage. With compute, and especially GPUs, becoming costly and hard to come by, the factory ensures efficient allocation, sharing, and auto-scaling of compute resources, including distribution and parallelism.

MLOps orchestration is improved because an AI factory helps move models and AI applications from prototype to production rapidly, securely, and reliably.

The factory helps performance and output integrity by mitigating business and ethical risks such as hallucinations, bias, toxicity, and inaccurate outputs, ensuring high performance, accuracy, and reliability. This is done by introducing central management and governance for the entire AI lifecycle, including guardrails embedded throughout the entire development, training, and deployment process.

Hallucination guardrails

Protecting against hallucinations, for example, can take place as early as the data pipeline. This requires a RAG workflow and MongoDB's unified data platform.

Structured and reliable data (such as product manuals, FAQs, pricing policies, customer data, etc.) is converted to embeddings and stored in MongoDB. When a user prompts a query, the relevant record is retrieved from the database and structured as natural text. This ensures the response is grounded in real facts, minimizing hallucinations.

AI factories improve compliance, privacy, and security by enforcing guardrails for secure model access, explainability, logging for audit, alignment with GDPR and **Financial Industry Regulatory Authority (FINRA)** regulations, and fairness.

Many banking systems still run on legacy stacks. AI factories improve integration between new and legacy systems by abstracting complexity through API bridges, wrappers, or fine-tuned connectors, easily and seamlessly.

Even after successful proofs of concept, most enterprises still fail to scale AI and create real business impact. The AI factory helps ensure production-grade delivery and management, so that enterprises see actual ROI.

An AI factory is a future-proof infrastructure with modularity and scalability that can be adapted to any AI operationalization need, such as AI agents.

Agents are autonomous AI systems that can perceive their environment, make decisions, and take actions toward a specific goal. Rather than following specific tasks, they can follow a set of objectives, adapt to changing inputs, and operate independently or alongside human teams. This helps speed up decision-making, enhance the customer experience, and improve operational resilience across the financial services value chain.

For financial services, AI agents can automate complex workflows, serve as always-on financial assistants, continuously monitor transactions and flag fraud, suggest investment strategies, personalize financial advisory, and more.

Leading FSI use cases where GenAI brings real value

The value of GenAI for private banks and financial institutions goes beyond relationship management. It can also be extended to use cases such as the following:

- **Smart call center analysis**: Using AI to transcribe, summarize, and analyze support calls in real time to identify sentiment, product pain points, and upsell opportunities, and to feed information to downstream applications for strategic insights

- **Virtual agent support**: Deploying AI-powered agents to handle routine queries, freeing up human agents for complex cases

- **Hyper-personalized product recommendations**: Combining behavioral data with customer information to recommend tailored credit cards, loans, or investment products

- **Fraud prediction and anomaly detection**: Detecting suspicious transaction patterns in real time, improving response times

Let's look at an example in detail.

Case study: A GenAI-driven smart call center analysis application

A large successful European bank built a GenAI call center analysis app to improve call center operations, simplify agent training, improve customer experience, and reduce costs. The GenAI application, deployed on-premises, summarized customer calls, analyzed sentiment and topics, and removed **personally identifiable information (PII)**. The data was fed to downstream applications, such as live agent support, customer profiles, auto-generated content, tailored recommendations, customized offers, and so on.

This resulted in 2x improvement in runtime, 60x faster call diarization, and 3x improvement in GPU utilization. Such agents can also access the MongoDB data platform to extract information that can assist with information retrieval and use.

What now? How enterprises can succeed with GenAI

Success with GenAI solutions isn't just about implementing the right technology. Rather, it hinges on engagement with people, securing C-suite alignment, building the right processes, and introducing governance strategies. Integrating GenAI into relationship manager workflows, or any other department, in a cooperative manner is foundational to its success, while driving success for the company and the individual employee as well.

Therefore, it's recommended to implement the following practices across people, processes, and technology:

- **Strategic infrastructure planning**: Developing a tailored deployment strategy across the cloud, on-premises, or hybrid, guided by regulatory, compliance, and resource needs. The data infrastructure should be designed to leverage existing systems while ensuring smooth integration into existing processes.

- **Robust governance and regulatory alignment**: Embedding internal policies and aligning with regulations such as the EU AI Act, to accelerate progress and minimize risks.

- **Driving adoption among users**: Engaging top-performing relationship managers in shaping the tool's functionality and user experience. This ensures and drives a sense of ownership. It includes highlighting the potential to enhance insights, upskill professional capabilities, improve productivity, and boost revenue, and piloting with high performers to generate quick wins, build credibility, and spark peer-driven momentum across the organization.

By anchoring GenAI solutions such as copilots in their digital strategy, banks can transform customer relationships and position themselves for sustainable, revenue-driving growth in an increasingly competitive and volatile landscape.

Summary

The transformation of wealth management through GenAI copilots represents a fundamental shift from the impossible catch-22 of scaling personalized service to an AI-powered solution that enhances both efficiency and client experience. With relationship managers currently spending more than half of their time on research and paperwork rather than client interaction, GenAI copilots offer a clear path to flip this ratio, enabling managers to focus on value-generating activities while AI handles data processing, sentiment analysis, and administrative tasks.

The technical foundation for this transformation requires a comprehensive AI factory approach, encompassing data pipelines, application orchestration, development workflows, and governance frameworks. MongoDB's unified data platform enables the real-time processing of structured and unstructured data necessary for contextual AI responses, while built-in guardrails ensure compliance with financial services regulations and protect against hallucinations. Real-world implementations have demonstrated significant business impact, with potential revenue uplifts of 10–25% per relationship manager and increases of 5–15% in active customers managed, alongside operational improvements such as 2x runtime improvements and 60x faster call processing.

The next chapter explores how to deliver business value with AI in insurance, examining the strategic integration of AI within the insurance sector to drive meaningful business outcomes. Moving beyond banking applications, it demonstrates how to architect AI-augmented application workflows that align with insurance business objectives, covering the evolution of data architectures and the practical applications of AI across underwriting, claims processing, and customer experience to transform insurance operations.

14

Delivering Business Value with AI in Insurance

When architecting for AI-augmented application workflows, it's important to keep your overall business objectives in mind. What business problems are you solving, and what are the most pressing challenges your organization is facing?

Different stakeholders across your organization may approach AI implementation from various perspectives. Technology teams driving platform consolidation and modernization may evaluate solutions through a technology-first lens, comparing platforms based on technical capabilities and cost. Data science and analytics teams may focus on testing or proving data hypotheses. Business product owners may prioritize enhancing application features and capabilities, hoping to augment data processing with AI.

Regardless of your role, the challenge is to help your organization leverage AI to make meaningful strides in business outcomes. This requires navigating multiple dimensions, including a clear understanding of business objectives to align AI initiatives with organizational goals, deep knowledge of the relevant data and workflows to ensure AI supports core business processes effectively, and thoughtful application of AI technologies to streamline data-intensive tasks and unlock new efficiencies.

Our end goal is to be able to gather, understand, interact with, and generate data faster by applying the right AI capabilities to the right points in the organization.

This version removes the specific role targeting and makes it applicable to anyone involved in AI implementation decisions, while maintaining the same key concepts and structure.

By the end of this chapter, you will understand the following:

- How data architectures have evolved from legacy systems to AI-ready infrastructures, and how to implement a converged datastore approach that unifies structured and unstructured data

- The spectrum of AI technologies available to insurance organizations, from traditional machine learning to agentic AI systems, and their practical applications across underwriting, claims processing, and customer experience

- Why domain-driven AI implementation aligns with business objectives and how to architect root domain entities that provide the rich context needed for intelligent decision-making

- Real-world examples of insurance organizations successfully implementing AI solutions

- The strategic importance of integrating AI directly into business applications rather than treating it as a separate initiative

The evolution of data architectures

We've been on a journey with data architectures in insurance. This evolution has moved through three distinct phases:

- **Legacy systems**: These were characterized by monolithic relational databases that were slow and expensive, with rigid schemas that were slow to adapt and had limited scalability

- **Microservices era**: This introduced domain datastores with faster development cycles, using JSON for data both in motion and at rest, APIs and events for communication, and domain-specific schemas

- **AI integration**: Now, we're entering an era where we need to architect data specifically for AI, with smart business applications and intelligent agents operating on converged datastores

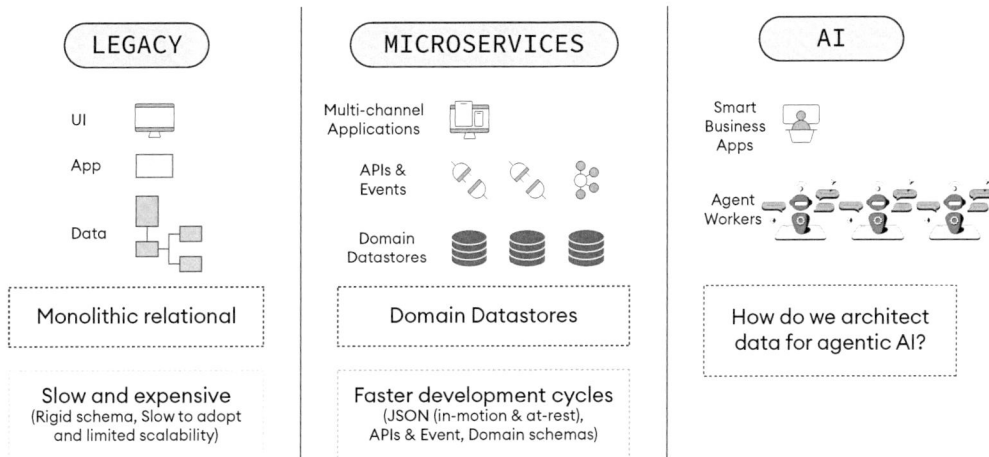

Figure 14.1: Data architecture evolution: from legacy systems to AI-ready infrastructure

Figure 14.1 illustrates the three-phase evolution of data architectures in insurance. Legacy systems show a traditional three-tier structure (UI, app, and data) with monolithic relational databases. The era of microservices introduces distributed domain datastores with multi-channel applications communicating through APIs and events. The AI phase depicts a new paradigm with smart business applications and multiple agent workers, raising the key question of how to properly architect data infrastructure to support agentic AI systems.

Technology has always driven advancements in how we transact business. Each phase has brought increased agility and capability, with the AI integration phase representing the most significant leap forward in terms of business value potential.

Having explored how data architectures have evolved to support AI capabilities, let's examine how these technical foundations translate into tangible business value through a concrete insurance example.

Claim handling as an example

Having explored how data architectures have evolved to support AI capabilities, let's examine how these technical foundations translate into tangible business value through a concrete insurance example. Common organizational goals for an insurer may include increasing operational excellence and customer centricity. Emphasizing efficiency and effectiveness in operations to maximize returns and reduce waste, and prioritizing investments that improve customer satisfaction and engagement.

How well your organization can process and resolve claims, for example, directly impacts the preceding objectives. Achieving this is directly coupled to how quickly, efficiently, and accurately you can process the data found within claim-handling application workflows.

Claim handling provides us with great opportunities to leverage AI in order to accelerate data processing hotspots, so that the organization can return meaningful value from the technology investment.

So what kinds of data in a claim-handling workflow are hard to work with? Unstructured data sources, such as damage photos, accident forms and reports, claim handler notes, traffic camera videos, and claim-handling guidelines and recommendations.

Are these data sources cumbersome for your employees to process? Consider the manual effort required: opening and reading forms, examining and interpreting images, and distilling and writing case-file notes before claims can move forward. During catastrophic events, this challenge multiplies exponentially with massive, sudden influxes of claims.

The insurance industry's challenge isn't a lack of data; it's the ability to process, understand, and act on that data at scale and with speed. This is where AI, in its various forms, offers transformative potential.

The spectrum of AI in insurance

Insurance organizations can leverage multiple types of AI to address different business challenges. Understanding the full spectrum of AI capabilities is essential for making strategic implementation decisions.

Traditional machine learning

Machine learning models trained on historical data can be used to make predictions and decisions within a business workflow, effectively replacing certain human tasks. These models excel at risk classification and pricing, detecting fraud based on patterns, segmenting and targeting customers, and triaging and routing claims.

While these AI models have been in use for years, the question now is: what about **generative AI (GenAI)**?

GenAI and LLMs

GenAI and LLMs give us core NLP capabilities that are particularly well-suited to augmenting data processing abilities. When applied to the claim-handling workflow, these technologies can dramatically transform how insurers process and understand unstructured information.

One of the most powerful applications is entity extraction, which helps interrogate and retrieve relevant information from unstructured sources such as PDF guidelines or large bodies of text found within accident forms. This capability allows claims processors to quickly identify key information such as dates, locations, policy numbers, and damage descriptions without manually scanning through lengthy documents.

Text and image classification takes this a step further, enabling claim handlers to automatically determine types of damage or characteristics found in damage photos. Combined with text summarization capabilities, which speed up the synthesis of large bodies of text or information across many sources, these tools can dramatically reduce the time spent on initial claim assessment and documentation review.

The technology also excels at text generation, helping generate case files and providing succinct instructions to workers based on larger bodies of guidelines. This ensures consistency in claim handling while reducing the cognitive load on adjusters. Additionally, interactive chat capabilities make previous or additional existing information available more quickly to both employees and customers, creating a more responsive and efficient service experience.

Agentic AI systems

At the most advanced end of the spectrum are agentic AI systems, autonomous systems that can perceive their environment, make decisions, and take actions to achieve specific goals. While still emerging and primarily deployed for specific, bounded tasks in production environments today, these systems represent the next evolution in AI capabilities. These are distinct from traditional LLMs in several key ways:

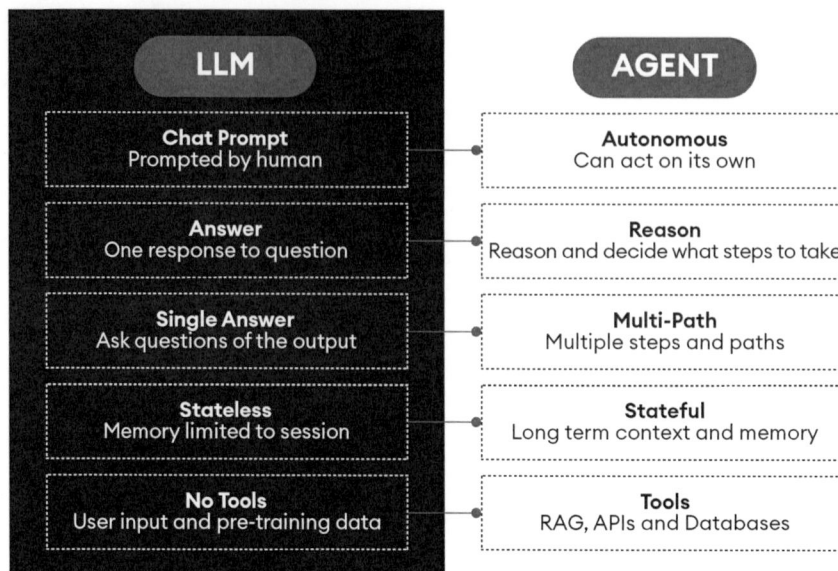

Figure 14.2: LLM vs. agentic AI systems: key differences and capabilities

This comparison chart highlights the fundamental differences between traditional LLMs and advanced agentic AI systems. The diagram shows five key distinctions:

- **Interaction mode:** LLMs are prompted by humans for each response, while agents can act autonomously to execute multi-step workflows once given an initial goal or objective

- **Response capability**: LLMs provide single answers versus agents that can reason through multi-step processes

- **Processing approach**: LLMs offer single-answer responses, while agents can explore multiple paths

- **Memory**: LLMs are stateless, while agents maintain long-term context and memory

- **Tool access:** LLMs lack tool access compared to agents that can use RAG, APIs, and databases

The choice of which AI approach to implement depends on the specific business challenge, data availability, and organizational readiness. Many insurance organizations will benefit from implementing a mix of these approaches across different business domains and use cases.

Understanding these fundamental differences between LLMs and agents is crucial because they determine how we architect AI solutions for insurance workflows. While LLMs excel at individual tasks such as document analysis or customer inquiries, the complex multi-step nature of insurance processes, from initial claim intake through final settlement, requires the autonomous decision-making and tool integration capabilities that only agentic systems can provide.

Agentic workflows in insurance

To understand how AI agents can deliver business value, let's examine a concrete example of an agentic workflow in insurance claims processing. These autonomous systems can perceive their environment, make decisions, and take actions. These capabilities make them particularly powerful for orchestrating complex insurance processes to reach your business goals of reducing operational expenses and increasing customer satisfaction.

This workflow demonstrates how the most advanced AI systems can orchestrate complex insurance processes by seamlessly connecting the following:

- **Structured data** (claim record)
- **Business workflow steps** (first notice of loss → identify and document damages → check coverage → determine and summarize coverage)
- **Unstructured data** (damage photos, policy forms, etc.)
- **User touchpoints** (customer mobile app, claim handler interface, etc.)

The workflow is shown in the following diagram:

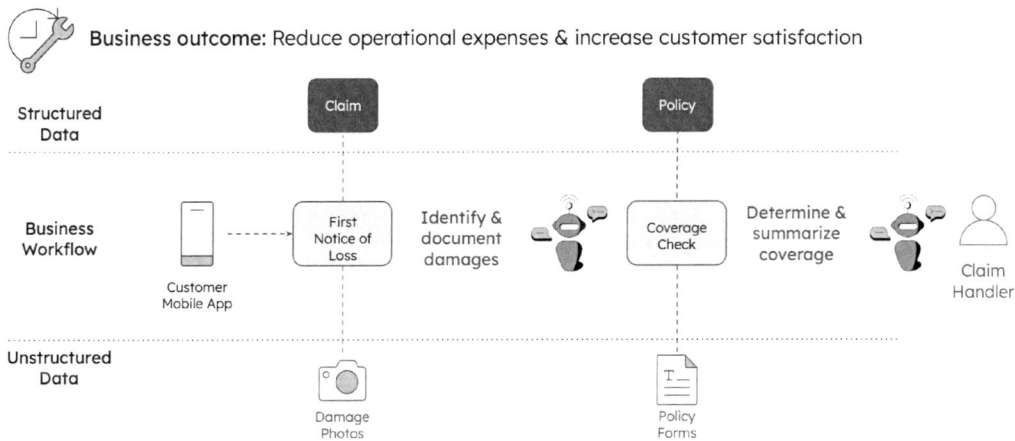

Figure 14.3: Agentic AI workflow for insurance claims processing

It illustrates how AI agents orchestrate an end-to-end insurance claims workflow, integrating structured data (claim records and policy information), business processes (from first notice of loss through coverage determination), unstructured data (damage photos and policy forms), and user touchpoints (customer mobile app and claim handler interface). The workflow shows AI agents operating at key decision points to automate processes while connecting customer experiences with backend systems.

This workflow demonstrates how AI agents can bridge the gap between customer experiences and backend processes, handling both structured and unstructured data seamlessly. The key advantage is that agents can operate autonomously across multiple systems and data types, reducing the need for human intervention in routine processes while still maintaining accuracy and compliance.

Architecting for applications

Your software delivery teams and the applications they support may be divided up by agile delivery domains. It's inside those domains and applications that you'll need to apply AI in order to effectively move the needle on organizational and process outcomes. In short, your AI belongs in your applications.

The data that supports those applications resides in operational data stores. If we want both our applications and our AI to work with real-time data, it should be accessible within the same underlying data store. What serves our apps should also serve our AI.

This integration of AI directly into business applications represents a critical shift from the experimental phase of AI adoption to the value-delivery phase. Rather than treating AI as a separate initiative, forward-thinking insurance organizations are embedding AI capabilities directly into their core business systems.

While this approach delivers significant business value, it requires careful attention to security considerations, including the following:

- Access controls and authentication
- Data protection and encryption
- Secure output handling and validation
- Zero-trust security principles
- Proper API controls and monitoring
- Regular security assessments

Organizations should implement these safeguards as part of their AI integration strategy to mitigate risks such as unauthorized access, data exposure, and potential system vulnerabilities.

The converged datastore

A **converged datastore** is an architectural approach that brings together APIs and events, users and agents, and structured and unstructured data in a unified system. This approach is particularly powerful for insurance applications where diverse data types must be processed efficiently.

For example, in a claims processing workflow, the following happens:

1. A customer reports first notice of loss and uploads photos through a mobile app.

2. The system stores both the structured claim data (ID, claimant info, and status) and unstructured data (damage photos with vector embeddings).

3. AI agents extract image metadata, update status summaries, and interact with both the claim data and the customer.

4. Claim handlers have access to the same unified data store, ensuring consistency.

A *Converged* Datastore: APIs & events, users & agents, structured & unstructured data

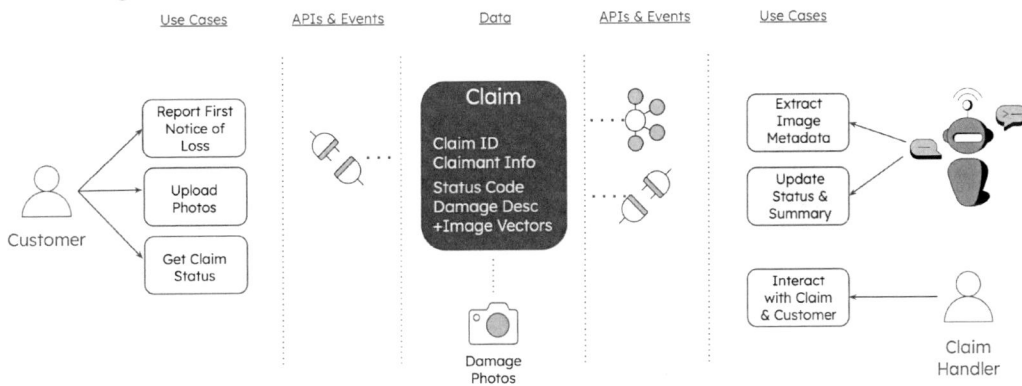

Figure 14.4: Converged datastore architecture for AI-enabled claims processing

This diagram shows how a converged datastore unifies APIs and events, users and agents, and structured and unstructured data in a single system. The workflow illustrates a customer reporting a claim and uploading photos, with the central claim datastore containing both structured data (claim ID and claimant info) and unstructured data (damage photos with vector embeddings), while AI agents process image metadata and interact with both customers and claim handlers through the unified data foundation.

The converged datastore concept addresses one of the most significant challenges in AI implementation: the integration of AI systems with existing operational systems. By providing a unified data foundation, it eliminates the need for complex data pipelines and reduces the latency between data creation and AI-driven insights.

Managing operational structured and unstructured data

Your application architecture needs to provide a way to store, serve, and update structured data as part of your workflow and to integrate the unstructured data. This may come in the form of both the raw data (PDFs, images, and notes) and the vector-encoding representation of it. You'll want the vector-encoding data to be as close as possible to the structured data that already may exist in your application. There are several reasons for this, including the following:

- **Performance**: Providing application-level **service-level agreements** (**SLAs**) utilizing efficient server compute
- **Security**: Providing consistent app tier-level security controls to determine who can access what data
- **Ease of application delivery and maintenance**: The fewer components and dependencies, the lower the complexity and cost of building, deploying, and maintaining effective software solutions that leverage AI

This integrated approach to data management is particularly important in insurance, where data privacy, security, and compliance requirements are stringent. By maintaining a unified approach to data governance across both structured and unstructured data, organizations can ensure that AI implementations meet regulatory requirements while still delivering business value.

Architecture features for agentic systems

Let's look at the architectural features we can expect to find in an agentic system. Putting focus on architectural significance, what's new, and what's changing is important to understanding not only what you can build, but how it will integrate into existing systems.

Root domain entity and domain schema

The converged datastore approach uses fewer but richer data objects that provide deep and immediate context. A **root domain entity** is essentially a comprehensive data container that holds everything related to a specific business concept in one place. For example, a claim entity would contain the following:

- Structured data (claim ID, dates, type codes, loss details, and claimant information)
- Unstructured data (damage photos, accident reports, and traffic camera videos)
- Vector embeddings of the unstructured content

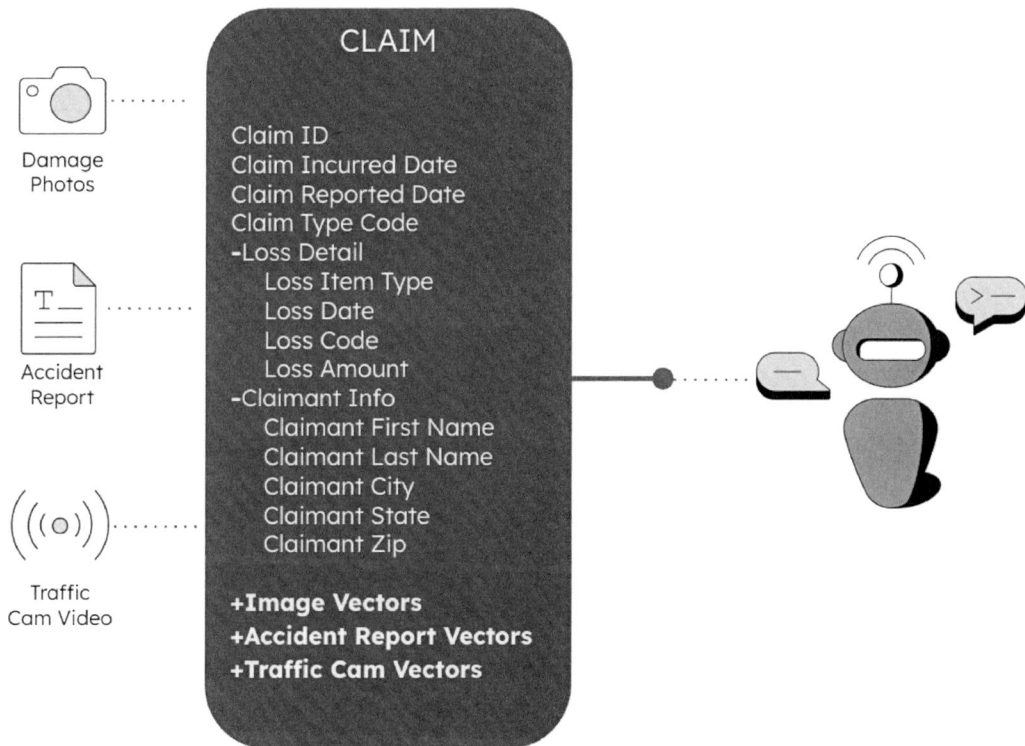

Figure 14.5: Root domain entity and domain schema

Figure 14.5 shows how unstructured data sources (damage photos, accident reports, and traffic camera videos) are integrated into a rich claim entity alongside structured data fields. This approach delivers fewer but richer data objects that provide deep and immediate context, using **JavaScript Object Notation (JSON)** as the AI standard format; this is the preferred data format for AI systems because it's flexible and easy to process while enabling real-time access across agents and use cases with low-latency performance.

Unified search across all data types

This rich data structure enables powerful new search capabilities. Instead of querying multiple systems, a claims adjuster can say, "Show me all Q4 claims over $15,000 with damage photos similar to this new claim", and get results that combine structured data filters with visual similarity matching in a single query.

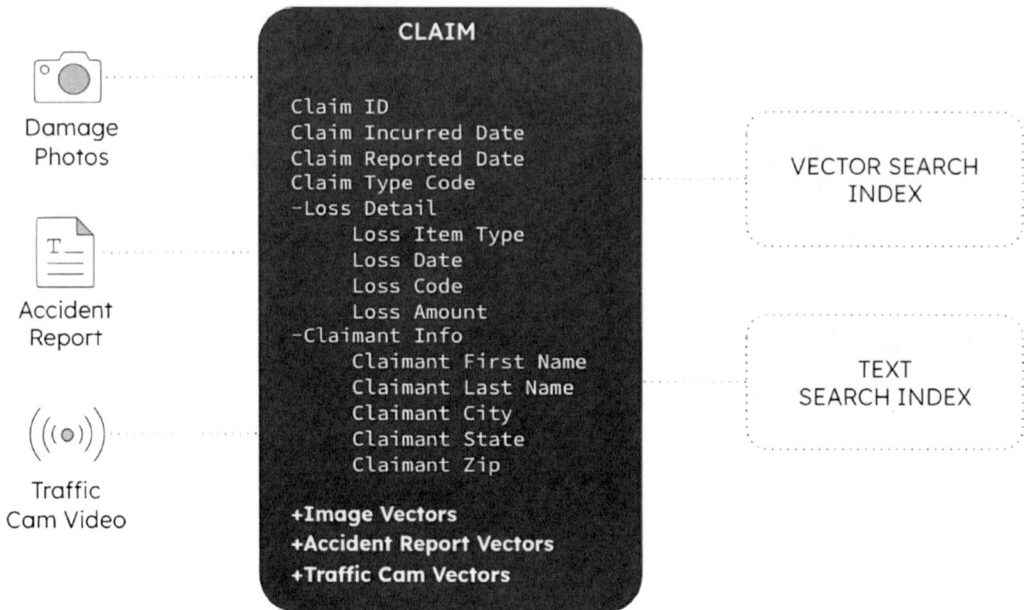

Figure 14.6: Vector, text, and hybrid search

Figure 14.6 illustrates how MongoDB Atlas automatically creates both vector and text search indexes from the CLAIM collections. When data changes, edits propagate automatically into all indexes, enabling queries using $vectorSearch (for finding similar images or content) and $search (for traditional text searching) within MongoDB's query language. This architecturally elegant approach allows you to traverse structured and unstructured data within the same query while maintaining low latency, low complexity, and a single security model.

Learn more about Atlas Vector Search at https://www.mongodb.com/products/platform/atlas-vector-search and Atlas Search at https://www.mongodb.com/products/platform/atlas-search.

Event-based architecture for autonomous actions

Beyond rich data models and unified search, agentic systems need to react automatically to changing conditions. This is where event-based architecture becomes essential.

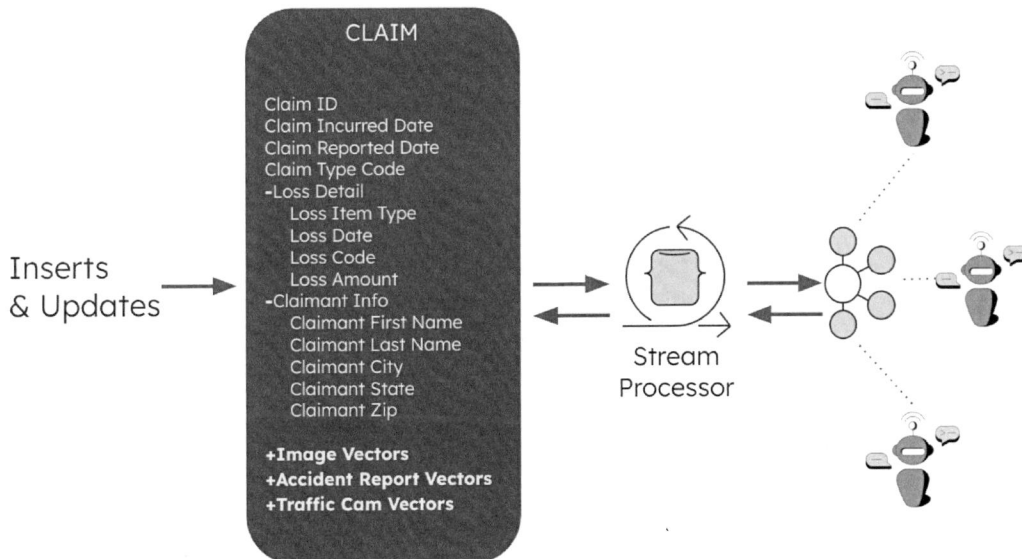

Figure 14.7: Event-based architecture for autonomous actions

Figure 14.7 shows how MongoDB Atlas supports persistent stream processing, allowing AI systems to process continuous streaming data using aggregation pipeline stages (MongoDB's powerful data processing framework that can filter, transform, and analyze data in real time). The stream processor component continuously monitors inserts and updates to CLAIM entities, automatically triggering responses by AI agents. This provides MongoDB Atlas deployment simplicity and security while enabling real-time responsiveness.

Learn more about Atlas Stream Processing here: `https://www.mongodb.com/products/platform/atlas-stream-processing`.

Key advantages of this unified approach are as follows:

- **One query, comprehensive results**: Find relevant information using any combination of structured data, text content, and visual similarity
- **Automatic synchronization**: When data changes, all search indexes update instantly
- **Real-time responsiveness**: AI systems react immediately to data changes
- **Consistent security**: One access control model across all data types and processes

Together these architectural features include rich domain entities, unified search capabilities, and event-driven responsiveness. They create the technical foundation for intelligent, autonomous systems. However, architectural elegance means nothing without measurable business impact. The real test of any AI implementation lies in whether it solves actual business problems and improves operational outcomes.

Now, let's examine how these architectural principles translate into practical business value through a concrete example of AI-enhanced claims processing.

AI-driven improvements in claim handling for better business outcomes

The integration of AI into claims processing represents one of the most immediate opportunities for insurance organizations to realize value from AI investments. By automating routine aspects of claims handling, organizations can reduce processing times, improve accuracy, and free up human adjusters to focus on complex cases and customer interactions that benefit from human judgment and empathy.

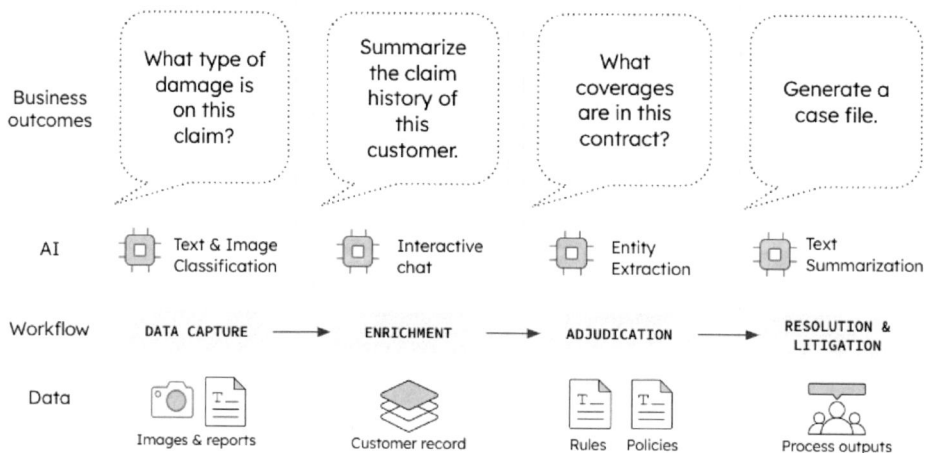

Figure 14.8: AI use cases aligned to the claim-handling workflow

Figure 14.8 shows practical use cases for core NLP capabilities that include text and image classification, interactive chat, entity extraction, and text summarization. When applied to a claim-handling workflow, for example, these capabilities can reduce data hotspots, resulting in lower processing times and costs, and improved customer experience.

Before AI can transform our organizations, we first have to bring it into our applications and move beyond experimentation to production deployment.

AI maturity and implementation strategy

Figure 14.9 shows the different stages of AI adoption within enterprises, from early interest to a pervasive and structural integration into processes and decisions. Many organizations struggle with moving out of Level 2, analytics experimentation, to Level 3, deploying AI features within business applications, in order to deliver meaningful business value and outcomes.

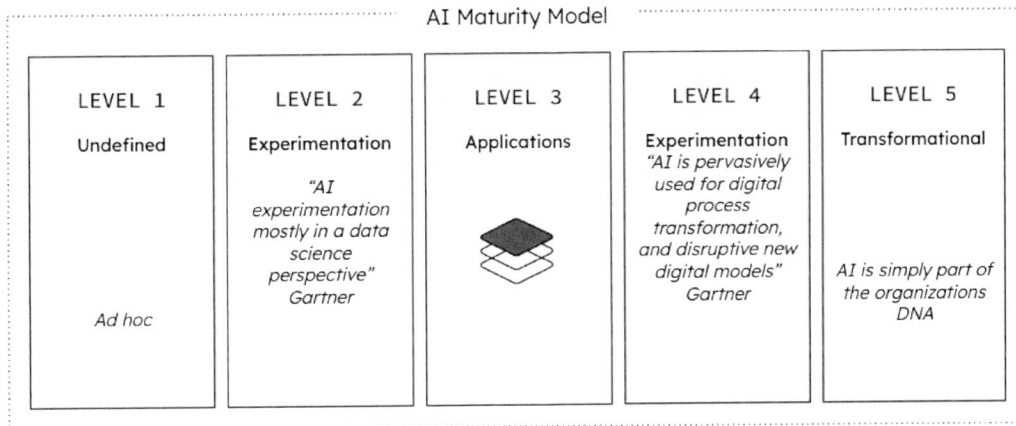

Figure 14.9: AI maturity levels from undefined to transformational

This maturity model provides a roadmap for insurance organizations looking to advance their AI capabilities. The key transition from experimentation to production implementation requires not just technical expertise but also organizational alignment, clear business objectives, and a willingness to reimagine existing processes.

The three layers of GenAI

Understanding the technical foundation of GenAI helps insurance organizations make strategic decisions about where to invest resources and how to build comprehensive AI capabilities. GenAI applications can be separated into three major layers:

- **Layer 1, compute and AI models:** The underlying processing power plus foundational and embedding models that provide the core AI capabilities.
- **Layer 2, tooling to fine-tune and build applications:** Tools that provide foundational models with context by feeding them proprietary data. This is the critical middle layer that bridges generic AI capabilities with specific business needs.
- **Layer 3, AI-powered apps and experiences:** The interface and experiences that end users interact with, plus app frameworks that simplify the process of building AI experiences.

Foundational models are extremely powerful, but being trained on public datasets, they lack the domain knowledge and data context needed to adequately support enterprise applications. This is where Layer 2 becomes crucial, the data and tooling that enable GenAI-enhanced applications to be fully operational, moving your organization from Level 2 experimentation into Level 3 production maturity.

A converged operational database stores proprietary structured and vector data, making it available to LLMs when an application makes a request. This effectively provides the context necessary for a foundational model to answer questions beyond its initial knowledge boundary.

While much attention focuses on foundational models, the middle-layer data and tooling often determine the success or failure of AI initiatives in production environments.

Figure 14.10 shows the three layers of GenAI in greater detail, showing structured data flowing from the application into the operational database, with raw unstructured data managed in object storage where it can be processed by applications. Part of this processing includes vectorization (converting unstructured content into numerical representations that AI can understand) and subsequent persistence of those vectors in the operational data store, where they can be readily accessed by the application.

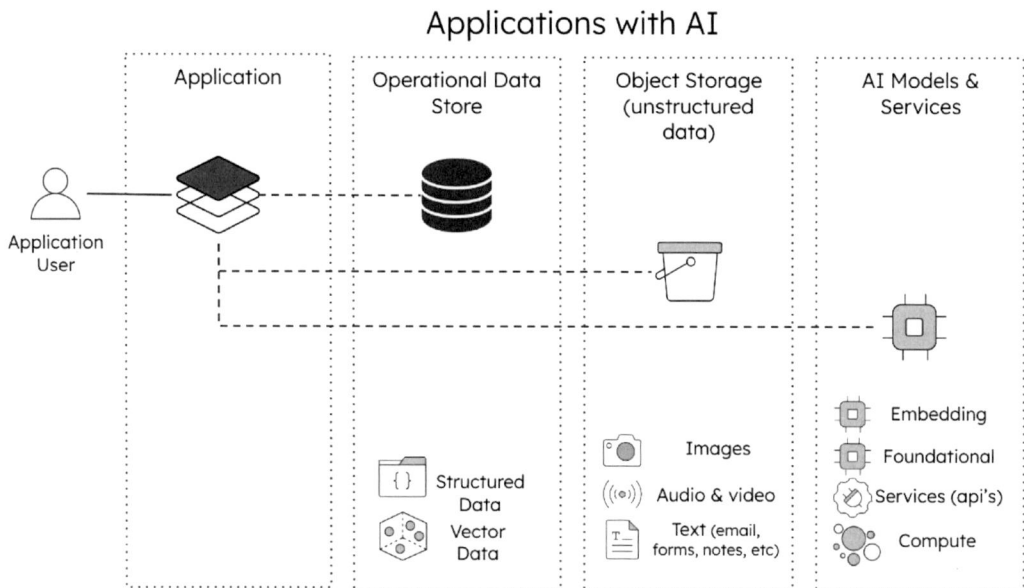

Figure 14.10: AI-enabled application architecture with integrated data and model services

This architecture provides a blueprint for insurance organizations looking to build AI-enhanced applications. The key insight is that AI capabilities should be integrated directly into business applications rather than existing as separate systems. This integration ensures that AI has access to real-time data and can deliver insights and actions within the context of existing business processes.

Domain-driven AI implementation

Insurance enterprises worldwide have embraced domain-driven design alongside aligned software delivery teams organized around core processing domains. With the shift to microservices and event-streaming architectures, AI capabilities can now supercharge this approach and accelerate the ability to interact with and serve up real-time data.

Working together: applications, data, and AI

Core insurance business capabilities organized and deployed by domain can be significantly enhanced when augmented by AI. This integration works best when AI implementations are as follows:

- **Domain-specific**: Tailored to specific business areas such as claims, underwriting, or customer service
- **Task-focused**: Directly addressing data processing bottlenecks where they naturally occur
- **Application-integrated**: Built into existing workflows rather than operating as separate systems

For this approach to be effective, both operational and vector data should be stored as close to applications as possible. This proximity enables the following:

- **Real-time context**: Decisions made based on current data
- **Optimal performance**: Reduced latency for time-sensitive insurance processes
- **Consistent security**: Unified access controls across all data types
- **Domain agility**: Quick adaptation to changing business requirements

Domain-based operational data stores help segment and enable stronger data lineage, data quality, and data governance for more trustworthy AI interactions. The architecture also relies on APIs and events for efficient processing both within individual domains and across domain boundaries.

Modernization and AI-forward architecture

Moving to a converged datastore architecture often requires modernizing existing systems. The recommended approach consolidates legacy complexity into a common, root domain schema:

- **Migrate data** from relational, hierarchical, and file-based systems to a single-view operational data layer
- **Create unified access** that can simultaneously serve APIs, AI agents, classical applications, and provide internal/external interoperability

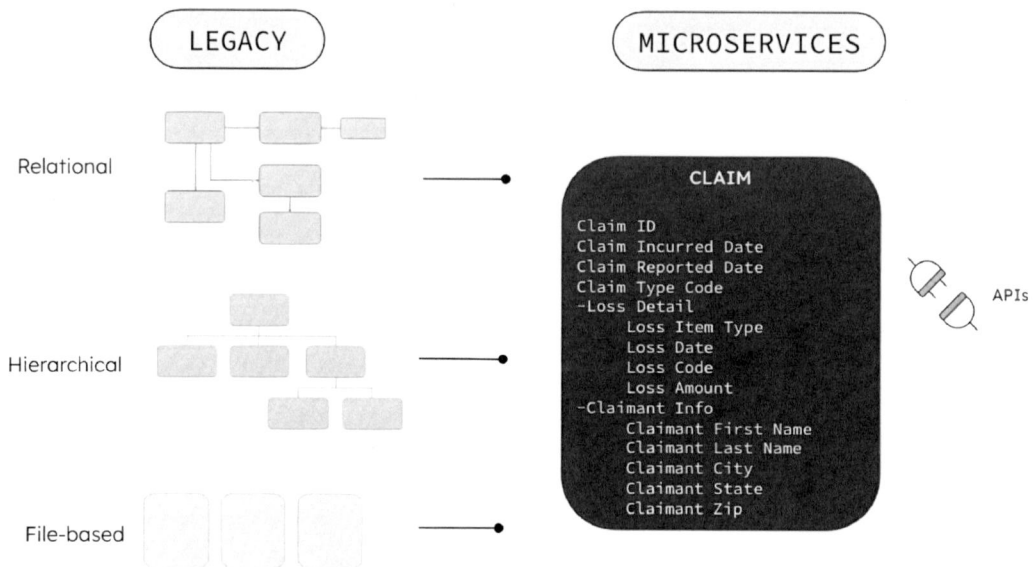

Figure 14.11: Legacy system modernization strategy for converged datastore architecture

This diagram illustrates the migration path from fragmented legacy systems (relational, hierarchical, and file-based) to a unified converged datastore approach. The strategy consolidates complex legacy data structures into a common root domain schema that can simultaneously serve APIs, agents, classical applications, and provide internal/external interoperability, enabling organizations to modernize incrementally while maintaining existing system functionality.

This modernization strategy acknowledges the reality that most insurance organizations operate with a mix of legacy and modern systems. Rather than requiring complete replacement, the converged datastore approach offers a pragmatic path forward, allowing incremental modernization while delivering value from AI investments.

AI-forward architecture

The future of insurance technology is an AI-forward architecture built on a converged datastore centered around core collections for enterprise root domain entities such as customer, submission, policy, and claim.

This architectural approach emphasizes the following:

- **Future-proof design**: Document model flexibility allows seamless integration of both structured and unstructured data without rigid schema constraints

- **Essential features**: Every component contributes directly to business value for AI-enabled insurance operations

- **Robust foundation**: Security, scale, and performance characteristics handle the demanding requirements of real-time AI processing

- **Reduced complexity**: Fewer objects and components create more maintainable and efficient systems

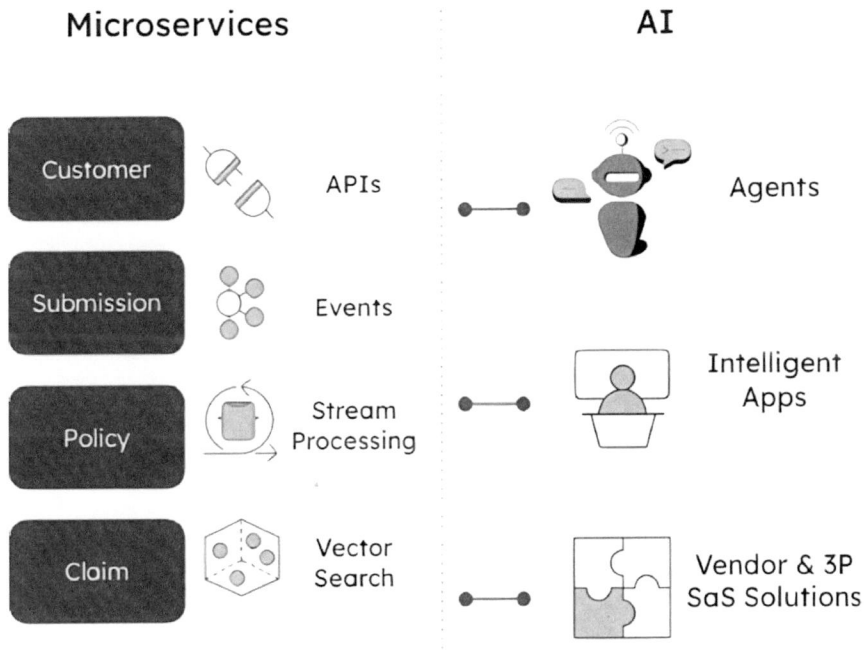

Figure 14.12: AI-forward architecture

This diagram shows an AI-forward architecture that consolidates core enterprise entities (customer, submission, policy, and claim) into a unified platform supporting APIs, events, stream processing, vector search, and text search capabilities. The architecture enables AI agents, intelligent applications, and vendor/SaaS solutions to operate seamlessly across a reduced complexity infrastructure, designed from the ground up to anticipate and enable AI capabilities rather than retrofitting legacy systems.

By designing systems with AI capabilities in mind from the beginning, insurance organizations can avoid retrofitting challenges and rapidly adopt new AI capabilities as they emerge, maintaining a competitive advantage in an increasingly AI-driven industry.

Underwriting and risk management

Few roles within insurance are as important as underwriters, who strike the right balance between profit and risk, bring real-world variables to actuarial models, and help steer product portfolios, markets, pricing, and coverages. Achieving equilibrium between exposures and premiums requires constantly gathering and analyzing information from multiple sources to build comprehensive risk profiles.

While many established insurers have access to a wealth of historical underwriting and claims data, challenges remain in integrating newer real-time data sources, keeping up with regulatory changes, and modeling what-if risk scenarios, which are tasks that still involve significant manual effort.

Advanced analytics

Traditional IT systems are slow to respond to changing data formats and requirements. The burden often falls on underwriters to summarize data and turn it into actionable information and insights.

LLMs are now being leveraged to do the following:

- Speed up data source wrangling and summarization
- Help underwriting teams make quicker decisions
- Reduce the manual effort required for data interpretation

By doing so, AI models are helping manage seasonal demands, market shifts, and staff availability impacts on the underwriting team workload and productivity. This saves underwriting time for high-value accounts where human expertise is truly needed.

Traditional AI models already play an important role in classifying and triaging risk in the following ways:

- Sending very low-risk policies to touchless automated workflows
- Routing low-to-moderate risk policies to trained service center staff
- Directing high-risk and high-value accounts to dedicated underwriters

Beyond triage, another challenge underwriters face lies in rate adjustments and policy renewals, which takes up a large portion of an underwriters' daily responsibilities and demands significant time and manual effort. Automated underwriting workflows leveraging AI can analyze and classify risk with far less manual effort, freeing up significant time and intellectual capital.

A converged datastore offers unparalleled ability to store data from vast amounts of sources and formats, responding quickly to requests for new data ingestion. As data and requirements change, the document model allows insurers to simply add more data and fields without costly change cycles associated with rigid database structures.

Learn more about automating digital underwriting with ML at `https://www.mongodb.com/solutions/solutions-library/machine-learning-underwriting-solution`.

Claim processing

Efficient claim processing is critical for insurers. Timely resolution and good communication throughout the process are key to maintaining positive relationships and customer satisfaction. Additionally, insurers must pay and process claims according to jurisdictional regulations, which may include penalties for non-compliance with specific timelines.

Processing claims accurately requires analyzing vast amounts of information. A typical automobile accident may include verbal and written descriptions from claimants and appraisers, along with unstructured content from police reports, traffic and vehicle dashboard cameras, photos, and vehicle telemetry data.

AI is helping insurers make sense of data faster and in real time. From natural language processing to image classification and vector embedding, all the pieces are now available for insurers to make a generational leap forward in transforming their IT systems and business workflows.

Generating accurate impact assessments for catastrophic events can now be done with far less time and greater accuracy by cross-referencing real-time and historical claims experience data, thanks to GenAI and the vector embedding of unstructured data.

Using vector embeddings from photo, text, and voice sources, insurers can now enhance inbound claims with richer metadata, enabling them to more quickly do the following:

- Classify and triage claims

- Route work to appropriate specialists

- Make prescriptive work assignments based on real-time workload and staff availability

Claim details are not always clear-cut, and parties don't always act in good faith. AI is helping insurers drive to resolution faster and even avoid litigation altogether through its ability to analyze more data more effectively and in less time.

Many insurers provide risk-assessment services using drones, sensors, or cameras to capture and analyze data. This data offers the promise of preventing losses altogether, lowering exposures, liability, and expenses. This is possible through a combination of vector embedding with traditional and GenAI models.

Customer experience

Accessing information consistently during customer service interactions, while expecting representatives to quickly interpret it, presents perennial challenges. The volume, variety, and complexity of insurance information make this particularly challenging, driving heavy investment in customer experience transformation:

- **24/7 virtual assistance**: AI-based chat agents can free up call center staff to work on more complex, high-touch cases. Handling routine inquiries can now extend to more complex scenarios thanks to vector-embedded content and LLMs.

- **Claims assistance**: GenAI can deliver specific claim-handling guidelines to staff in real time, while traditional ML models can interrogate real-time information streams to alert customers or claim-handlers to quality, content, or compliance issues. These capabilities allow insurers to process more claims faster while significantly reducing errors.

- **Customer profiling**: Every interaction is an opportunity to learn more about customers. Technologies such as voice-to-text streaming, vector embedding, and GenAI help insurers build more robust customer profiles in near-real time.

According to the Coalition Against Insurance Fraud, the U.S. insurance industry lost over $308 billion to fraud in 2022 [1]. With the vector embedding of unstructured data sources, semantic similarity searches across both vector and structured metadata, and traditional ML models, insurers can detect and prevent fraud in ways that were never before possible.

While these AI capabilities offer significant potential, insurance executives need concrete evidence that similar organizations have successfully implemented these technologies and achieved measurable results. The theoretical benefits of AI become compelling only when supported by real-world implementations that demonstrate clear ROI and operational improvements.

The following examples show how insurance companies and related industries have moved beyond experimentation to production-scale AI deployments. They provide practical blueprints for implementation and quantifiable business outcomes.

Real-world examples of domain-specific AI

To bring the earlier concepts to life, let's look at how domain-specific AI is already making a measurable impact across the insurance industry. These real-world examples show how insurers are applying AI to solve complex problems in underwriting, risk assessment, and compliance, turning advanced technologies such as real-time data analysis RAG into practical business outcomes.

> **AI-powered risk intelligence platform transforms insurance underwriting with AI and MongoDB Atlas, slashing costs by 30%**
>
> An AI-powered risk intelligence platform helps insurance companies and underwriters build confidence in coverage decisions by providing real-time insights on individuals and businesses using AI. Powered by MongoDB Atlas, this platform analyzes vast amounts of public data to identify risks and opportunities for insurance underwriting, offering a comprehensive view of policyholder relationships and potential fraud indicators. The platform enables insurers to streamline **know your customer** (**KYC**) processes and enhance due diligence for complex commercial policies.
>
> This example has been anonymized for editorial clarity. To learn more, see: `https://mdb.link/building-trust-with-relationship-intelligence`.

> **A leading AI-powered third-party cyber risk management platform accelerates vendor evaluation with AI**
>
> An AI-powered third-party cyber risk assessment platform enables insurance companies to evaluate cyber insurance applications and assess policyholder security postures in minutes. By leveraging MongoDB Atlas for efficient data storage and retrieval, this advanced AI platform can process vast amounts of cybersecurity information, delivering actionable underwriting insights in minutes. This streamlined approach significantly reduces policy evaluation time and enhances overall cyber insurance risk assessment accuracy. The platform uses sophisticated models and RAG techniques to provide highly accurate and contextually relevant intelligence for cyber insurance underwriters. This not only accelerates policy approval decisions but also ensures that insurance companies are equipped with the most precise cyber risk evaluations for premium pricing. Risk assessments generated from analysis are 80% faster than manual underwriting methods with no loss in accuracy. This example has been anonymized for editorial clarity. To learn more, see: `https://mdb.link/transforming-cyber-risk-intelligence`.

These real-world examples demonstrate how insurance and related industries are already realizing significant business value from AI implementations. By studying these success stories, insurance organizations can identify patterns and approaches that might apply to their own underwriting challenges and risk assessment processes.

Practical AI use cases in insurance

Having explored the architectural foundations and strategic approaches to AI implementation, let's examine concrete examples that demonstrate these concepts in action. The following use cases showcase how insurance organizations are applying AI technologies to solve specific business challenges, providing practical blueprints that can guide similar implementations across the industry.

Claim management using LLMs and Vector Search for RAG

By converting claim data into vector embeddings, MongoDB's Atlas Vector Search accelerates information retrieval, making it quicker and easier to find relevant details. LLMs then analyze these embeddings to extract valuable insights and context, optimizing claim processing. This combined approach enhances accuracy, efficiency, and overall claims management.

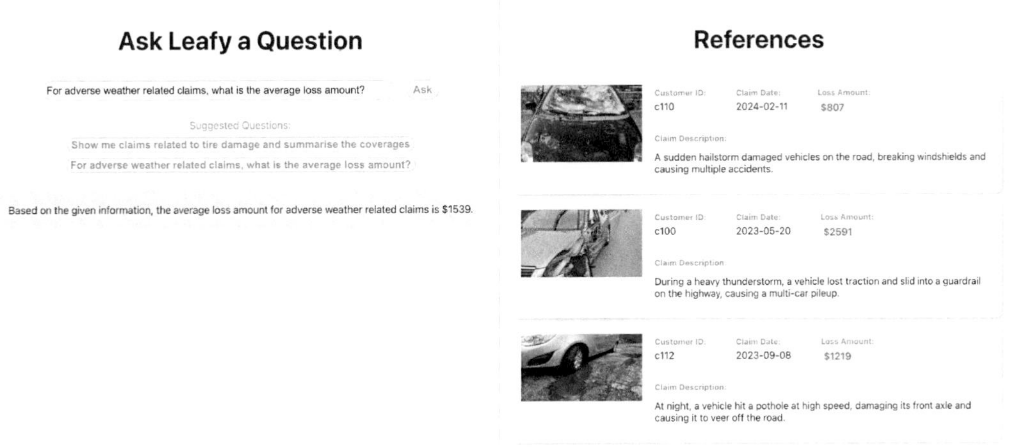

Figure 14.13: Atlas Vector Search provides answers to user questions about insurance claims, including calculations and detailed claim examples

This interface demonstrates how MongoDB's Atlas Vector Search enables natural language querying of insurance claims data. Users can ask questions such as `"For adverse weather-related claims, what is the average loss amount?"` and receive contextual answers with supporting claim examples, photos, and detailed loss information. The system combines vector embeddings with LLMs to provide accurate, evidence-based responses for claims analysis and management.

Learn more at `https://www.mongodb.com/solutions/solutions-library/claim-management-llms-vector-search`.

AI-enhanced claim adjustment for auto insurance

By leveraging AI and vector image search, this solution automates auto insurance claim adjustments. Accident photos are compared to a database of past claims, significantly accelerating damage estimates while maintaining consistency throughout the claims process.

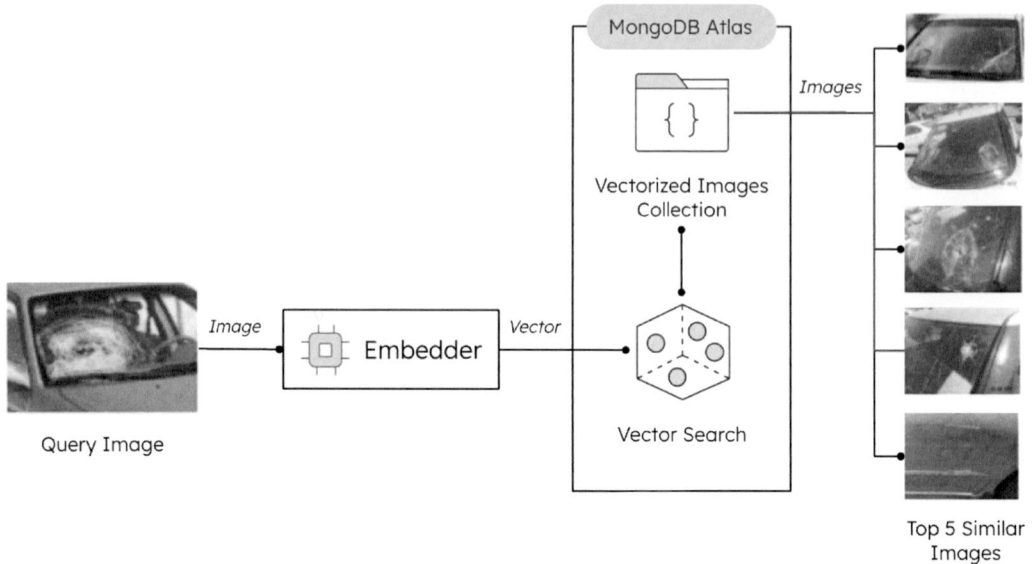

Figure 14.14: AI-enhanced auto insurance claim adjustment using vector image search

This diagram illustrates an automated claim adjustment system where accident photos are processed through an embedding model to create vector representations, then searched against a collection of vectorized images in MongoDB Atlas. The system performs similarity matching to return the top 5 most similar damage images from historical claims, enabling rapid and consistent damage assessment.

Learn more at `https://www.mongodb.com/docs/atlas/architecture/current/solutions-library/insurance-image-search/`.

PDF search application with Vector Search and LLMs

PDFs are traditionally hard to search, making it difficult for insurance workers to find information quickly. This solution converts PDFs into a searchable format using tools such as Superduper, allowing users to quickly retrieve information and streamline insurance work.

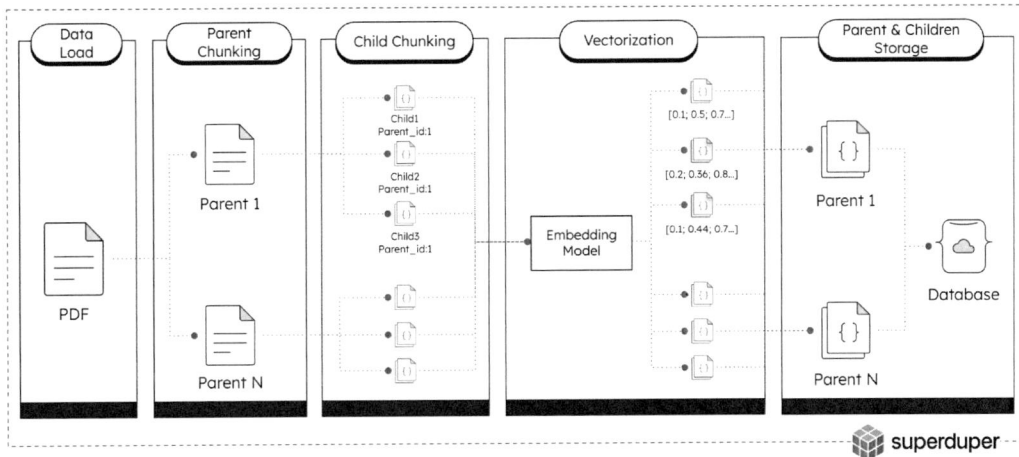

Figure 14.15: PDF search application pipeline with Vector Search and LLMs

This workflow diagram shows the process of converting PDFs into searchable content through a five-stage pipeline: data load, parent chunking, child chunking, vectorization using an embedding model, and storage in a database. The system breaks down PDF documents into hierarchical chunks, creates vector embeddings for semantic search capabilities, and stores both parent and child document structures to enable efficient retrieval and LLM-powered search functionality.

Learn more here: https://www.mongodb.com/docs/atlas/architecture/current/solutions-library/pdf-search/.

The future of AI in insurance

As AI technologies continue to mature, we're seeing expansion into new and innovative use cases beyond current implementations:

Predictive analytics for customer engagement

AI-powered predictive analytics can anticipate customer needs, preferences, and behaviors based on historical data and trends. By leveraging predictive models, insurers can identify at-risk customers, anticipate churn, and proactively engage with customers to prevent issues and enhance satisfaction.

These capabilities enable a shift from reactive to proactive customer engagement, improving customer retention, increasing lifetime value, and enabling more efficient allocation of customer service resources.

Crop insurance and precision farming

AI is being used in agricultural insurance to assess crop health, predict yields, and mitigate risks associated with weather events and crop diseases. By combining satellite imagery, weather data, soil sensors, and historical yield information, AI systems can provide granular risk assessments at the field level, enabling insurers to offer customized policies that reflect the specific risk profile of each farming operation.

Predictive maintenance for property insurance

AI-powered predictive maintenance solutions, leveraging **Internet of Things (IoT)** sensors installed in buildings and infrastructure, are being used in property insurance to prevent losses and minimize damage to insured properties. These systems can detect early warning signs of equipment failure, water leaks, and electrical issues before they cause significant damage.

Usage-based insurance (UBI) for commercial fleets

AI-enabled telematics devices installed in commercial vehicles collect data on driving behavior, including speed, acceleration, braking, and location. ML algorithms analyze this data to assess risk and determine insurance premiums, representing a fundamental shift from static risk assessments to dynamic pricing based on actual driving behavior.

Insurance organizations that establish strong AI foundations today will be well positioned to capitalize on these emerging opportunities. The most successful organizations will view AI not as a standalone technology initiative but as a fundamental capability that transforms how they operate, serve customers, and manage risk.

For more information and resources, visit the *MongoDB for Insurance* page: `https://www.mongodb.com/solutions/industries/insurance`.

Summary

In this chapter, we explored the strategic integration of AI within the insurance sector to drive meaningful business outcomes. It traced the evolution of data architectures from legacy systems to AI-ready infrastructures built on converged datastores, highlighting AI's potential to transform data processing, particularly in managing unstructured data in claims management.

The chapter covered a range of AI technologies, from traditional ML to generative and agent-based systems, showing how they enhance decision-making, automate processes, and improve efficiency across underwriting, claims, and customer experience. It demonstrated that successful AI implementation requires understanding business workflows first, recognizing the interplay between structured and unstructured data, and designing around root domain entities within a converged datastore approach. Most importantly, organizations must focus on delivering value through business applications rather than isolated AI experiments to move beyond experimentation and truly transform operations with measurable business value.

The following chapter shifts from strategic overview to focused implementation, examining how these architectural principles are applied in practice to transform underwriting processes from weeks-long quote cycles into real-time decisions. It outlines a 10-step AI pipeline automating the underwriting workflow and presents business impact metrics showing major improvements in turnaround time, cost efficiency, and underwriting capacity.

References

1. *Coalation Against Insurance Fraud*: `https://insurancefraud.org`

15

Automating Insurance Underwriting with Fireworks AI and MongoDB

While the previous chapter explored the broad landscape of AI applications transforming the insurance industry, from data architecture evolution to intelligent business applications, this chapter examines a specific, high-impact implementation that exemplifies how AI can revolutionize core insurance operations. The underwriting process, traditionally one of the most time-consuming and labor-intensive aspects of commercial insurance, demonstrates how the AI-ready data architectures and intelligent agents discussed previously can deliver immediate, measurable business value through automation that maintains accuracy while dramatically improving speed.

Consider this hypothetical scenario: At 2:47 P.M., a broker emails a quote request for a $15M construction company. By 2:53 P.M., a comprehensive quote with full underwriting analysis arrives in their inbox. This six-minute turnaround represents a fundamental shift from traditional quote cycles to real-time processing, showcasing the practical application of the architectural principles and AI capabilities covered in earlier chapters.

By the end of this chapter, you will have a clear understanding of the following:

- The technical architecture that enables real-time insurance automation, combining Fireworks AI's inference capabilities with MongoDB Atlas's intelligent document storage and retrieval systems
- The complete 10-step AI pipeline that transforms unstructured broker emails into structured quotes, from email parsing through risk assessment to final quote generation

- How RAG principles ensure that AI decisions are grounded in authoritative underwriting documents while maintaining compliance and accuracy standards

- The production-grade implementation details, including vector search architecture, structured output generation, and cost-effective scaling strategies that make sub-30-minute quotes economically viable

- Real-world application examples demonstrating how the system processes actual quote requests, from initial email parsing through final quote delivery with full audit trails

- The broader implications for insurance industry transformation, including impacts on underwriters, brokers, and carriers that extend beyond simple process automation to fundamental business model evolution

Understanding the importance of speed

In commercial insurance, time is everything. When a broker submits a quote request for a new commercial policy, they're racing against the clock in a highly competitive market where the fastest response often wins the deal. This reality has created an industry paradox where speed determines success, yet the fundamental processes that drive the business remain stubbornly anchored in outdated methodologies that prioritize thoroughness over agility.

AI has reduced the average underwriting decision time from 3–5 days to 12.4 minutes for standard policies, while maintaining 99.3% accuracy rates [1]. Yet many carriers continue operating with manual processes, creating competitive vulnerabilities as InsurTech companies capture business with streamlined, automated operations.

Manual underwriting workflows contain systematic inefficiencies where a large portion of an underwriter's time is spent on manual data processing. The process involves email chaos with unstructured communications, document hunts through fragmented systems, manual calculations across multiple rate tables, and approval hierarchies that create bottlenecks. These inefficiencies result in processing just 2–3 quotes per underwriter daily, with variable accuracy and inconsistent guideline application.

The broken workflow

Today's underwriting process is a case study in inefficiency, involving eight disconnected steps that transform what should be minutes of work into weeks of delays:

1. **Email chaos:** Brokers send unstructured emails with client details buried in paragraphs. Information arrives in inconsistent formats, often missing critical underwriting data.

2. **Manual data entry:** Underwriters manually extract company names, industry classifications, revenue figures, and coverage limits, often introducing transcription errors that affect final quotes.

3. **Document hunt:** This involves searching through multiple PDF manuals, rate sheets, and guidelines stored across different systems with inconsistent organization.

4. **Fragmented analysis:** Risk assessment involves checking multiple databases and historical data across siloed systems that don't communicate with each other.

5. **Manual calculations:** This involves referencing various rate tables and applying multiple modifiers, a time-consuming, error-prone process.

6. **Review bottlenecks:** Complex cases require multiple approval levels, often involving senior underwriters who may not be immediately available.

7. **Response generation:** This involves writing quote response emails from scratch, explaining complex terms in broker-friendly language.

8. **Follow-up chaos:** This includes managing multiple quote versions, deadline tracking, and broker communications manually.

The result is 2 or 3 quotes processed per underwriter per day, with high error rates and inconsistent quality.

The vision

Building on the AI-ready data architectures discussed in *Chapter 14, Delivering Business Value with AI in Insurance*, this underwriting solution demonstrates how to apply the converged datastore principles to solve a critical business problem: transforming weeks-long quote processes into real-time decisions.

We'll explore a practical implementation using **Fireworks AI**, a high-performance inference platform optimized for fast, cost-effective **large language model (LLM)** deployment, and MongoDB Atlas's document-oriented database with built-in vector search capabilities. This combination enables the semantic understanding and real-time processing essential for intelligent automation.

Consider a system where the following applies:

- Unstructured broker emails are instantly parsed and understood
- Relevant underwriting guidelines are automatically retrieved and applied
- Risk assessments are generated with full citation trails
- Quotes are produced with the same accuracy as experienced underwriters
- The entire process is auditable and compliant

We'll begin by outlining the key concepts of this system, followed by a practical, real-world example demonstrating the system's actual implementation and how its components interact.

Setting up the core technical components

Fireworks AI provides the high-performance inference engine that powers the system's NLP. The Llama 3.3 70B model processes unstructured broker communications and generates structured outputs. Model selection criteria include inference speed, accuracy on extraction tasks, and cost efficiency for production scaling.

As discussed previously, MongoDB Atlas provides a document-oriented database with built-in vector search capabilities that enable semantic document retrieval. For underwriting specifically, this means storing policy documents, rate manuals, and regulatory guidelines with vector embeddings for context-aware information access during quote processing.

Document architecture

The MongoDB collections store various types of underwriting knowledge, such as policy information, rating manuals, and regulatory guidelines. These are converted to vector embeddings, which enables quick semantic search using RAG later on.

The system's intelligence relies on a sophisticated semantic search implementation:

```
# Assemble vector-search pipeline
pipeline = [
    {
        "$vectorSearch": {
            "queryVector": query_embedding,    # the user's embedding
            "path": vector_field,              # field that stores each
doc's embedding
            "numCandidates": limit * 10,       # oversampling for recall
            "limit": limit,                    # top-k to return
            "index": "vector_index"            # name of Atlas search index
        }
    }
]


# Execute search and fetch results
results = list(collection.aggregate(pipeline))
```

To retrieve the most relevant document, the pipeline compares the query embedding against every stored embedding in vector_index, ranks the candidates by similarity score, and returns the highest-scoring match (or the top-k if multiple results are requested).

The following diagram illustrates the complete AI-powered underwriting system architecture, showing how Fireworks AI processes broker emails while MongoDB Atlas provides semantic search across underwriting documents:

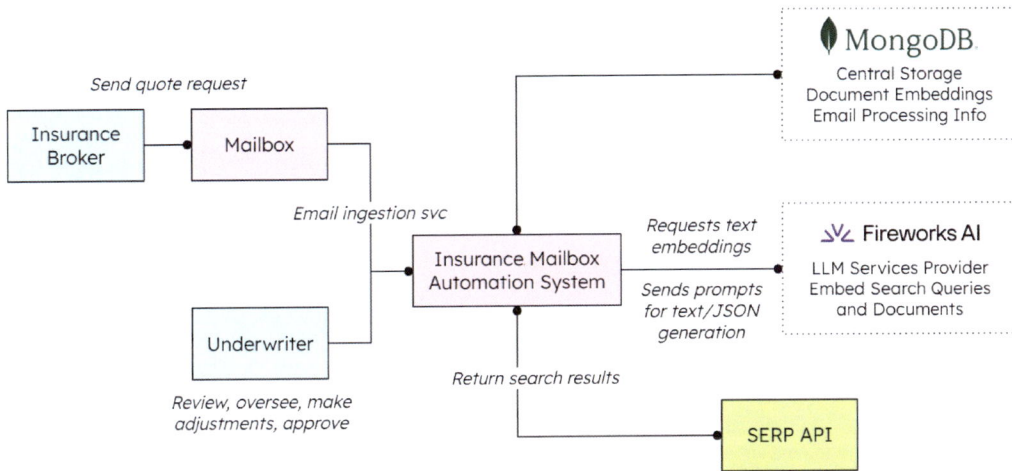

Figure 15.1: Insurance underwriting system architecture

The system includes an **Insurance Broker** sending quote requests to a **Mailbox**, which feeds into an **Insurance Mailbox Automation System**. The system connects to MongoDB for **Central Storage** (Document Embeddings, Email Processing Info) and Fireworks AI for **LLM Services** (Embed Search Queries and Documents). An **Underwriter** reviews and approves decisions, with connections to the **SERP API** for additional data sources.

The 10-step AI pipeline: From email to quote

The processing pipeline transforms unstructured emails into structured quotes through 10 intelligent steps, each powered by the Fireworks-MongoDB combination:

1. **Intelligent email information extraction:** The journey begins when a broker's email hits the system. Using Fireworks' natural language understanding, the platform extracts structured information from unstructured text:

   ```
   # Email extraction using structured output
   email_info = pipeline.extract_email_info(email_content)
   # Returns: {
   #    "client_name": "ABC Construction Corp",
   #    "industry": "Commercial Construction",
   #    "coverage_requested": {
   ```

```
#        "type": "General Liability",
#        "limits": "$2M/$4M"
#    },
#    "annual_revenue": 15000000,
#    "employee_count": 85
# }
```

2. **Automated industry classification**: Once it has gathered the company details, the system determines the precise **Business Industry Classification (BIC)** code by querying MongoDB's industry classification documents:

    ```
    # Semantic search for industry classification
    industry_results = vector_search(
        query=f"Industry classification for {company_industry}",
        collection="bic_codes"
    )
    bic_code = llm_client.classify_industry(industry_results, company_
    description)
    ```

3. **Base rate discovery**: With the BIC code identified, it retrieves industry-specific base rates from the rating manuals stored in MongoDB:

    ```
    # Vector search for base rates
    base_rate_docs = vector_search(
        query=f"Base rates for BIC code {bic_code}",
        collection="rating_manuals",
        filters={"document_type": "base_rates"}
    )
    ```

    The remaining steps showcase the sophisticated interplay between AI reasoning and document retrieval.

4. **Revenue estimation**: When revenue isn't provided, the AI-powered underwriting automation system attempts to estimate it based on industry benchmarks, company size, and other available data points. However, revenue estimates are flagged for underwriter review due to the inherent uncertainty in predicting company financials from limited data.

5. **Base premium calculation**: With industry classification (BIC code), base rates, and revenue established, the system calculates the foundational premium by applying the retrieved rate to the company's annual revenue.

6. **Premium modifiers:** Risk factors are applied by querying modifier tables and letting Fireworks reason about their applicability.

7. **Authority checks:** The system determines approval requirements by cross-referencing coverage limits with authority matrices.

8. **Coverage analysis:** Recommended endorsements and limitations are identified through a semantic search of coverage guidelines.

9. **Risk assessment:** External data sources are integrated to provide comprehensive risk profiles.

10. **Response email:** The system generates professional, broker-friendly quote emails with comprehensive coverage details, premium breakdowns, and underwriting explanations in clear, accessible language.

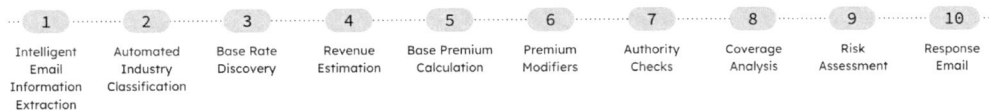

1	2	3	4	5	6	7	8	9	10
Intelligent Email Information Extraction	Automated Industry Classification	Base Rate Discovery	Revenue Estimation	Base Premium Calculation	Premium Modifiers	Authority Checks	Coverage Analysis	Risk Assessment	Response Email

Figure 15.2: AI-powered insurance quote generation pipeline

This flowchart illustrates a 10-step automated pipeline that transforms unstructured email inquiries into structured insurance quotes.

The RAG advantage

The following steps and code illustrate the complete RAG workflow. It first locates the most relevant underwriting documents with a vector similarity search, threads their content into the prompt as trusted context, and then instructs the model to return a schema-validated JSON answer:

1. Retrieve source documents most relevant to the user prompt:

```
relevant_docs = self.retrieve_relevant_documents(prompt, limit=max_
documents)
```

2. Concatenate their content into a single context block:

```
doc_content = "\n\n".join(
    f"Document: {d.get('name','')}\n{d.get('content','')}" for d in
relevant_docs
)
```

3. Build an augmented prompt that embeds this context ahead of the user question:

```
augmented_prompt = f"""Use the following documents as reference.

Documents:
{doc_content}

Question/Task:
{prompt}
"""
```

4. Ask the LLM for a structured JSON answer that conforms to a predefined schema:

```
response = self.client.chat.completions.create(
    model=self.model,
    messages=[{"role": "user", "content": augmented_prompt}],
    response_format={"type": "json_object",
                     "schema": schema_model.model_json_schema()}
)
```

5. Parse and return the model output:

```
return json.loads(response.choices[0].message.content)
```

Relevant documents are fetched first, then injected directly into the prompt so the model must cite them when forming its reply.

In the next section, we'll see how MongoDB can provide the perfect infrastructure.

Using MongoDB Atlas for modern database infrastructure

In this system, MongoDB Atlas is used as a document-oriented datastore, enabling context-aware retrieval and supporting real-time AI-driven workflows.

The foundation of the system's intelligence lies in MongoDB Atlas's vector search capabilities. We've implemented a sophisticated embedding strategy using Nomic AI embeddings via Fireworks:

```
def generate_embeddings(self, input_texts: List[str], prefix: str = "") ->
List[float]:
        """Generate embeddings from Fireworks python library"""
        start_time = time.time()

        if prefix:
```

```
            input_texts = [prefix + text for text in input_texts]

        response = self.client.embeddings.create(
            input=input_texts,
            model=self.embedding_model,
        )

        return response.data[0].embedding
```

This code demonstrates how the system converts text into searchable vectors. Every underwriting document, rate manual, and policy guideline gets processed through this embedding function during setup, creating a semantic search index that allows the AI to find relevant information based on meaning rather than exact word matches. When a quote request comes in, user queries go through the same embedding process to find the most applicable underwriting rules.

Inference layer implementation: Fireworks AI

Fireworks AI was selected as the inference engine based on its performance. It runs the inference layer through its **FireOptimizer** adaptation engine, which auto-tunes hardware mapping, quantization, and adaptive speculative execution for each workload. This approach has delivered up to 3× lower generation latency and roughly 4× per-token cost savings in production tests, while customers such as Cursor have confirmed a 2× speed gain with a single-click deployment, which proves that the platform meets the strict latency and budget requirements of underwriting flows.

Fireworks' **JSON** mode ensures that the language model generates machine-readable outputs, eliminating the need for additional parsing:

```
# Guaranteed structured output
response = self.client.chat.completions.create(
    model="accounts/fireworks/models/llama-v3p3-70b-instruct",
    messages=[{"role": "user", "content": prompt}],
    response_format={"type": "json_object"},
    temperature=0.1  # Low temperature for consistent outputs
)
```

Using Fireworks' JSON response mode forces the model to emit a strict, machine-readable object, so downstream services can consume the data without brittle post-processing. Because JSON is a universal interchange format, the output slots directly into existing pipelines and APIs, letting developers wire AI capabilities into production systems with minimal glue code.

The Fireworks pricing model allows organizations to process high volumes of quotes economically:

- **Token efficiency**: Optimized prompts reduce token usage by 40%
- **Batch processing**: Background processing of quotes reduces per-request costs
- **Intelligent caching**: Common industry patterns are cached to reduce repeated inference

Together, these cost optimizations enable insurance carriers to achieve unprecedented scale without proportional cost increases. The system's efficiency improvements mean that processing 1,000 quotes per day costs roughly the same as processing 100, creating a compelling economic case for automation that transforms underwriting from a cost center into a competitive advantage.

Exploring the results

This implementation demonstrates measurable changes in underwriting operations, particularly in processing speed, scalability, and cost efficiency.

Quantitative impact

Automation significantly changes the operational baseline for underwriting workflows. The following metrics compare traditional manual processes with outcomes observed in an AI-assisted implementation:

Metric	Before (manual process)	After (AI-powered)	Improvement
Average quote turnaround	20–30 days	15–30 minutes	98% faster
Daily quote capacity	5–10 quotes/ underwriter	Thousands of quotes/system	100–1,000x increase
Processing cost per quote	$125 (labor + overhead)	$12 (compute + overhead)	90% reduction
High-risk detection rate	60% (manual review)	89% (AI flagging)	+29 percentage points
Compliance consistency	Variable	100% (standardized)	Eliminated variance

Table 15.1: Quantitative impact comparison – manual vs. AI-powered underwriting performance metrics

The data reveals a fundamental transformation. The 98% speed improvement combined with 100–1,000x capacity increases demonstrates that automation enables qualitatively different business capabilities, while the 90% cost reduction and improved accuracy metrics show this transformation is both economically compelling and operationally superior.

Qualitative transformation

Beyond the numbers, this platform has transformed the underwriting profession itself.

For **underwriters,** the platform fundamentally elevates their role by freeing them from repetitive data entry tasks, allowing them to focus their expertise on complex risk analysis and strategic decision-making. AI provides comprehensive risk profiles with supporting documentation, enabling more informed and confident underwriting decisions. The system continuously learns from underwriter feedback, improving its recommendations over time and creating a collaborative human-AI partnership.

Brokers experience immediate benefits through real-time status updates and rapid quote responses that meet modern client expectations. Full visibility into underwriting decisions and reasoning helps brokers better serve their clients by providing clear explanations of coverage recommendations and pricing rationale. Most importantly, faster quote turnaround times give brokers a significant competitive advantage in winning new business.

Insurance carriers gain unprecedented market agility with the ability to respond to new opportunities immediately rather than being constrained by processing bottlenecks. The system's scalability allows carriers to handle seasonal peaks and market fluctuations without hiring additional staff, while standardized underwriting processes reduce regulatory risk and ensure consistent application of guidelines across all decisions.

Now that we have a clear idea of the benefits, let's take a closer look at how it all works.

Diving deep into the technical innovation

Let's look in-depth at what makes the Fireworks and MongoDB implementation such an innovative solution.

Production-grade RAG implementation

The RAG system represents a production-ready implementation of advanced AI techniques:

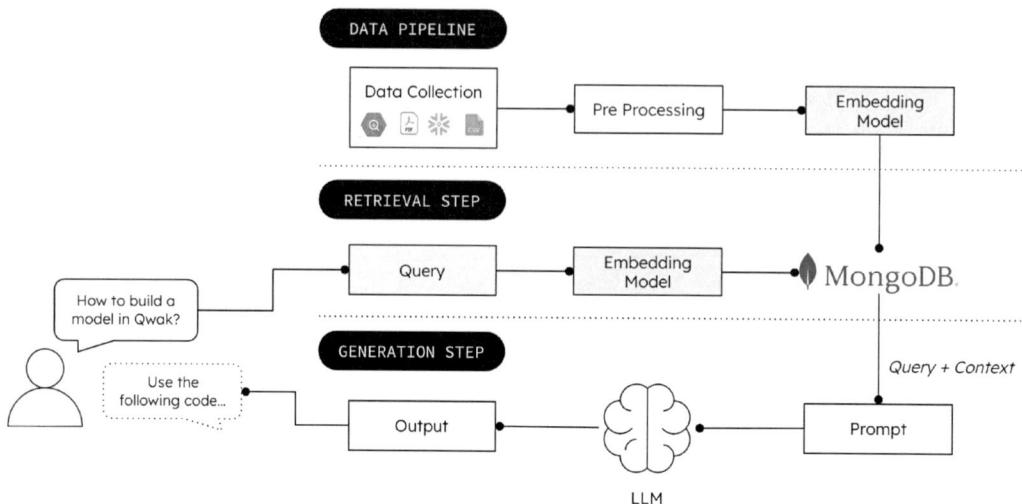

Figure 15.3: The production-grade RAG implementation workflow

The RAG system is a robust and production-ready implementation of cutting-edge AI methodologies. This system is meticulously engineered to address the limitations of standalone LLMs by seamlessly integrating an information retrieval mechanism with a powerful text generation module. This architecture allows the model to access and incorporate relevant information from external knowledge sources in real time, leading to more accurate, contextually rich, and informative generated responses.

The core components of our RAG implementation include a highly efficient document indexing and retrieval pipeline and a sophisticated generation model fine-tuned for incorporating retrieved information. The retrieval component is designed for speed and accuracy, capable of efficiently searching through a vast corpus of documents and identifying the most pertinent information for a given query. This involves advanced techniques for semantic understanding and vector embeddings to capture the underlying meaning of both the query and the documents.

Once the relevant information is retrieved, it is carefully injected into the prompt provided to the generation model. This process ensures that the model has access to the necessary context to generate a well-informed and grounded response. The generation module leverages state-of-the-art transformer architectures and is specifically trained to effectively utilize the retrieved information, avoiding common pitfalls such as ignoring the context or generating contradictory statements.

By combining the strengths of information retrieval and GenAI, this production-grade RAG system delivers significant advantages over traditional LLMs. It enhances the accuracy and factual correctness of generated text, reduces the likelihood of hallucination, and allows the model to provide responses that are grounded in up-to-date and specific information. This makes it a powerful solution for a wide range of applications, including question answering, content creation, chatbots, and knowledge-intensive tasks.

Real-world application: A quote request journey

Let's follow a typical quote request through the system to see the technology in action. This example demonstrates key steps from the 10-step AI pipeline described earlier in the chapter, focusing on the most critical processes to illustrate how the system handles real-world scenarios.

Let's begin with the email that kickstarts the whole process:

```
Subject: Quote Request - ABC Construction Corp

Hi there,

I need a quote for ABC Construction Corp. They're a mid-size commercial
construction company based in Texas, doing about $15M in annual revenue.
They need General Liability coverage with $2M/$4M limits, plus Auto
Liability for their fleet of 25 vehicles.

The company has been in business for 12 years, 85 employees. They've had
two small workers comp claims in the past 3 years but nothing major.
They're looking for coverage to start March 1st.

This is somewhat urgent; they're shopping around and want to make a
decision by end of week.

Thanks,
Sarah Johnson
ABC Insurance Brokerage
```

This email contains all the essential data points the AI system needs to generate an accurate quote, though they're embedded in natural, conversational language. Notice how the email clearly states the company's annual revenue ($15M), employee count (85), specific coverage requirements (General Liability with $2M/$4M limits plus Auto Liability), and fleet size (25 vehicles). The AI will also extract critical risk indicators such as the company's 12-year operating history and loss experience (two small workers' comp claims), plus operational details such as the Texas location and March 1st effective date. Even subtle cues, such as *somewhat urgent* and *end of week* for the decision timeline, help the system prioritize this request appropriately.

Now, we'll follow the step-by-step processing with Fireworks and MongoDB to see exactly how the AI transforms this unstructured email into actionable underwriting data, using the same pipeline steps we outlined earlier:

1. **Intelligent email information extraction**: NLP extracts structured information from unstructured broker communications, identifying client details, coverage requirements, and urgency indicators with high accuracy. In Sarah's email, the AI identifies *ABC Construction Corp* as the client name, parses *$15M in annual revenue* into a numerical value, and extracts specific coverage needs from phrases such as *General Liability coverage with $2M/$4M limits, plus Auto Liability for their fleet of 25 vehicles*:

```python
# Fireworks extracts structured data
extracted_info = {
    "client_name": "ABC Construction Corp",
    "industry": "Commercial Construction",
    "annual_revenue": 15000000,
    "employee_count": 85,
    "coverage_requested": {
        "type": "General Liability + Auto Liability",
        "limits": "$2M/$4M"
    },
    "fleet_size": 25,
    "urgency": "urgent",
    "loss_history": "Two small workers comp claims in past 3 years",
    "broker_contact": {
        "name": "Sarah Johnson",
        "brokerage": "ABC Insurance Brokerage"
    }
}
```

2. **Automated industry classification**: Semantic search (vector search) through BIC code databases determines precise industry categorization by matching company descriptions with standardized classification systems:

```
# MongoDB vector search finds relevant BIC codes
industry_docs = vector_search(
    query="Commercial construction company building contractor",
    collection="bic_codes"
)
# Returns: BIC Code 44 - Construction/Contracting
```

3. **Base rate discovery**: Vector search retrieves industry-specific base rates from rating manuals, ensuring accurate foundational pricing based on established underwriting guidelines. Using the determined BIC code of 44 for construction, the system retrieves the specific base rate of $8.50 per $1,000 of revenue that applies to ABC Construction Corp's general liability coverage:

```
# Retrieve construction industry base rates
rate_docs = vector_search(
    query="Base rates BIC 44 construction general liability",
    collection="rating_manuals"
)
# Returns: $8.50 per $1000 of revenue for construction GL
```

4. **Risk assessment**: It analyzes risk factors through document retrieval and AI reasoning. The AI specifically processes Sarah's mention of *two small workers' comp claims in the past 3 years* and the company's 12-year operating history to determine risk modifiers:

```
# Vector search for construction risk factors
risk_docs = vector_search(
    query="Construction company risk factors workers comp claims",
    collection="underwriting_guidelines"
)
# AI analyzes: Previous claims suggest 15% modifier increase
```

5. **Response email/quote generation**: The final step is producing a comprehensive quote with full documentation and professional formatting. The final quote directly addresses Sarah's timeline (*end of week*) and incorporates all the specific details from her email (the March 1st start date, the exact coverage limits requested, and the fleet size) into a professional response:

```
Subject: Quote for ABC Construction Corp - General Liability
Coverage

Dear Sarah,

Thank you for your quote request for ABC Construction Corp. We're
pleased to provide the following quote:

**Coverage Summary:**
- General Liability: $2,000,000 / $4,000,000
- Auto Liability: $1,000,000 Combined Single Limit
- Effective Date: March 1, 2024

**Premium Calculation:**
- Base Premium (GL): $127,500
  (Based on $15M revenue × $8.50 per $1000 - BIC Code 44)
- Loss History Modifier: +15% ($19,125)
- Auto Liability Premium: $18,750 (25 vehicles × $750 base rate)
- **Total Annual Premium: $165,375**

**Underwriting Notes:**
- Previous workers compensation claims reviewed and factored into
pricing
- Construction operations fall within our standard appetite
- No additional endorsements required for this risk profile

This quote is valid for 30 days. Please let me know if you need any
modifications or have questions.

Best regards,
Automated Underwriting System
```

That completes the automated underwriting process, from Sarah's initial email to a comprehensive, professional quote ready for delivery. What traditionally would have taken days or weeks of manual work was accomplished in under 6 minutes, demonstrating the transformative power of AI-driven automation in insurance operations.

This entire process is completed in under 6 minutes with the following technical metrics:

- **MongoDB queries**: 8 vector searches
- **Fireworks API calls**: 10 completion requests
- **Average tokens used/query**: 15,847 (input: 9,234; output: 6,613)
- **Vector Search accuracy**: 94% relevance score average
- **Citations generated**: 23 supporting document references

In summary, a process that once required extensive manual effort is now executed with unprecedented speed and precision, delivering accuracy, efficiency, and reliability that set a new standard for modern underwriting.

Transforming daily operations

Before this solution, an underwriter would spend their day differently. Their previous daily routine might look like this:

- 8:00 A.M.: Review 15 new email quote requests
- 8:30 A.M.: Begin manual data entry for first quote
- 10:00 A.M.: Search rating manuals for appropriate rates
- 11:30 A.M.: Calculate base premium and modifiers
- 1:00 P.M.: Lunch break
- 2:00 P.M.: Continue with second quote request
- 4:00 P.M.: Review and approval process
- 5:30 P.M.: Draft response email

This results in 2–3 quotes processed per day.

Now, with the help of Fireworks and MongoDB, the current daily routine looks more like this:

- 8:00 A.M.: Review 25 AI-processed quotes from the overnight batch
- 8:30 A.M.: Focus on three complex risks requiring human judgment
- 10:00 A.M.: Review and approve 15 standard quotes (2 minutes each)
- 11:00 A.M.: Deep-dive risk analysis on challenging cases
- 1:00 P.M.: Lunch break
- 2:00 P.M.: Broker relationship management and market analysis
- 4:00 P.M.: Training session on new AI features
- 5:00 P.M.: Strategic planning for portfolio management

This results in 15+ quotes processed and the strategic work completed.

So that's how one person's day might change. Let's consider the impact it could have across the entire industry.

Industry impact and implications

Beyond the quantitative improvements, this AI-powered platform has fundamentally transformed the daily experience of insurance professionals across the value chain. For underwriters, the change represents a complete elevation of their professional role. Rather than spending hours on repetitive data entry and manual document searches, underwriters can now focus their expertise on complex risk analysis and strategic decision-making that truly requires human judgment. The AI provides comprehensive risk profiles with supporting documentation, enabling more informed and confident underwriting decisions while continuously learning from its feedback to improve recommendations over time. This creates a collaborative human-AI partnership where technology amplifies human expertise rather than replacing it.

Brokers have experienced equally dramatic improvements in their ability to serve clients and compete effectively. Real-time status updates and rapid quote responses allow them to meet the increasingly demanding expectations of modern clients who expect immediate service. The system's transparency into underwriting decisions and reasoning enables brokers to provide clear, detailed explanations of coverage recommendations and pricing rationale, strengthening client relationships through improved communication. Most importantly, the dramatic reduction in quote turnaround times gives brokers a significant competitive advantage in winning new business, as they can often deliver quotes while competitors are still gathering information.

Insurance carriers benefit from unprecedented operational flexibility and market responsiveness. The system's ability to process quotes immediately allows carriers to respond to new market opportunities without the traditional delays that could result in lost business. Scalability becomes a strategic advantage rather than a constraint, as carriers can handle seasonal peaks, catastrophic events, and market fluctuations without the expense and complexity of hiring additional staff. Perhaps most significantly, standardized underwriting processes reduce regulatory risk and ensure consistent application of guidelines across all decisions, providing both operational efficiency and compliance confidence.

Broader technology adoption

The success of this AI-powered underwriting solution is creating a ripple effect throughout the insurance industry, driving broader AI adoption across multiple operational areas. Claims processing has emerged as the next major frontier, with insurers implementing automated claim assessment and settlement systems that can evaluate damage photos, process documentation, and even authorize payments for straightforward claims without human intervention. Policy administration is being transformed through AI-powered systems that can handle policy changes, renewals, and modifications in real time, dramatically reducing the administrative burden on both insurers and policyholders. Customer service operations are increasingly leveraging intelligent chatbots and support automation that can handle complex inquiries, guide customers through policy options, and provide 24/7 support with human-level understanding and empathy. Fraud detection has become significantly more sophisticated through advanced pattern recognition systems that can identify fraudulent claims by analyzing subtle patterns across vast datasets that would be impossible for human reviewers to detect.

Regulatory considerations

As AI becomes more prevalent throughout the insurance industry, regulatory frameworks are rapidly evolving to address new challenges and ensure consumer protection. Algorithmic transparency has become a critical focus, with regulators increasingly requiring explainable AI decisions that allow both regulators and consumers to understand how automated systems reach their conclusions, particularly in areas affecting coverage and pricing. Bias prevention has emerged as a major concern, with new monitoring requirements designed to detect and prevent discriminatory pricing practices that could unfairly impact protected classes or create unintended disparities in coverage access. Data privacy protections have been enhanced significantly, with stricter requirements for how customer information is collected, stored, and used in AI systems, reflecting growing concerns about the vast amounts of personal data these systems can process. Professional liability standards are being redefined to address the unique challenges of AI-assisted underwriting, establishing new frameworks for accountability when automated systems make decisions that affect coverage and claims.

Summary

The transformation we've achieved with Fireworks AI and MongoDB represents a fundamental shift in insurance operations, demonstrating how AI-powered platforms can revolutionize traditional processes without sacrificing accuracy or compliance. Our implementation proves that speed truly is a competitive advantage, reducing quote turnaround from weeks to minutes while achieving 98% faster processing, 90% cost reduction, and 100–1000x capacity increases. The combination of intelligent automation, semantic search, and explainable AI creates a foundation where human expertise is amplified rather than replaced, freeing underwriters to focus on complex risk analysis and strategic decision-making.

The success of this platform extends beyond operational metrics to fundamental business model evolution. By enabling real-time underwriting decisions grounded in comprehensive data analysis, we've created a system that transforms insurance from a reactive to a proactive industry. The architectural principles demonstrated here (document-oriented data foundations, vector search capabilities, and RAG-powered decision making) provide a blueprint that organizations can adapt to drive their own competitive transformation.

Moving forward, these same principles of AI-powered transformation are revolutionizing healthcare delivery, where the potential for positive impact extends far beyond business metrics to fundamental improvements in human health and wellbeing. The next chapter explores how converged data architectures and intelligent automation are addressing healthcare's most pressing challenges, from provider burnout to patient care coordination.

References

1. *How Artificial Intelligence Is Transforming the Insurance Underwriting Process*: https://biztechmagazine.com/article/2025/03/how-artificial-intelligence-transforming-insurance-underwriting-process

16

AI-Powered Transformation of Healthcare and Life Sciences

Healthcare currently generates more clinical data than ever before, including **electronic health records (EHRs)**, wearable devices, advanced imaging, and genomic sequencing. Yet, healthcare professionals feel increasingly disconnected from actionable insights. This isn't a technological failure but a fragmented success, where each system excels individually but fails to work harmoniously, creating healthcare's digital debt. As we rush toward an AI-powered future with GenAI and autonomous agents promising to revolutionize care delivery, we risk compounding this fragmentation exponentially by creating *agentic silos*: disconnected AI systems operating in isolation without the complete clinical context.

The transformation of healthcare through AI represents both our greatest opportunity and our most critical challenge. While AI agents can automate documentation, coordinate care, and provide decision support that augments clinical expertise, their effectiveness depends entirely on access to unified, comprehensive patient data. This chapter explores how healthcare organizations can build the intelligent data foundations necessary to support coordinated AI systems that enhance rather than fragment clinical care, moving from reactive data archaeology to proactive intelligence activation.

In this chapter, you will learn about the following:

- The evolution from GenAI to autonomous agents requires unified data foundations to prevent dangerous agentic silos that operate without the complete clinical context
- Traditional interoperability solutions, such as **Health Level Seven's (HL7's) Fast Healthcare Interoperability Resources (FHIR)** and vendor APIs, fall short of AI-era requirements, creating compliance without meaningful data accessibility
- Document-based data models provide the flexibility to combine healthcare standards with AI-ready architectures while maintaining semantic integrity
- The facade pattern enables the strategic use of standards as interface layers without forcing internal data rigidity, preserving organizational data ownership
- Multi-agent architectures can orchestrate specialized AI roles across clinical workflows while maintaining human oversight and regulatory compliance
- Future-proof healthcare data foundations must accommodate emerging data types, AI capabilities, and regulatory changes while preserving clinical relationships

Understanding the AI revolution in healthcare

The numbers tell a stark story: healthcare professionals now spend more time inputting information into electronic systems than delivering direct patient care. This administrative overload affects provider well-being, directly undermines patient care quality, and contributes to the burnout epidemic that threatens healthcare's human foundation.

But here's what makes this crisis particularly urgent: we're about to compound it exponentially. As healthcare organizations rush to implement AI solutions on fragmented data foundations, they risk creating what we call agentic silos. These are autonomous AI systems that operate with incomplete clinical context, potentially scaling dangerous blind spots while appearing to save time. Each AI agent trained on isolated data becomes confident in its limited view, missing critical interactions and context that exist in other systems.

The 47-minute problem

Consider this illustrative scenario that represents thousands of daily occurrences across healthcare systems. Dr. Sarah Chen is a pediatric specialist preparing for a complex autism evaluation. She spends 47 minutes hunting through 7 different systems to gather the patient information needed for a 15-minute consultation. Down the hall, care coordinator Maria manually compiles patient summaries from five separate databases for tomorrow's multidisciplinary team meeting. In the emergency department, Dr. Williams documents the same patient information in three different systems to satisfy various regulatory and operational requirements.

This scenario repeats thousands of times daily across healthcare systems worldwide, representing more than operational inefficiency; it's a crisis of human potential. When skilled clinicians spend their expertise as data archaeologists rather than patient advocates, the entire healthcare ecosystem suffers.

This administrative burden drives healthcare's urgent search for transformative solutions. GenAI and autonomous agents promise to finally deliver on digital transformation goals, but only if implemented thoughtfully. LLMs can process unstructured clinical notes, understand medical context, and generate intelligent insights from complex patient data. AI agents can automate documentation, coordinate care, and provide decision support that augments clinical expertise.

The potential is transformative. The stakes couldn't be higher. Before exploring how healthcare's data fragmentation crisis intersects with emerging AI capabilities, it's essential to understand the evolution of AI in healthcare and where we're heading. The AI landscape is advancing rapidly from simple automation tools to sophisticated autonomous systems that will fundamentally reshape how healthcare is delivered.

Why traditional solutions fall short

Healthcare has invested heavily in solving data fragmentation through interoperability standards such as **HL7 FHIR**, specialized integration platforms, and vendor-specific APIs. While these approaches provide compliance and basic data exchange, they create new problems for the AI era:

- Standards excel at specific purposes but lack the flexibility for AI applications
- Implementation complexity creates vendor lock-in disguised as interoperability
- Organizations achieve technical compliance without meaningful data accessibility

Most healthcare organizations rely on specialized, domain-driven solutions that handle interoperability superficially. These *black-box* approaches create new silos while maintaining compliance, achieving technical interoperability without true data ownership or control.

Meanwhile, focusing only on API-level integration limits how organizations can use their own data. When data ownership resides in vendor systems rather than organizational control, healthcare systems cannot adapt quickly to new AI capabilities, changing regulations, or evolving care models.

Demystifying the AI terminology

Let's look at some of the important terminology used in healthcare-centered AI applications. While you may be familiar with these concepts, their specific applications and implications in healthcare contexts warrant examination:

- **GenAI** represents the current mainstream of AI adoption in healthcare. It serves as an intelligent assistant that can do the following:

    - Summarize complex medical literature and research findings
    - Generate patient education materials tailored to specific conditions
    - Create clinical documentation from voice recordings or structured data
    - Provide differential diagnosis suggestions based on patient presentations
    - Translate medical information across languages and literacy levels

    GenAI excels at specific, bounded tasks but requires human direction and oversight. A physician might ask a GenAI system to "summarize the latest research on diabetes treatment options for elderly patients", and receive a comprehensive, well-structured response. However, the physician must still interpret this information within the specific clinical context and make treatment decisions.

- **AI agents** in healthcare represent a significant evolution beyond GenAI, functioning as autonomous digital assistants capable of handling multi-layered tasks independently. Unlike GenAI, which responds to specific prompts, AI agents can plan, execute, and adapt their actions to achieve defined objectives. Take the following example:

    - Review a patient's complete medication list, identify potential drug interactions based on the patient's medical history, suggest appropriate alternatives, and generate new prescription orders for physician approval
    - Monitor patient vital signs from connected devices, recognize concerning patterns, alert appropriate clinical staff, and initiate protocol-driven interventions

- Coordinate care across multiple specialists by analyzing appointment availability, patient preferences, clinical urgency, and scheduling optimal care sequences

- Process insurance pre-authorization requests by gathering required clinical documentation, submitting forms, and following up on approvals

The key distinction is autonomy. AI agents can operate independently within defined parameters, making decisions and taking actions without constant human intervention.

- **Agentic AI** represents the systems architecture that enables multiple AI agents to work together as a coordinated ecosystem. Rather than using isolated tools, agentic AI creates interconnected networks of autonomous agents that can communicate, share insights, and collaborate on complex healthcare objectives. Consider a hospital implementing agentic AI across multiple departments:

  - **Emergency department agent**: Processes incoming patients, triages based on symptoms and vital signs, and initiates diagnostic protocols

  - **Laboratory agent**: Receives test orders, prioritizes based on clinical urgency, processes results, and alerts clinicians to critical values

  - **Pharmacy agent**: Reviews medication orders, checks for interactions and allergies, manages inventory, and coordinates with nursing for administration

  - **Care coordination agent**: Monitors patient progress, identifies discharge readiness, coordinates with specialists, and arranges follow-up care

When the emergency department agent identifies a patient needing urgent surgery, it automatically coordinates with the laboratory agent for pre-operative testing, the pharmacy agent for medication preparation, and the care coordination agent for surgical scheduling and post-operative planning.

Next, let's see how these tools can be used to help transform healthcare.

The transformative opportunity of GenAI

Market analysts expect significant growth in agentic AI adoption by 2028, with healthcare representing one of the most promising opportunities for meaningful impact. Amanda Saunders from NVIDIA observes the following:

"Agentic AI is already transforming enterprises and is likely to be a multitrillion-dollar opportunity. Healthcare IT leaders should lean in to learn how AI agents can help transform work across drug discovery, patient care, operations, and so much more. [1]"

While there is vast potential for agentic AI in healthcare, successful implementation requires recognizing both its capabilities and limitations. Agentic AI will primarily help in alleviating computational workload and administrative tasks, but complex clinical decisions will still require human expertise and judgment.

Even technology developers acknowledge that autonomous AI is not yet ready to independently handle critical aspects of care such as prescribing medications, making diagnostic decisions, or managing complex patient interactions.

Healthcare leaders must strike a thoughtful balance between deploying agentic systems and maintaining meaningful human collaboration. The goal is not to replace clinical expertise but to amplify it, enabling healthcare professionals to operate at the top of their training while AI handles routine tasks and provides intelligent support.

Building the right architecture for healthcare AI

To achieve this balanced human-AI collaboration effectively, healthcare organizations must address a fundamental prerequisite: ensuring that AI agents have access to complete, unified patient contexts. The effectiveness of agentic AI directly correlates with the quality and comprehensiveness of the data it can access.

This creates an important strategic consideration: healthcare organizations implementing agentic AI without addressing data fragmentation may achieve local improvements while missing the transformative potential of coordinated intelligent care. The key is building data foundations that enable AI agents to work together effectively, rather than creating isolated pockets of automation.

This architectural challenge (transitioning from fragmented data systems to unified foundations that support coordinated AI) represents healthcare's next major opportunity for innovation.

Imagine replacing Dr. Chen's 47-minute data archaeology with an AI agent trained on just one of those seven systems. The time savings are instant. The blind spots are invisible: an AI agent analyzing imaging data might miss a critical drug interaction documented in a separate system, or recommend treatments that contradict care plans it cannot access. The potential for harm scales silently. Unlike human errors that are typically isolated incidents, AI agents can replicate the same dangerous blind spot across thousands of patients before anyone realizes the pattern.

This represents AI's central paradox in healthcare: the more autonomous our systems become, the more critical it becomes to unify the data they rely on. An AI agent without the complete clinical context is inefficient and dangerous. It may recommend treatments that contradict other care plans, miss critical drug interactions, or duplicate interventions because it cannot see the full patient picture.

We call this phenomenon *agentic sprawl*: a future where every department has its own AI, but no one truly sees the full patient. To understand how AI fragmentation develops, we must examine the underlying data architecture challenges that create these disconnected AI ecosystems.

The challenge of healthcare data architectures

Modern healthcare is drowning in data, yet often starved for actionable insights. The COVID-19 pandemic dramatically exposed the urgent need for readily available, complete, and reliable data throughout the healthcare spectrum, from individual clinical care to national research and strategic planning, by revealing gaps in data infrastructure and accelerating digital innovation in health systems [2].

Healthcare standards serve as the agreed-upon language enabling interoperability across systems, ensuring the semantic integrity of clinical data. These standards are about establishing a shared understanding of what each piece of data means. They guarantee the semantic integrity of data across diverse systems and stakeholders. Without this shared understanding, we risk misinterpretations, errors, and, ultimately, compromised patient care.

Standards are essential. However, standards alone can't fully address the evolving and varied needs of modern healthcare organizations. Standards are typically designed for a specific purpose, each with inherent strengths and specific limitations. The insights shared in resources such as Alastair Allen's *FHIR + openEHR — 2022* article highlight how different standards offer complementary strengths [3]. But healthcare requires data for so much more, and standards primarily define how data is structured or shared; they rarely address the deeper challenge of how that data should be optimally stored, queried, or leveraged to meet the demands of modern healthcare innovation.

Specifically, healthcare organizations face several practical challenges that standards can't solve on their own:

- **Application-specific needs**: Different applications need data in different formats to create user-friendly interfaces and support specialized clinical workflows. Standards define how data enters the system, but they rarely match how applications need to organize or present that data.

- **Evolving standards**: Standards are constantly changing, requiring ongoing investments to stay current. Organizations often avoid these costs by sticking with older versions. This creates technical debt, data versioning conflicts, and even more data silos.

- **Implementation complexity**: Standards can be complex and difficult to implement correctly. As a result, organizations often choose ready-made black-box solutions that handle interoperability superficially, rather than deeply embedding standards into their systems.

- **Organizational silos:** Data governance is not just a technical challenge; it's an organizational one. Data silos often reflect departmental silos, with different teams having their own data, priorities, and incentives. Overcoming these barriers requires strong leadership, clear data governance policies, and a culture of data sharing.

Theoretically, standards such as openEHR, with their focus on structured clinical data, could solve many of these problems. However, even organizations that adopt openEHR often find themselves adding layers of complexity. Vendors introduce specialized caches, build fast views for specific applications, and develop complex architectures to meet diverse usages and performance needs, especially to support cross-patient and analytical queries. While often necessary, these additions can significantly increase costs and complexity, and may even reintroduce data silos. This shows that even the best standards rarely provide a one-size-fits-all solution, and real-world implementations often require a more adaptable approach.

Preparing for the healthcare data needs of the future

The challenges we've discussed so far are significant, but they're just a prelude to the healthcare data tsunami ahead. For example, genomic data today is rarely integrated with clinical records, limiting the real-world impact of precision medicine. To realize healthcare's full potential, organizations must first address this critical integration gap:

- **Precision medicine** is evolving beyond genomics to include proteomics, metabolomics, transcriptomics, imaging, digital pathology, clinical records, and real-time patient data from wearables. It also considers lifestyle factors and **social determinants of health (SDOH)** such as housing, environment, and healthcare access. However, effectively capturing, integrating, and analyzing such complex datasets far exceeds the capabilities of traditional healthcare data architectures, requiring far greater agility, scalability, and integrative capacity.

- **The AI explosion:** AI is transforming every aspect of healthcare, from diagnostics and drug discovery to personalized treatment and predictive analytics. But AI models require vast amounts of data for training, and they generate complex outputs (such as risk scores and treatment recommendations) that need to be stored and integrated with other patient information.

- **The unstructured data goldmine:** Clinical notes, research papers, patient conversations – unstructured data contains a wealth of valuable information that is often locked away in text documents. NLP and other AI techniques can help us unlock this goldmine, but we need systems that can store and manage unstructured data effectively.

In short, the future of healthcare will be defined by the ability to harness a diverse and ever-expanding range of data types.

A document-based, AI-ready approach

Given these challenges, what is an effective way forward? The answer is a practical approach designed to strategically leverage healthcare standards within a flexible architecture. A document-based model provides the necessary agility, empowering organizations to combine standardized data and essential extensions seamlessly, without the need for continuous restructuring of storage models.

In essence, a **document-based data model** stores data as a collection of documents, where each document can be thought of as a self-contained unit. These documents can contain a mix of structured, semi-structured, and unstructured data. Unlike traditional relational databases that enforce a rigid schema, document databases offer a flexible schema that allows documents to evolve over time without requiring costly schema migrations. This makes them well suited for handling the diverse and evolving data types found in healthcare. Specifically, it does the following:

- **Aligns with healthcare standards**: Standards such as HL7 FHIR and openEHR define complex, hierarchical data structures naturally represented in JSON format.

- **Handles diverse data types**: Easily accommodates structured data from EHRs, unstructured text from clinical notes, image metadata, genomic data, sensor data from wearables, and AI-generated insights.

- **Schema flexibility**: Allows for iterative data model evolution without requiring disruptive migrations. As new data types emerge and data requirements change, the schema can be adapted accordingly.

- **Improved performance**: Document databases typically provide faster query performance for queries involving the retrieval of entire documents. Performance is further enhanced by optimized disk access, as related data is stored contiguously, resulting in efficient retrieval and reduced latency. Additionally, this approach is cost-effective due to advanced storage-layering strategies, automatically placing frequently accessed data on higher-performance storage tiers.

- **Developer-friendly**: The flexible schema and JSON-based representation simplify development, enabling faster cycles, reduced complexity, and improved productivity.

The solution is not to discard standards but to use them as components within a more flexible architecture. Rigid architectures often provided by many vendors often impose constraints that undermine the agility required in healthcare. The growing complexity of healthcare data demands a new approach. The document model provides this foundation. For more information on the document model, see *Chapter 3, The System of Action*.

Healthcare standards, while crucial for interoperability, often introduce implementation complexity. As mentioned previously, organizations frequently turn to off-the-shelf black-box solutions that superficially handle interoperability rather than embedding standards deeply into their data strategy.

But let's be clear: adopting a document model isn't about discarding standards. Instead, it's about strategically leveraging them. The key lies in the **facade pattern**, a software design approach that provides a simplified interface to complex underlying systems. Think of it as using standards as translators, ensuring different systems can communicate without dictating the core structure of your data. This means that rather than forcing all your data into rigid, predefined molds, you embrace a flexible document format for storage, allowing for a rich mix of structured, semi-structured, and unstructured information.

Then, when it's time to exchange data or connect with external systems, standards such as FHIR act as the interface layer, not the internal structure. This approach delivers the best of both worlds by providing seamless interoperability and full ownership of your data. It's the essence of the facade pattern, exposing standard-compliant views without forcing internal rigidity.

Some architectures, such as openEHR, take the opposite approach. They use the standard itself as the foundational data model. While this can offer strong consistency and semantic structure, it often introduces rigidity and places long-term control in the hands of the standard's constraints. However, the same guiding principle applies: organizations must retain ownership of their data model and ensure flexibility for future needs. Ultimately, how you model and query data, not just which API you expose, determines how well your system adapts to new requirements.

Enhancing flexibility and interoperability with the facade model

The following `DiagnosticReport` example demonstrates this approach in practice, showing how a document model accommodates both FHIR-compliant clinical data and additional operational metadata:

```
{
  "_id": {"$oid": "65ea3df8fde80681cde96175"},
  "metadata": {
    "documentVersion": "1.0",
    "fhirVersion": "4.0.1",
    "lastUpdate": "2024-03-07T22:07:02Z",
    "tenant_id": "TenantA",
```

```
      "uuid": "urn:uuid:0081fd71-59c0-4995-94e0-ce8628dc0529",
      "searchParameters": [
        {"key": "code", "value": "34117-2"},
        {"key": "date", "value": "2004-09-08T20:32:52-04:00"},
        {"key": "patient", "value": "Patient/1"},
        {"key": "status", "value": "final"}
      ],
      "vectorSearchEmbeddings": {
        "model": "text-embedding-3-small",
        "vector": [-0.01741, -0.02967, 0.01068, /* truncated for brevity */]
      },
      "applicationFields": {
        "reviewStatus": "pending",
        "priorityLevel": "high",
        "assignedTo": "Reviewer123"
      }
    },
    "fhirResource": {
      "resourceType": "DiagnosticReport",
      "id": "DiagnosticReport/7",
      "status": "final",
      "category": [
        {"coding": [{"system": "http://loinc.org", "code": "34117-2",
"display": "History and physical note"}]}
      ],
      "code": {"coding": [{"system": "http://loinc.org", "code": "34117-2",
"display": "History and physical note"}]},
      "subject": {"reference": "Patient/1"},
      "encounter": {"reference": "Encounter/7"},
      "effectiveDateTime": "2004-09-08T20:32:52-04:00",
      "issued": "2004-09-08T20:32:52.360-04:00",
      "performer": [{"reference": "Practitioner/62", "display": "Dr.
Waltraud488 Gaylord332"}],
      "presentedForm": [{
        "contentType": "text/plain",
        "data": "Encoded clinical note content here."
      }]
    }
  }
}
```

In this sample you can see:

- **FHIR resource layer:** This contains standardized clinical data (`DiagnosticReport`).
- **Metadata layer:** This includes custom fields (`documentVersion` and `tenant_id`) and search parameters for optimized querying.
- **Application-specific fields:** These fields, such as `reviewStatus` and `priorityLevel`, enable additional operational workflows outside FHIR standards.
- **Vector embeddings:** These facilitate advanced semantic searches and AI-driven functionalities by embedding clinical information in vector format. For a detailed explanation of how vector embeddings work and their role in AI systems, see *Chapter 2, What Sets GenAI, RAG, and Agentic AI Apart.*

This structure exemplifies the facade pattern by harmoniously integrating standard clinical data with additional metadata and application-specific details without compromising interoperability.

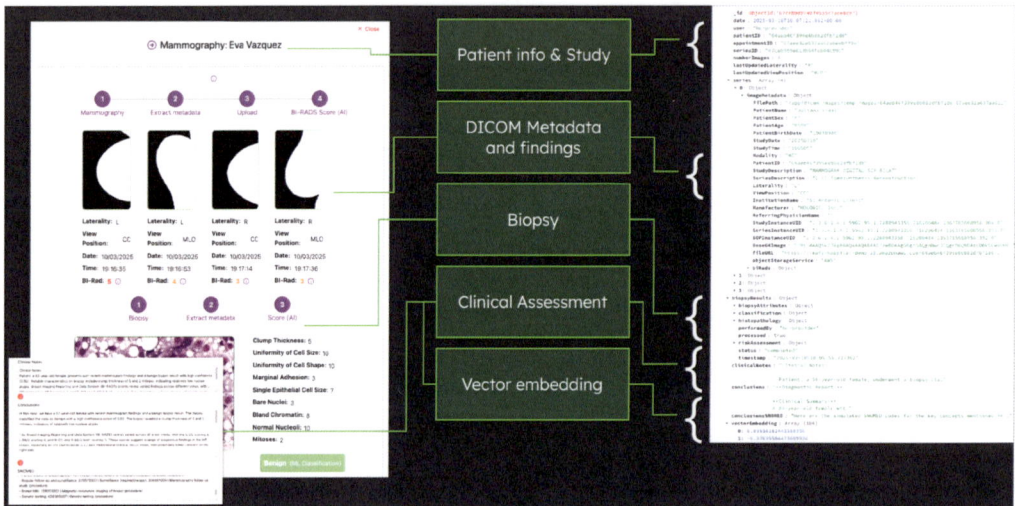

Figure 16.1: Medical data integration and vector embedding architecture for AI-enhanced healthcare analytics

This diagram demonstrates how MongoDB's flexible document model stores and integrates diverse healthcare data types, including patient information, **Digital Imaging and Communications in Medicine (DICOM)** metadata, biopsy results, and clinical assessments. Each data category is stored as MongoDB documents that can be enhanced with vector embeddings for AI-powered semantic search and analysis. The architecture shows how MongoDB's schema-flexible approach accommodates varied medical data formats while enabling advanced search capabilities through embedded vectors for improved clinical insights and decision support.

As we've seen, the facade pattern allows standards to do what they do best, that is, enable communication, without forcing internal uniformity. With document-oriented storage as the foundation, systems gain the freedom to evolve, integrate new data modalities, and respond to emerging needs without re-engineering their entire infrastructure.

The new stack for healthcare AI

This hybrid approach, with documents at the core and standards at the edge, sets the stage for the next leap: AI agents that operate not just on data but on contextual intelligence. In oncology, for instance, a single case might involve dozens of interconnected artifacts: FHIR-based clinical notes, DICOM imaging metadata, whole-genome sequencing, PDF pathology reports, and model-generated risk scores. Trying to unify all of that in a relational or standards-bound schema would either fail or require prohibitive effort. But stored as nested documents, each with rich metadata, relationships, and embeddings, you enable AI systems to traverse that complexity, reason across modalities, and provide clinically useful insights.

This is not a theoretical possibility; it's already happening. In pilot programs across cancer centers, document-based repositories are enabling oncologists to query patients with radiology growth patterns matching specific molecular subtypes, while pathologists surface similar tissue slides using vector search regardless of diagnostic labels. Care teams can now link patient-reported outcomes with wearable data, NLP-analyzed notes, and drug response records in a single query, creating comprehensive views that were previously impossible to achieve.

By taking an incremental, phased approach to implementation, healthcare organizations can balance immediate operational needs with long-term strategic goals. The result is a data architecture that delivers immediate value through standardization while maintaining the flexibility to adapt to tomorrow's healthcare challenges, whether they involve new data types, advanced application requirements, or emerging AI capabilities.

This balanced strategy, respecting standards while embracing adaptability, ultimately enables healthcare organizations to achieve the dual goals of operational efficiency and clinical innovation. Moreover, all these factors contribute to a significantly lower **total cost of ownership (TCO)**.

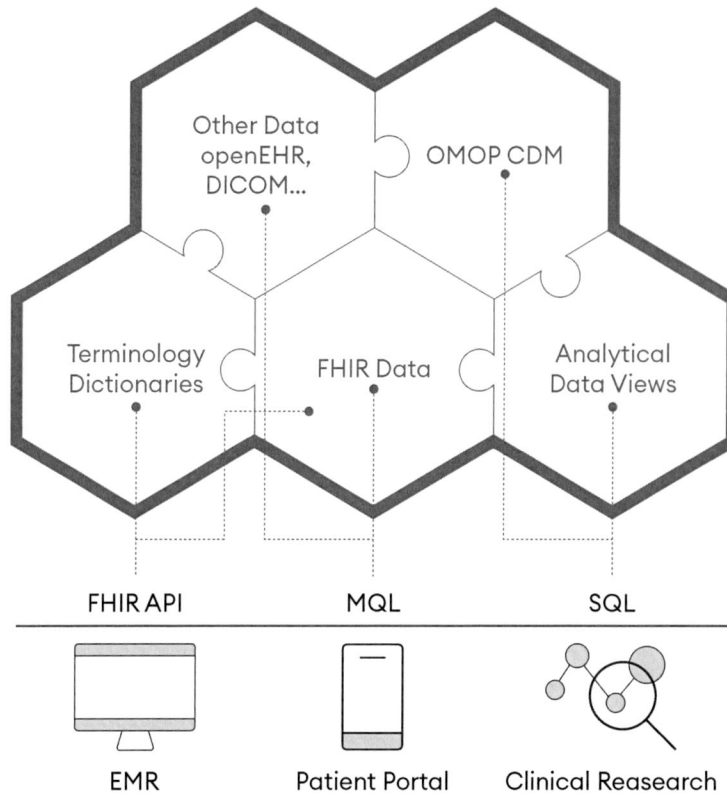

Figure 16.2: FHIR-centered approach with MongoDB's flexible document model

This diagram illustrates how MongoDB's document model enables healthcare organizations to integrate diverse data sources, including FHIR data, terminology dictionaries, the OMOP CDM, analytical data views, and other healthcare standards (such as openEHR and DICOM). The central FHIR data hub connects to various access methods (FHIR API, MQL, and SQL) and serves multiple endpoints, including EMR systems, patient portals, and clinical research applications. This flexible approach balances standardization with adaptability for evolving healthcare data requirements.

By taking control of your data strategy, embracing the document model, and leveraging standards strategically, you create a future-proof foundation for healthcare innovation. This means building systems that can accommodate new data types without architectural overhauls, integrate emerging AI capabilities without vendor lock-in, and scale computational resources based on clinical demand rather than technical limitations. A truly future-proof foundation adapts to regulatory changes, evolving standards, and breakthrough technologies while preserving the clinical context and data relationships that make healthcare intelligence possible. This foundation sets the stage for the intelligent care coordination that transforms healthcare delivery.

Implementation architecture patterns

Successful AI-powered care coordination implementations follow consistent architectural patterns that can be adapted across different healthcare settings and clinical specialties.

- **Document-oriented data foundation**: Healthcare information naturally exists in hierarchical, interconnected relationships that are preserved through document-oriented data models. Patient records contain nested information where problems encompass interventions and interventions include outcomes, maintaining clinical context while enabling efficient queries.

- **Vector search integration**: Semantic search capabilities enable natural language queries across clinical documentation, making similar cases and relevant protocols discoverable even when described using different terminology. This capability proves essential for specialty care areas where clinical knowledge must be shared across providers with varying experience levels.

- **Multi-modal data processing**: Modern healthcare generates diverse data types, including structured assessments, narrative notes, family communications, and multimedia observations that must work together to support comprehensive care decisions. Successful platforms accommodate this diversity while maintaining appropriate relationships and clinical context.

- **Real-time processing architecture**: Clinical decisions occur in real time, requiring systems that can process new information continuously and provide immediate access to updated insights. This responsiveness proves crucial for coordinated care scenarios where multiple providers must adapt their interventions based on shared observations.

Together, these enable a much more coordinated approach to care.

AI-powered care coordination

The evolution from fragmented healthcare systems to intelligent coordination platforms represents one of healthcare's most significant opportunities for transformation. AI-powered care coordination addresses the fundamental challenge of making diverse clinical information accessible and actionable across multidisciplinary teams, enabling providers to focus on patient care rather than administrative burden while improving care quality and outcomes.

Healthcare coordination requires sophisticated orchestration capabilities that can handle complex clinical scenarios, process diverse data types, and maintain human oversight throughout automated workflows. Multi-agent architectures provide the framework for managing these interactions while ensuring clinical accuracy and regulatory compliance.

Orchestrating specialized agent roles in clinical workflows

Different aspects of clinical information processing require specialized capabilities and domain knowledge. A comprehensive care coordination platform employs multiple AI agents, each optimized for specific healthcare tasks:

- **Clinical query processing agents** understand healthcare-specific language and intent, translating natural language questions into structured queries that can be executed against clinical data. When a provider asks, `"Which patients need attention this week?"` the agent interprets this as requiring analysis of progress trends, upcoming assessments, family concerns, and care plan deadlines.

- **Context synthesis agents** gather comprehensive patient information from multiple sources, understanding the relationships between different types of clinical data. These agents recognize that patient progress might be influenced by medication changes, family circumstances, educational settings, or social factors, collecting relevant context from diverse documentation sources.

- **Clinical reasoning agents** apply healthcare-specific logic to analyze retrieved information, identifying patterns and trends that might influence care decisions. These agents understand clinical significance, distinguishing between statistically significant changes and clinically meaningful improvements that warrant intervention modifications.

- **Documentation agents** maintain audit trails and citations for all AI-generated insights, ensuring that recommendations can be traced to specific observations, assessments, or clinical guidelines. This capability proves essential for regulatory compliance and clinical accountability.

The coordination of multiple AI agents requires sophisticated workflow management that can adapt to different clinical scenarios while maintaining consistency and reliability:

- **Sequential processing workflows** handle complex queries that require multiple analysis steps, with each agent building upon the results of previous processing stages. This pattern proves effective for comprehensive patient assessments that must integrate information from multiple clinical domains.

- **Parallel processing workflows** enable simultaneous analysis of different aspects of patient care, improving response times for urgent clinical queries. Multiple agents can simultaneously analyze behavioral data, medication effectiveness, and family reports to provide rapid, comprehensive assessments.

- **Adaptive workflows** modify their processing approach based on the type of clinical question, available data sources, and urgency requirements. Emergency scenarios trigger accelerated workflows that prioritize immediate safety considerations, while routine progress reviews employ comprehensive analysis patterns.

It's not just the workflows that make a difference. One of the crucial benefits of these agents is the way they process language in this specific professional context.

Natural language clinical intelligence

The transformation of clinical information access through natural language processing represents one of the most immediate benefits of intelligent care coordination platforms. Rather than requiring providers to navigate complex database structures, natural language interfaces enable clinicians to interact with patient data conversationally.

Clinical context understanding

Healthcare providers communicate in clinical language that doesn't map directly to database queries. Advanced natural language processing systems must understand medical terminology, temporal relationships, and clinical significance to provide accurate responses to provider questions.

Effective clinical communication requires responses appropriate for specific roles and decision contexts. The same clinical question requires different levels of detail and focus depending on whether it's asked by a direct care provider, clinical supervisor, or family member.

Role-adapted response generation should provide the following:

- **Technical terminology and quantitative metrics for providers**
- **Summary focus**: Key insights and action items for supervisors
- **Family communication**: Accessible language with progress explanations
- **Regulatory format**: Compliance-focused documentation for audits

This role-specific approach ensures that AI-generated insights match the decision-making context and information needs of each stakeholder, maximizing both efficiency and clinical safety.

Semantic search capabilities

Vector-based semantic search enables clinicians to find relevant information even when specific terminology varies between providers or documentation systems. This capability proves particularly valuable in specialized care areas where progress manifests through subtle changes across multiple domains.

Semantic search can identify connections between seemingly unrelated observations, such as correlating behavioral improvements with communication progress or linking environmental modifications to reduced challenging behaviors. These insights often emerge from patterns that individual providers might not notice but become apparent through comprehensive data analysis.

CentralReach's impact on autism and IDD care

Let's now consider the benefits of AI-powered care coordination in real-world implementations across healthcare organizations. These deployments demonstrate measurable improvements in clinical efficiency, care quality, and provider satisfaction.

CentralReach provides a compelling example of AI-powered care coordination addressing critical healthcare challenges. Operating in autism and **Intellectual and Developmental Disability (IDD)** care (a sector facing acute provider shortages), CentralReach has developed solutions that significantly reduce administrative burden while improving care delivery.

The care gap challenge, as Chris Sullens, CEO of CentralReach, explains it, is as follows:

"One in 36 children are diagnosed with autism, and of those 2+ million children, less than half are estimated to be served today predominantly because there aren't enough clinicians to deliver care. At CentralReach, we refer to this as the Autism and IDD Care gap and it drives our mission to deliver the best technology possible to compress the amount of time a provider's team, especially the therapists, spends on administrative tasks."

AI-enhanced clinical workflows on CentralReach's platform demonstrate how AI can transform routine clinical tasks. David Stevens, head of AI at CentralReach, describes the impact:

"It surfaces all that information and puts it right at your fingertips. You don't have to hunt and peck, or worry if someone filled out the right field or not. In that classic parlance, the AI doesn't just find the needle in the haystack, it burns the haystack down."

The platform enables natural language queries across comprehensive clinical datasets, allowing providers to ask questions such as *"how is my client progressing on this skill?"* and receive synthesized responses that integrate multiple data sources and clinical observations.

CentralReach's Care360 initiative represents the evolution toward comprehensive care coordination, unifying datasets into holistic learner profiles that support multidisciplinary team collaboration. This approach eliminates redundant data entry while ensuring that each provider has access to the comprehensive context for their interventions.

For more information about this story, visit `https://venturebeat.com/data-infrastructure/ai-boosted-autism-and-idd-care-centralreach-and-mongodb-transform-how-care-is-delivered/`.

Using GenAI for visual diagnostics

Consider this scenario that reflects a common challenge faced by radiologists. Dr. Martinez studies a chest CT while the prior-study icon spins across three PACS servers with the image in view, but the story remains out of reach. The 8 mm nodule in the right upper lobe sits isolated from the patient's smoking history locked in the EMR, the pathology report from last month's biopsy stored in another system, and the oncology notes that could transform this finding from a routine follow-up to an urgent intervention.

At that moment, she experiences healthcare's visual version of the 47-minute problem: not hunting through seven text-based systems like Dr. Chen, but navigating imaging silos that fragment the complete clinical picture into disconnected visual pieces.

But replacing Dr. Martinez's system-hopping for a single-vision AI creates a subtler hazard. You gain speed but lose the smoking history, the EGFR result, and the nuance. In imaging, half-knowledge is dangerous because diagnostic accuracy depends on the complete clinical context. An AI system that sees nodule growth but misses the patient's immunosuppression status might recommend aggressive follow-up when watchful waiting is appropriate, or conversely, might underestimate cancer risk in a high-risk patient, potentially delaying life-saving interventions.

Modern radiology faces this exact challenge: how to harness AI's pattern recognition capabilities while ensuring access to the complete clinical context that transforms pixels into patient care. The solution requires unified data architectures that connect imaging insights with comprehensive patient stories.

GenAI transforms medical imaging by bridging the gap between what systems can see and what clinicians need to know. These systems process multiple data types simultaneously, that is, images, metadata, clinical history, and comparative studies, creating unified patient contexts that enable both human expertise and AI capabilities to function optimally.

The model sees an 8 mm spiculated nodule, knows the 30-pack-year history, and, citing Fleischner Society guidelines (established medical recommendations for pulmonary nodule management), suggests a three-month follow-up:

```
PRELIMINARY AI IMPRESSION
8mm solid pulmonary nodule, RUL, spiculated.
Given smoking history, repeat CT in 3 months per Fleischner.
[Radiologist review required]
```

This automated generation demonstrates how document-oriented architectures enable AI systems to access complete clinical contexts rather than isolated image data, which is exactly the unified foundation that prevents agentic silos from forming.

One of AI's most transformative capabilities addresses imaging's fundamental challenge: understanding how findings evolve over time. When integrated with comprehensive data repositories, AI systems can automatically retrieve relevant prior studies and highlight critical changes that inform current interpretation.

Consider Dr. Martinez reviewing follow-up scans: May shows the original 6 mm nodule, July reveals growth to 7 mm, and October measures 8 mm. To Dr. Martinez, the AI analysis feels like having last year's films permanently mounted on today's lightbox, but annotated in real time with growth calculations, doubling time estimates, and guideline-based recommendations.

This **temporal intelligence** becomes possible only when imaging data connects seamlessly with complete patient histories.

Medical visual question-answering

Medical visual question-answering represents the ultimate expression of integrated clinical intelligence, enabling clinicians to interact with imaging data through natural language while accessing complete patient contexts. This technology transforms the traditional relationship between radiologists and imaging systems from passive viewing to active diagnostic collaboration.

When an emergency physician asks, `"Is there evidence of intracranial hemorrhage?"` the system canvasses density patterns, anatomical landmarks, and mass effect indicators, responding within seconds: `"No acute bleed, no midline shift, study negative"`.

The system is able to correlate visual findings with clinical context drawn from unified patient data.

Applying vector embeddings

Vector embeddings transform medical images into mathematical fingerprints that enable semantic search across vast imaging repositories. Think of pathology slides chopped into small tiles, each assigned a vector fingerprint that lets computers spot family resemblances among tumors that human observers might miss.

When Dr. Martinez encounters a rare adenocarcinoma variant, vector search can instantly locate similar cases from thousands of prior studies, providing visual references and diagnostic guidance that would be impossible to find through traditional text-based searches. Unified repositories turn those fingerprints into a clinical Google, surfacing twin tumors in seconds.

This technology demonstrates how unified data architectures enable new forms of clinical reasoning. Only when pathology images, clinical metadata, and diagnostic outcomes exist within integrated repositories can vector embeddings provide meaningful clinical insights rather than isolated pattern matching.

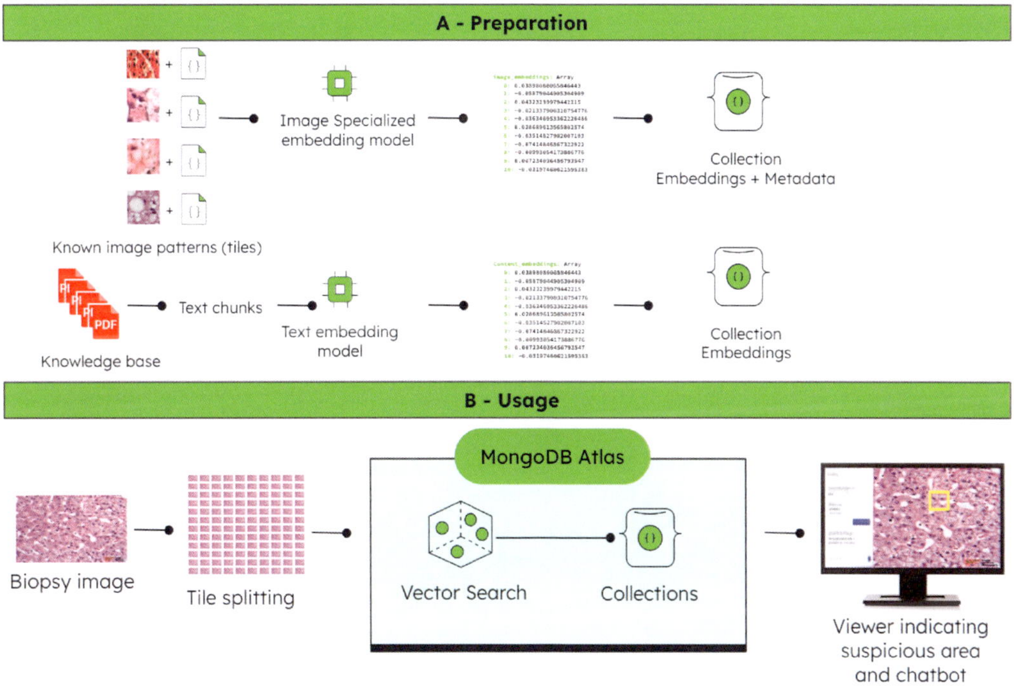

Figure 16.3: Vector embeddings workflow for medical image analysis using MongoDB Atlas

This two-phase workflow demonstrates how vector embeddings enable semantic search of medical images. Phase A (**Preparation**) shows the process of converting medical images and knowledge base data through image-encoding models to create vector embeddings stored as collections. Phase B (**Usage**) illustrates how query images are processed through tile splitting and vector search in MongoDB Atlas collections, with results displayed in a viewer interface for detecting suspicious areas and tumors. This approach transforms visual medical data into mathematical representations for AI-powered diagnostic assistance.

Medical imaging AI represents both a compelling application and a crucial test case for healthcare's broader transformation. When imaging systems can seamlessly access patient histories, correlate findings with clinical context, and integrate insights with care coordination platforms, they demonstrate the unified intelligence that defines healthcare's digital future.

Radiology is just the scout. By 2028, a scan will pull its own priors, flag growth, and ping oncology for biopsy before the patient even leaves CT.

This imaging transformation shows how unified data architectures enable AI capabilities that enhance rather than fragment clinical care, while providing a practical model for healthcare's evolution toward truly integrated, intelligent care delivery systems.

Extending intelligence to life sciences

While our exploration has focused on healthcare delivery and clinical workflows, the architectural principles we've developed, that is, unified data foundations, semantic intelligence, and document-oriented flexibility, extend naturally beyond patient care settings. Life sciences organizations face remarkably parallel challenges: complex, hierarchical data structures that resist traditional relational approaches, the need for semantic relationships across diverse information types, and the imperative to eliminate administrative friction that diverts expertise from core scientific work.

The same fragmentation patterns that plague clinical systems, where critical information lives in disconnected silos, manifest throughout the pharmaceutical development life cycle, from molecular research through regulatory approval. The facade strategies and vector search capabilities that enable clinical intelligence prove equally transformative when applied to drug discovery, regulatory processes, and market authorization workflows.

In life sciences, transforming vast amounts of data into actionable insights is critical throughout the entire medicine life cycle, from basic research to market. With the rise of precision medicine and genomics, AI is playing a transformative role by tailoring treatments to individual patients based on genetic, environmental, and lifestyle factors. GenAI accelerates drug discovery, analyzes genomic data for personalized treatment pathways, and optimizes clinical trials.

Revolutionizing CSRs with GenAI and MongoDB

The pharmaceutical industry faces immense pressure to expedite the regulatory approval process for new drugs and therapies. A critical component of this process is the creation of **clinical study reports (CSRs)**, which are comprehensive documents that are often hundreds of pages long. These reports serve as the primary evidence submitted to regulatory bodies such as the U.S. **Food and Drug Administration (FDA)** and **European Medicines Agency (EMA)** to demonstrate a drug's safety and efficacy. They detail the methodology, execution, and results of clinical trials, providing the complete scientific foundation upon which drug approval decisions are made.

Traditionally, compiling a CSR has been a labor-intensive task, often requiring several weeks to complete and involving multidisciplinary teams of clinical researchers, biostatisticians, medical writers, and regulatory specialists. This prolonged timeline not only delays the introduction of potentially life-saving treatments to patients who urgently need them, but also incurs significant costs associated with extended R&D cycles and longer time-to-market.

The process of generating CSRs is complex, involving the integration of vast amounts of clinical data. This includes statistical outputs, safety analyses, efficacy summaries, and detailed narratives that must conform to strict regulatory formatting requirements. Manual methods are time-consuming and error-prone, which can further delay regulatory approvals or trigger costly requests for additional information from regulatory agencies. The need for compliance with stringent regulatory standards, such as those set by the FDA and EMA, adds another layer of complexity to the document creation process. Any deviation from prescribed formats or missing information can result in submission delays or rejections.

GenAI, integrated with modern database platforms such as MongoDB Atlas, offers a groundbreaking solution to these challenges by automating the CSR creation process. This approach can reduce the time required to generate CSRs from weeks to mere minutes, allowing pharmaceutical companies to accelerate their time to market for new drugs.

The combination of GenAI with flexible, scalable database environments supports the dynamic and varied data structures inherent in clinical trials. This flexibility is crucial for managing the diverse data types involved in CSR generation, including text, tables, and complex statistical data. By using GenAI models, companies can automate the drafting of CSRs, producing high-quality, compliant documents that require minimal human intervention.

These AI models can automate the importation and transformation of data tables, generate accurate narratives, and ensure that the final documents meet the compliance standards required by regulatory bodies. Advanced search capabilities further enhance this process by enabling the retrieval of relevant data with high precision, which the AI uses to generate consistent and accurate content.

The same approach described for CSRs can provide an end-to-end solution that covers a wide range of regulatory documents, including **clinical trial narratives (CTNs)**, **summary clinical safety (SCS)**, and **summary clinical efficacy (SCE)**. However, certain document types may require specialized approaches: abbreviated CSRs for early-phase or discontinued studies may need different templates, synoptic CSRs for non-efficacy studies require condensed formats, and regulatory submissions involving novel therapeutics or breakthrough designations may demand additional documentation beyond standard AI automation capabilities. Despite these exceptions, this comprehensive coverage ensures that companies can automate the majority of their regulatory submissions, reducing the risk of human error and speeding up the entire process.

By integrating GenAI with modern database platforms, pharmaceutical companies can transform their approach to generating CSRs. This solution offers unparalleled speed, accuracy, and compliance, enabling companies to bring new treatments to market faster while maintaining the highest standards of quality and regulatory adherence. The result is a more efficient drug development process that ultimately benefits patients by accelerating access to innovative therapies.

Novo Nordisk accelerates drug approvals with NovoScribe and GenAI

Novo Nordisk, a global leader in healthcare, is transforming how it brings new medications to market using GenAI and cloud-based database solutions. Known for its pioneering work in diabetes care, Novo Nordisk produces 50% of the world's insulin and serves millions of patients worldwide.

With the introduction of NovoScribe (an internal AI-powered tool built on Amazon Bedrock, LangChain, and MongoDB Atlas), the company has significantly reduced the time required to generate CSRs, which is a critical step in the regulatory approval process. The app was built by a small team of three: Louise Lind Skov, Waheed Jowiya, and Tobias Kröpelin. NovoScribe has enabled Novo Nordisk to reduce the time to compile CSRs from 12 weeks to just 10 minutes. This innovation is helping Novo Nordisk get new medicines to patients faster, enhancing both the speed and quality of their regulatory submissions. The system automates complex data retrieval and analysis, allowing the company to scale its operations efficiently and securely across multiple cloud platforms.

Learn more about this story here: `https://www.mongodb.com/solutions/customer-case-studies/novo-nordisk`.

From CentralReach reducing autism care administrative burden to Novo Nordisk accelerating drug approvals, these implementations demonstrate a consistent pattern: unified data foundations enable AI systems to enhance human expertise rather than create isolated automation.

Looking ahead to intelligent healthcare

We began by looking at Dr. Chen's 47-minute struggle: a skilled pediatric specialist reduced to a data archaeologist, hunting through seven disconnected systems for information that should flow seamlessly. Her story revealed healthcare's central problem: we generate more clinical data than ever before, yet clinicians have never felt more disconnected from actionable insights.

This journey through healthcare's AI transformation revealed that unified data foundations enable comprehensive clinical intelligence. Whether it is Dr. Martinez accessing complete clinical context for imaging interpretation, care coordination agents synthesizing information across specialties, or Novo Nordisk reducing regulatory report compilation from 12 weeks to 10 minutes, success depends on AI systems having access to complete, unified patient contexts.

Document-oriented architectures preserve healthcare's natural information hierarchies while enabling AI innovation. The facade strategy, using standards as interfaces rather than structural constraints, enables FHIR compliance while supporting vector embeddings, semantic search, and intelligent applications. This approach eliminates the data duplication and ETL complexity that plague traditional approaches while enabling rapid adaptation to new requirements.

Vector embeddings transform medical images into searchable clinical intelligence, while multi-agent architectures coordinate specialized AI capabilities under human oversight. Natural language interfaces replace complex database navigation with conversational intelligence that understands clinical context and intent.

For healthcare providers, this means returning focus to patient care. Instead of 47 minutes of system archaeology, comprehensive clinical intelligence flows through natural language interactions while AI handles routine documentation and provides intelligent insights that augment clinical expertise.

For healthcare organizations, unified platforms enable operational efficiency that scales with demand rather than complexity. The same infrastructure supporting current operations adapts seamlessly to new AI capabilities and evolving clinical requirements. For patients, AI-enhanced healthcare delivers more personalized care through providers with complete information, intelligent coordination across specialists, and diagnostic insights from comprehensive analysis rather than isolated observations.

In the very near future, in the state-of-the-art healthcare systems, as we have seen before, scans will pull their own priors and ping oncology for biopsy before patients leave CT. Care coordination agents will synthesize information across specialties, flagging interactions and optimizing treatment sequences. Clinical documentation will emerge automatically while maintaining audit trails for compliance and quality improvement.

This isn't science fiction; it's the logical evolution of unified data foundations and AI capabilities implemented today by forward-thinking healthcare organizations. When healthcare data exists within intelligent platforms that preserve clinical context while enabling sophisticated analysis, the transformation from fragmented care to coordinated intelligence becomes inevitable.

The healthcare organizations implementing these foundations today will define tomorrow's standard of care. They will demonstrate that technology serves its highest purpose when it amplifies human expertise, preserves clinical relationships, and enables providers to operate at the top of their training while AI handles complex data integration and analysis.

For more information and resources, visit the *MongoDB for Healthcare* page at `https://www.mongodb.com/solutions/industries/healthcare`.

Summary

In this chapter, we demonstrated how skilled clinicians become data archaeologists rather than patient advocates, hunting through fragmented systems for essential information. As healthcare rushes toward an AI-powered future with GenAI and autonomous agents, there's a dangerous risk of creating agentic silos, where disconnected AI systems operate without the complete clinical context, potentially scaling harm invisibly while appearing to save time.

The solution lies in unified data foundations built on document-oriented architectures that preserve healthcare's natural information hierarchies while enabling AI innovation. By implementing the facade pattern, using standards such as HL7 FHIR as interface layers rather than structural constraints, healthcare organizations can achieve interoperability while maintaining data ownership and flexibility. Real-world implementations such as CentralReach demonstrate how AI-powered care coordination, natural language clinical intelligence, and unified medical imaging can transform administrative burden into clinical insight. The transformation from Dr. Chen's 47-minute struggle to intelligent, coordinated care delivery represents healthcare's next great leap forward, with success dependent on AI agents having access to complete, unified patient contexts rather than isolated data fragments.

Part 3, The Future of Intelligent Enterprise charts the future trajectory of intelligent enterprises through the lens of modern AI protocols and architectures. It introduces frameworks such as **Model Context Protocol (MCP)** and Causal AI as foundational elements for building adaptive, explainable, and interoperable systems. The next chapter explores how **enterprise document management (EDM)** is evolving from static storage to intelligent infrastructure, demonstrating how modern platforms leverage AI to classify, enrich, and activate unstructured content across business workflows at scale.

References

1. *Agentic AI In Healthcare*: https://medicalfuturist.com/agentic-ai-in-healthcare/
2. *Increased importance of digital medicine and eHealth during the Covid-19 pandemic*: https://www.tandfonline.com/doi/full/10.1080/02813432.2020.1770466
3. *FHIR + openEHR*: https://www.better.care/news/fhir-openehr/

Part 3:
The Future of Intelligent Enterprise

This set of chapters looks ahead to how AI systems, and the enterprise platforms they rely on, must evolve. From rethinking legacy document stores to implementing causal intelligence, Model Context Protocol, and agentic orchestration at scale, this part outlines the architectural patterns and operating models that will define the next generation of intelligent enterprise systems.

This part of the book includes the following chapters:

- *Chapter 17, Enterprise Document Management with Encore and MongoDB*
- *Chapter 18, Democratizing Agentic AI for Enterprise with Dataworkz and MongoDB*
- *Chapter 19, Outlook: Beyond Today's AI*

17

Enterprise Document Management with MongoDB and AI

The transformation to intelligent enterprise begins with a fundamental truth: AI is only as powerful as the data it can access and understand. While organizations have spent decades accumulating vast repositories of information, much of this critical business intelligence remains trapped in legacy systems that were never designed for the AI era.

The final part of the book explores how enterprise platforms must evolve to support truly intelligent operations: from reimagining how we store and access unstructured content, to democratizing agentic AI capabilities, to implementing the next generation of causal and orchestrated intelligence systems. Each transformation builds upon the last, creating the foundation for enterprises that don't just use AI tools but operate as intelligent systems themselves.

We begin with perhaps the most overlooked yet fundamental challenge: transforming the vast archives of *dark data* that exist in every organization into AI-ready intelligent content platforms.

But that's changing fast. AI is finally able to bridge the structured/unstructured data gap. Thanks to platforms such as **Encore**, built on MongoDB, **enterprise document management (EDM)** is becoming a dynamic, AI-powered foundation for productivity, compliance, and customer experience.

By the end of this chapter, you will understand the following:

- Why traditional EDM systems created massive stores of inaccessible dark data that limited decision-making
- How unstructured data has outpaced structured data in both growth and relevance
- Why AI is uniquely suited to transform passive documents into active, intelligent content assets
- How MongoDB-powered platforms such as Encore deliver value through flexible architecture and native AI integrations
- What organizations are achieving through modern EDM use cases such as claims processing, customer support, and audit readiness
- How document-oriented architectures and integrated vector search enable AI-driven content management
- How Encore's integration with AWS Bedrock enables instant content intelligence without complex configuration
- What the last mile of AI transformation involves, and why content readiness is the critical factor
- How to frame EDM modernization as a business value accelerator rather than a storage upgrade
- Why EDM's role is increasingly important as AI becomes central to enterprise operations

The digital filing cabinet era

Traditional EDM systems were built for a different era. They were designed to file away scanned documents, meet compliance requirements, and, if you were lucky, let you find and retrieve a document. Content was indexed through rigid taxonomies based on traditional SQL database structures. Search relied on simple keyword queries against limited index fields, often yielding frustrating results when working with large document repositories. These systems couldn't understand content, provide dynamic search, process natural language, or integrate into AI workflows. At best, they were digital filing cabinets.

The hidden costs of legacy systems

The limitations of traditional EDM went far beyond inconvenience. They created a measurable business impact that most organizations never fully calculated. When teams searched, for example, for *contracts from Q3*, typical systems returned hundreds of irrelevant files mixed with relevant ones, forcing manual sorting through large volumes of false positives. Knowledge workers spent up to 3.6 hours daily just hunting for information, representing millions in lost productivity for larger organizations [1].

Compliance became a recurring nightmare. When auditors arrived, teams scrambled for weeks gathering documentation that should have been instantly accessible. Version control chaos meant critical decisions were made using outdated information, with multiple document versions scattered across email, shared drives, and local storage. The hidden costs were staggering; document retrieval failures represent massive productivity losses for enterprises, with the time spent searching translating to millions in lost value for larger organizations.

Legacy architectural constraints

Traditional EDM platforms built on relational databases created fundamental architectural limitations that became increasingly problematic as content volumes and organizational complexity grew. Understanding these constraints helps explain why many organizations struggle with document management transformation.

Schema rigidity represented the most significant limitation. Every new document type or metadata field required careful database schema planning, often involving system downtime during implementation. This created a fundamental mismatch: business documents are inherently varied and unpredictable, while relational structures demand consistency and predefined relationships. PDFs, images, emails, and multimedia content had to be force-fitted into tabular structures, often losing valuable contextual information in the process.

Scalability bottlenecks emerged as repositories grew. Traditional architectures struggled with geographic distribution, making it difficult for global organizations to provide consistent document access across time zones. Performance degraded predictably as complex joins and **atomicity, consistency, isolation**, and **durability (ACID)** compliance requirements created computational overhead that worsened with volume. The familiar experience of search timeouts during peak-usage periods became a standard frustration.

Integration complexity compounded these issues. Each business system required point-to-point connections to the document repository, creating maintenance-intensive architectures. When underlying systems changed (which they frequently did), integrations broke, requiring constant IT attention that diverted resources from value-adding capabilities.

Modern alternatives address these constraints through various approaches: document-oriented databases that handle unstructured content natively, cloud-native architectures that scale dynamically, microservices designs that reduce integration complexity, and distributed systems that support global operations. The key insight isn't that relational databases are inherently flawed, but that EDM requirements have evolved beyond what traditional architectures were designed to handle.

When digital promises failed to deliver

The promise of digital transformation often collided with implementation realities. Organizations invested heavily in enterprise content management systems only to discover that digitizing broken processes simply created faster ways to be inefficient. McKinsey research shows that 66% of enterprise software projects experience cost overruns, demonstrating systemic implementation challenges across the industry [2].

Organizations experienced costly document management failures, part of the broader pattern where large IT projects regularly exceed budgets and fail to deliver promised benefits. The fundamental issue wasn't the technology; it was that legacy EDM architectures couldn't evolve with business needs or integrate with emerging AI capabilities.

The result? Mountains of dark data that remained effectively inaccessible for search or decision-making [3].

The unstructured data challenge

Here's the challenge: unstructured data doesn't follow schemas. It lives in PDFs, images, and emails, scattered across systems, often without reliable metadata. It's difficult to search, govern, or analyze without purpose-built infrastructure.

This creates a roadblock for AI. **Large language models (LLMs)** require context-rich, well-organized data. Poorly labeled or inaccessible content prevents AI from delivering meaningful value.

The numbers tell the story: unstructured data now comprises up to 90% of all enterprise information, including emails, documents, videos, social media content, and sensor outputs. This data type grows 55–65% [4] annually, significantly outpacing structured data growth.

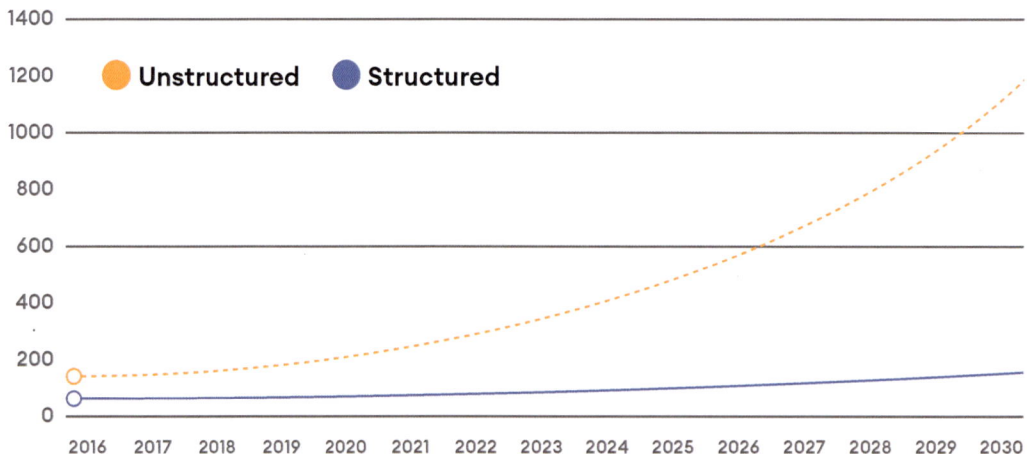

Figure 17.1: A graph showing the growth of unstructured versus structured data

Figure 17.1 demonstrates this exponential growth pattern. The dashed orange line shows unstructured data rising dramatically from under 200 units in 2016 to over 1,000 units by 2029, while the blue line representing structured data remains relatively flat, growing only modestly from approximately 100 to 200 units over the same period.

Despite its volume and potential value, unstructured data often remains siloed, unclassified, and underutilized, posing challenges for organizations aiming to leverage AI and analytics. As businesses increasingly adopt AI technologies, the ability to effectively manage and analyze unstructured data becomes crucial. Without robust strategies to process and interpret this vast information reservoir, enterprises risk missing out on critical insights and falling behind in the competitive landscape.

Redefining document management with Encore

Today, organizations need more than just content storage; they require systems that can extract key insights from unstructured data, feed those insights into downstream automation and analytics, and ensure compliance without creating excessive operational burden. That's where AI comes in. When AI can understand your archives, your documents stop languishing as passive, opaque records and become active business assets. Let's look at some real-world wins for AI in this area.

Claims processing

Insurance claims often involve a flood of documents, including accident reports, estimates, medical records, photos, emails, and more. Traditionally, teams spent hours tracking down files and piecing everything together.

With Encore, those documents are ingested the moment they arrive via email, third-party portals, or branch uploads. Encore automatically tags and organizes them, extracts key details such as claim numbers and dates, and presents everything in a clear, searchable timeline.

Now, a processor can simply say, *Show me all documents for John Doe's March 2024 auto claim*, and get an instant summary with relevant documents and missing info flagged.

This results in faster claim resolution, improved accuracy, and happier customers.

Call center support

Support agents are under pressure to answer tough questions while juggling outdated systems and scattered documents. A large percentage of support calls cannot be resolved solely with data available in business applications. Many critical policy and claim document details exist only in stored document images. That's a recipe for long hold times and frustrated callers.

Encore simplifies the chaos by centralizing policy documents, past interactions, FAQs, and call notes in one smart content hub. When a customer asks, `"Am I covered for windshield damage?"`, the agent can search that exact question and instantly get the right excerpt, plus related cases and similar queries.

This results in quicker answers, shorter calls, and a better customer experience.

Compliance and audit readiness

When audits or compliance checks occur, teams often scramble to locate years of documentation, such as forms, certifications, and approvals, which are often buried in siloed systems.

Encore streamlines the audit process. As documents are uploaded or captured, Encore indexes and classifies them, linking each to the right process or case. During an audit, teams can instantly pull up exactly what's needed, see summaries, and even flag missing items such as unsigned forms or expired documents.

This results in faster audit responses, fewer compliance gaps, and peace of mind.

Building a platform for new EDM with MongoDB and Encore

What makes Encore so different? At its core, Encore reimagines EDM from the ground up. Built on MongoDB, it breaks free from the rigid structures of traditional content platforms. Documents are treated as flexible, intelligent data objects, not just as attachments with a name and a date.

Figure 17.2: Encore's AI-powered content intelligence platform

This diagram illustrates Encore's approach to transforming unstructured enterprise content into intelligent business assets. On the left, diverse document types, emails, images, and files from across the organization flow into Encore's cloud-native platform. The system then processes this scattered content through AI-powered classification and organization, delivering three core intelligent capabilities on the right: **enabling agentic AI** for autonomous content processing, **AI analysis** for automated insights and summarization, and **enterprise search** for instant content discovery. This visualization demonstrates how modern EDM platforms such as Encore break free from traditional digital filing cabinet limitations to create active, intelligent content ecosystems that fuel AI-driven business operations and decision-making.

Even before we bring AI into the discussion, MongoDB's NoSQL architecture and rich search feature set offer tangible advantages to traditional EDM platforms. Atlas's **faceted search** capability, for example, provides an intuitive level of content filtering that legacy systems don't provide.

In progressing to AI capabilities, Encore leverages MongoDB's support for vector embeddings and vector search, tools that then let Encore take full, native advantage of the AWS Bedrock LLM and GenAI suite. With virtually no additional configuration or setup, users find their unstructured content unlocked to the power of AI.

Here's what Encore and MongoDB together immediately provide:

- **Flexibility**: Store and evolve your content without redesigning your database
- **Real-time search and access**: Retrieve exactly what you need, instantly
- **AI-driven insights**: Classify, extract, and summarize content automatically, with no more manual tagging or hunting through folders

This is the EDM that was built for the age of AI. Encore does not simply allow you to manage your content, but also to activate it.

The urgent case for EDM modernization

Organizations are sitting on mountains of documents, and most of them are still unsearchable, unstructured, and underutilized. Whether it's for customer service, compliance, claims processing, or audits, teams are wasting time digging through static files.

The business case for modernizing legacy document management extends far beyond simple storage improvements. Organizations that embrace intelligent content platforms realize transformative value across multiple operational dimensions, from process automation to enhanced security frameworks.

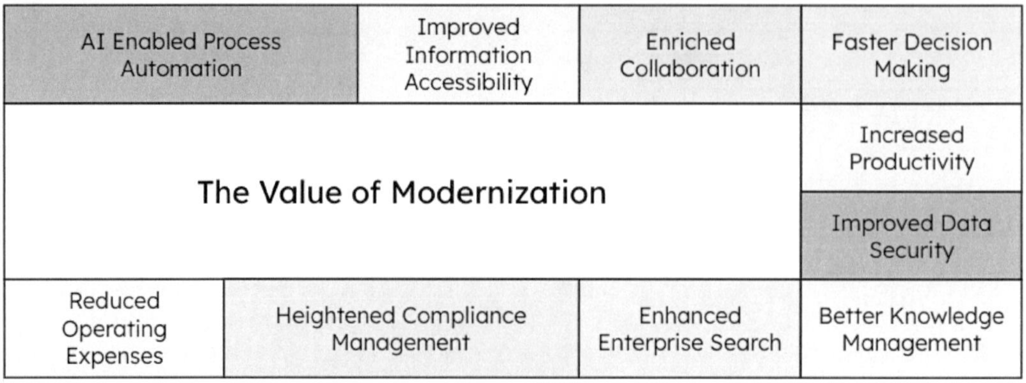

AI Enabled Process Automation	Improved Information Accessibility	Enriched Collaboration	Faster Decision Making
The Value of Modernization			Increased Productivity
			Improved Data Security
Reduced Operating Expenses	Heightened Compliance Management	Enhanced Enterprise Search	Better Knowledge Management

Figure 17.3: The value of modernization for EDM

This diagram illustrates the comprehensive business benefits realized when organizations modernize their document management infrastructure with AI-powered platforms. The transformation creates interconnected value chains where improvements amplify each other. **AI-enabled process automation** serves as the catalyst. When documents are automatically categorized and routed, **information accessibility** improves naturally. This enhanced findability directly enables **enriched collaboration**, as teams spend less time searching and more time working together on content. The result is **faster decision-making**, since critical information surfaces when needed. These operational gains create a productivity multiplier effect. Time saved on document tasks compounds across every employee interaction. Meanwhile, data security and compliance management work in tandem. The same AI systems that organize content for accessibility also identify sensitive information for protection. The financial benefits interconnect, as reduced operating expenses from automation enable investment in strategic initiatives, while enhanced search and knowledge management prevent duplicated efforts. These interconnected improvements demonstrate why modern EDM represents a strategic business investment rather than a simple technology upgrade.

AI can solve this problem, but only if it has access to quality, readable, structured content. AI initiatives typically fail not due to weak models but because the data isn't adequately prepared. Unstructured content is the *last mile* of AI transformation, and Encore, powered by MongoDB, bridges the gap. It enables organizations to modernize their content infrastructure, unlock hidden value, and accelerate the path to enterprise AI.

Modern solutions such as Encore demonstrate how MongoDB's document-oriented architecture enables organizations to move beyond traditional digital filing systems. When combined with AI capabilities, these platforms transform legacy archives into searchable, intelligent content repositories that can actively support business operations rather than simply storing documents.

Summary

The transformation of EDM from dusty digital filing cabinets to AI-powered intelligent content platforms represents a fundamental shift driven by the urgent need to unlock dark data. With 90% of enterprise information trapped as inaccessible unstructured content growing at 55–65% annually, organizations face a critical choice: evolve their document management approach or watch valuable business intelligence remain buried in legacy systems. Modern EDM platforms such as Encore, built on MongoDB's flexible document-oriented architecture, demonstrate how AI can transform passive storage into active business assets through automated classification, vector search capabilities, and seamless integration with AWS Bedrock for GenAI functionality.

Real-world applications across claims processing, call center support, and compliance management prove that intelligent document platforms deliver immediate, measurable value by dramatically reducing search times, improving accuracy, and streamlining audit processes. The combination of modern document-oriented architectures with AI-powered content intelligence enables organizations to move beyond rigid, schema-dependent systems toward dynamic platforms that understand, classify, and synthesize information autonomously. This evolution positions EDM as the critical last mile of AI transformation, where proper data preparation determines whether enterprise AI initiatives succeed or fail in delivering tangible business outcomes.

The next chapter explores how organizations can democratize agentic AI across their enterprise with MongoDB's partner, Dataworkz, moving beyond document management to build intelligent agents that work autonomously to achieve specific business objectives and deliver immediate operational transformation.

References

1. *Report: Employees spend 3.6 hours each day searching for info, increasing burnout*: https://venturebeat.com/business/report-employees-spend-3-6-hours-each-day-searching-for-info-increasing-burnout/

2. *Delivering large-scale IT projects on time, on budget, and on value*: https://www.mckinsey.com/capabilities/mckinsey-digital/our-insights/delivering-large-scale-it-projects-on-time-on-budget-and-on-value

3. *Dark Data*: https://www.gartner.com/en/information-technology/glossary/dark-data

4. *The Future of Data: Unstructured Data Statistics You Should Know*: https://www.congruity360.com/blog/the-future-of-data-unstructured-data-statistics-you-should-know/

18

Democratizing Agentic AI for Enterprise with Dataworkz and MongoDB

The buzz around AI is louder than ever, yet most organizations struggle to translate its potential into tangible, immediate business value. The core problem often lies in decision-making, as companies get stuck waiting for perfect data infrastructure, attempting massive transformations that take years, or deploying isolated solutions that don't scale.

Agentic AI systems work autonomously to achieve specific business objectives, making decisions and taking actions without constant human oversight. This shift to proactive intelligence enables organizations to implement AI solutions that deliver immediate value while building toward more sophisticated automation.

Successful AI adoption doesn't require massive upfront investments or years-long development cycles. Through real-world case studies spanning financial services, developer operations, and brand management, we'll explore how organizations at different maturity levels are deploying agentic AI solutions that transform specific business processes and deliver measurable ROI in weeks, not years.

In this chapter, you will learn about the following:

- Ways organizations across the data maturity spectrum can implement AI solutions tailored to their current capabilities and infrastructure

- The role of agentic AI in delivering immediate business value through real-world applications in financial services, DevOps, and brand messaging

- The Client Insight Engine's ability to transform financial advisor training through dynamic scenario generation and personalized feedback

- How DevOps Efficiency Agent eliminates developer productivity bottlenecks by automating administrative tasks and streamlining workflows

- How Brand Messaging Agent ensures consistent communications at scale using sophisticated RAG and agent orchestration

- Simple, effective AI implementations that provide measurable ROI without massive upfront investments or complex development cycles

- The support modern data architectures, such as MongoDB Atlas, provide for rapid AI development and deployment across diverse use cases

- The future trajectory of agentic AI, which points toward autonomous systems acting as virtual employees and trusted partners

Tailoring AI for every organization

Successfully implementing AI isn't a one-size-fits-all endeavor. Organizations exist across a spectrum of data maturity, each with unique challenges and opportunities. Understanding where your organization sits on this spectrum is crucial for developing an AI strategy that delivers immediate impact with your current capabilities. Here's how it plays out across the spectrum:

- **Nascent organizations**: If you're grappling with fragmented data, limited infrastructure, and a shortage of in-house technical talent, your focus should be on establishing foundational data practices and demonstrating quick, impactful wins to build momentum and internal buy-in for AI adoption.

- **Evolving organizations**: If you're characterized by siloed data systems, a proliferation of point solutions that don't integrate seamlessly, and difficulty scaling initial AI successes across the enterprise, your priority should be unifying data, optimizing existing investments, and building scalable AI frameworks.

- **Mature organizations**: These organizations are data-rich and often equipped with significant technological capabilities, yet may still struggle with issues such as model explainability, achieving real-time insights from complex data flows, or fully automating sophisticated processes without extensive human oversight. For these firms, the challenge is often about unlocking deeper intelligence and achieving full operational efficiency.

The key to democratizing AI within your organization is implementing solutions that are right-sized for your current stage. A crucial enabler is adopting modern data architectures. Technologies such as **MongoDB vector search**, for instance, offer the flexibility and scalability required to handle diverse data types and support the dynamic needs of AI-driven insights, making rapid AI development and deployment feasible regardless of your maturity level.

The following case studies demonstrate how organizations at different maturity stages have successfully implemented agentic AI solutions.

Case study 1: Client Insight Engine – agentic AI for financial advisors

A leading example of Dataworkz's agentic AI in action is the **Client Insight Engine**. This solution addresses a critical need within financial services: the continuous, practical skill development of financial advisors in an ever-evolving regulatory and market landscape. Traditional training methods often fall short in providing the dynamic, hands-on experience necessary to build confidence and refine the nuanced art of financial advice.

The Client Insight Engine operates through a multi-agent architecture that integrates various data sources and processing capabilities. As illustrated in *Figure 18.1*, the system begins with the organization's existing data assets, including PDFs and Salesforce records, which feed into a coordinated network of specialized RAG applications. The central Dataworkz agent orchestrates interactions between different tools, from report analysis to document processing to Salesforce integration, synthesizing responses from each component to deliver comprehensive insights through the API to external applications.

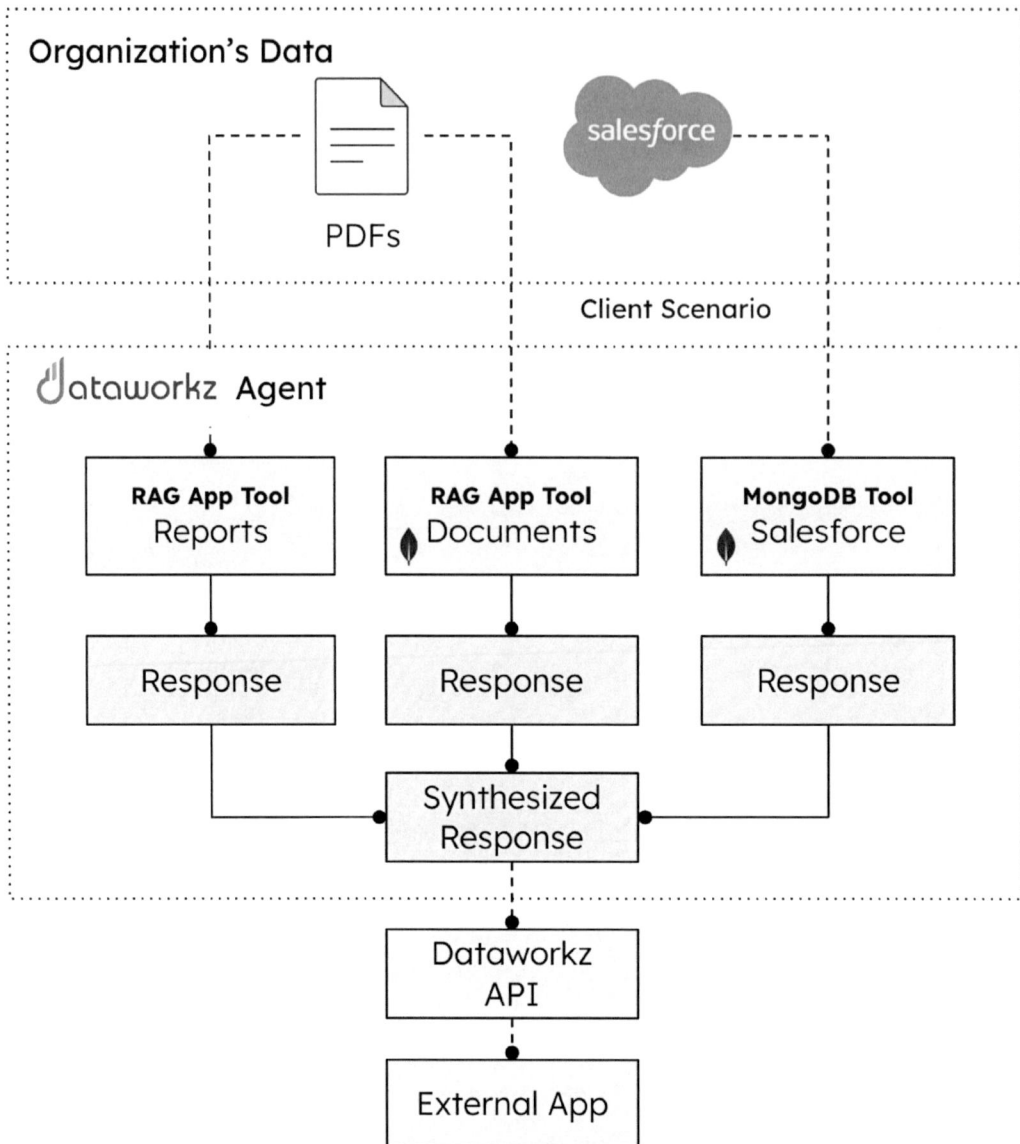

Figure 18.1: Client Insight Engine architecture

The primary goal of the Client Insight Engine is straightforward yet profound. It enhances advisor proficiency, ensures unwavering compliance, and ultimately, significantly improves client outcomes. It achieves this by moving beyond static learning to an autonomous, interactive coaching system powered by agentic AI.

Here's how you can leverage its agentic components to transform your advisor training:

- **Dynamic scenario generation**: You can generate an unlimited supply of realistic and diverse client scenarios tailored to your specific learning objectives, current market conditions, and individual advisor needs. This creates a truly dynamic practice environment that evolves with your training requirements.

- **Real-time performance analysis**: As your advisors navigate simulated client interactions, you can monitor their responses against your established framework of best practices, regulatory compliance guidelines, and effective client engagement strategies. The system analyzes performance in real time using guidelines you provide directly to the agent.

- **Personalized feedback and guidance**: You can move beyond simple *correct/incorrect* assessments to provide your advisors with specific, actionable suggestions for improvement. The system explains *why* certain approaches are more effective and how to change the sentiment of responses to be more professional. This gives you the ability to offer personalized coaching that's available 24/7.

- **Integration**: You can leverage your existing internal knowledge bases, industry best practices, and real-world case studies to inform scenario generation and feedback mechanisms. Through RAG technology, you can find and utilize the most similar scenarios from your advisor's experience.

By deploying the Client Insight Engine, you can deliver significant and immediate value for both individual advisors and your financial firm as a whole: accelerated skill development, increased confidence, enhanced compliance, consistent quality of advice, stronger client retention, and ultimately, business growth.

Case study 2: DevOps Efficiency Agent – supercharging developer productivity

Beyond external-facing solutions, agentic AI holds significant potential for internal operational efficiency. For large enterprises, particularly in the realm of software development and IT operations, significant developer time is often consumed by administrative overhead, information retrieval, and routine task automation. Dataworkz addresses this challenge with solutions such as its **DevOps Efficiency Agent**, an example of how agentic AI drives efficiency for home office associates, particularly developers.

The DevOps Efficiency Agent streamlines developer workflows by orchestrating interactions across multiple enterprise platforms. As shown in *Figure 18.2*, the system integrates seamlessly with your existing tools, such as Confluence, Jira, and Slack, through a centralized Dataworkz agent. When a user submits a query through the Slack bot interface, the agent intelligently selects the appropriate tool based on context, severity, and keywords, then either retrieves existing information or creates new items as needed before including relevant links in the response.

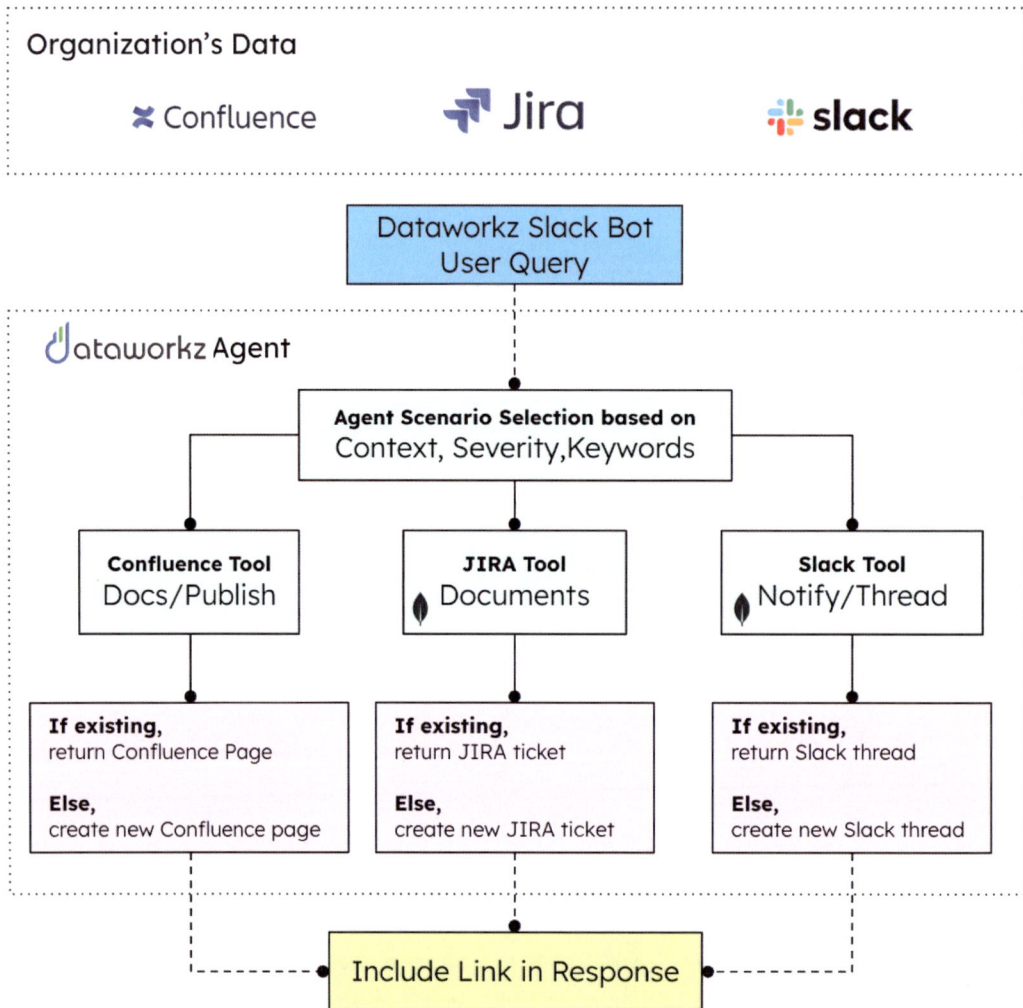

Figure 18.2: DevOps Efficiency Agent workflow

Consider the typical workflow for an enterprise developer: navigating multiple platforms such as internal knowledge bases, task tracking systems, code repositories, and service management tools. Each context switch, each search, and each manual ticket creation consumes valuable time, time that could be spent innovating and building. Studies show that a substantial portion of a developer's day, potentially 25% for a large organization with thousands of developers, is diverted to these non-coding tasks. This represents a massive untapped efficiency gain.

The DevOps Efficiency Agent is designed to be an intelligent copilot for development and operations teams. It's an internal-facing agent that streamlines complex workflows, automates mundane administrative tasks, and provides instant access to critical information scattered across disparate systems. It acts as an intelligent intermediary between developers and the tools they use daily, offering the following:

- **Intelligent information retrieval and contextual Q&A**: Developers can interact conversationally with the AI agent to query information stored across various repositories such as internal knowledge bases, code repositories, task management systems, and service management systems. The agent uses its understanding of natural language and its ability to access and synthesize information from these cross-domain data sources to provide precise, actionable responses.

- **Automated administrative task execution**: The agent empowers developers and stakeholders to automate common, time-consuming administrative tasks. For instance, a developer can simply ask the agent to `create a draft incident ticket for a "Sev 2" issue affecting the "Analytics Reporting" service`, and the agent will interact with the service management system to create a ticket in a draft state, prepopulating fields and associating relevant data. It can also manage routine releases to lower environments, all using existing drafts as a reference point.

The DevOps Efficiency Agent delivers substantial, measurable value for organizations by providing significant time savings, reduced context switching, improved information accessibility, enhanced developer experience, and faster incident resolution and change management.

Case study 3: Brand Messaging Agent – ensuring on-brand communications at scale

Given how quickly business needs evolve, maintaining a consistent and authentic brand message across all communications is crucial for credibility and recognition. Yet, for large organizations, ensuring every internal email, external social media post, or client communication adheres to a specific style guide can be a challenge. Dataworkz leverages agentic AI to tackle this head-on with solutions such as the **Brand Messaging Agent**, enabling organizations to create content that consistently reflects a unique and established brand persona.

The Brand Messaging Agent operates through a sophisticated content generation pipeline that ensures stylistic consistency across all communications. As illustrated in *Figure 18.3*, the system begins by ingesting your organization's existing content assets in various formats (Word documents, PDFs, and Markdown files). When you submit a content request, the Dataworkz agent first classifies the intent (whether you're creating a blog post, LinkedIn update, speech, or email), then uses both RAG technology for contextual research and LLM capabilities for intent analysis. The interactive layer generates drafts according to your specific style guide, allows for user confirmation and refinement, and finally, outputs the content in your preferred format.

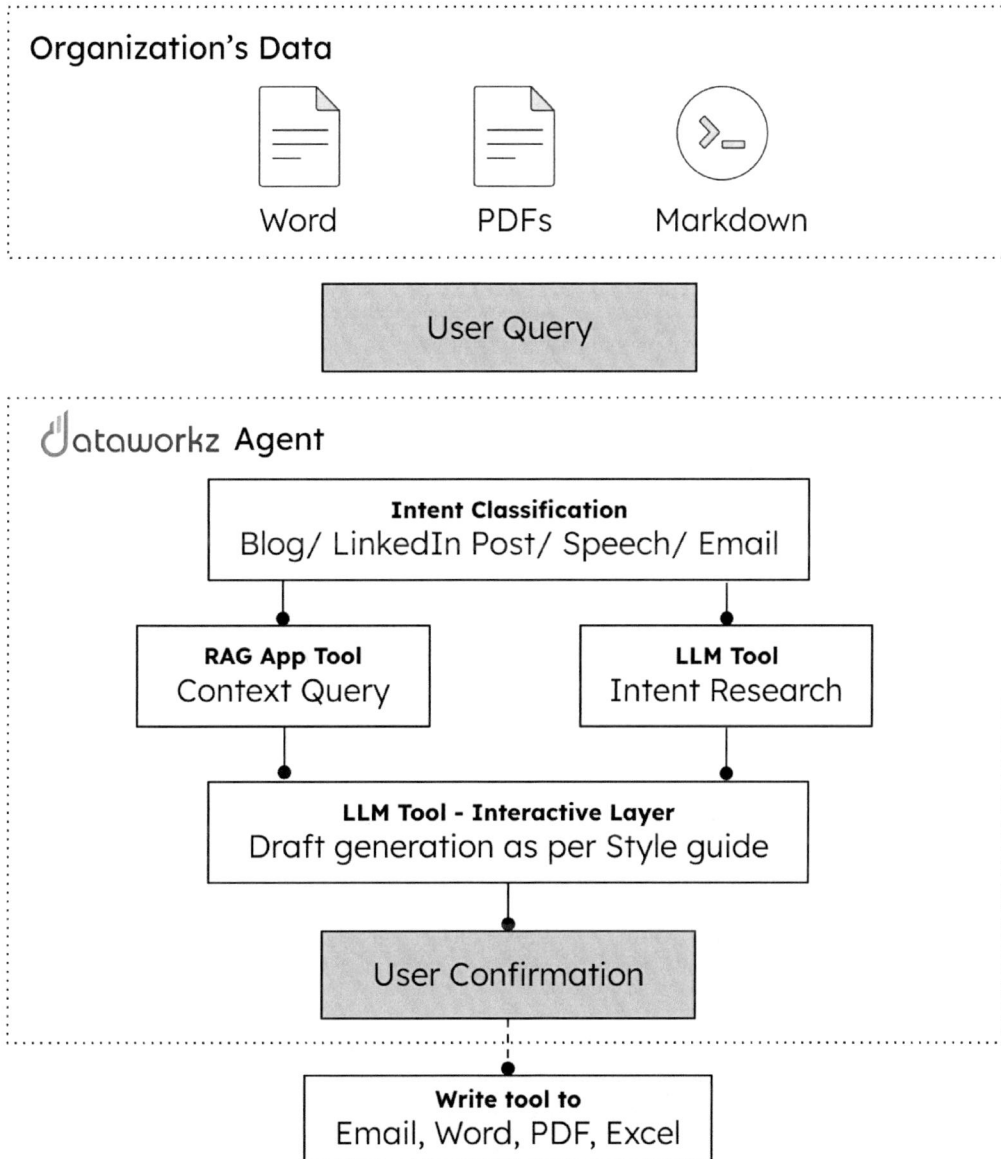

Figure 18.3: Brand Messaging Agent architecture

The objective is simple: empower various teams, from marketing and communications to internal stakeholders, to generate content that sounds and feels exactly right, every time. This isn't just about grammar or spelling; it's about nuance, tone, specific phrasing, and even formatting, all of which contribute to a distinct brand identity.

The Brand Messaging Agent is an intelligent system that combines RAG with sophisticated agent orchestration to achieve this level of stylistic consistency. It's designed to replicate the unique communication style of a specific persona, let's call it *Alex*, ensuring every piece of content speaks with the authoritative yet approachable tone that Alex embodies.

Here's how this agentic solution works:

- **Dedicated contextual AI applications**: For each type of content that Alex might create (e.g., internal team updates, public-facing thought leadership articles, and sales outreach messages), Dataworkz builds a specialized RAG application using our contextual AI framework. Each of these applications is meticulously configured with Alex's specific style guide for that content type, along with a comprehensive collection of its past communications as a reference knowledge base.

- **Intelligent agent orchestration**: When a user requests to generate a specific type of content on a particular topic, the central Brand Messaging Agent steps in. This agent intelligently identifies the appropriate RAG application tailored for the requested content type, then sends the user's topic as a query. The RAG application, acting as a highly informed curator, retrieves the most stylistically and topically similar examples from Alex's archive of past content.

- **GenAI with contextual guidance**: Finally, the agent takes the user's original request, along with the rich, stylistically relevant examples retrieved by the MongoDB-powered RAG application, and instructs a GenAI model to create new content. This content not only addresses the user's specific topic but also aligns with Alex's established style, tone, and even preferred formatting.

The Brand Messaging Agent delivers tangible value by ensuring consistent brand identity, accelerating content creation, reducing the risk of off-brand messaging, empowering non-expert users, and enabling scalability in communication efforts.

These three case studies demonstrate a crucial insight. Agentic AI solutions don't require years of development or massive infrastructure overhauls to deliver meaningful business impact. Whether you're training financial advisors, streamlining developer workflows, or maintaining brand consistency, the key lies in identifying specific pain points and implementing targeted solutions that work with your existing systems. This practical approach to AI implementation forms the foundation of a framework that any organization can follow to achieve similar results.

Implementing effective AI solutions with Dataworkz and MongoDB

A common misconception is that impactful AI requires years of complex development and massive upfront investments. However, the case studies we've explored demonstrate a different reality. Simple, effective AI solutions can deliver immediate, measurable business value. The key is focusing on pragmatic implementation that makes AI accessible and useful across all parts of your organization.

Turning your AI strategy into action

You can achieve measurable results by following a framework that emphasizes rapid deployment over perfect solutions. Start with your current capabilities and iterate based on results.

The following key principles outline a framework for effective implementation:

- **Identify high-impact use cases**: Pinpoint specific pain points or opportunities where AI can deliver clear, measurable value quickly.

- **Leverage existing data**: Unlock the value of existing, often siloed, data by using modern engineering techniques to ingest, transform, and unify sources, from structured databases to semi-structured cloud storage and SaaS applications, making it AI-ready for immediate use.

- **Agile prototyping and iteration**: Prioritize rapid prototyping and iterative development to quickly see working AI solutions, demonstrate value early, and provide feedback that refines the agent's capabilities throughout its lifecycle. This agile approach minimizes risk and accelerates time-to-value. With flexible A/B testing, you can ensure that your applications are performing optimally.

- **Focus on user adoption**: An AI tool is only as good as its adoption. You should prioritize intuitive no-code and low-code interfaces with seamless integration into existing workflows. For financial advisors, developers, and communications teams alike, this means conversational AI and user experiences that feel natural and assistive, ensuring that tools are actually used and embraced, rather than becoming technical curiosities.

- **Architectural considerations**: The foundation of any successful AI implementation is a scalable architecture. You can design and implement scalable data solutions, often leveraging technologies such as MongoDB Atlas with vector search to power AI applications. Its flexible document model and scalability make it suitable for storing the diverse data needed by AI agents, from user interactions to knowledge bases, facilitating rapid AI development and deployment.

These implementation principles provide a practical roadmap for deploying agentic AI solutions that deliver immediate value. However, as organizations begin to experience the transformative power of these autonomous systems, it's worth considering where this technology is headed and how it will reshape enterprise operations in the years to come.

Future directions for enterprise agentic AI

The trajectory of AI in enterprise points toward increasingly sophisticated and autonomous agentic systems that act as virtual employees. Solutions like Dataworkz, powered by MongoDB, envision a future where AI agents are not merely tools but integral, proactive partners in enterprise operations.

While AI will continue to augment human capabilities, agentic AI will increasingly take on more complex, proactive roles. Imagine agents autonomously monitoring real-time market sentiment, identifying emerging risks, or initiating preliminary compliance checks without direct human prompts.

This isn't about replacing human expertise but elevating it. AI agents will become trusted partners, handling routine or data-intensive tasks, allowing human professionals to focus on strategic thinking, complex problem-solving, and relationship building. The case studies covered in this chapter are all microcosms of this, freeing up human talent while simultaneously improving output quality.

Dataworkz is committed to making advanced AI accessible to all types of organizations, from large financial institutions to bustling IT departments and dynamic marketing teams. We believe that the benefits of agentic AI should not be exclusive to tech giants.

As AI systems gain more autonomy, ethical considerations become paramount. Organizations implementing agentic AI must prioritize responsible development practices, ensuring fairness, transparency, and robust security in all enterprise applications. Explainable AI architectures that allow stakeholders to understand how decisions are made become increasingly critical for fostering trust and accountability in autonomous systems.

Summary

This chapter addressed a critical challenge facing organizations today: how to move beyond AI hype and pilot projects to implement solutions that deliver tangible, immediate business value. The core problem isn't technical capability but implementation paralysis; companies get stuck waiting for perfect data infrastructure, attempting massive transformations that take years, or deploying isolated solutions that don't scale across the enterprise.

We explored how agentic AI offers a fundamentally different approach, moving from reactive models to proactive intelligence that works autonomously to achieve specific business objectives. Through three comprehensive case studies, we demonstrated real-world applications: the Client Insight Engine transforms financial advisor training through dynamic scenario generation and personalized feedback; the DevOps Efficiency Agent eliminates developer productivity bottlenecks by automating administrative tasks across multiple platforms such as Confluence, Jira, and Slack; and the Brand Messaging Agent ensures consistent communications at scale using sophisticated RAG and agent orchestration techniques. The implementation framework we presented emphasizes identifying high-impact use cases, leveraging existing data assets, agile prototyping and iteration, focusing on user adoption, and building on robust architectural foundations using modern technologies such as MongoDB Atlas with vector search capabilities.

In the next chapter, we'll explore the technological foundations that will enable this future vision, examining how emerging standards such as the **Model Context Protocol (MCP)** are revolutionizing AI integration and paving the way for even more advanced intelligent architectures powered by developments in causal AI and context-aware systems.

19

Outlook: Beyond Today's AI

When we began this book, we knew there was a risk that by the time it reached readers, the technology would have shifted. That's the pace of AI. But architectural principles endure beyond any single model release. That's why we focused on concepts built to remain relevant and adaptable for years to come.

Over these chapters, we've traced the trajectory from modernized infrastructures to the living, breathing reality of intelligent architectures: systems that perceive, adapt, and evolve. And we've seen industries prove these concepts in the wild, turning them from abstraction into operational advantages.

This isn't speculation. These patterns are already moving into production. The question is no longer if they will shape enterprise systems, but how quickly leaders will adapt them. The future won't be won by monoliths or narrow point solutions. It belongs to intelligent architectures built for context, interoperability, and continuous evolution. Self-configuring adaptability will emerge as agents gain awareness of their network topology and environments (without the pain of earlier eras). As software grows more capable, connectivity will emerge with it. Systems will increasingly capture the intent of their creators' as much as the code, words, or images used to describe them.

And so, this last chapter is not intended to just serve as a conclusion. It's the starting point for what comes next. The decisions you make today will determine whether your systems can keep pace with what's already on the horizon.

From tools to context: The rise of intelligent architectures

Traditional software systems perform isolated tasks. Intelligence, when present, is brittle and reactive. Legacy *systems of record* could only track what happened. For decades, those systems of record defined enterprise IT. They still have their place, but the next wave of enterprise systems will decide what should happen next.

Intelligent architectures are emerging that can:

- **Perceive** and interpret their environments, adjusting to change without manual coding, e.g., reconfiguring automatically when moved to a new deployment environment.
- **Adapt** their behavior based on real-time data, e.g., adjusting ingest functions to handle a new smart meter.
- **Interact** with humans and other systems through multi-modal input, e.g., a surgeon shifting between voice, video, and typed input during surgery.
- **Learn** from prior outcomes and optimize future performance.

These shifts mirror human behavior, not as isolated functions but as modular, memory-rich, goal-driven collaborators. In the enterprise, this means architecting systems where data access, reasoning, tool execution, and decision rights are built into the architecture itself.

MCP: Building blocks for contextual intelligence

One of the most important accelerants of this shift to autonomous agents is the **Model Context Protocol (MCP)**. Proposed by Anthropic in 2024 [1] and quickly adopted by multiple organizations, including MongoDB, MCP defines a standard for how intelligent agents access tools, manage permissions, and retain memory across tasks.

Unlike traditional ETL-like approaches (where mapping context to data could take months or years), MCP bypasses that burden. Consider legacy master data management projects, where global product IDs had to be painstakingly reconciled across brands and countries. MCP sidesteps that complexity by allowing LLMs to interpret context directly and act accordingly, reducing integration time dramatically.

In practice, MCP provides:

- A structured way for agents to discover and invoke external tools
- Clear authorization boundaries that define when and how those tools can be used
- Persistent context that allows agents to learn from past interactions

Think of MCP as a shared language between AI agents and the tools they operate. Rather than relying on one-off integrations, it enables a composable ecosystem where context and governance are built into every interaction.

MongoDB's MCP Server embodies this approach by acting as a connective tissue between agentic interfaces (such as IDEs, support tooling, internal copilots) and a composable library of MongoDB capabilities. Agents can, for example:

- List Atlas clusters or collections
- Create or manage database users
- Read, write, or index data in MongoDB collections
- Describe schemas or suggest performance optimizations

MongoDB MCP Server

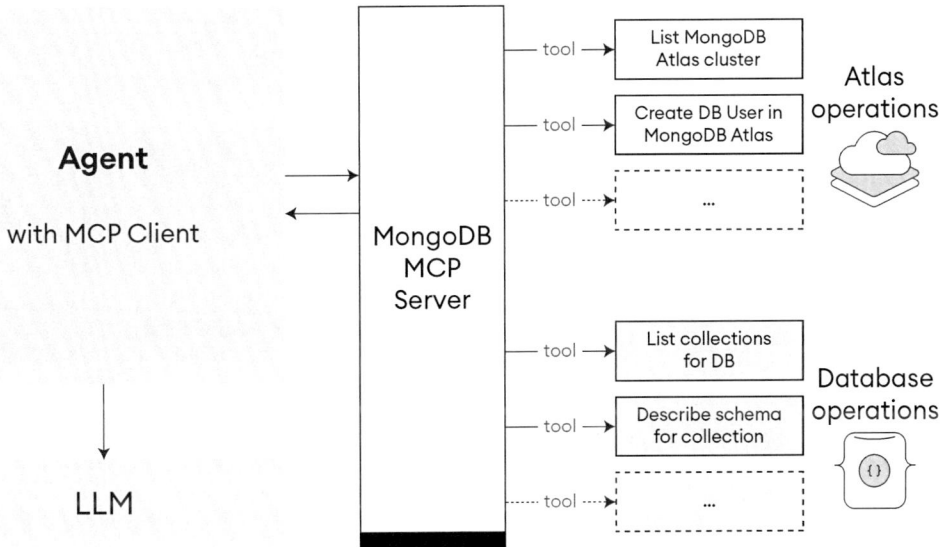

Figure 19.1: How the MongoDB MCP Server enables contextual tool access for intelligent agents

Figure 19.1 shows how the MongoDB MCP Server links Atlas administration with database operations, enabling secure, policy-aware workflows for intelligent agents.

With MCP, these operations become secure, policy-aware workflows. They don't simply connect tools; they coordinate them with memory, real-time adaptation, and accumulated experience. All of it stays within defined limits.

Causal AI: Beyond prediction, toward impact

Prediction alone won't define the next phase of enterprise AI. To shape outcomes, systems must understand *why* events occur, not just what might happen next.

Causal AI maps represent cause-and-effect relationships, enabling interventions that are both explainable and outcome-driven. It shifts systems from reacting to patterns toward shaping decisions. In financial services, instead of just flagging a portfolio as underperforming, a causal system could pinpoint the exact drivers (macroeconomic indicators, sector shifts, portfolio composition) and simulate the impact of interventions such as reallocation or hedging *before* taking action. In customer experience, it might reveal that churn is driven less by pricing and more by delayed onboarding, making it clear which lever to pull.

Causal AI enables clearer decision-making by making outcomes traceable, explainable, and accountable. But the challenges are significant: they demand cleaner data, stronger model design, and judgment that blends statistical inference with domain expertise.

As autonomy grows, so will the demand for explainability. In high-stakes industries, leaders will insist on systems that can show not only what they recommend but why that recommendation will work and how it will change the outcome. In enterprise architectures, causal AI will sit alongside predictive and generative systems, providing the reasoning layer that links perception to action. Its integration will depend on:

- **Data readiness**: Robust, well-governed datasets that support causal inference.
- **Simulation environments**: Safe sandboxes for testing interventions before deployment.
- **Governance frameworks**: Policies that ensure causal models reflect ethical, regulatory, and business constraints.

In enterprise architectures, causal AI acts less as a new feature and more as a trust accelerator. When systems can explain their reasoning in human terms, stakeholders are more likely to adopt and rely on them for critical decisions.

Memory architectures: Persistent context for intelligent agents

As agents become more capable, they shift from stateless utilities to highly contextual collaborators. Like people, they develop histories, preferences, and a sense of continuity, but only if their architectures are designed to remember. Without that, they operate like amnesiacs, waking up fresh with every interaction.

Software agents also face the same mundane hazards as any hosted service: power outages, network hiccups, or even a rogue cleaner unplugging a server. Unlike a fleet of identical, stateless containers that can be swapped out without consequence, intelligent agents depend on the context they have built over time. That's where memory enters architecture.

Traditional databases offer **CRUD** (**create**, **read**, **update**, **delete**). Agents require something more, which we can summarize as **RALF: remember**, **adapt**, **learn**, **forget**. They need flexible, bias-aware, high-performance data layers that can survive failures, bridge across multiple instantiations, and maintain context over time. These are not the strengths of old-school RDBMS. They are the hallmarks of modern document databases such as MongoDB, especially when combined with:

- **Vector databases** for semantic recall (for example, MongoDB Atlas Vector Search)
- **RAG pipelines** for dynamic context injection
- **Agent memory frameworks** such as LangGraph, MemGPT, or MongoDB's own agent memory functions

Together, these patterns enable agents to recall prior interactions, personalize over time, and maintain a goal-oriented state. They also bring responsibility: preventing stale or biased knowledge, enforcing privacy, and designing lifecycles that can explain why something was remembered or forgotten.

The payoff is worth it. Memory turns agents from reactive tools into proactive collaborators. In customer service, they won't ask the same question twice. In industrial maintenance, they will anticipate failures based on years of performance data. And in every domain, they will act with the context and continuity needed to make better decisions, more reliably, over time.

Constitutional AI: Governing intelligence with principles

If causal AI is about reasoning, constitutional AI is about values. It ensures intelligent systems are not only capable but also guided by principles that can be read, debated, and improved over time.

Developed and popularized by Anthropic, constitutional AI trains models not only on human feedback or ground truth but also on a written set of guiding rules, a kind of *constitution* that shapes how systems behave, respond, and reason about their actions [2]. They might include commitments to helpfulness, harmlessness, honesty, fairness, and deferring to human judgment in moments of ambiguity.

The approach arose partly from the limits of **reinforcement learning from human feedback (RLHF)**. While RLHF works, it is costly, opaque, and heavily dependent on the quality of human raters. The result often sounds polite, but it is not consistently aligned. Constitutional AI moves alignment upstream. Instead of depending on human judgment at every turn, it allows models to critique their own outputs against explicit principles and adjusts its own responses against these principles, enabling:

- **Scalability**: Once the principles are written, they can be applied broadly without the need for millions of manual annotations
- **Transparency**: Behavior can be traced back to written rules rather than hidden scoring functions
- **Consistency**: Responses remain more stable across edge cases and over time

But that doesn't mean the hard questions go away. Who decides which principles matter most? How are conflicts resolved? How do we handle cultural nuances? Even a rule like *"avoid causing offense"* can mean very different things in different industries or regions.

Still, the architectural implication is clear. Governability must be built into the design rather than added as an afterthought. Just as MCP standardizes how agents act and causal AI structures how they reason, constitutional AI sets the standards by which their actions are judged. Together, these elements create the scaffolding for AI systems that are powerful, explainable, and trusted by design.

Multi-agent systems: From solo models to cooperative intelligence

If a single AI model can learn, reason, plan, and act, what happens when you put hundreds of them together, each with its own role, memory, and perspective?

This is no longer a theoretical question. Multi-agent systems are already operating in the real world: in manufacturing, coordinating predictive maintenance, process optimization, and quality control; in healthcare, integrating inputs from multiple specialties for coordinated care; and in finance, distributing portfolio management and risk assessment across specialized agents. These implementations show how quickly multi-agent architectures are moving from experiment to production.

The pattern is straightforward yet transformative. Multiple interacting agents, each optimized for a specific function, collaborate to solve problems beyond the reach of any single model. Projects such as AutoGPT, BabyAGI, OpenDevin, and ChatDev have demonstrated this by simulating workflows with defined roles (planner, coder, critic, tester), passing tasks in iterative loops. Research groups at Stanford, Berkeley, and Google DeepMind are now investigating both the potential and the hazards of scaling this pattern.

The advantages are compelling:

- **Task decomposition** into specialized roles
- **Parallel execution** that speeds up workflows
- **Cross-checking** to reduce errors
- **Emergent creativity** through agent-to-agent interaction

Yet with complexity comes risk. Multi-agent systems can generate feedback loops, unanticipated dependencies, or strategies that satisfy immediate objectives while missing intended outcomes.

For these systems to function, they require a shared environment where agents can store, read, and update context in real time. MongoDB supports this through flexible document schemas for varied agent outputs, change streams for immediate event propagation, vector search for semantic coordination, and role-based access controls to maintain boundaries. In practice, principles of distributed computing are being applied to reasoning entities as well as services.

Multi-agent systems also do not stand alone. They depend on the governance frameworks, causal reasoning, and memory architectures described earlier in this chapter. This is where those elements converge. Intelligent architectures prove themselves at scale when they operate as interdependent societies rather than isolated performers.

Looking back to look forward: Patterns in the field

As we reach the final stretch, it is worth pausing to reflect on the journey. Across these chapters, we have traced one of the most significant shifts in modern computing: the operationalization of AI into the fabric of real-world systems. What began as academic research has matured into an architectural discipline that is layered, nuanced, and ready for scale, one where intelligent agents, retrieval-based grounding, and multimodal data integration converge to support decision-making, personalization, optimization, and discovery across industries.

This book was not written to predict the future of AI in abstract terms. Instead, its purpose has been to offer practitioners, architects, and decision-makers a practical and conceptual foundation for understanding how today's AI systems are built, what differentiates performant from brittle architectures, and how these systems are being deployed at scale across sectors as diverse as manufacturing, media, retail, finance, insurance, and healthcare.

In this concluding section, we distill the key ideas explored throughout the book. We do so by revisiting both the core architectural principles laid out in the early chapters and the domain-specific deployments discussed in the second half.

Foundational architecture: From theory to practice

The first half of this book defined the architectural primitives and system-level concepts that enable generative and agentic AI. We began by disentangling terminology that is often misused or misunderstood: **generative AI (GenAI)**, **retrieval-augmented generation (RAG)**, and agentic systems.

Each of these represents a distinct architectural class. GenAI systems, built atop **large language models (LLMs)**, produce coherent and contextually plausible outputs but lack grounding by default. RAG systems augment generative models with access to external knowledge, retrieved in real time and appended to the model's context window. This pattern introduces traceability and factual grounding, mitigating hallucination and enabling explainable outputs.

Agentic systems extend this further. Rather than operating on a single input-output cycle, agents maintain memory, invoke tools, coordinate across steps, and even interact with other agents. They are context-aware not only in the narrow sense of a prompt but in the broader sense of evolving state and goal orientation. These systems bring us closer to autonomous software, though always bounded by policy, memory, and architecture.

To support these systems, this book explored in depth the role of vector embeddings, numerical representations of semantics that allow systems to search, cluster, and reason over unstructured content. Embeddings enable semantic search, personalized recommendations, document classification, and cross-modal alignment between text, images, and structured data. We showed how embeddings become foundational in both RAG and agentic architectures, especially when stored in vector-enabled document databases.

Through this lens, we introduced the concept of systems of action: databases designed not just to store data but to enable real-time decisions, automation, and collaboration between humans and AI agents. We explored how document-oriented architectures provide the flexibility needed to handle diverse data types while maintaining the performance characteristics required for intelligent applications.

This foundational half of the book closed with treatments of trustworthy AI and modernization. We established that successful AI implementation requires not just technical capability but governance structures that ensure fairness, transparency, and regulatory compliance. We then demonstrated how AI can accelerate modernization efforts, transforming legacy code and systems through intelligent automation. In doing so, we established the architectural context required to understand the applications explored in *Part 2: Real-World Case Studies and Implementations*.

Industry applications: Validation through diversity

The second half of this book shifted from foundation to application. Each chapter was grounded in a specific sector, but together, these use cases revealed architectural patterns that transcend domain. What varied was not the structure of the systems but the shape of the data, the regulatory constraints, and the operational requirements. From this comparative analysis, a set of shared design principles emerged.

Manufacturing demonstrated AI's most tangible impact on physical operations. Here, intelligent systems transform supply chains from reactive to predictive, optimizing inventory through multi-criteria classification that incorporates both quantitative metrics and qualitative insights from customer reviews and supplier communications. The standout architecture was the multi-agent system coordinating predictive maintenance, process optimization, and quality assurance, each with independent memory and feedback loops, unified by shared context in a document database. Manufacturing also revealed how GenAI can preserve institutional knowledge that would otherwise be lost when experienced workers retire, transforming institutional knowledge into searchable, actionable insights. In automotive applications, we explored how AI powers next-generation in-cabin experiences and autonomous fleet management, requiring real-time coordination across systems with different data velocities without creating dangerous agentic silos.

Media and telecommunications showcased how sectors grappling with declining referral traffic and platform dependencies leverage AI for transformation. Here, AI-augmented search transforms traditional keyword matching into intent-driven experiences that understand user context and preferences. Content personalization emerged as a critical differentiator, with RAG systems enabling the generation of dynamic, tailored experiences at scale. Search generative experiences demonstrated how traditional information retrieval could evolve into conversational, context-aware interactions that reduce bounce rates and deepen user engagement. In telecommunications, agentic AIOps frameworks showed how complex network operations could be automated and optimized, with real-time fraud detection systems processing millions of events. These sectors highlighted a crucial insight: the same architecture that powers content recommendation can also drive operational excellence, depending on the data sources and interface requirements.

Retail revealed AI's power to transform every aspect of the customer journey. Here, AI-augmented search enables customers to find products through natural language queries, moving beyond simple keyword matching to understand intent and context. Personalized marketing and content generation demonstrated the scalability benefits of AI, with systems capable of creating tailored experiences for millions of customers simultaneously. Demand forecasting and predictive analytics showed how retailers could shift from reactive to proactive planning, optimizing inventory and supply chain management through intelligent prediction. The digitization of in-store interactions revealed how physical retail could benefit from the same intelligence as digital channels, bridging the gap between online and offline experiences through technologies such as digital receipts and real-time personalization. Conversational and agentic chatbots emerged as transformative tools for customer service, providing autonomous, context-aware assistance that continuously learns and adapts to customer needs.

Financial services presented perhaps the most complex regulatory and security requirements, demanding solutions that balance innovation with compliance. Here, we traced the evolution from predictive analytics to GenAI to agentic systems, showing how each stage builds upon the previous to create more sophisticated capabilities. The transformation of credit applications demonstrated how AI can make financial services more inclusive while maintaining risk management standards. Enterprise knowledge management systems showed how GenAI could revolutionize internal operations, helping employees access and synthesize vast amounts of regulatory and procedural information. Customer experience transformation emerged as a key theme, with AI-powered interactions providing personalized, real-time support while maintaining the trust and security standards essential to financial services. Advanced applications in **environmental, social, and governance (ESG)** analysis, payments processing, and capital markets demonstrated the breadth of AI's potential impact across the entire financial ecosystem. A critical insight from this sector was the importance of semantic data protection, approaches that preserve the meaning and utility of data while protecting sensitive information.

Insurance revealed how AI transforms one of the world's most data-intensive industries. Here, we explored domain-driven AI implementation, showing how converged datastores enable unified handling of structured policy data and unstructured documents like photos and reports. The underwriting automation case study demonstrated perhaps the most dramatic transformation in the book, reducing quote cycles from weeks to minutes while maintaining accuracy and compliance. This showcased how the combination of RAG architectures with high-performance inference could deliver transformative business value. Claims processing illustrates the power of AI in handling complex workflows that involve multiple data types and stakeholders. Agentic systems coordinated between customer communications, damage assessments, policy interpretation, and regulatory compliance, demonstrating how autonomous agents could orchestrate sophisticated business processes. The insurance sector validated a key architectural principle: successful AI applications must be embedded directly into business workflows rather than operating as separate systems.

Healthcare represented both our greatest opportunity and most critical challenge, where AI mistakes could affect human lives. Here, we explored how fragmented data systems create the *47-minute problem*, with skilled clinicians spending more time hunting for information than delivering patient care. Document-oriented architectures and the facade pattern can preserve healthcare standards such as HL7 FHIR while enabling AI innovation. AI-powered care coordination showed how multi-agent systems could synthesize information across specialties while maintaining human oversight and regulatory compliance. Medical imaging AI revealed the importance of unified clinical context, showing how diagnostic accuracy depends on complete patient information rather than isolated image analysis. Natural language clinical intelligence transformed provider-data interactions from complex database queries to conversational clinical communication. The healthcare transformation validated our core thesis: AI agents require unified, comprehensive data contexts to be effective and safe. Fragmented systems create dangerous agentic silos where AI operates without complete clinical pictures.

Partner ecosystem: Specialized excellence on unified foundations

Throughout our industry exploration, we witnessed how a thriving partner ecosystem extends platform capabilities into domain-specific applications. **Cognigy** demonstrated how conversational AI could scale to handle thousands of interactions per minute during crisis scenarios, transforming customer communication from reactive support to intelligent, contextual engagement. **RegData** showed how semantic data protection could enable AI innovation while maintaining strict security standards, proving that compliance and capability need not be opposing forces.

Iguazio transformed wealth management through GenAI copilots that allow relationship managers to shift from administrative tasks to high-value client interactions. This initiative delivered measurable improvements in both productivity and client satisfaction. **Fireworks AI** enabled real-time insurance underwriting through high-performance inference capabilities, turning weeks-long processes into minute-long decisions without sacrificing accuracy. **Encore** revolutionized document management by transforming static storage into intelligent, AI-powered content platforms that activate rather than merely archive organizational knowledge.

Dataworkz demonstrated how agentic AI could be democratized across organizations of varying technical maturity, providing tailored solutions that deliver immediate business value regardless of existing infrastructure sophistication. Throughout these partnerships, a clear pattern emerged: transformative AI applications arise when unified data architectures meet specialized domain expertise, creating solutions that neither component could deliver alone.

Universal patterns across domains

Despite the diversity of use cases, several principles recurred across every chapter and every partner implementation:

- **Context is a first-class citizen**. Grounding LLMs in semantically relevant data is the difference between novelty and utility. Every successful implementation prioritized rich, comprehensive context over model sophistication.
- **Memory is infrastructure**. Long-running agents need persistent, queryable, and inspectable memory. Whether it is vector search for knowledge reuse or persistent agent state, the systems that remember deliver more contextually intelligent outcomes.
- **Retrieval is a control surface**. What an LLM knows is no longer limited to its training weights; it is mediated by what it can retrieve. RAG architectures proved essential for grounding AI in organizational knowledge.

- **Architecture is destiny**. From document management to underwriting automation, those who build flexible, modular systems adapt fastest. System outcomes, accuracy, traceability, and performance are determined less by which model is chosen and more by how the components interact.

- **Governance is no longer optional**. The more we automate, the more we must make values and policies machine-readable. Constitutional AI, semantic data protection, and explainable decision-making emerged as critical requirements across regulated industries.

- **Composability wins**. From semantic pipelines in healthcare to configurable AI factories in banking, plug-and-play architectures enable experimentation without chaos. The most successful organizations built systems where components could be mixed, matched, and evolved independently.

- **Unified data foundations enable specialized applications**. Every industry, every partner, every use case succeeded because of flexible, unified data architectures that could adapt to diverse requirements without compromising performance or consistency.

This book has provided not just a vocabulary but a reference architecture. It has shown how GenAI, RAG, and agentic systems can be made composable, observable, and scalable, regardless of domain. As AI adoption deepens, success will depend less on having the right model and more on applying the right systems thinking. This approach must be grounded in clarity, built on open data principles, and aligned with a clear operational purpose.

Final thought: Architecture is the intelligence

We are standing at the edge of a new paradigm in AI, not just more capable models, but more intentional architectures. The trajectory is clear: from isolated predictions to integrated, contextual, and governed systems that can reason, act, and adapt in dynamic environments. It is against this backdrop that we witness the transition from **systems of record** to **systems of action**.

References

1. *Introducing the Model Context Protocol*: https://www.anthropic.com/news/model-context-protocol

2. *Constitutional AI: Harmlessness from AI Feedback*: https://www.anthropic.com/research/constitutional-ai-harmlessness-from-ai-feedback

Afterword

As we write this, we're struck by how far this project has come since it was first suggested that we turn our scattered industry insights into a cohesive guide. What began as an effort to organize our existing knowledge has evolved into something we never expected: a comprehensive framework that bridges the gap between AI theory and production reality.

The process of writing also changed how we saw our own experiences. What began as documenting case studies soon turned into recognizing the deeper forces at play. We realized that decisions about data, governance, and system design consistently shaped outcomes. Rather than a set of disconnected stories, the chapters revealed a bigger picture. The real breakthroughs came from aligning technology choices with business realities.

What we learned

Writing this book reinforced three critical insights that weren't obvious when we began. First, successful AI implementation centers on data architecture. Every transformative application we studied, from real-time fraud detection to clinical report generation, succeeded because organizations invested in unified and flexible data foundations before they worried about model selection.

Second, GenAI, RAG systems, and agentic architectures represent fundamentally different approaches to system design. Each has distinct requirements for data management, governance, and operational oversight. The companies that thrive understand these differences and choose their architectural patterns deliberately.

Finally, AI agents require comprehensive context to be both effective and safe. The most dangerous implementations we encountered weren't those that failed to produce intelligent outputs, they were systems that operated with incomplete information. Whether in healthcare, financial services, or manufacturing, fragmented data creates fragmented intelligence, and fragmented intelligence creates operational risk.

Architectural insights

It became clear very early in this journey that infrastructure choices had a major impact on the ability of customers to get a GenAI-powered application into production. In every implementation we studied, applications built on old but familiar technology such as RDBMS created so much headwind in tech sprawl and operational complexity that projects quickly withered and died.

It was also apparent that document-oriented databases had emerged as the unifying platform for the modern age. The clues had been there all along, surfacing as we traced the technical requirements across industries. Vector embeddings, operational data, analytical workloads, and agentic memory all converged on the same architectural pattern. Flexible schemas could evolve with intelligent applications while maintaining the performance characteristics required for real-time decisions.

This convergence suggests something profound about the future of enterprise software. We are witnessing the emergence of what we have called *systems of action*: platforms designed not just to store data, but to enable intelligent collaboration between humans and AI agents. The implications extend far beyond any single technology stack.

Beyond case studies

The industries covered in this book (manufacturing, media, retail, financial services, insurance, and healthcare) represent just the beginning. As we've traveled and spoken with technology leaders across sectors, similar patterns have emerged everywhere. Transportation companies are optimizing logistics networks, energy firms are coordinating distributed generation, and educational institutions are personalizing learning experiences at scale.

The architectural principles remain consistent. The implementation details vary, but the core requirements for trustworthy, scalable, intelligent systems remain remarkably stable across domains. This gives us confidence that the frameworks presented here will stay relevant as AI capabilities continue to evolve.

Our partner ecosystem validated this belief. Companies such as Cognigy, RegData, Iguazio, Fireworks AI, Encore, and Dataworkz did more than provide specialized capabilities. They showed how unified data architectures enable rapid innovation across diverse use cases. Their success stories reinforce a key thesis: transformative AI applications arise when flexible platforms meet domain expertise.

What's next

If you have made it this far, you are likely facing your own AI implementation decisions. Our advice is straightforward: understand your use case and use it to inform your architecture. If your use case needs GenAI, then you'll need a solution that integrates capabilities such as vector search, embedding, and re-ranking, along with the basics such as flexible schemas, security, and performance, in one unified platform. The most compelling AI demonstration becomes irrelevant if it cannot access the information it needs to operate safely and effectively in production.

Focus on creating unified, comprehensive data contexts before worrying about model selection or interface design. Invest in governance structures that can evolve with your AI capabilities. Design for agent coordination, even if you are starting with simple automation. Most importantly, remember that trustworthy AI is not just about algorithmic fairness; it is about systems that humans can understand, monitor, and control.

The technology landscape will continue to evolve rapidly. What will not change is the need for AI systems that are grounded in complete information, governed by clear policies, and designed to augment rather than replace human judgment.

The future belongs to organizations that can move quickly while maintaining safety, scale efficiently while preserving quality, and innovate continuously while building trust. The architectural principles and implementation patterns in this book provide a roadmap for that future.

We are excited to see what you will build next!

Connect with us at `industry.solutions@mongodb.com` to share your AI implementation experiences, or visit `https://www.mongodb.com/resources/use-cases/artificial-intelligence` for additional resources, case study updates, and community discussions.

Index

‹packt›

Subscribe to our online digital library for full access to over 7,000 books and videos, as well as industry leading tools to help you plan your personal development and advance your career. For more information, please visit our website.

Why subscribe?

- Spend less time learning and more time coding with practical eBooks and Videos from over 4,000 industry professionals
- Improve your learning with Skill Plans built especially for you
- Get a free eBook or video every month
- Fully searchable for easy access to vital information
- Copy and paste, print, and bookmark content

At www.packtpub.com, you can also read a collection of free technical articles, sign up for a range of free newsletters, and receive exclusive discounts and offers on Packt books and eBooks.

Other Books You May Enjoy

If you enjoyed this book, you may be interested in these other books by Packt:

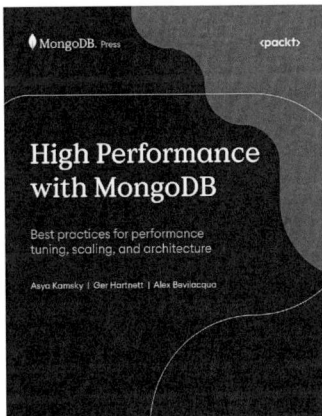

High Performance with MongoDB

Asya Kamsky, Ger Hartnett, Alex Bevilacqua

ISBN: 978-1-83702-263-2

- Diagnose and resolve common performance bottlenecks in deployments
- Design schemas and indexes that maximize throughput and efficiency
- Tune the WiredTiger storage engine and manage system resources for peak performance
- Leverage sharding and replication to scale and ensure uptime
- Monitor, debug, and maintain deployments proactively to prevent issues
- Improve application responsiveness through client driver configuration

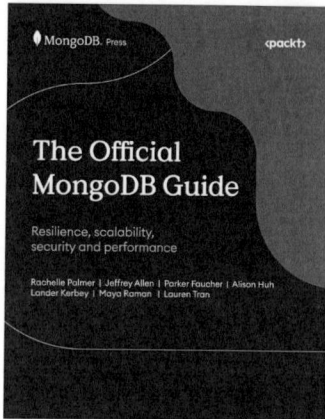

The Official MongoDB Guide

Rachelle Palmer, Jeffrey Allen, Parker Faucher, Alison Huh, Lander Kerbey, Maya Raman, Lauren Tran

ISBN: 978-1-83702-197-0

- Build secure, scalable, and high-performance applications
- Design efficient data models and indexes for real workloads
- Write powerful queries to sort, filter, and project data
- Protect applications with authentication and encryption
- Accelerate coding with AI-powered and IDE-based tools
- Launch, scale, and manage MongoDB Atlas with confidence
- Unlock advanced features like Atlas Search and Atlas Vector Search
- Apply proven techniques from MongoDB's own engineering leaders

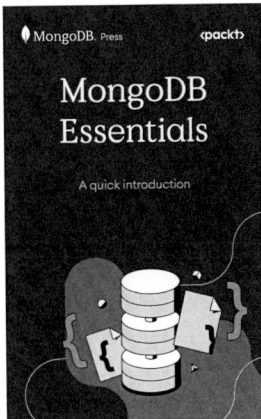

MongoDB Essentials

ISBN: 978-1-80670-609-9

- Understand MongoDB's document model and architecture
- Set up MongoDB local deployments quickly
- Design schemas tailored to application access patterns
- Perform CRUD and aggregation operations efficiently
- Use tools to optimize query performance and scalability
- Explore AI-powered features such as Atlas Search and Atlas Vector Search

Packt is searching for authors like you

If you're interested in becoming an author for Packt, please visit authors.packt.com and apply today. We have worked with thousands of developers and tech professionals, just like you, to help them share their insight with the global tech community. You can make a general application, apply for a specific hot topic that we are recruiting an author for, or submit your own idea.

Share your thoughts

Now you've finished *Architectures for the Intelligent AI-Ready Enterprise*, we'd love to hear your thoughts! Scan the QR code below to go straight to the Amazon review page for this book and share your feedback or leave a review on the site that you purchased it from.

https://packt.link/r/1806117150

Your review is important to us and the tech community and will help us make sure we're delivering excellent quality content.

Download a free PDF copy of this book

Thanks for purchasing this book!

Do you like to read on the go but are unable to carry your print books everywhere?

Is your eBook purchase not compatible with the device of your choice?

Don't worry, now with every Packt book you get a DRM-free PDF version of that book at no cost.

Read anywhere, any place, on any device. Search, copy, and paste code from your favorite technical books directly into your application.

The perks don't stop there, you can get exclusive access to discounts, newsletters, and great free content in your inbox daily.

Follow these simple steps to get the benefits:

1. Scan the QR code or visit the link below:

https://packt.link/free-ebook/9781806117154

2. Submit your proof of purchase.
3. That's it! We'll send your free PDF and other benefits to your email directly.